Oracle8i Certified Professional SQL and PL/SQL Exam Guide

Jason S. Couchman

Osborne/**McGraw-Hill**

New York   Chicago   San Francisco
Lisbon   London   Madrid   Mexico City   Milan
New Delhi   San Juan   Seoul   Singapore   Sydney   Toronto

Osborne/**McGraw-Hill**
2600 Tenth Street
Berkeley, California 94710
U.S.A.

To arrange bulk purchase discounts for sales promotions, premiums, or fund-raisers, please contact Osborne/**McGraw-Hill** at the above address. For information on translations or book distributors outside the U.S.A., please see the International Contact Information page immediately following the index of this book.

Oracle8i Certified Professional SQL and PL/SQL Exam Guide

1234567890 FGR FGR 01987654321
Book p/n 0-07-219154-6 and CD p/n 0-07-219155-4
parts of
ISBN 0-07-219153-8

Publisher
　Brandon A. Nordin

Vice President & Associate Publisher
　Scott Rogers

Acquisitions Editor
　Jeremy Judson

Project Editor
　Julie M. Smith

Acquisitions Coordinator
　Ross Doll

Technical Editors
　Sheldon Barry
　Carol Rosenow

Copy Editors
　Bart Reed
　Marilyn Smith

Proofreader
　Linda Medoff

Indexer
　Jack Lewis

Computer Designers
　Carie Abrew, Michelle Galicia
　Roberta Steele, George Toma Charbak

Illustrators
　Beth E. Young
　Alex Putney

Series Design
　Jani Beckwith

This book was composed with Corel VENTURA™ Publisher.

To Joseph Manning

About the Author

Jason S. Couchman is a database consultant and the author of *Oracle8i Certified Professional DBA Certification Exam Guide*, also from Oracle Press. He is a regular presenter on Oracle and OCP at international Oracle user conferences and meetings. His work has been published by Oracle Magazine, Harvard Business School Publishing, and Gannett Newspapers, among others.

ORACLE®

Certified Professional

About the Oracle Certification Exams

The expertise of Oracle database administrators (DBAs) is integral to the success of today's increasingly complex system environments. The best DBAs operate primarily behind the scenes, looking for ways to fine-tune day-to-day performance to prevent unscheduled crises and hours of expensive downtime. They know they stand between optimal performance and a crisis that could bring a company to a standstill. The Oracle Certified Database Administrator Track provides DBAs with tangible evidence of their skills with the Oracle database.

The Oracle Certified Professional (OCP) Program was developed by Oracle to recognize technical professionals who can demonstrate the depth of knowledge and hands-on skills required to maximize Oracle's core products according to a rigorous standard established by Oracle. By earning professional certification, you can translate the impressive knowledge and skill you have worked so hard to accumulate into a tangible credential that can lead to greater job security or more challenging, better-paying opportunities.

Oracle Certified Professionals are eligible to receive use of the Oracle Certified Professional logo and a certificate for framing.

Requirements for Certification

To become an Oracle Certified Database Administrator, you must pass five tests. These exams cover knowledge of the essential aspects of the SQL language, Oracle administration, backup and recovery, and performance tuning of systems. The certification process requires that you pass the following five exams:

- Exam 1: Introduction to Oracle-SQL and PL/SQL (1Z0-001)

- Exam 2: Oracle8i Architecture and Administration (1Z0-023)

- Exam 3: Oracle8i Backup and Recovery (1Z0-025)

- Exam 4: Oracle8i Performance Tuning (1Z0-024)

- Exam 5: Oracle8i Network Administration (1Z0-026)

If you fail a test, you must wait at least 30 days before you retake that exam. You may attempt a particular test up to three times in a twelve-month period.

Recertification

Oracle announces the requirements for upgrading your certification based on the release of new products and upgrades. Oracle will give six months advance notice when an exam version is due to expire.

Exam Format

The computer-based exams are multiple-choice tests, consisting of 60–90 questions that must be completed in 90 minutes.

20% OCP Exam Discount Offer

You can receive a 20% exam discount when you register for a FREE membership to Oracle Technology Network (OTN) at **http://technet.oracle.com/membership**. OTN is your definitive source for Oracle technical information. As a member, you will be part of an online community with access to:

- Oracle Certified Professional (OCP) discounts and training offers

- Free software downloads

- OTN sponsored eSeminars and conferences

- Discussion forums on key technology topics

Contents

PART II
OCP Oracle8*i* DBA Practice Exams

Preface

y interest in Oracle certification began in 1996 when I read about the Oracle DBA certificate offered by the Chauncey Group. I found it difficult to prepare for that certification exam for two reasons. First, there was an absence of practice questions readily available. Second, preparation for the exam involved reviewing six or seven different manuals and Oracle Press books, none of which were particularly suited to the task. Judging from the response to the proliferation of titles now available in the OCP Exam Guide Series from Oracle Press, it would seem others have had similar experiences.

This book is divided into two units, the first containing preparatory material for the Oracle8i Introduction to SQL and PL/SQL exam—part of Oracle's Oracle8i DBA certification track. The first unit has six chapters, each containing several discussions that focus on a particular topic or subtopic objective listed by the Oracle Certified Professional Oracle8i DBA Track Candidate Guide. (For a complete listing of all the topics on the candidate guide, check the Introduction.) These discussions are followed by a For Review section, each listing the three or four most important concepts for you to retain from the discussion. After the review, you'll see two to six exercise questions in exam-based multiple-choice or short answer format. Following the questions you will find an answer key for those questions, which should help you master the material even more quickly. Thus, with this book you're never more than a few pages away from demonstrating what you've learned about Oracle8i SQL and

PL/SQL for the OCP exam. At the end of each chapter, you will find a short summary of what was covered in the chapter, followed by a Two-Minute Drill. The Two-Minute Drill contains another bullet list of fast facts to review, or "crib notes" for the days leading up to your OCP exam. The chapters conclude with 12-20 short-answer and exam-based multiple-choice questions designed to help you further to test your understanding of the materials you learned in the chapter.

The second unit consists of one chapter containing three full-length practice exams. Each test contains exam-based multiple choice and scenario-based questions that are designed to help you strengthen your test-taking skills for the OCP exams. You will also find answers and in-depth explanations for every question in the practice exams in the back of that chapter, along with a reference back to the exam topic and subtopic objectives from the OCP Candidate Guide. This feature should help you determine your areas requiring further improvement with pinpoint accuracy.

Finally, a note about updates and errata. Because OCP covers such vast ground in a short time, this has become a living text. If you feel you have encountered difficulties due to errors, you can either check out **www.exampilot.com** to find the latest errata, or send me an email directly at **jcouchman@mindspring.com**. Good luck!

Acknowledgments

here are many people I would like to thank for their help with writing this book. My first and most heartfelt thanks goes to the dedicated readers of my other books who took time out of their busy schedules to send feedback on the book. I have listened to your praise and constructive criticism, and made every effort to correct and amplify my work based on the points you made. Please, keep the email coming—it is by far the most effective way to make the book better!

Ulrike Schwinn has been a loyal associate, colleague, and friend during my ongoing effort to help 80,000+ readers get Oracle certified. Thanks also to Julia Johnson, Mike Serpe, Jim DiIanni, and Chris Pirie from Oracle University for their feedback and assistance with overall direction for the OCP DBA track. As always, thanks to the fine folks at Osborne—Scott Rogers, Jeremy Judson, Ross Doll, Sheldon Barry, Carol Rosenow, and Julie Smith. Special thanks to the folks in production as well—and to both Bart Reed and Marilyn Smith for their thorough copy edit and for accommodating some important last-minute changes.

The last person I'd like to thank is Joseph Manning, the man to whom my eighth book is dedicated. Joseph was a professor of Computer Science at Vassar College when I was part of that program many years ago. Thinking back to that first day of Computer Science 123, when I sat in the back of his class, I can still feel the rush of excitement about computer technology that only comes when you have someone who can explain difficult concepts with the flair and wit that Joseph possesses.

Unfortunately, Vassar College no longer enjoys his expert talent, but Vassar's loss is University College Cork's gain. Its probably for the best, though—you can take the Irishman out of Ireland (for a little while, at least), but you'll never take Ireland out of the Irishman. Joseph, thanks for being such a great teacher and an even better colleague and friend!

Introduction

he Oracle Certified Professional DBA certification exam series from Oracle Corporation is a great opportunity for you to demonstrate your expertise on the use of Oracle database software. Called OCP, it represents the culmination of many people's request for objective standards in Oracle database administration, one of the hottest markets in the software field. The presence of OCP on the market indicates an important reality about Oracle as a career path. Oracle is mature, robust, and stable for enterprise-wide information management. However, corporations facing a severe shortage of qualified Oracle professionals need a measurement for Oracle expertise.

The OCP certification core track for DBAs consists of five tests in the following areas of Oracle8i: SQL and PL/SQL, database administration, performance tuning, network administration, and backup/recovery, with the current content of those five exams covering Oracle through Oracle8i.. As of this printing, each test consists of about 60 multiple choice questions pertaining to the recommended usage of Oracle databases. You have about 90 minutes to take each exam. Obtaining certification for Oracle8i through the core track is contingent on taking and passing *all five* core examinations. This book will help you prepare for the first exam in that track, which incidentally is the first exam in the Internet Developer track as well.

Why Get Certified?

If you are already an Oracle professional, you may wonder, "Why should I get certified?" Perhaps you have a successful career as an Oracle DBA or developer, enjoying the instant prestige your resume gets with that one magic word on it. With market forces currently in your favor, you're right to wonder. But, while no one is saying you don't know Oracle when you put the magic word on your resume, can you prove how well you *do* know Oracle without undergoing a technical interview? I started asking myself that question last year when Oracle certification began to emerge. I was surprised to find out that, after years of using Oracle, developing Oracle applications, and administering Oracle databases for Fortune 500 companies, there were a lot of things about Oracle I *didn't* know. And the only reason I know them now is because I took the time and effort to become certified.

If you're looking for another reason to become certified in Oracle, consider the experience of computer professionals with Novell NetWare experience in the late 1980s and early 1990s. Back then, it seemed that anyone with even a little experience in Novell could count on a fantastic job offer. Then Novell introduced its CNE/CNA programs. At first, employers were okay with hiring Novell professionals whether they had a certificate or not. As time went on, however, employers no longer asked for computer professionals with Novell NetWare *experience*—they asked for CNEs and CNAs. A similar phenomenon can be seen in the arena of Microsoft Windows NT, where the MCSE has already become the standard by which those professionals are measuring their skills. Furthermore, with the latest economic downturn in the technology-driven US economy comes the possibility of involuntary IT job changes. If you want to stay competitive in the field of Oracle database administration or development through those changes, your real question shouldn't be *whether* you should become certified, but *when*.

If you are not in the field of Oracle development or database management, or if you want to advance your career using Oracle products, there has never been a better time to do so. OCP is already altering the playing field for DBAs and developers by changing the focus of the Oracle skill set from "how many years have you used it" to "do you know *how* to use it?" That shift benefits organizations using Oracle as much as it benefits the professionals who use Oracle because the emphasis is on *skills*, not attrition.

Managers who are faced with the task of hiring Oracle professionals can breathe a sigh of relief with the debut of OCP as well. By seeking professionals who are certified, managers can spend less time trying to determine if the candidate possesses the Oracle skills for the job, and more time assessing the candidate's work habits and compatibility with the team.

The Oracle Certified Professional Oracle8i DBA Track Candidate Guide

The following topic areas are covered in OCP Exam 1. Note that these concepts are taken directly from the Oracle OCP Candidate Guide for OCP Exam 1 and are current as of the publication of this book. It is essential that you begin your preparation for the OCP DBA certification exams by understanding the test contents. You can download the most current OCP Candidate Guide for the Oracle8i DBA track from the Oracle University website, **http://www.oracle.com/education/certification**. The Candidate Guide publishes the topic areas for each exam corresponding to chapter and section discussions in this book.

The topics and subtopics are as follows:

1. Overview of Relational Databases, SQL, and PL/SQL

    1.1. Discuss the theoretical and physical aspects of a relational database

    1.2. Describe the Oracle implementation of the RDBMS and ORDBMS

    1.3. Describe the use and benefits of PL/SQL

2. Writing Basic SQL Statements

    2.1. List the capabilities of SQL `select` statements

    2.2. Execute a basic `select` statement

    2.3. Differentiate between SQL statements and SQL*Plus commands

3. Restricting and Sorting Data

    3.1. Limit the rows retrieved by a query

    3.2. Sort the rows retrieved by a query

4. Single-Row Functions

    4.1. Describe various types of functions available in SQL

    4.2. Use character, number, and date functions in `select` statements

    4.3. Describe the use of conversion functions

5. Displaying Data from Multiple Tables

    5.1. Write `select` statements to access data from more than one table using equality and nonequality joins

How Should You Prepare for the Exam?

If you spend your free time studying things like the maximum number of nested subqueries permitted in SQL, you are probably ready to take the OCP Oracle8i SQL and PL/SQL exam now. For the rest of us, Oracle and other companies offer classroom- and computer-based training options to learn Oracle. Now, users have another option—this book! By selecting this book, you demonstrate two excellent characteristics—that you are committed to a superior career using Oracle products, and that you care about preparing for the exam correctly and thoroughly. And by the way, the maximum number of subqueries permitted in SQL is 255, and it is on the OCP Oracle8i SQL and PL/SQL exam. That fact, along with thousands of others, is covered extensively in this book to help you prepare for, and pass, the OCP Oracle8i SQL and PL/SQL exam.

DBA Certification Past and Present

Oracle certification started in the mid 1990s with the involvement of the Chauncey Group International, a division of Educational Testing Service. With the help of many Oracle DBAs, Chauncey put together an objective, fact-based and scenario-based examination on Oracle database administration. This test did an excellent job of measuring knowledge of Oracle7, versions 7.0 to 7.2. Consisting of 60 questions, Chauncey's exam covered several different topic areas, including backup and recovery, security, administration, and performance tuning, all in one test.

Oracle Corporation has taken DBA certification ahead with the advent of OCP. Their certification examination is actually five tests, each consisting of about 60 questions. By quintupling the number of questions you must answer, Oracle requires that you have unprecedented depth of knowledge in Oracle database administration. Oracle has also committed to including scenario-based questions on the OCP examinations, and preparation material for these new questions is included in this book as well. Scenario-based questions require you to not only know the facts about Oracle, but also understand how to apply those facts in real-life situations.

Oracle's final contribution to the area of Oracle certification is a commitment to reviewing and updating the material presented in the certification exams. Oracle-certified DBAs will be required to maintain their certification by retaking the certification exams periodically—meaning that those who certify will stay on the cutting edge of the Oracle database better than those who do not.

The Next Steps

Next, you should be sure to understand the test interface you will encounter on exam day. Figure 1-1 is contains a diagram of the actual test graphical user

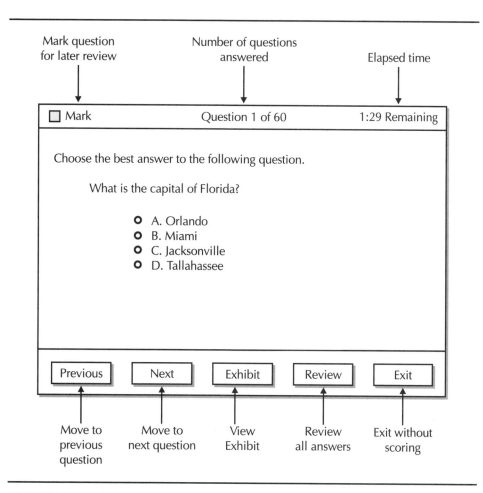

Mark question for later review

Number of questions answered

Elapsed time

☐ Mark   Question 1 of 60   1:29 Remaining

Choose the best answer to the following question.

What is the capital of Florida?

- A. Orlando
- B. Miami
- C. Jacksonville
- D. Tallahassee

| Previous | Next | Exhibit | Review | Exit |

Move to previous question

Move to next question

View Exhibit

Review all answers

Exit without scoring

FIGURE I-1. *Sylvan Prometric exam interface illustration*

interface. Now we'll delve into an explanation of the interface. The top of the interface tells you how much time has elapsed and the number of questions you have answered. You can use the checkbox in the upper left-hand corner of the interface to mark questions you would like to review later. In the main window of the interface you'll find the actual exam question, along with your possible choices. Generally, the interface allows the user to select only one answer (unless the question specifically directs you to select more answers). In this case, the interface will allow you to select only as many answers as the question requests. After answering a question, or marking the question for later review, the candidate can move onto the next question by clicking the appropriate button in the lower left-hand corner. To return to the previous question on the OCP exam, hit the next button over to the left. You can score your questions at any time by pressing the grade test button on the bottom right-hand side. The final point feature to cover is the exhibit button. In some cases, you may require the use of an exhibit to answer a question. If the question does not require use of an exhibit, the button will be grayed out.

Once you've completed all questions on the exam, the Sylvan Prometric interface will display a listing of all the answers you selected, shown in Figure 1-2. The questions you marked for later review will be highlighted, and the interface will guide you through review of all those questions you marked. You can review individual questions, or simply have Sylvan Prometric grade your exam.

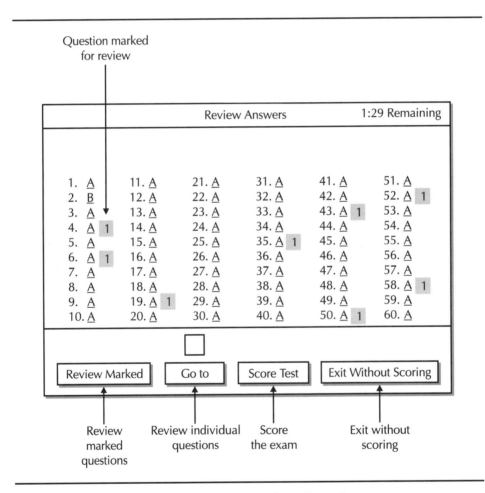

FIGURE 1-2. *Sylvan Prometric answer interface illustration*

The Assessment Test indicates your performance by means of a grade window, such as the one displayed in Figure 1-3. It details the number of questions you answered correctly, along with your percentage score based on 100 percent. You will be shown a section-by-section breakdown of how you did according to the topics covered on the exam as published in the OCP DBA Candidate Guide from Oracle. Finally, a bar graph indicates where your performance falls in comparison to the maximum score possible on the exam. The OCP exam reports your score immediately after you exit the exam, so you will know right then whether you pass or not in a similar fashion as the assessment test. Both interfaces offer you the ability to print a report of your score.

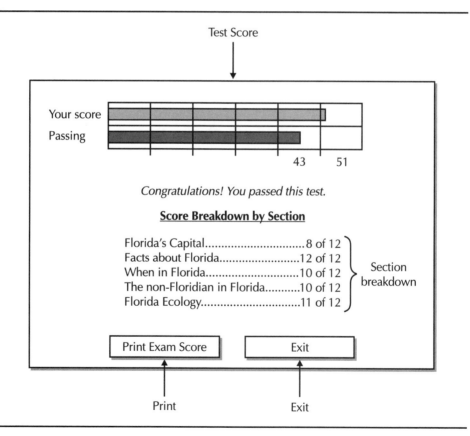

FIGURE 1-3. *Sylvan Prometric score interface illustration*

Strategies for Improving Your Score

When OCP exams were first released, the score range for each OCP Exam was between 200 and 800. However, Oracle has vacillated on whether to scale the OCP exam score, and has experimented lately with reporting only a raw score of the number of questions you answered correctly. However, the bottom line is still the same. Since there are typically 60 questions on an OCP exam, you want to make sure you get at least 75%, or 45 of the questions right in order to pass. Given the recent use of questions with two or even three correct answers on OCP exams, you need to be careful to select *all* correct answer choices on a question or else you may not get full credit for a correct answer. *There is no penalty for wrong answers.* Some preliminary items are now identified for you to take the OCP exams. The first tip is, *don't wait until you're the world's foremost authority on Oracle to take the OCP Exam.* If your OCP exam is scaled as it was when the exams were first released, the passing score for most exams is approximately 650. You have to get 45-50 questions right, or about 75 to 80 percent of the exam. So, if you are getting about four questions right out of five on the assessment test or in the chapters (more on chapter format in a minute), you should consider taking the OCP exam. Remember, you're certified if you pass with 77% or 96% correct answers.

If you can't answer the question within 30 seconds, mark it with the checkbox in the upper left-hand corner of the OCP interface for review later. The most significant difference between the OCP interface and the assessment test interface is a special screen appearing after you answer all the questions. This screen displays all your answers, along with a special indicator next to the questions you marked for review. This screen also offers a button for you to click in order to review the questions you marked. You should use this feature extensively. If you spend only 30 seconds answering each question in your first pass on the exam, you will have at least an hour to review the questions you're unsure of, with the added bonus of knowing you answered all the questions that were easiest to you first.

Third, *there is no penalty for guessing.* If you answer the question correctly, your score goes up, if not, your score doesn't change. If you can eliminate any choices on a question, you should take the chance in the interest of improving your score. In some questions, the OCP exam requires you to specify two or even three choices—this can work in your favor, meaning you need to eliminate fewer choices to get the question right.

OCP for the Experienced DBA

Here are some notes on taking OCP exams tailor-made for users with specific levels of expertise:

- **Advanced (3-5 years continuous Oracle DBA experience):** Take the database administration exam first, then take the exams in any order you wish. This is especially recommended for readers who are more experienced with database administration, because chances are you will do well on the matters tested in that exam. Many test takers go for OCP Exam 1 on SQL and PL/SQL first, thinking it is the easiest exam. This is a trap. OCP Exam 1 asks many questions that may challenge your understanding of obscure single-row functions or complex use of PL/SQL, and we believe for this reason that OCP Exam 1 is a "weeder" exam.

■ **Intermediate (1-3 years continuous Oracle DBA experience):** As with advanced-level DBAs, you may benefit from taking the database administration exam first to get a success under your belt, and taking OCP Exam 1 after you've had the chance to review the chapters covering that exam in this book.

■ **Beginner (less than 1 year continuous Oracle DBA experience):** Take the exams in sequential order as listed above, because each subsequent chapter of this Guide builds on information presented in the previous chapters. As such, you should read the Guide from beginning to end, and take the tests accordingly. Taking the exams in this manner will maximize your use of the Guide and your results on the tests. Also, stick around in your current job until you have 12-18 months experience – the combination of OCP plus experience will prove a winning combination as you hunt for a better career opportunity.

■ **No experience with Oracle:** Begin your exposure to the world of Oracle with another book, such as *Oracle: A Beginner's Guide*, by Corey and Abbey, also from Oracle Press. Then, use this book to prepare for taking the exams in sequential order as listed above, because each subsequent chapter of this Guide builds on information presented in the previous chapters. As such, you should read the Guide from beginning to end, and take the tests accordingly. Taking the exams in this manner will maximize your use of the Guide and your results on the tests. However, don't be surprised if your job search still takes awhile—most employers want to see at least six months of experience plus certification. If you're having trouble gaining experience, try sending me an email for some tailor-made advice.

A Note about Updates and Errata

If you have comments about the book or would like to contact me about it, please do so by email at **jcouchman@mindspring.com**. You can also find related information such as posted updates, corrections, and amplifications at **www.exampilot.com**. Check back on this site and email me often, as new issues arise all the time in the pursuit of OCP. Plus, I love hearing about OCP success stories – especially yours!

PART

I

Preparing for OCP
DBA Exam 1: SQL
and PL/SQL

CHAPTER
1

Selecting Data from Oracle

n this chapter, you will learn about and demonstrate knowledge in the following areas:

- Overview of SQL and PL/SQL
- Writing basic SQL statements
- Restricting and sorting row data
- Using single-row functions

The first exam in the OCP series covers your understanding of basic areas of database usage and design. Every Oracle user, developer, and DBA should have complete mastery in these areas before moving into other test areas. This unit assumes little or no prior knowledge of Oracle on your part in order to help you go from never having used Oracle to having enough expertise in the Oracle server product to maintain and enhance existing applications and develop small new ones. The chapters in this unit will function as the basis for understanding the rest of the book. This chapter will introduce Oracle and cover several aspects of data retrieval from the Oracle database, including selecting rows, limiting the selections, and using single-row functions. This chapter covers material comprising 17 percent of the test content of OCP Exam 1.

Try Following Along on Your Own Database!   As we move through the chapter, you will see examples of SQL statements issued on an Oracle database. For the most part, you can follow along with most of these examples on your own working database if you want. If the following instructions look like a foreign language to you, show this page to your Oracle DBA and ask for his or her help:

1. On the command line of your machine hosting Oracle, change the directory to $ORACLE_HOME/rdbms/admin.

2. Log into Oracle as a privileged user, such as SYSTEM, who is allowed to create other users.

3. Issue the command @utlsampl.sql. This command runs the utlsampl. sql script, which creates objects owned by the user SCOTT/TIGER that we will use in the examples throughout the rest of the book. If you have more experiece with Oracle and wish to create your own user ID, you can run the demobld.sql script instead of utlsampl.sql to create the demonstration tables I reference later in the text.

TIP
Some of the more trivial examples in the chapter may use tables not created by `utlsampl.sql`*. These examples will be noted in the text. No script is available for creating those examples. If you want to use these tables, you have to create them yourself. Instructions for creating tables appear in Chapter 3.*

Overview of SQL and PL/SQL

This section covers the following topics as an overview of SQL and PL/SQL:

- Theoretical and physical aspects of relational databases

- Oracle's RDBMS and ORDBMS implementations

- Usage and benefits of PL/SQL

Welcome to the world of Oracle databases. This section will cover a great deal of the introductory material you need to get started with Oracle in preparation for using query operations to obtain data from the database. This section will cover the theoretical and physical aspects of relational databases, as well as Oracle's RDBMS and ORDBMS implementations. Finally, the use and benefits of PL/SQL will be explained.

Theoretical and Physical Aspects of Relational Databases

Oracle finds its roots in relational database theory, as conceived by E. F. Codd in the 1950s, and extends those theories into an infinite variety of directions, such as data warehousing, online transaction processing, and Web-enabled applications. Undoubtedly, the popularity of this software is part of the reason you are reading this book. This book has the answers to your questions about what an Oracle database is, how it works, and what you can do with it, all of which you'll need to know in order to pass OCP DBA Exam 1.

Software-development companies have taken many different approaches to information management. In years gone by, the more popular software packages for data storage and retrieval focused on flat-file systems as the storage means of choice while simultaneously requiring you to define how information is stored and retrieved, using a programming language such as COBOL. Some early breeds of flat-file systems included hierarchical storage systems, where data records were stored in a hierarchy similar to the hierarchical directory structure you might see on your PC's hard drive in Windows Explorer. These applications ran on mainframes, and brand names of these older data-management packages included IMS from IBM and IDMS from Computer Associates. The language most often used to develop mechanisms to add or manage data in those systems was COBOL.

Those older flat-file systems were great for certain tasks, such as defining parent/child relationships. A parent/child relationship might include the relationship of salespeople within a food service distribution company to the company's customers or the tracking number for an invoice as it relates to product line items on the customer's order from that food service distribution company. However, one drawback to flat-file systems stems from the fact that a parent/child relationship cannot model every possible type of data relationship. Within the food service company example, a customer's order may list many different products. Each of those products themselves will probably appear on many different orders. In this case of a "many products to many orders" relationship, which way should the hierarchy be designed? What should be the parent and what should be the child? The usual solution was to create two separate hierarchies—one with product as parent; the other with order as parent. Unfortunately, this often meant maintaining much of the same information in two (or more) places. Keeping data content consistent across multiple places where it is kept makes storage and retrieval complex. Another shortcoming of hierarchical databases using flat-file systems is that they are not easily adaptable to changing business needs. If the food service distributor creates a new sales system that calls for joint ownership of customer accounts by multiple salespeople, the hierarchical database will need to be redesigned.

Motivated by dissatisfaction with the cumbersome characteristics of hierarchical flat-file databases, E. F. Codd, a computer scientist working for IBM in the 1950s, developed an alternative: the *relational* model. Instead of storing data in hierarchies, Codd proposed storing related data items, such as control numbers and ordered products, in tables. If the tables were designed according to a few simple principles, they were both intuitive and extremely efficient in storing data, as Codd discovered. A single data item could be stored in only one place. Over time, many software makers recognized the significance of Codd's work and began developing products that adhered to Codd's model. Since the 1980s, virtually all database software products (including Oracle's) conform to the relational model.

Central to the success of the relational model is the use of a relational database management system, or *RDBMS*, for storing, retrieving, and manipulating data in a database. Earlier products required organizations to have many COBOL programmers on staff to code mechanisms for managing data-retrieval routines that interact directly with the files of the database. In contrast, the RDBMS handles these tasks automatically using a functional programming language called *SQL* (pronounced either "sequel" or as the letters spelled out). SQL stands for "structured query language," and it allows users to request the data they want according to strict comparison criteria. The following code block shows a typical SQL statement:

```
SQL> SELECT EMPNO, ENAME, SAL FROM EMP
  2  WHERE ENAME = 'FARBISSINA';
```

TIP
The preceding block was taken directly from SQL*Plus. The "2," which indicates that you are typing in the second line, is written automatically by SQL*Plus. As such, you do not actually need to type "2" yourself.

Behind the scenes, an RDBMS translates this statement into a series of operations that will retrieve the actual data from a file somewhere on the machine hosting your database. This step is called *parsing.* After parsing is complete, the RDBMS executes the series of operations to complete the requested action. That series of operations may involve some or all of the following tasks:

- Implicit datatype conversion
- Disk reads or disk writes
- Filtering table data according to search criteria
- Index lookups for faster response time
- Sorting and formatting data returned

TIP
An index is a special database object that can be used to enhance performance of certain RDBMS operations. A datatype is literally a definition of the "type" of data being stored in the table's column. You'll learn more about both these topics in later chapters.

RDBMS vs. Flat File System Quick Reference

The following table shows a quick comparison of flat-file systems to relational database management systems:

Task	Flat File System	RDBMS
Handles parent/child data relationships?	Yes	Yes
Handles other types of data relationships?	Not well	Yes
Handles data manipulation easily?	No	Yes
Easily adaptable to changing business needs?	No	Yes
Handles data retrieval easily?	Sometimes	Yes
Handles data retrieval quickly?	Sometimes	Sometimes

For Review

1. Understand the tasks an RDBMS completes behind the scenes when users request certain pieces of data.

2. Be sure you can describe the features, advantages, and disadvantages of flat-file systems and relational database management systems.

Exercises

1. **You are exploring theoretical aspects of the Oracle RDBMS. Which of the following choices identifies an aspect of data management that the Oracle RDBMS does not handle on your behalf?**

   A. Datatype conversion

   B. Disk reads

   C. Sorting and formatting return data

   D. Defining required information via SQL

2. **You are evaluating the use of Oracle to replace legacy pre-relational systems in your organization. In comparison to the Oracle RDBMS, which**

of the following aspects of pre-relational database systems did those systems handle as well as their relational counterpart?

A. Many-to-many data relationships

B. Parent-child relationships

C. Adaptability to changing business needs

D. Data manipulation

3. What is the name of the scientist who first conceptualized the use of relational database management systems? _____

Answer Key

1. D. **2.** B. **3.** E. F. Codd.

Oracle's RDBMS and ORDBMS Implementations

Oracle **8** and higher │ Although every relational database offers an RDBMS that accepts basically the same types of SQL statements, not all databases have the same components. An Oracle database is considerably more complicated than some other PC-based databases you may have seen, such as Microsoft Access or even SQL Server. The components of an Oracle database are broken into three basic areas, corresponding to the three basic areas of host machines that run Oracle databases. In this section, pay close attention to how each component in each part of the Oracle database interacts with a component in another part. Figure 1-1 illustrates the various elements of the Oracle database, whereas the following discussions identify and describe each component. The components are as follows:

Memory	The Oracle System Global Area (SGA)
Disk	Oracle datafiles, redo logs, control files, password files, and parameter files
Processes	Threads in the `oracle.exe` background process (Windows) or individual processes (UNIX) and the server process

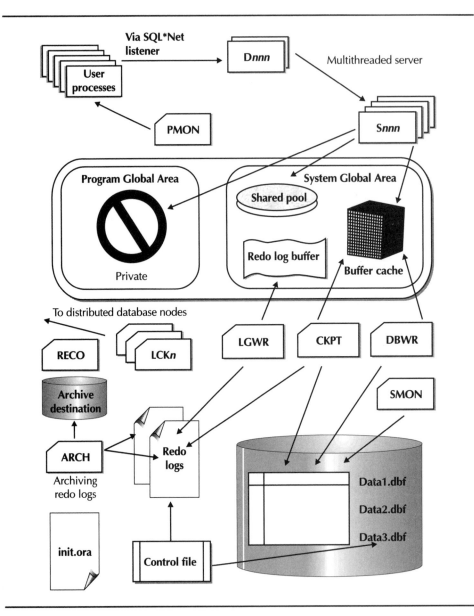

FIGURE 1-1. *Oracle server architecture*

Oracle SGA

Oracle's memory component, the System Global Area (SGA), consists of several elements, each of which is designed for a specific purpose.

Buffer Cache   The buffer cache stores Oracle data in memory for users to view or change. In this way, users never make changes directly to disk files. Instead, Oracle reads the appropriate data into memory for the user process to change, and it writes the changes back to disk at some point later. The buffer cache follows a modified least recently used (LRU) algorithm to determine when data in this area can be eliminated when more space is needed in the buffer cache to make room for user data requested.

Log Buffer   The log buffer stores special information called *redo*, which helps Oracle reconstruct data changes in the event of a system failure. Redo information is written to the log buffer by users making data changes and is stored in the log buffer until Oracle can write the redo information to disk.

Shared Pool   The shared pool stores many items that are "mission critical" to the operation of your Oracle database. Components of the shared pool include the library cache, for storing parsed SQL statements for reuse by other users; the dictionary or row cache, for storing Oracle data dictionary information in memory where it can be accessed quickly; and latches and other database-control mechanisms.

TIP
The Oracle data dictionary is a set of information stored in Oracle that tells you all kinds of important things about your database. The data dictionary is used frequently by users and Oracle processes alike, so it is important for overall database performance to store dictionary information in memory whenever possible. Hence, you can see the need for the dictionary cache in your shared pool.

Oracle **8i** and higher   **Large Pool**   The fourth and less frequently used component of Oracle's SGA is the large pool, which is used to support parallel database operations and parallel database recovery. It also supports storage of session User Global Area, or UGA, information when the multithreaded server architecture is used. Introduced in Oracle8, this component is optional for Oracle database operation.

Other Memory Areas   There are other components to the SGA in Oracle8i and later versions, such as the Java pool and large pool, that are not shown in Figure 1-1. The items not included in this discussion and/or the figure are excluded because a detailed examination of these topics is not necessary for passing the OCP exam on SQL and PL/SQL. This figure and the current discussion are merely meant to give you the larger picture of Oracle before digging into a meaningful discussion of SQL queries.

Oracle Disk Components

The Oracle disk components store all kinds of vital information in your Oracle database. You cannot run Oracle without having all your disk components (except password files) in their proper places.

Datafiles   This mandatory disk component is used for storing Oracle dictionary and application database objects. These components often grow extremely large in size. Information in the buffer cache and the dictionary cache in memory comes from datafiles on disk.

Redo Logs   This mandatory disk component is used for storing redo information on disk. Information from the log buffer in memory eventually gets written here.

Control Files   This mandatory disk component is used for storing vital information about the location of Oracle disk components on the host system. The physical locations of both datafiles and redo logs in the server's file system are stored in your control file. There can be one or many control files in an Oracle database. If there is more than one control file, each will be an identical copy. Oracle reads the control files every time you start the database and updates the control files when redo logs or datafiles are added or moved.

Password Files   This optional disk component is used for securing privileged user connection information to allow the database to be managed remotely via Enterprise Manager, Oracle's database-management tool. It also controls the number of the privileged system-management connections that can be made to the database at the same time. Without a password file, you may only administer your database by connecting directly to the machine hosting the Oracle database and using management tools such as SQL*Plus directly from the host machine.

Parameter Files   This mandatory disk component is used for configuring how Oracle will operate while it is running. A parameter file contains many parameters and their set values. Oracle reads the parameter file when you start the database. Some Oracle professionals refer to the parameter file as the `init.ora` file. You may maintain one or many parameter files for a database, corresponding to different instance configurations you may want to implement at various times.

Oracle Server and Background Processes

The final component of Oracle to be covered is the set of elements that comprise Oracle on your host system's CPU. The Oracle server process reads data from datafiles into the buffer cache on behalf of user processes. It can either be shared between multiple users or be dedicated to one user. The Oracle database also has one background process in Windows environments—oracle.exe. If you hit CTRL-ALT-DELETE on your system hosting the Oracle database, click on the Task Manager button to bring up the Task Manager, and then click on the Processes tab, you will see this process running on your Windows machine. In Windows, this process has many threads that handle other important activities your database is engaged in at all times in the background. If you want to find information in Windows about services setup for use with Oracle software, you can look in Start | Settings | Control Panel. For NT, the Services icon lists all the Windows services available on the machine. For Windows 2000, you can double-click on the Administrative Tools icon to find the Services icon. On UNIX machines, Oracle consists of multiple background processes. If the database is running on a UNIX machine, you can usually see its background processes if you issue the command ps -fu oracle on your UNIX command line.

What an ORDBMS Is

Oracle **8i** and higher | As object-oriented programming has gained popularity, Oracle has adjusted its relational database-management paradigm to include support for object-relational database design. This methodology incorporates the best features of object programming with the best features of relational programming and allows the developer to draw from both when designing a system in Oracle. Some of the features supported on the object side include the following:

- Storing user-defined datatypes in the database as object tables

- Associating methods to the object table definition

- Extending the relational design to include object-relational features such as columns of user-defined datatypes

For Review

Know the three components of the Oracle database, and be able to name each of the elements in each component.

Exercises

1. You are examining the components of an Oracle database. Which of the following choices identifies an aspect of Oracle that resides on the disk of the machine hosting the Oracle database?

    A. SGA

    B. Datafile

    C. Background process

    D. Java pool

2. You are interested in seeing Oracle running on your Windows-based host machine. In which of the following areas would you look?

    A. Control Panel | Services Icon

    B. Desktop

    C. Windows Explorer

    D. Start menu

3. You are interested in seeing Oracle running on your UNIX machine. Which of the following commands might you use?

    A. ls

    B. grep

    C. ps

    D. df

Answer Key
1. B. 2. A. 3. C.

Usage and Benefits of PL/SQL

PL/SQL is Oracle's own language for developing database applications. In addition to supporting all SQL operations that Oracle SQL supports, PL/SQL adds programming language extensions such as conditional statement processing, loops, variables, cursor operations, abstract datatypes, modularization, encapsulation, overloading, and more. The following lists frequently cited reasons why PL/SQL developers use the language:

- **PL/SQL is easy to learn and use.**   Professionals with even a modest programming background can usually pick up PL/SQL syntax before too long and develop programs of moderate complexity without much effort. Professionals without a programming background can learn PL/SQL with more effort spent learning basic constructs, such as variable declaration, conditional statement processing, and so on.

- **PL/SQL is stored in the Oracle database.**   This means that you only have to compile the code into the Oracle database to make that code available to every user on the system. There is no need for an extended deployment as with traditional client/server applications. The result is code that runs quickly and works natively with your Oracle data.

- **PL/SQL integrates well with the Oracle database.**   No special command syntax is needed to perform SQL operations involving data in the Oracle database. No colons, question marks, or other "odd characters" are required to prefix variables as in other languages. One exception to this rule relates to trigger development, which is a hybrid between a database object and PL/SQL.

- **PL/SQL is especially adept at processing large blocks of data.**   Oracle PL/SQL provides a special construct called a `cursor for` loop, which allows you to query several rows of table data and then process through each row of that data in an iterative fashion. This feature allows you to process large amounts of data in bulk.

- **PL/SQL comes with lots of Oracle-supplied code to assist in performing tasks.**   Oracle distributes several packages of PL/SQL code with every database shipped. This code enables you to perform highly specialized operations, such as file input/output (or I/O), retrieving Web pages into your database, job scheduling, dynamic SQL, interprocess communication, resource management, and much more. You can refer to these Oracle-supplied packages just like any other PL/SQL program.

- **PL/SQL supports named and anonymous programs.**   There are many different types of named programs you can develop in PL/SQL, including stored procedures, functions, and packages. These code blocks are actually compiled and stored in the database and are available for later use. You can also write anonymous programs, which are compiled at the time you submit the code for execution, and executed, but not stored in the database.

■ **PL/SQL can be integrated into database tables via triggers.**   Oracle integrates PL/SQL programmatic activity into database tables via triggers. This feature allows you to develop applications that utilize complex business rules for regulating data inside the database, thus reducing the potential for corrupt or inappropriate data from users.

■ **PL/SQL supports encapsulation and modularization.**   *Encapsulation* involves using one named PL/SQL program to call another named PL/SQL program. *Modularization* involves breaking down a large task into several smaller components and then writing named PL/SQL programs to handle those smaller tasks. The result is code that's easier to read and maintain.

■ **PL/SQL supports overloading.** *Overloading* occurs when you have a package containing procedures or functions with the same name that accept different variables of different datatypes. When you call the overloaded procedure, Oracle dynamically decides which version of the procedure to use based on the datatype of the variable you pass.

■ **PL/SQL allows programmers to package their Oracle code.**   Oracle PL/SQL supports a construct called a *package*. This feature allows you to logically group several procedures or functions that work together into one single construct. Procedures grouped together using packages perform better than they would individually because all procedures in the package will be loaded into memory as soon as one of the procedures is referenced. In contrast, stand-alone procedures are only loaded into memory when called. This reduces the overhead Oracle requires for memory management, thus improving performance.

■ **PL/SQL supports advanced datatypes.**   PL/SQL gives users the ability to define abstract datatypes such as records, allowing you some object-oriented flexibility in your procedural code. PL/SQL also offers table constructs for variable definition and use, approximating the use of arrays. Finally, PL/SQL allows you to declare REF datatypes, which gives PL/SQL the ability to use datatypes similar to pointers in C and C++.

For Review

Be sure you understand the benefits of PL/SQL programming before you begin Chapter 5.

Exercises

1. **You develop a PL/SQL package for use with Oracle. Which of the following choices identifies where that code is stored?**

    A. As an executable file on the host system

    B. As uncompiled code in the database

    C. As compiled code in the database

    D. As a flat file, sent to the database when you want to run the program

2. **You want to develop a PL/SQL package containing different procedures with the same name but different variable datatypes. What is the name of the PL/SQL feature that allows this?**

    A. Packaging.

    B. Overloading.

    C. Encapsulation.

    D. This functionality is not possible in PL/SQL.

3. **What is the name of the special loop that makes PL/SQL especially adept at processing large numbers of data records?** _____

Answer Key

1. C. **2.** B. **3.** The `cursor for` loop.

Writing Basic SQL Statements

This section will cover the following areas related to selecting rows:

- Capabilities of SQL `select` statements

- Executing `select` statements

- Differentiating between SQL and SQL*Plus commands

    This section starts your approach to Oracle systems. You will learn what SQL provides you in the Oracle working environment and how to develop the all-important `select` statement, used for obtaining data from Oracle. You will also learn how to distinguish SQL commands from SQL*Plus commands. This skill is important as you use SQL*Plus for developing and running queries and because there are certain SQL*Plus commands you must know for passing the OCP exam.

Capabilities of SQL Select Statements

If you've already developed SQL code for other database applications, you're in for some good news. Oracle SQL complies with the industry accepted standards, such as ANSI SQL92. But before exploring SQL `select` statements in detail, consider the following overview of all the statement categories available in SQL and their associated usage:

- **`select`** Used for data retrieval and query access. Many developers consider this statement to be part of data manipulation language (DML) operations against the database. However, Oracle does not. When OCP refers to DML statements, you should make a mental note that Oracle is not referring to the `select` command.

- **`insert`, `update`, `delete`** Used for data manipulation language (DML) operations against the Oracle database, including adding new records, changing existing records, and removing records, respectively.

- **`create`, `alter`, `drop`** Used for data definition language (DDL) operations against the Oracle database, including adding, modifying, and removing database objects such as tables, indexes, sequences, and so on, respectively.

- **`commit`, `rollback`, `savepoint`** Used for transaction-control activities inside a user's session, including saving changes, discarding changes, and marking logical breakpoints within the transaction, respectively.

- **`grant`, `revoke`** Used for data control language (DCL) operations against your Oracle database, where you might need to control user access to data.

Many developers, designers, DBAs, and power users begin their experience with Oracle using an existing Oracle application in an organization. The first tool many people see for selecting data directly from the Oracle relational database management system is SQL*Plus. When users first start SQL*Plus, in most cases, they must enter their Oracle username and password in order to begin a session with the Oracle database. There are some exceptions to this rule that utilize the password authentication provided with the operating system. The following example shows how you might begin a session with Oracle on the UNIX command line:

```
$/home/jason> sqlplus scott/tiger
```

TIP

*From Windows, you can click on Start | Programs |
Oracle ORACLE_HOME | Application Development |
SQL*Plus or double-click on the SQL*Plus icon on
your desktop if one appears there. On most systems,
ORACLE_HOME will be replaced with the name
of the Oracle software home location, such as
OraHome81.*

Class in Session

When you log into Oracle via SQL*Plus, you create a session with the database. A
session is an interactive runtime environment similar to a command-line environment,
such as UNIX or DOS, in which you enter commands to retrieve data. Oracle
performs a series of activities to obtain the data you ask for based on the SQL
command you enter. Think of it as a conversation, which, in turn, implies *language*.
Remember, you communicate with Oracle using the structured query language, SQL,
to obtain the information you need.

TIP

*To connect to the database, you must be granted
permission to do so—simply having a user ID and
password isn't enough. For more information on
permissions, see Chapter 4.*

SQL is a *functional* programming language, which means that you specify the
types of things you want to see happen in terms of the results you want. You define
the result you want, and Oracle determines how to get it for you. Take another look
at the `select` statement I showed you earlier:

```
SQL> SELECT EMPNO, ENAME, SAL FROM EMP
  2  WHERE ENAME = 'FARBISSINA';
```

This statement asks Oracle to provide data from the EMP table, where the value
in a certain column called ENAME equals FARBISSINA. We don't care how Oracle
gets it, just so long as Oracle returns only the record from table EMP we asked for.
Contrast this approach to other languages you may have heard about or programmed
in, such as C++ and COBOL. These languages are often referred to as *procedural*
or *iterative* programming languages because the code written in these languages
implies an end result by explicitly defining the *process* for obtaining the result.
The following block of code from an imaginary procedural programming language

similar to C illustrates how the same function may be handled by explicitly defining the means to the end:

```
Include <stdio.h>
Include <string.h>
Include <rdbms.h>

Int *empno;
Char *statement;

Type emp_rec is record (
Int            empno;
Char[10]       emp_name;
Int            sal; )

Void main() {
  login_to_oracle(scott,tiger);
  Access_table(emp);
  Open(statement.memaddr);
  Strcpy("SELECT EMPNO, ENAME, SAL FROM EMP WHERE
         ENAME = 'FARBISSINA'",statement.text);
  parse(statement);
  execute(statement);
  for (I=1,I=statement.results,I+1)
    fetch(statement.result[I],emp_rec);
    printf(emp_rec);

  close(statement.memaddr);
  }
```

Of course, this C-like block of code will not compile anywhere but in your imagination, but the point of the example is clear—other languages make you define the process, whereas SQL lets you define the result.

For Review

1. What is SQL?

2. What is SQL capable of?

3. How does SQL compare to other programming languages you might use, such as Java and C?

Exercises

1. **You are determining which type of SQL statement to use in your Oracle database. Which of the following choices identifies the type of statement you would use when trying to obtain data from the database?**

    A. select

    B. update

    C. insert

    D. delete

2. **Which of the following choices identifies a functional programming language?**

    A. C

    B. Java

    C. COBOL

    D. SQL

3. **Identify a command that is part of SQL's data control language (DCL).**

    _____

Answer Key

1. A. **2.** D. **3.** grant or revoke

Executing select Statements

The most common type of SQL statement executed in most database environments is the select statement, which queries a table in the database for requested data. Tables in Oracle are similar in concept to spreadsheets. Examine the following code block, where you will see a select statement in the context of a session with Oracle:

```
C:\> c:\oracle\ora81\bin\sqlplus scott/tiger
SQL*Plus: Release 8.1.7.0.0 - Production on Tue Feb 03 18:53:11 2000
Copyright (c) Oracle Corporation 1979, 2000.  All rights reserved.
Connected to: Oracle8i Release 8.1.7.0.0
With the distributed and replication options
PL/SQL Release 8.1.7.0.0 Production

SQL> select * from emp;
    EMPNO ENAME    JOB         MGR HIREDATE   SAL COMM DEPTNO
--------- -------- --------- ----- --------- ---- ---- ------
     7369 SMITH    CLERK      7902 17-DEC-80  800         20
     7499 ALLEN    SALESMAN   7698 20-FEB-81 1600  300    30
     7521 WARD     SALESMAN   7698 22-FEB-81 1250  500    30
     7566 JONES    MANAGER    7839 02-APR-81 2975         20
     7654 MARTIN   SALESMAN   7698 28-SEP-81 1250 1400    30
```

7698	BLAKE	MANAGER	7839	01-MAY-81	2850		30
7782	CLARK	MANAGER	7839	09-JUN-81	2450		10
7788	SCOTT	ANALYST	7566	19-APR-87	3000		20
7839	KING	PRESIDENT		17-NOV-81	5000		10
7844	TURNER	SALESMAN	7698	08-SEP-81	1500	0	30
7876	ADAMS	CLERK	7788	23-MAY-87	1100		20
7900	JAMES	CLERK	7698	03-DEC-81	950		30
7902	FORD	ANALYST	7566	03-DEC-81	3000		20
7934	MILLER	CLERK	7782	23-JAN-82	1300		10

TIP

For the purposes of preparing for OCP, any version of Oracle8i (8.1.5, 8.1.6, or 8.1.7) should be sufficient, though many of the questions for OCP seem to show a slight bias toward Oracle8i version 8.1.6.

The first part, containing the copyright information, is a welcome message from SQL*Plus. If you wanted, you could suppress this information in your call to SQL*Plus from the operating system command line by entering sqlplus −s and pressing ENTER, where the −s extension indicates SQL*Plus should run in silent mode. This is sometimes useful for batch programs that write output to an automated feed file, where you don't want a lot of extraneous junk in the feed because an error will result. We'll explore some other SQL*Plus commands that help you control the appearance of your output later in the chapter. The bold line in the block illustrates a simple SQL select statement. In essence, you're asking Oracle to return all data from all columns in the EMP table. Oracle replies with the contents of the EMP table. The main components of a select statement are listed next, and *both* are required in every select statement you issue on the database:

- **The select, or *column*, clause** This clause contains columns or expressions containing data you want to see, separated by commas. The preceding query uses a *wildcard* (*) character, indicating we want data from every column in the table.

- **The from, or *table*, clause** This clause tells Oracle what table to get the data from.

TIP

*Always use a semicolon (;) to end SQL statements when entering them directly into SQL*Plus. You can use a slash (/) in some situations, such as for SQL*Plus batch scripts, but be careful—a slash at the end of a SQL statement already ended with a semicolon makes the statement run twice!*

A Note About Columns and Datatypes

Tables in the Oracle database are comprised of columns, each storing a unit of information for the row. These units taken together across a single row comprise a record stored in the table. Review the first record in the preceding code block for EMPNO 7369, which is listed here:

```
    EMPNO ENAME     JOB         MGR HIREDATE   SAL COMM DEPTNO
--------- --------  ---------   ----- --------- ---- ---- ------
     7369 SMITH     CLERK      7902 17-DEC-80  800           20
```

Each column identifies an aspect of this unique employee. EMPNO identifies his employee number, ENAME identifies his name, and so on. The information stored in each column of the table for this fellow must correspond to the datatype defined for that column. For example, column EMPNO is defined as a NUMBER column, meaning that only numbers of a certain size can be stored for records in that column. No text, date, or nonnumerical information can be stored in EMPNO, because doing so would violate the column's stated datatype. I'll refer to a column's datatype frequently throughout the rest of the book, so it's worth your time to master this fundamental concept. The column datatypes permitted in Oracle tables that we'll work with most frequently are listed here:

- **NUMBER**   A datatype used for storing numerical data. No dashes, text, or other nonnumerical information is allowed in columns of this datatype.

- **DATE**   A datatype used for storing date information. Internally, Oracle stores dates as numbers, which it can then convert into any DATE format you want. By default, DATE information is displayed in DD-MON-YY format (for example, 25-DEC-79).

- **VARCHAR2**   A datatype used for storing text data. Any text character (including special characters, numbers, dashes, and so on) can be stored in a VARCHAR2 column.

- **CHAR**   A datatype used for storing text data. Any text character (including special characters, numbers, dashes, and so on) can be stored in a CHAR column.

TIP: The main difference between VARCHAR2 and CHAR columns is the amount of space required for storing text data, which is greater for CHAR columns than for VARCHAR2 columns. This is because CHAR columns have a fixed length and always store the same number of bytes, whereas VARCHAR2 has a variable length and only contains the number of bytes you provide it.

Datatypes for storing other types of information exist in Oracle; however, there aren't as many of them as you might encounter in database products from other vendors. For example, Oracle has no currency datatype. Monetary values are treated simply as numbers, and as such they can be stored in a column defined as the NUMBER datatype.

TIP
Another datatype we'll observe from time to time in the book is the ROWID datatype. This is a special datatype used by Oracle to format the information used to display the physical location of the row on disk.

The "Schema" of Things

Take a look at the following code block:

```
SQL> select empno, ename, sal
  2  from scott.emp;
    EMPNO ENAME            SAL
--------- ---------- ---------
     7369 SMITH            800
     7499 ALLEN           1600
     7521 WARD            1250
     7566 JONES           2975
     7654 MARTIN          1250
     7698 BLAKE           2850
     7782 CLARK           2450
     7788 SCOTT           3000
     7839 KING            5000
     7844 TURNER          1500
     7876 ADAMS           1100
     7900 JAMES            950
     7902 FORD            3000
     7934 MILLER          1300
```

Notice anything different about the way table EMP is referenced in this table clause? It has the name of the owner, SCOTT, prefixed to it. Oracle developers and DBAs refer to the concept of referencing the table owner as well as the table itself as a *schema*. When you, the user logging into an Oracle database, are granted the ability to create database objects such as tables, the objects you create will belong to you. In other words, they are part of your schema. The identity you use when you log into your database to run `demobld.sql` determines the schema that all those tables will belong to.

When the table you reference in a query isn't prefixed with the schema it belongs to, Oracle assumes the table exists in your schema and tries to query it. If the table doesn't exist in your schema, you must prefix the table name with the schema information, separating the schema owner from the table name with a period.

TIP
A schema is a logical grouping of database objects based on the user who owns the objects.

Prefixing Columns with Table Names

The same aliasing concept works in the column clause, too—you can prefix the column name with the table name separated by a dot (.) in the table clause for your query. Make sure you understand how to specify a schema owner, the table name, and the column name in a `select` statement in SQL*Plus. The following code block demonstrates the most formal usage for prefixing with appropriate schema and table information:

```
SELECT table_name.column_name, table_name.column_name
FROM schema.table_name;
```

Arithmetic and Table Data

Oracle lets you perform arithmetic operations on your numeric table data as well. The operators used in Oracle are the same as in daily use (+ for addition, – for subtraction, * for multiplication, and / for division). Say, for example, you are performing a simple annual review that involves giving each user a cost-of-living increase in the amount of 8 percent of his or her salary. The process involves multiplying each person's salary by 1.08. Oracle makes the work easy if you use arithmetic expressions, as shown here:

```
SQL> select empno, ename, sal, sal*1.08
  2  from emp;
     EMPNO ENAME             SAL   SAL*1.08
--------- ---------- --------- ---------
      7369 SMITH             800        864
      7499 ALLEN            1600       1728
      7521 WARD             1250       1350
      7566 JONES            2975       3213
      7654 MARTIN           1250       1350
      7698 BLAKE            2850       3078
      7782 CLARK            2450       2646
      7788 SCOTT            3000       3240
      7839 KING             5000       5400
      7844 TURNER           1500       1620
      7876 ADAMS            1100       1188
```

```
7900 JAMES           950        1026
7902 FORD           3000        3240
7934 MILLER         1300        1404
```

Operator Precedence

There's usually at least one question on OCP dealing with operator precedence—that high-school math concept regarding which calculation to do first. An easy way to remember operator precedence in mathematics is to use the acronym PEMDAS. You can remember PEMDAS using the mnemonic "Please Excuse My Dear Aunt Sally." PEMDAS stands for parentheses, exponents, multiplication and division, addition and subtraction. Therefore, $2 / 10 + 36 * (84 - 6)$ is 2808.2, whereas $2 / 10 + 36 * 84 - 6$ is 3018.2.

2 + 2 and the DUAL Table

As mentioned earlier, every `select` statement must have a column clause and a table clause. However, you might not always want to perform arithmetic calculations on data from an actual table. Say, for example, you simply want to add 2 + 2. Conveniently, the column clause in a `select` statement needn't contain actual column names. It can contain fixed numbers or other types of expressions instead. But what about the table clause? Because you're using fixed numbers, you don't want data from a real table. So why not use a fake one? You can use a special table called *DUAL* to fill in the table clause without Oracle actually using its data. Take a look at the following block:

```
SQL> select 2 + 2 from dual;
     2+2
---------
       4
```

The DUAL table consists of one column, called *DUMMY*, containing one value, X. Execute a `select * from DUAL` statement and see for yourself that there is no meaningful data stored here. It simply exists as a SQL construct to support the requirement of a table specification in the `from` clause. The DUAL table is owned by the Oracle built-in user SYS.

Handling NULL Values

Sometimes a query for information will produce a "nothing" result. In database terms, *nothing* is called *NULL*. In set theory, the mathematical foundation for relational databases, NULL represents the value of an empty dataset, or a dataset containing no values. Put another way, NULL is *not* the blank character displayed when you press the spacebar! NULL is the absence of information. Unless specified otherwise, a column in a table is designed to accommodate the placement of nothing into the column. An example of retrieving NULL is listed in the MGR column of the following code block on EMPNO 7839:

```
SQL> select empno, ename, mgr
  2  from emp;
     EMPNO ENAME             MGR
  --------- ---------- ---------
      7369 SMITH            7902
      7499 ALLEN            7698
      7521 WARD             7698
      7566 JONES            7839
      7654 MARTIN           7698
      7698 BLAKE            7839
      7782 CLARK            7839
      7788 SCOTT            7566
      7839 KING
      7844 TURNER           7698
      7876 ADAMS            7788
      7900 JAMES            7698
      7902 FORD             7566
      7934 MILLER           7782
```

However, there are times when you may want to substitute a value in place of NULL. Oracle provides this functionality with a special function, called nvl(). Assume that you do not want to see blank spaces for manager information. Instead, you want the output of the query to contain a zero where a NULL value is listed. The query in the following code block illustrates how you can obtain the desired result:

```
SQL> select empno, ename, nvl(mgr,0)
  2  from emp;
     EMPNO ENAME      NVL(MGR,0)
  --------- ---------- ----------
      7369 SMITH            7902
      7499 ALLEN            7698
      7521 WARD             7698
      7566 JONES            7839
      7654 MARTIN           7698
      7698 BLAKE            7839
      7782 CLARK            7839
      7788 SCOTT            7566
      7839 KING                0
      7844 TURNER           7698
      7876 ADAMS            7788
      7900 JAMES            7698
      7902 FORD             7566
      7934 MILLER           7782
```

Notice that the column specified in `nvl( )` contains an actual value. That value is what Oracle returns; when the column is NULL, the special string is returned. The `nvl( )` function can be used on columns of all datatypes, but remember this: *The value specified to be returned if the column value is NULL must be the same datatype as the column specified.* The basic syntax for `nvl( )` is as follows:

```
NVL(column_name, value_if_null)
```

The distinct Keyword

If you look back at the code block that lists all the employees in the EMP table, you'll notice something interesting in the JOB column. Many of the employees have the same job title. Sometimes, you might want to see only the unique values for a column that you know will contain many repeated values. In order to do so, Oracle offers the `distinct` keyword. To obtain the unique values for a column containing duplicates, you simply precede the column reference with the `distinct` keyword in your column clause, like this:

```
SQL> select distinct job
  2  from emp;
JOB
---------
ANALYST
CLERK
MANAGER
PRESIDENT
SALESMAN
```

TIP
In order for the `distinct` keyword to work, it must appear directly after the `select` keyword in your SQL query.

Changing Output Headings with Aliases

In every result set Oracle returns in response to your SQL `select` commands, Oracle creates headings for each column so that you know what the data is. By default, Oracle reprints the column name exactly as you defined it in the `select` statement, including functions if there are any. Unfortunately, this method often leaves you with a bad description of the column data. Oracle truncates the expression to fit a certain width corresponding to the datatype of the column returned, making the problem even worse. Fortunately, you can use *aliases* in your column clause to solve this problem. In a column alias, you give the column another name that Oracle will use when the `select` statement results are displayed. This feature gives you the ability to fit more descriptive names into the space allotted. Here's an example:

```
SQL> select empno, ename, nvl(mgr,0) as mgr
  2  from emp;
    EMPNO ENAME            MGR
--------- ---------- ---------
     7369 SMITH           7902
     7499 ALLEN           7698
     7521 WARD            7698
     7566 JONES           7839
     7654 MARTIN          7698
     7698 BLAKE           7839
     7782 CLARK           7839
     7788 SCOTT           7566
     7839 KING               0
     7844 TURNER          7698
     7876 ADAMS           7788
     7900 JAMES           7698
     7902 FORD            7566
     7934 MILLER          7782
```

TIP
You can omit the as *keyword in the column alias
and still wind up with substantially the same result.*

Column aliases are useful for adding meaningful headings to output from SQL
queries. Aliases can be specified in two ways: either by naming the alias after the
column specification separated by a space or by using the as keyword to mark the
alias more clearly. Here's the general rule:

```
SQL> -- SELECT column_name_or_operation alias, ...;
SQL> SELECT nvl(mgr,0) MGR
  2  FROM EMP;
```

or

```
SQL> -- SELECT column_name_or_operation  AS alias, ...;
SQL> SELECT nvl(mgr,0) AS MGR
  2  FROM EMP;
```

Putting Columns Together with Concatenation
You can also glue together column data to produce more interesting or readable
output. This is called *concatenation*. The concatenation operator is two pipe characters
put together: ||. You can also use the concat( ) operation, passing it the two
column names. In the following example, the ENAME column is concatenated with
a text expression and the JOB column using both available methods to produce a
meaningful result:

```
SQL> select ename || ', who is the ' ||
  2  concat(job,' for the company')
  3  as "Name and Role"
  4  from emp;
Name and Role
------------------------------------------------
SMITH, who is the CLERK for the company
ALLEN, who is the SALESMAN for the company
WARD, who is the SALESMAN for the company
JONES, who is the MANAGER for the company
MARTIN, who is the SALESMAN for the company
BLAKE, who is the MANAGER for the company
CLARK, who is the MANAGER for the company
SCOTT, who is the ANALYST for the company
KING, who is the PRESIDENT for the company
TURNER, who is the SALESMAN for the company
ADAMS, who is the CLERK for the company
JAMES, who is the CLERK for the company
FORD, who is the ANALYST for the company
MILLER, who is the CLERK for the company
```

TIP
Use column aliases to name your concatenated column to make the output more readable and meaningful.

For Review

1. Understand the two components of `select` statements and what a schema is.

2. Know how to perform arithmetic on selected columns and on numeric expressions in Oracle and know what the DUAL table is.

3. Know both methods used for concatenating columns and how to define column aliases. Also, know what the `distinct` keyword is and how it is used.

4. Be able to define what NULL means in the context of Oracle SQL and how to use the `nvl( )` function.

5. Be sure you understand the correct operator precedence using the acronym PEMDAS.

Exercises

1. You are identifying a table for use in your `select` clause that was not created by you. Which of the following choices identifies the reference that must be included in your `select` statement so that Oracle knows where to look for the information?

   A. Alias

   B. Schema

   C. Expression

   D. Session

2. Use the following code block to answer this question:

```
SQL> select empno, ename, mgr
  2  from emp;
    EMPNO ENAME            MGR
--------- ---------- ---------
     7369 SMITH           7902
     7499 ALLEN           7698
     7521 WARD            7698
     7566 JONES           7839
     7654 MARTIN          7698
     7698 BLAKE           7839
     7782 CLARK           7839
     7788 SCOTT           7566
     7839 KING
     7844 TURNER          7698
     7876 ADAMS           7788
     7900 JAMES           7698
     7902 FORD            7566
     7934 MILLER          7782
SQL> select empno, ename, nvl(mgr,'none') as mgr
  2  from emp;
```

   Which of the following choices describes what Oracle will return as the output in the MGR column for KING's record from this query?

   A. Oracle returns NULL in the MGR column for KING's record.

   B. Oracle returns MGR in the MGR column for KING's record.

    C. Oracle returns NONE in the MGR column for KING's record.

    D. Oracle returns an error.

3. **You are concatenating information from two columns in a SQL query. Which of the following choices best identifies the special character required for this operation?**

    A. @

    B. #

    C. ||

    D. /

4. **Provide the name of the table containing no meaningful information that can be used to fulfill the table clause requirement for select statements when you perform arithmetic operations on fixed numeric expressions:**

    _____

Answer Key

1. B. **2.** D. Remember, the datatype in the nvl ( ) function must match the datatype for the column. **3.** C. **4.** DUAL

Differentiating Between SQL and SQL*Plus Commands

Although the SQL*Plus work environment works well when you don't make mistakes, it is unforgiving to the fat-fingered once you have pressed ENTER to move to the next input line. So far, this limitation hasn't presented much difficulty because our queries haven't been very long. However, as the queries you write get more and more complicated, you will grow frustrated. SQL*Plus does allow some correction of entered statements with a special command called change, abbreviated as c. Consider the following example, which illustrates this point:

```
SQL> SELECT empno, ename, NVL(mgr,'none') mgr,
  2  hiredate, sal, comm, deptno
  3  FROM EMP;
SELECT empno, ename, NVL(mgr,'none') mgr,
                          *
ERROR at line 1:
ORA-01722: invalid number
SQL> 1
```

```
1> SELECT empno, ename, NVL(mgr,'none') mgr,
SQL> c/'none'/0
1> SELECT empno, ename, NVL(mgr,0) mgr,
SQL> /
```

EMPNO	ENAME	JOB	MGR	HIREDATE	SAL	COMM	DEPTNO
7369	SMITH	CLERK	7902	17-DEC-80	800		20
7499	ALLEN	SALESMAN	7698	20-FEB-81	1600	300	30
7521	WARD	SALESMAN	7698	22-FEB-81	1250	500	30
7566	JONES	MANAGER	7839	02-APR-81	2975		20
7654	MARTIN	SALESMAN	7698	28-SEP-81	1250	1400	30
7698	BLAKE	MANAGER	7839	01-MAY-81	2850		30
7782	CLARK	MANAGER	7839	09-JUN-81	2450		10
7788	SCOTT	ANALYST	7566	19-APR-87	3000		20
7839	KING	PRESIDENT	0	17-NOV-81	5000		10
7844	TURNER	SALESMAN	7698	08-SEP-81	1500	0	30
7876	ADAMS	CLERK	7788	23-MAY-87	1100		20
7900	JAMES	CLERK	7698	03-DEC-81	950		30
7902	FORD	ANALYST	7566	03-DEC-81	3000		20
7934	MILLER	CLERK	7782	23-JAN-82	1300		10

In this example, the select statement contains a datatype mismatch error in the nvl( ) function. Oracle notices the error and alerts you to it with the ORA-01722 error message. Other error messages that may be produced include the following:

ORA-00904: invalid column name

This error indicates that the column you referenced does not exist or was misspelled.

ORA-00923: FROM keyword not found where expected

This error indicates that the from keyword was not included or was misspelled.

ORA-00942: table or view does not exist

This error indicates that the table or view typed in does not exist. Usually, the ORA-00942 error message indicates a typo in the name of the table or view, or that the schema owner was not specified in front of the table name. This error is fixed either by correcting the typing problem or by adding the schema owner onto the front of the table name. (An alternative solution for the latter case involves creating synonyms for tables that are accessible to other users. This solution will be discussed later in the book.)

In any case, the method used to correct the typing problem is to first type the line number containing the error to activate that line for editing. In the preceding example, we did so by typing the number 1, shown in bold. Then we used the `change` command, also shown in bold, observing the proper syntax:

 `c/old_value/new_value`

After the change is made to the *first* appearance of *old_value* in the current line, Oracle redisplays the current line with the change made. Note that the change will be made to the first appearance of *old_value* only. If the change must be made to a specific place in the line, more characters can be added to the *old_value* parameter, as appropriate. Finally, the corrected text can be reexecuted by entering a slash (/) at the prompt, as indicated, or by entering the command `run` on the SQL*Plus command line.

TIP

*If you ever get confused about the difference between the use of the slash and semicolon, remember that the slash command reruns the code currently in your SQL*Plus operating buffer, whereas the semicolon is used to end a SQL statement you type into the buffer.*

Using a Text Editor

Oracle makes provisions for you to use your favorite text editor to edit the statement created in `afiedt.buf`, the file in which SQL*Plus stores the most recently executed SQL statement. You simply type `edit` (abbreviated `ed`). This action causes Oracle to bring up the SQL statement from `afiedt.buf` into the operating system's default text editor. On UNIX systems, that text editor is usually VI or EMACS, whereas Windows environments use Notepad. To change the text editor used, issue the `define_editor='youreditor'` statement on the SQL*Plus prompt.

TIP

*You can also define your text editor in the SQL*Plus GUI interface using the Tools | Environment menu option.*

Using a text editor rather than the line editor native to SQL*Plus offers many benefits. By using a text editor you know well, you can create a familiarity with SQL*Plus that is useful for adapting to the application. Second, it is helpful with large queries to have the entire block of code in front of you and immediately accessible.

Writing SQL Commands in Scripts

You can write entire queries in a text editor first and then load the queries into SQL*Plus if you want to. When you do this, try to remember to save the script with a `.sql` extension so that SQL*Plus can identify it easily. Two commands are available to load the file into SQL*Plus. The first is `get`. The `get` command opens the text file specified and places the contents in `afiedt.buf`. Once the script is loaded, you can execute the command using the slash (/) command. Alternatively, you can use the `@` or `start` command, which loads SQL statements from the named file into `afiedt.buf` and executes them in one step. The methods are shown in the following example, with a script called `select_emp.sql`:

```
SQL*Plus: Release 8.1.7.0.0 - Production on Tue Feb 03 18:53:11 1999
Copyright (c) Oracle Corporation 1979, 1998.  All rights reserved.
Connected to Oracle8i Release 8.1.7.0.0
With the distributed and replication options
PL/SQL Release 8.1.7.0.0 - Production
SQL> GET select_emp
SELECT * FROM emp
SQL> /
     EMPNO ENAME    JOB          MGR HIREDATE    SAL COMM DEPTNO
--------- -------- ---------- ----- --------- ---- ---- ------
      7369 SMITH    CLERK       7902 17-DEC-80  800           20
      7499 ALLEN    SALESMAN    7698 20-FEB-81 1600  300      30
      7521 WARD     SALESMAN    7698 22-FEB-81 1250  500      30
      7566 JONES    MANAGER     7839 02-APR-81 2975           20
      7654 MARTIN   SALESMAN    7698 28-SEP-81 1250 1400      30
      7698 BLAKE    MANAGER     7839 01-MAY-81 2850           30
      7782 CLARK    MANAGER     7839 09-JUN-81 2450           10
      7788 SCOTT    ANALYST     7566 19-APR-87 3000           20
      7839 KING     PRESIDENT        17-NOV-81 5000           10
      7844 TURNER   SALESMAN    7698 08-SEP-81 1500    0      30
      7876 ADAMS    CLERK       7788 23-MAY-87 1100           20
      7900 JAMES    CLERK       7698 03-DEC-81  950           30
      7902 FORD     ANALYST     7566 03-DEC-81 3000           20
      7934 MILLER   CLERK       7782 23-JAN-82 1300           10
SQL> @select_emp
SELECT * FROM emp
     EMPNO ENAME    JOB          MGR HIREDATE    SAL COMM DEPTNO
--------- -------- ---------- ----- --------- ---- ---- ------
      7369 SMITH    CLERK       7902 17-DEC-80  800           20
      7499 ALLEN    SALESMAN    7698 20-FEB-81 1600  300      30
      7521 WARD     SALESMAN    7698 22-FEB-81 1250  500      30
      7566 JONES    MANAGER     7839 02-APR-81 2975           20
      7654 MARTIN   SALESMAN    7698 28-SEP-81 1250 1400      30
      7698 BLAKE    MANAGER     7839 01-MAY-81 2850           30
```

```
7782 CLARK     MANAGER     7839 09-JUN-81 2450          10
7788 SCOTT     ANALYST     7566 19-APR-87 3000          20
7839 KING      PRESIDENT        17-NOV-81 5000          10
7844 TURNER    SALESMAN    7698 08-SEP-81 1500     0    30
7876 ADAMS     CLERK       7788 23-MAY-87 1100          20
7900 JAMES     CLERK       7698 03-DEC-81  950          30
7902 FORD      ANALYST     7566 03-DEC-81 3000          20
7934 MILLER    CLERK       7782 23-JAN-82 1300          10
```

Notice that the .sql extension was left off the end of the filename in the line with the get command. SQL*Plus assumes that all scripts containing SQL statements will have the .sql extension, so it can be omitted in the get and the @ commands. You can store SQL commands in text files with other extensions, such as .txt and .lst, but if you do, you have to specify the full filename, including the extension, in the get command. Notice also that after the file is brought in using get, it can then be executed using the slash (/) command. Later in that same code block, we use the @ command to read the same file into afiedt.buf. The contents of the buffer are executed in the same step, which eliminates the need for entering the slash (/) command. Again, we omit the .sql extension. Finally, if you don't specify the path when typing the filename for the get or @ command, Oracle assumes the file is in whatever directory you were in when you started running SQL*Plus.

TIP
*When typing SQL statements in a script that you intend to execute in SQL*Plus, do not put a semicolon (;) at the end of these SQL statements. Instead, put a slash (/) character as the first character on the last line in the script. Do this if you encounter problems where Oracle says it encountered an invalid character (the semicolon) in your script.*

Other SQL*Plus Commands to Know
The rest of this discussion focuses on identifying other important commands you should know in SQL*Plus, both for your job and for passing the OCP exam. Let's now take a look at explanations for important SQL*Plus commands to know about.

DESCRIBE *tablename*   This command returns a description of *tablename*, including all columns in that table, the datatype for each column, and an indication of whether the column permits storage of NULL values. This command is synonymous with its abbreviation, desc. Here's an example:

```
SQL> describe emp
Name                                Null?    Type
----------------------------------- -------- -------------
EMPNO                               NOT NULL NUMBER(4)
ENAME                                        VARCHAR2(10)
JOB                                          VARCHAR2(9)
MGR                                          NUMBER(4)
HIREDATE                                     DATE
SAL                                          NUMBER(7,2)
COMM                                         NUMBER(7,2)
DEPTNO                                       NUMBER(2)
```

LIST   This command is used to list the contents of the current SQL*Plus working buffer, organized by line number. SQL*Plus buffers the last SQL command you issued. If you haven't entered a SQL command yet, the SP2-0223: No lines in SQL buffer error message is displayed. The current line available for editing and other changes is indicated by an asterisk next to the line number. Here's an example:

```
SQL> select empno, ename
  2  from emp
  3  where empno < 7700;
    EMPNO ENAME
--------- ----------
     7369 SMITH
     7499 ALLEN
     7521 WARD
     7566 JONES
     7654 MARTIN
     7698 BLAKE
6 rows selected.
SQL> list
  1  select empno, ename
  2  from emp
  3* where empno < 7700
```

DEL *number*   This command deletes line *number* from the SQL*Plus working buffer (not *number* lines!). Each line in the buffer is preceded by a line number. If you want to delete multiple lines, list each line to be removed, separated by a space. Here's an example:

```
SQL> del 3
SQL> list
  1  select empno, ename
  2* from emp
```

APPEND *string*   This command adds *string* specified to the current line. Blank spaces are permitted in the string, and a leading blank space should be included if the current string already has information in it. The current line is indicated with an asterisk (*) in the output of the append command. See the following append command for displaying current line information along with the contents of the SQL*Plus working buffer:

```
SQL> append  where empno < 7700
   2* from emp where empno < 7700
```

CLEAR BUFFER   This command clears the contents of the SQL*Plus buffer. Here's an example:

```
SQL> clear buffer
Buffer cleared
```

INPUT   When entered at the SQL prompt, this command allows you to add contents to your SQL*Plus operating buffer at the current line. If the buffer was cleared, you start at the first line. If the buffer has something in it, you start at the beginning of a new line at the end of the buffer. Here's an example:

```
SQL> input
   1  select ename, sal
   2  from emp
   3  where empno < 7600;
ENAME             SAL
---------- ---------
SMITH             800
ALLEN            1600
WARD             1250
JONES            2975
```

RUN   This command executes the contents of the SQL*Plus buffer. Here's an example:

```
SQL> run
   1  select ename, sal
   2  from emp
   3* where empno < 7600
ENAME             SAL
---------- ---------
SMITH             800
ALLEN            1600
WARD             1250
JONES            2975
```

number string   When a number is entered in SQL*Plus followed by a string of
characters, SQL*Plus adds the *string* you specify to the operating buffer as the
line *number* you indicated. If the line number already exists, Oracle replaces it.
If the line number indicated is not contiguous with the existing lines in the buffer,
SQL*Plus adds the string as the last line number in the buffer. Here's an example:

```
SQL> 6 new line being added
SQL> list
  1   select ename, sal
  2   from emp
  3   where empno < 7600
  4*  new line being added
SQL> 2 from jason.emp
SQL> list
  1   select ename, sal
  2   from jason.emp
  3   where empno < 7600
  4*  new line being added
```

SPOOL {filename|OFF|OUT}   This command writes all output shown in
SQL*Plus following issuance of the spool *filename* command to a text file
identified by *filename*. If no filename extension is specified, SQL*Plus appends
the .1st extension. When the off or out keyword is specified, spooling SQL*Plus
output to a file is turned off. Here's an example:

```
SQL> spool jason.out
SQL> select ename, sal
  2   from emp
  3   where empno < 7600;
ENAME               SAL
---------- ---------
SMITH                800
ALLEN               1600
WARD                1250
JONES               2975
SQL> spool off
SQL> exit
C:\WINDOWS> type jason.out
SQL> select ename, sal
  2   from emp
  3   where empno < 7600;
ENAME               SAL
---------- ---------
SMITH                800
ALLEN               1600
WARD                1250
JONES               2975
SQL> spool off
```

SAVE *filename*   This command places the contents of your SQL*Plus buffer into a text file called `filename`. If no filename extension is specified, SQL*Plus appends `.sql`.

EXIT   This command exits the SQL*Plus interface and returns to the operating system.

TIP
*You can see that having the ability to edit your SQL commands using your favorite text editor is a handy feature of SQL*Plus that makes it possible to avoid learning all of SQL*Plus's commands. Nevertheless, be sure you understand the basics of entering SQL using SQL*Plus before taking the OCP exam.*

For Review

1. Be sure you know the two mechanisms available for entering and modifying SQL statements within SQL*Plus.

2. Know how to use the `edit` command in the SQL*Plus command line and how to load and run the contents of SQL scripts into SQL*Plus.

3. Understand how to use the other SQL*Plus commands identified in this section.

Exercises

1. **You are modifying a text string on line 3 of your SQL*Plus buffer. Which of the following choices best identifies the method you must use if the `edit` command is used?**

   A. Modify the code block using your favorite text editor.

   B. First refer to the line number; then use the `change` command.

   C. First delete the line using the `del` command; then refer to the line number.

   D. Load the SQL you intend to modify using the `input` command.

2. **You would like to list the columns found in an Oracle table. Which of the following SQL*Plus commands are useful for this purpose?**

      A. `get`

      B. `input`

      C. `describe`

      D. `spool`

3. **This command displays the contents of your SQL*Plus buffer:**

    _____

4. **This is the name of the file Oracle stores the contents of your SQL*Plus buffer in:** _____

Answer Key

1. A. **2.** C. **3.** `list` **4.** `afiedt.buf`

Restricting and Sorting Row Data

This section will cover the following areas related to restricting and sorting row data:

- Sorting return data with the `order by` clause
- Limiting return data with the `where` clause

    Obtaining all output from a table is great, but usually you must be more selective in choosing output. Most database applications contain a lot of data. How much data can a database contain? Some applications contain tables with a million rows or more, and the most recent release of Oracle8i will store over 512 petabytes ($512 \times 1{,}024^5$ bytes) of data. Of course, this is only a theoretical limit—the real amount of data you can store with Oracle depends on how much disk space you give Oracle to use. But, needless to say, manipulating vast amounts of data like that requires you to be careful. Always ask for *exactly* what you want, and no more. This section tells you how.

Sorting Return Data with the order by Clause

Notice that Oracle does not return data requested in a particular order on any particular column, either numeric or alphabetical. According to the fundamentals of relational database theory, a table is by definition an *unordered* set of row data. That's fine for the ivory tower, but it's not always useful in real-world situations.

Oracle allows you to order the output from `select` statements using the `order by` clause. This clause can impose a sort order on one or many columns in ascending *or* descending order in each of the columns specified. The general syntax for the `order by` clause is to include both the clause and the column(s) or column alias(es) by which Oracle will order the results, each optionally followed by a special clause defining the direction of the order (`asc` for ascending and `desc` for descending). The default value is `asc`, and the output for `desc` is as shown here:

```
SQL> select * from emp
  2   order by ename desc;

EMPNO ENAME      JOB         MGR HIREDATE    SAL  COMM  DEPTNO
----- ---------- ---------- ---- --------- ----- ----- -------
 7521 WARD       SALESMAN   7698 22-FEB-81  1250   500      30
 7844 TURNER     SALESMAN   7698 08-SEP-81  1500     0      30
 7369 SMITH      CLERK      7902 17-DEC-80   800             20
 7788 SCOTT      ANALYST    7566 19-APR-87  3000             20
 7934 MILLER     CLERK      7782 23-JAN-82  1300             10
 7654 MARTIN     SALESMAN   7698 28-SEP-81  1250  1400       30
 7839 KING       PRESIDENT       17-NOV-81  5000             10
 7566 JONES      MANAGER    7839 02-APR-81  2975             20
 7900 JAMES      CLERK      7698 03-DEC-81   950             30
 7902 FORD       ANALYST    7566 03-DEC-81  3000             20
 7782 CLARK      MANAGER    7839 09-JUN-81  2450             10
 7698 BLAKE      MANAGER    7839 01-MAY-81  2850             30
 7499 ALLEN      SALESMAN   7698 20-FEB-81  1600   300       30
 7876 ADAMS      CLERK      7788 23-MAY-87  1100             20
```

TIP
When NULL data appears in a column Oracle is attempting to sort in ascending order, Oracle lists the NULL records at the end of the list. When sorting in descending order, Oracle places the NULL data at the top of the list.

The `order by` clause can be useful in simple reporting. It can be applied to columns that are of NUMBER, text (VARCHAR2 and CHAR), and DATE datatypes. You can even use numbers to indicate, positionally, the column on which Oracle should order the output from a statement. For example, if you issue a statement similar to the one in the following code block, the order for the output will be as shown (the number 2 indicates that the second column specified in the statement should be used to define the order in the output):

```
SQL> select empno, ename from emp
  2 order by 2 desc;
 EMPNO ENAME
 ------ --------
   7521 WARD
   7844 TURNER
   7369 SMITH
   7788 SCOTT
   7934 MILLER
   7654 MARTIN
   7839 KING
   7566 JONES
   7900 JAMES
   7902 FORD
   7782 CLARK
   7698 BLAKE
   7499 ALLEN
   7876 ADAMS
SQL> select ename, empno from emp
  2  order by 2 desc;
ENAME       EMPNO
--------- ------
MILLER       7934
FORD         7902
JAMES        7900
ADAMS        7876
TURNER       7844
KING         7839
SCOTT        7788
CLARK        7782
BLAKE        7698
MARTIN       7654
JONES        7566
WARD         7521
ALLEN        7499
SMITH        7369
```

TIP
You can also sort by column alias.

For Review

1. Know how to put row data returned from a `select` statement into order and know the various sort orders (ascending and descending) that can be used with this option. Know also that Oracle can sort based on multiple columns.

2. Be sure you understand both the positional and named way to specify the column on which the sort order should be defined.

Exercises

1. Use the following code block to answer this question:

```
EMPNO ENAME            MGR
--------- ---------- ---------
     7369 SMITH           7902
     7566 JONES           7839
     7782 CLARK           7839
     7698 BLAKE           7839
     7876 ADAMS           7788
     7934 MILLER          7782
     7499 ALLEN           7698
     7654 MARTIN          7698
     7521 WARD            7698
     7900 JAMES           7698
     7844 TURNER          7698
     7788 SCOTT           7566
     7902 FORD            7566
```

Which of the following choices identifies the `order by` clause that produced the output shown in the preceding code block?

A. order by empno asc

B. order by ename desc

C. order by hiredate asc

D. order by mgr desc

2. You are sorting data in a table in your `select` statement in descending order. The column you are sorting on contains NULL records. Where will the NULL records appear?

A. At the beginning of the list

B. At the end of the list

C. In the middle of the list

D. The same location they are listed in the unordered table

3. Identify the default sort order used by Oracle when no sort order is specified: _____

Answer Key

1. D. **2.** A. **3.** Ascending.

Limiting Return Data with the where Clause

The where clause in Oracle select statements is where things really become interesting. This important clause in select statements allows you to single out a few rows from hundreds, thousands, or even millions like it. The where clause operates on a basic principle of comparison. Here's an example:

```
SQL> select * from emp
  2  where empno = 7844;
   EMPNO ENAME       JOB          MGR HIREDATE     SAL  COMM  DEPTNO
   ------ ---------  ---------  ----- ---------  ----- ----- -------
    7844 TURNER      SALESMAN    7698 08-SEP-81  1500      0      30
```

Assuming the EMPNO column contains all unique values, instead of pulling all rows from EMP, Oracle pulls just one row for display. To determine what row to display, the where clause performs a comparison operation as specified by the query—in this case, the comparison is an equality operation: where empno = 7844. However, equality is not the only means by which Oracle can obtain data. Some other examples of comparison are demonstrated in Table 1-1. Every comparison between two values in Oracle boils down to one or more of the operations from that table.

$x = y$	Comparison to see if x is equal to y.
$x > y$	Comparison to see if x is greater than y.
$x >= y$	Comparison to see if x is greater than or equal to y.
$x < y$	Comparison to see if x is less than y.
$x <= y$	Comparison to see if x is less than or equal to y.
$x <> y$	Comparison to see if x is not equal to y.
$x \mathrel{!=} y$	
$x \mathrel{\char`\^=} y$	

TABLE 1-1. *Comparison Operations in Oracle*

`like`	A special comparison used in conjunction with search wildcards. Two wildcards exist in Oracle. The first, percent (%), is for multiple characters, as in `'%ORA%'` for all columns or rows containing string ORA. The second, underscore (_), is used for single-character substitution, as in `'OR_CLE'` for all strings where the user may have mistyped "I" instead of "A."
`soundex`	A special function used to introduce "fuzzy logic" into text string comparisons by allowing equality based on similarly spelled words.
`between`	A range comparison operation that allows for operations on dates, numbers, and characters that are similar to the following numeric comparison: y "is between" x and z.
`in`	A special comparison that allows you to specify multiple equality statements by defining a set of values, any of which the value can be equal to. An example of its usage would be x `in (1,2,3,4,5)`.

TABLE 1-1.   *Comparison Operations in Oracle* (continued)

Getting Even More Selective

Multiple comparisons can be placed together using the list of operations given in Table 1-2. The operator is listed along with the result that is required to fulfill the criteria based on the presence of this operator. For example, the `and` keyword can be used to join two comparisons together, forcing Oracle to return only the rows that fulfill both criteria. In contrast, the `or` keyword allows for a much looser joining of two comparisons, allowing Oracle to return records that fulfill one criteria or the other. In this case, if a record fulfills the criteria of both comparisons, Oracle will return the record as well.

x `and` y	Both comparisons in x and y must be true.
x `or` y	One comparison in x or y must be true.
`not` x	The logical opposite of x.

TABLE 1-2.   *Keywords for Joining Comparisons Together*

---

x is NULL   Returns TRUE if the value is NULL. This operator resolves the problem where comparing variable *x* to NULL produces a NULL result rather than TRUE.

TABLE 1-2.   *Keywords for Joining Comparisons Together* (continued)

For Review

1. Be able to define what a `where` clause is, as well as the principle of comparison upon which the clause operates to determine data to return to the user.

2. Know all the operations available to assist in the purpose of comparison. Also, be sure you know which operations allow you to specify more than one comparison in the `where` clause.

Exercises

1. **You are defining a SQL statement to return a limited number of rows based on specific criteria. Which of the following choices identifies the clause you will use to define the search criteria?**

   A. `select`

   B. `from`

   C. `where`

   D. `order by`

2. **This is the principle upon which the search criteria available within SQL `select` statements operate: _____**

3. **This is the operation used when you want to determine whether a NULL value appears in a column (two words): _____**

Answer Key

1. C. **2.** Comparison. **3.** `is NULL`.

Using Single-Row Functions

This section will cover the following areas related to using single-row functions:

■ Explanations of various single-row functions

■ Using functions in `select` statements

■ Date functions

■ Conversion functions

Dozens of functions are available in Oracle that can be used for many purposes. Some functions in Oracle are designed to alter the data returned by a query, such as the `nvl()` function already presented. The functions in this category are designed to work on columns of any datatype to return information in different ways. Other single-row functions operate on only one or two datatypes. This section will explain the use of various important single-row functions in the Oracle database. Single-row functions are those designed to operate on individual column records in a row, for every row returned in the result set. You'll also see how these functions are used in SQL commands. Date and conversion functions will be covered in some detail as well.

Various Single-Row Functions Explained

One commonly used single-row function is `decode()`. The `decode()` function works on the same principle as the `if-then-else` statement works in many common programming languages, including PL/SQL. You can pass a variable number of values into the call to the `decode()` function, which will appear in the column clause of your `select` statement. Your first item will always be the name of the column you want to decode. Next, you identify the first specific value Oracle should look for in that column. After that, you pass in the substitute you want Oracle to return if the first specific value is encountered. From there, you can then define as many specific value-substitute pairs as you would like. Once all value-substitute pairs have been defined, you can optionally specify a default value Oracle will return if the column value doesn't match a specified value. Take a look at the following code block to get a better idea how this works:

```
SELECT decode(column_name,
              value1, substitute1,
              value2, substitute2,
              ... ,
              return_default)
FROM ... ;
```

The decode( ) function allows for powerful transformation of data from one value to another. Some examples of decode( ) in action will appear shortly. This function is presented first because, like nvl( ), decode( ) can operate on virtually every datatype in Oracle. From this point on, all functions described have limitations on the datatypes on which they can perform their operations.

Text Functions

Several functions in Oracle manipulate text strings. These functions are similar in concept to nvl( ) and decode( ) in that they can perform a change on a piece of data, but the functions in this family can change only VARCHAR2 and CHAR data. Some examples follow:

lpad(x,y[,z]) rpad(x,y[,z])	Returns data in string or column x padded on the left or right side, respectively, to width y. The optional value z indicates the character(s) that lpad( ) or rpad( ) will use to pad the column data. If no character z is specified, a space is used.
lower(x) upper(x) initcap(x)	Returns data in string or column x in lowercase or uppercase characters, respectively, or changes the initial letter in the data from column x to a capital letter.
length(x)	Returns the number of characters in string or column x.
substr(x,y[,z])	Returns a substring of string or column x, starting at the character in position number y to the end, which is optionally defined by the character appearing in position z of the string.
instr(x,y)	Determines whether a substring y given can be found in string x.

The trim( ) Function

Oracle **8i**
and higher

A new feature in Oracle8i is a single-row function called trim( ), which behaves like a combination of ltrim( ) and rtrim( ). The trim( ) function accepts a string describing the data you would like to trim from a column value using the following syntax: trim([[keyword]'x' from] column). Here, keyword is replaced by leading, trailing, or both, or it's omitted. Also, x is replaced with the character to be trimmed, or it's omitted. If x is omitted, Oracle assumes it must trim whitespace. Finally, column is the name of the column in the table to be trimmed. Note that `trim( )` only removes trailing or leading instances of the character specified. If that character appears somewhere in the string, `trim( )` will not remove it. The following code block illustrates the use of `trim( )`:

```
SQL> select col_1,
  2   trim(both '_' from col_1) as trimmed
  3   from example;
LASTNAME TRIMMED
-------- ---------
__thr_   thr
@_593__  @_593
Booga__  Booga
```

> **TIP**
> *The table used in the preceding code block is not created by `utlsampl.sql` or `demobld.sql` and will not exist in your database unless you create and populate it yourself. Instructions for creating tables and adding data to them appear later in the book.*

Arithmetic Functions

Other functions are designed to perform specialized mathematical functions, such as those used in scientific applications like sine and logarithm. These operations are commonly referred to as *arithmetic* or *number operations*. The functions falling into this category are listed next. These functions are not all that are available in Oracle, but rather are the most commonly used ones that will likely appear on OCP Exam 1:

`abs(x)`	Obtains the absolute value for a number. For example, the absolute value of −1 is 1, whereas the absolute value of 6 is 6.
`round(x,y)`	Rounds x to the decimal precision of y. If y is negative, it rounds to the precision of y places to the left of the decimal point. For example, `round(134.345,1)` = 134.3, `round(134.345,0)` = 134, `round(134.345,-1)` = 130. This can also be used on DATE columns.
`ceil(x)`	Similar to executing `round` on an integer (for example, `round(x,0)`, except `ceil` always rounds up. For example, `ceil(1.4)` = 2. Note that rounding "up" on negative numbers produces a value closer to zero (for example, `ceil(-1.6)` = −1, not −2).

floor(*x*)	Similar to ceil, except floor always rounds down. For example, floor(1.6) = 1. Note that rounding "down" on negative numbers produces a value further away from zero (for example, floor(-1.6) = -2, not -1).
mod(*x*,*y*)	The modulus of *x*, defined in long division as the integer remainder when *x* is divided by *y* until no further whole number can be produced. For example, mod(10,3) = 1, and mod(10,2) = 0.
sign(*x*)	Displays an integer value corresponding to the sign of *x*: 1 if *x* is positive, -1 if *x* is negative.
sqrt(*x*)	The square root of *x*.
trunc(*x*,*y*)	Truncates *x* to the decimal precision of *y*. If *y* is negative, it truncates to *y* number of places to the left of the decimal point. This can also be used on DATE columns.
vsize(*x*)	The storage size in bytes for value *x*.

List Functions

The final category of number functions discussed here is the set of list functions. These functions are actually used for many different datatypes, including CHAR, VARCHAR2, NUMBER, and DATE. Let's now take a look at the list functions available in Oracle:

greatest(*x*,*y*,...)	Returns the highest value from the list of text strings, numbers, or dates (*x,y*...)
least(*x*,*y*,...)	Returns the lowest value from the list of text strings, numbers, or dates (*x,y*...)

For Review

1. Be sure you can identify the character, math, and date functions available in SQL, as shown in this discussion. Know the two functions that allow you to transform column values regardless of the datatype.

2. Know how to use the trim( ) function, which is new in Oracle8i.

3. Understand the list functions presented in this discussion that perform operations on specified sets of information.

Exercises

1. Input for a math function is –97, and the information passed into that
function was –97.342. Which of the following choices identifies the
single-row function that produced this output?

    A. abs( )

    B. ceil( )

    C. mod( )

    D. sqrt( )

2. You want to determine the size in bytes of a particular column value.
Which of the following single-row functions might be useful for doing so?

    A. vsize( )

    B. trunc( )

    C. trim( )

    D. greatest( )

3. Which of the single-row functions covered in this discussion operates in
a way similar to an **if-then-else** expression?

    _____

Answer Key

1. B. **2.** A. **3.** decode( ).

Using Functions in select Statements

Let's take a look at the functions introduced in the preceding discussion in action. The
first example details use of the decode( ) function. Assume that you select data from
the EMP table. The data in the JOB column identifies the role each employee performs
for the company. Instead of displaying the job title, the following code block lets you
write out a verb that describes the role that employee serves so that you know that no
slackers exist in the company:

```
SQL> select ename || ' does the ' ||
  2  decode(job, 'ANALYST','analyzing','CLERK','filing',
  3  'MANAGER','managing','PRESIDENT','bossing around',
```

```
   4  'SALESMAN','golfing','goofing off') as functions
   5  from emp;
FUNCTIONS
--------------------------------
SMITH does the filing
ALLEN does the golfing
WARD does the golfing
JONES does the managing
MARTIN does the golfing
BLAKE does the managing
CLARK does the managing
SCOTT does the analyzing
KING does the bossing around
TURNER does the golfing
ADAMS does the filing
JAMES does the filing
FORD does the analyzing
MILLER does the filing
```

This decode( ) command has 12 variables. The first is the name of the column to be decoded and must always be present. The next two variables identify, respectively, a value that could be found in the JOB column (ANALYST, in this case) and what decode( ) should substitute if the value is found. This matching of potential values with appropriate substitutes continues until you identify all cases you would like to decode. The last variable, which is optional, is used for the default substitute value.

Text Function Examples

Now let's look at some text (character) function examples. The first of these examples is for rpad( ) and lpad( ). As shown in the following code, these two functions can be used to place additional filler characters on the right and left sides of data in a column out to a specified column width:

```
SQL> select ename || ' does the ' ||
   2  RPAD(decode(job, 'ANALYST','analyzing','CLERK','filing',
   3  'MANAGER','managing','PRESIDENT','bossing around',
   4  'SALESMAN','golfing','goofing off'), 10, '-') as functions
   5  from emp
   6  where empno < 7600;
FUNCTIONS
-----------------------------
SMITH does the filing----
ALLEN does the golfing---
WARD does the golfing---
JONES does the managing--
```

TIP
This example also illustrates another important principle—the output from one SQL function can be used as input for another!

Some of the simpler character functions are shown next. The following examples show single-row functions that are sometimes referred to as "case translators" because they perform a simple translation of case based on the text string passed:

```
SQL> SELECT lower(ename) as one,
  2  upper(ename) as two,
  3  initcap(ename) as three
  4  FROM emp;
ONE        TWO        THREE
---------- ---------- ----------
smith      SMITH      Smith
allen      ALLEN      Allen
ward       WARD       Ward
jones      JONES      Jones
martin     MARTIN     Martin
blake      BLAKE      Blake
clark      CLARK      Clark
scott      SCOTT      Scott
king       KING       King
turner     TURNER     Turner
adams      ADAMS      Adams
james      JAMES      James
ford       FORD       Ford
miller     MILLER     Miller
```

Another straightforward and useful character function is the `length( )` function, which returns the length of a text string:

```
SQL> select ename, length(ename) as length
  2  from emp;
ENAME        LENGTH
--------- ---------
SMITH             5
ALLEN             5
WARD              4
JONES             5
MARTIN            6
BLAKE             5
CLARK             5
```

```
SCOTT               5
KING                4
TURNER              6
ADAMS               5
JAMES               5
FORD                4
MILLER              6
```

TIP
If the string includes spaces, double quotes, or other special characters, all those special characters are counted as part of the length!

Another extraordinarily useful function related to character strings is the substr() function. This function is commonly used to extract data from a longer text string. The substr() function takes as its first variable the full text string to be searched. The second variable contains an integer that designates the character number at which the substring should begin. The third parameter is optional and specifies how many characters to the right of the start of the substring will be included in the substring. Observe the following output to understand the effects of omitting the third parameter:

```
SQL> select ename, substr(ename,2,3)
  2  from emp;
ENAME       SUB
---------   ---
SMITH       MIT
ALLEN       LLE
WARD        ARD
JONES       ONE
MARTIN      ART
BLAKE       LAK
CLARK       LAR
SCOTT       COT
KING        ING
TURNER      URN
ADAMS       DAM
JAMES       AME
FORD        ORD
MILLER      ILL
SQL> select ename, substr(ename,2)
  2  from emp;
ENAME       SUBSTR(EN
---------   ---------
SMITH       MITH
ALLEN       LLEN
```

```
WARD      ARD
JONES     ONES
MARTIN    ARTIN
BLAKE     LAKE
CLARK     LARK
SCOTT     COTT
KING      ING
TURNER    URNER
ADAMS     DAMS
JAMES     AMES
FORD      ORD
MILLER    ILLER
```

Arithmetic Function Examples

The number (math) functions are frequently used in scientific applications. The first function detailed here is the abs ( ) function, or *absolute value* function, which calculates how far away from zero the parameter passed lies on the number line:

```
SQL> SELECT ABS(25), ABS(-12) FROM DUAL;
ABS(25) ABS(-12)
------- --------
     25       12
```

The next single-value function is the ceil ( ) function, which automatically rounds the number passed as its parameter up to the next highest integer:

```
SQL> SELECT CEIL(123.323), CEIL(45),
  2   CEIL(-392), CEIL(-1.12) FROM DUAL;
CEIL(123.323) CEIL(45) CEIL(-392) CEIL(-1.12)
------------- -------- ---------- -----------
          124       45       -392          -1
```

The next single-value function is the floor ( ) function. The floor ( ) function is the opposite of ceil ( ), rounding the value passed down to the next lowest integer:

```
SQL> SELECT FLOOR(123.323), FLOOR(45), FLOOR(-392),
  2   FLOOR(-1.12) FROM DUAL;
FLOOR(123.323) FLOOR(45) FLOOR(-392) FLOOR(-1.12)
-------------- --------- ----------- ------------
           123        45        -392           -2
```

The next function covered in this section is related to long division. The function is called mod ( ), and it returns the remainder (or *modulus*) for a number and its divisor:

```
SQL> SELECT MOD(12,3), MOD(55,4) FROM DUAL;
MOD(12,3)   MOD(55,4)
---------   ---------
        0           3
```

After that, look at round ( ). This important function allows you to round a number off to a specified precision:

```
SQL> SELECT ROUND(123.323,2), ROUND(45,1),
  2  ROUND(-392,-1), ROUND (-1.12,0) FROM DUAL;
ROUND(123.323,2) ROUND(45,1) ROUND(-392,-1) ROUND(-1.12,0)
---------------- ----------- -------------- --------------
          123.32          45           -390             -1
```

The next function is called sign ( ). It assists in identifying whether a number is positive or negative. If the number passed is positive, sign ( ) returns 1; and if the number is negative, sign ( ) returns –1. If the number is zero, sign ( ) returns 0:

```
SQL> SELECT SIGN(-1933), SIGN(55), SIGN(0) FROM DUAL;
SIGN(-1933) SIGN(55) SIGN(0)
----------- -------- -------
         -1        1       0
```

The next example is the sqrt ( ) function. It is used to derive the square root for a number:

```
SQL> SELECT SQRT(34), SQRT(9) FROM DUAL;
SQRT(34) SQRT(9)
-------- -------
5.830951       3
```

The next single-value number function is called trunc ( ). Similar to round ( ), trunc ( ) truncates a value passed into it according to the precision that is also passed in:

```
SQL> SELECT TRUNC(123.232,2), TRUNC(-45,1),
  2  TRUNC(392,-1), TRUNC(5,0) FROM DUAL;
TRUNC(123.232,2) TRUNC(-45,1) TRUNC(392,-1) TRUNC(5,0)
---------------- ------------ ------------- ----------
          123.23          -45           390          5
```

The final single-row operation that is covered in this section is the vsize ( ) function. This function is not strictly for numeric datatypes. The vsize ( ) function gives the size in bytes of any value for VARCHAR2, CHAR, NUMBER, DATE, ROWID, and other column datatypes:

```
SQL> SELECT VSIZE(384838), VSIZE('ORANGE_TABBY'),
  2  VSIZE(sysdate) FROM DUAL;
VSIZE(384838) VSIZE('ORANGE_TABBY') VSIZE(SYSDATE)
------------- ---------------------- --------------
            4                      12              8
```

For Review

1. Be sure you understand the purpose of the decode ( ) statement and that it accepts all the common Oracle datatypes. Make sure you can set up a call to this function correctly.

2. Know how to use the text functions. Also, make sure you understand how to combine two functions using the output of one function as input for the other.

3. Understand the use of the math functions. Be sure you know how to utilize them on real columns and how to use them on fixed expressions using the DUAL table.

Exercises

1. Use the following output to answer the question (assume that the information shown comes from the EMP table we've been using in the chapter):

```
ENAME
----------
SMITH-dog-
ALLEN-dog-
WARD-dog-d
JONES-dog-
MARTIN-dog
BLAKE-dog-
CLARK-dog-
SCOTT-dog-
KING-dog-d
TURNER-dog
ADAMS-dog-
JAMES-dog-
FORD-dog-d
MILLER-dog
```

Which of the following choices identifies the SQL statement that produced this output?

A. `select trim(trailing '-dog' from ename) as ename from emp;`

B. `select rpad(ename, 10, '-dog') as ename from emp;`

C. `select substr(ename, 1, 10) as ename from emp;`

D. `select lpad(ename, 10, '-dog') as ename from emp;`

2. Use the following code block to answer the question:

```
SQL> select _____(-45) as output from dual;
OUTPUT
------
   -45
```

Which of the following choices identifies a single-row function that could not have produced this output?

A. `abs()`

B. `ceil()`

C. `floor()`

D. `round()`

3. For a certain row in a table, a VARCHAR2 column contains the value SMITHY, padded to the right with seven spaces by the application. When the `length()` function processes that column value, what will be the value returned?

A. 5

B. 6

C. 12

D. 13

Answer Key

1. B. 2. A. 3. D.

Date Functions

To start our discussion of date functions, you should be aware that there is a special keyword that can be specified to give Oracle users the current date. This keyword is sysdate. In the same way you calculated simple arithmetic earlier in the chapter using the DUAL table, so, too, can you execute a select statement using sysdate to produce the current date. Here's an example:

```
SQL> SELECT sysdate FROM DUAL;
SYSDATE
---------
15-MAR-01
```

TIP
The DATE information you obtain when using the keyword sysdate will be the date according to the server hosting the Oracle database. Therefore, the date information returned could differ from the date information for your client PC.

The date functions available in Oracle can operate on columns of the DATE datatype. The date functions available in Oracle are very useful for executing well-defined operations on DATE data in a table or on constant values. Make sure you understand these functions for OCP. The functions that can be used on DATE columns are listed here, along with their definitions:

add_months(x, y)	Returns a date corresponding to date x plus y months.
last_day(x)	Returns the date of the last day of the month that contains date x.
months_between(x, y)	Returns a number of months between y and x as produced by $x - y$. This function can return a decimal value.
new_time(x, y, z)	Returns the current date and time for date x in time zone y as it would be in time zone z.
next_day(x)	Identifies the name of the next day from the given date, x.

Let's look at date information and the associated functions in more detail. As I mentioned earlier, Oracle stores dates as integers, representing the number of days since the beginning of the Julian calendar. This method allows for easy format changes and inherent millennium compliance. The first function is the `add_months()` function. This function takes as input a date and a number of months to be added. Oracle then returns the new date, which is the old date plus the number of months:

```
SQL> SELECT ADD_MONTHS('15-MAR-00',26)
  2  FROM DUAL;
ADD_MONTHS('15
--------------
    15-MAY-02
```

The next function, `last_day()`, helps determine the date for the last day in the month for the date given:

```
SQL> SELECT LAST_DAY('15-MAR-00') FROM DUAL;
LAST_DAY('15-M
--------------
    31-MAR-00
```

The next date function determines the number of months between two different dates given. The name of the function is `months_between()`. The syntax of this command is tricky, so it will be presented here. The syntax of this command is `months_between(x, y)`, and the return value for this function is $x - y$:

```
SQL> SELECT MONTHS_BETWEEN('15-MAR-00','26-JUN-99') FROM DUAL;
MONTHS_BETWEEN
--------------
    8.6451613
```

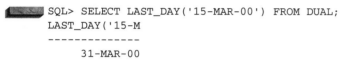

TIP
In general, you should try to specify the values passed into months_between( )*, such that the first value is larger than the second. If you pass a second value that is greater than the first, a negative number will be returned.*

The last example of a date function is `new_time()`. It accepts three parameters—the first being a date and time, the second being the time zone the first parameter belongs in, and the last parameter being the time zone you would like to convert to. Each time zone is abbreviated in the following way: *X*ST or *X*DT, where *S* and *D* stand for standard and daylight saving time, respectively, and *X* stands for the first letter of the time zone (for example, *Atlantic, Bering, Central, Eastern, Hawaii, Mountain, Newfoundland, Pacific,* or *Yukon*). There are two exceptions: Greenwich mean time is indicated by GMT, whereas Newfoundland standard time does not use daylight saving. Take a look at the following example:

```
SQL> ALTER SESSION
  2   SET NLS_DATE_FORMAT = 'DD-MON-YYYY HH24:MI:SS';
Session altered.
SQL> SELECT NEW_TIME('15-MAR-1999 14:35:00','AST','GMT')
  2   FROM DUAL;
NEW_TIME('15-MAR-199
--------------------
15-MAR-1999 18:35:00
```

None of the queries used to demonstrate the date functions have required that much precision so far, except for this one. In order to demonstrate the full capability of Oracle in the new_time( ) function, we altered the format Oracle uses to display date information—also known as the National Language Set (NLS) date format. The alter session set NLS_DATE_FORMAT command can be used to display the full date and time for the query. The next discussion contains information you may find useful in defining date format masks for NLS_DATE_FORMAT.

For Review

1. Understand that dates are stored as numbers in Oracle to allow the database to display the date information into multiple formats.

2. Know that the date format is defined by the alter session set nls_date_format command.

3. Be able to identify and use the date functions described in this section to return information about dates. Also, know that only the months_between( ) function returns information in a datatype other than DATE.

Exercises

1. **You issue the following query in Oracle:**

   ```
   SQL> select sysdate from dual;
   SYSDATE
   ------------------------------
   THURSDAY, MARCH 15 2001 10:35AM
   ```

   What format mask was used for generating this output?

   A. DD, MONTH DAY RRRR HH:MI

   B. DAY, MONTH DD YYYY HH:MIAM

      C. DAY, MON DD RR HH:MIAM

      D. MONTH, DAY DD YYYY HH24:MI

2. **You issue the following query in Oracle:**

```
SQL> select months_between('15-MAR-83', '15-MAR-97') from dual;
```

What will Oracle return?

      A. 14

      B. −14

      C. 168

      D. −168

3. **Which command is used for adjusting your date format for the duration of your connection with Oracle (two words)?** _____

Answer Key

1. C. This question was a little tricky—we'll cover date format conventions in the next discussion of the chapter. **2.** D. **3.** `alter session`.

Conversion Functions

Other functions are designed to convert columns of one datatype to another type. These functions do not actually modify the stored data in the table itself; they just return the converted values to the SQL*Plus session. Several different conversion functions are available in the Oracle database, as listed here:

`to_char(x)`	Converts the noncharacter value x to a character or converts a date to a character string using formatting conventions (see the next section, "Date-Formatting Conventions")
`to_number(x)`	Converts nonnumeric value x to a number
`to_date(x[,y])`	Converts the nondate value x to a date using the format specified by y
`to_multi_byte(x)`	Converts the single-byte character string x to multibyte characters according to national language standards

`to_single_byte(x)`	Converts the multibyte character string *x* to single-byte characters according to national language standards
`chartorowid(x)`	Converts the string of characters *x* into an Oracle ROWID
`rowidtochar(x)`	Converts ROWID value into the string of characters *x*
`hextoraw(x)`	Converts the hexadecimal (base-16) value *x* into a raw (binary) format
`rawtohex(x)`	Converts the raw (binary) value *x* into a hexadecimal (base-16) format
`convert(x[,y[,z]])`	Executes a conversion of alphanumeric string *x* from the current character set (optionally specified as *z*) to the one specified by *y*
`translate(x,y,z)`	Executes a simple value conversion for character or numeric string *x* into something else based on the conversion factors *y* and *z*

Date-Formatting Conventions

You can use the `to_char( )` function to convert DATE column information into a text string. The format is `to_char(column_name, 'date_format_mask')`. Some of the more popular format masks available in Oracle include the following:

- **DD**   Shows the two-digit date.

- **DAY**   Shows the day spelled out.

- **MON**   Shows a three-letter month abbreviation, such as MAR for March.

- **MONTH**   Shows the month spelled out.

- **YY**   Shows the two-digit year (not millennium compliant).

- **YYYY**   Shows the four-digit year (not millennium compliant).

- **RR**   Shows the two-digit year (millennium compliant).

- **RRRR**   Shows the four-digit year (millennium compliant).

- **HH**   Shows the two-digit hour in A.M./P.M. format (must be used with the MIAM mask, explained three bullets down).

- **HH24**   Shows the two-digit hour in 24-hour format (cannot be used with the MIAM mask).

- **MI**   Shows the two-digit minute (use with HH24 mask).

- **MIAM**   Shows the two-digit minute in A.M./P.M. format (do not use with the HH24 mask).

- **SS**   Shows the two-digit second.

TIP
Oracle stores hour and minute information, as well as the day, month, and year, for a DATE column. Therefore, if you want to compare dates, you need to reset your expectations about what you're actually comparing or else you will often have problems because the times don't match on dates that are otherwise the same. Use the trunc( ) *function to avoid this problem!*

Demonstrating Single-Row Functions, Continued

The following text illustrates the most commonly used procedures for converting data in action. These are the to_char( ), to_number( ), and to_date( ) functions. The first one demonstrated is the to_char( ) function. In the example of new_time( ), the date function described earlier, the alter session set nls_date_format statement was used to demonstrate the full capabilities of Oracle in both storing date information and converting dates and times from one time zone to another. That exercise could have been accomplished with the use of the to_char( ) conversion function as well. Using to_char( ) in this manner saves you from converting nls_date_format, which, once executed, is in effect for the rest of your session, or until you execute another alter session set nls_date_format statement. Rather than using this method, you may want to opt for the less permanent option offered by the to_char( ) function, as shown here:

```
SQL> SELECT TO_CHAR(NEW_TIME(TO_DATE('15-MAR-2000 14:35:00',
  2  'DD-MON-YYYY HH24:MI:SS'),'AST','GMT'))
  3  FROM DUAL;
NEXT_DAY('15-MAR-200
--------------------
15-MAR-2000 18:35:00
```

Note that this example also uses the to_date( ) function, another conversion function in the list to be discussed. The to_date( ) function is very useful for converting numbers, and especially character strings, into properly formatted DATE fields.

The next function to consider is `to_number( )`, which converts text or date information into a number:

```
SQL> SELECT TO_NUMBER('49583') FROM DUAL;
TO_NUMBER('49583')
------------------
            49583
```

Although there does not appear to be much difference between the output of this query and the string that was passed, the main difference is the underlying datatype. Even so, Oracle is intelligent enough to convert a character string consisting of all numbers before performing an arithmetic operation using two values of two different datatypes, as shown in the following code:

```
SQL> SELECT '49583' + 34 FROM DUAL;
'49583'+34
----------
     49617
```

For Review

1. Be sure you can identify the datatype-conversion functions. Also, know which of the functions are most commonly used.

2. Understand the situations in which Oracle performs implicit datatype conversion.

Exercises

1. **You wish to use a format mask for date information in Oracle. In which of the following situations is this format mask not appropriate?**

   A. `to_date( )`

   B. `to_char( )`

   C. `alter session set nls_date_format`

   D. `to_number( )`

2. **State the reason why using `to_number( )` to convert a numeric text string into an actual number is unnecessary in the Oracle database (three words):** _____

Answer Key

1. D. **2.** Implicit datatype conversion.

Chapter Summary

This chapter ambitiously takes you from an introduction to the Oracle database through some intermediate techniques used in `select` statements. You learned about the theory behind relational database systems such as Oracle's and how they differ from earlier systems for data storage and retrieval. The concept of a table was presented, along with common Oracle datatypes used in those tables. The chapter also described the basic architecture of an Oracle database system, and covered such factors as what an object-relational RDBMS is and some of the features for developing code in Oracle's proprietary programming language, PL/SQL. You then focused your attention on the use of `select` statements. We discussed the use of the column, table, and comparison clauses (`select`, `from`, and `where`, respectively) as well as the use of the `order by` clause. The chapter wrapped up intermediate coverage of queries by introducing a multitude of single-row functions.

Two-Minute Drill

- Data is retrieved from Oracle using `select` statements.

- The syntax for a `select` statement consists of `select ... from ...;`.

- When you're entering a `select` statement from the prompt using SQL*Plus, a semicolon (;) at the end of the statement or a slash (/) at the beginning of the first empty line appearing after the statement in your operating buffer must be used to terminate the statement.

- Arithmetic operations can be used to perform math operations on data selected from a table or on numbers using the DUAL table.

- The DUAL table is a table with one column and one row used to fulfill the syntactic requirements of SQL `select` statements.

- Values in columns for particular rows may be empty (NULL).

- If a column contains a NULL value, you can use the `nvl( )` function to return meaningful information instead of an empty field.

- Aliases can be used in place of the actual column name or to replace the appearance of the function name in the header.

■ Output from two columns can be concatenated together using a double-pipe (| |).

■ SQL commands can be entered directly into SQL*Plus on the command line.

■ You can edit mistakes in SQL*Plus with the change command. If a mistake is made, the change (c/old/new) command is used.

■ Alternatively, the edit (ed) command can be used to make changes in your favorite text editor.

■ You can specify your favorite text editor by issuing the define _editor command at the prompt.

■ The order by clause in a select statement is a useful clause to incorporate a sort order into the output of a file.

■ The sort orders that can be used are ascending and descending, abbreviated as asc and desc, respectively. The order is determined by the column identified in the order by clause.

■ The where clause is used in SQL queries to limit the data returned by a query.

■ The where clauses contain comparison operations that determine whether a row will be returned by a query.

■ The logical comparison operations include =, >, >=, <, <, <=, <>, !=, ^=.

■ In addition to the logical operations, there is a comparison operation for pattern matching, called like. The % and _ characters are used to designate wildcards.

■ The range operation is called between.

■ The fuzzy logic operation is called soundex.

■ The where clause can contain one or more comparison operations linked together by using and or or and preceded by not.

■ SQL functions are broken down into character functions, number functions, and date functions.

■ Several conversion functions are available for transforming data from text to numeric datatypes and back, numbers to dates and back, text to ROWID and back, and so on.

■ Use the acronym PEMDAS to remember the correct order for operator precedence.

Fill-in-the-Blank Questions

1. This term refers to a logical grouping of tables according to the user who created the tables: _____

2. When you want to perform an operation on two expressions, you can query this table: _____

3. The function that allows for complex substitutions of column data based on value is called: _____

4. A command-line tool you will use frequently to access Oracle is called

   _____

5. The function whose work is performed by placing two pipe characters (| |) together is called _____

6. The Oracle component handling the actual obtainment of data you request is called _____

7. The command set you request data from Oracle with is called

   _____

Chapter Questions

1. **Which of the following statements contains an error?**

   A. `select * from EMP where EMPNO = 493945;`

   B. `select EMPNO from EMP where EMPNO = 493945;`

   C. `select EMPNO from EMP;`

   D. `select EMPNO where EMPNO = 56949 and ENAME = 'SMITH';`

2. **Which of the following statements correctly describes how to specify a column alias?**

   A. Place the alias at the beginning of the statement to describe the table.

   B. Place the alias after each column, separated by a space, to describe the column.

   C. Place the alias after each column, separated by a comma, to describe the column.

   D. Place the alias at the end of the statement to describe the table.

3. **The `nvl( )` function does what?**

   A. Assists in the distribution of output across multiple columns

   B. Allows you to specify alternate output for non-NULL column values

   C. Allows you to specify alternate output for NULL column values

   D. Nullifies the value of the column output

4. **Output from a table called PLAYS with two columns, PLAY_NAME and AUTHOR, is shown next. Which of the following SQL statements produced it?**

```
PLAY_TABLE
------------------------------------
"Midsummer Night's Dream", SHAKESPEARE
"Waiting For Godot", BECKETT
"The Glass Menagerie", WILLIAMS
```

   A. `select PLAY_NAME|| AUTHOR from PLAYS;`

   B. `select PLAY_NAME, AUTHOR from PLAYS;`

   C. `select PLAY_NAME||', ' || AUTHOR from PLAYS;`

   D. `select PLAY_NAME||', ' || AUTHOR play_table from PLAYS;`

5. **Issuing `define _editor="emacs"` will produce which outcome?**

   A. The EMACS editor will become the SQL*Plus default text editor.

   B. The EMACS editor will start running immediately.

   C. The EMACS editor will no longer be used by SQL*Plus as the default text editor.

   D. The EMACS editor will be deleted from the system.

6. **Which function can best be categorized as similar in function to an `IF-THEN-ELSE` statement?**

   A. `sqrt( )`

   B. `decode( )`

    C. new_time( )

    D. rowidtochar( )

7. **Which three of the following are number functions? (Choose three of the four.)**

    A. sinh( )

    B. to_number( )

    C. sqrt( )

    D. round( )

8. **You issue the following statement. What will be displayed if the employee number selected is 60494?**

```
SELECT DECODE(empno,38475, 'Terminated',60494, 'LOA', 'ACTIVE')
FROM emp;
```

    A. 60494

    B. LOA

    C. Terminated

    D. ACTIVE

9. **Which of the following is a valid SQL statement?**

    A. select to_char(nvl(sqrt(59483), '0')) from dual;

    B. select to_char(nvl(sqrt(59483), 'INVALID')) from dual;

    C. select (to_char(nvl(sqrt(59483), '0')) from dual;

    D. select to_char(nvl(sqrt(59483), 'TRUE')) from dual;

10. **What is the appropriate table to use when performing arithmetic calculations on values defined within the `select` statement (not pulled from a table column)?**

    A. EMP

    B. The table containing the column values

    C. DUAL

    D. An Oracle-defined table

11. **Which of the following keywords are used in `order by` clauses? (Choose two.)**

    A. `abs`

    B. `asc`

    C. `desc`

    D. `disc`

12. **Which of the following statements are *not* true about `order by` clauses?**

    A. Ascending or descending order can be defined with the `asc` or `desc` keyword.

    B. Only one column can be used to define the sort order in an `order by` clause.

    C. Multiple columns can be used to define sort order in an `order by` clause.

    D. Columns can be represented by numbers indicating their listed order in the `select` clause within `order by`.

13. **Which of the following lines in the `select` statement shown in the following code block contain an error?**

    ```
    select decode(EMPNO, 58385, 'INACTIVE', 'ACTIVE') empno
    from EMP
    where substr(ENAME,1,1) > to_number('S')
    and EMPNO > 02000
    order by EMPNO desc, ENAME asc;
    ```

    A. `select decode(EMPNO, 58385, 'INACTIVE', 'ACTIVE') empno`

    B. `from EMP`

    C. `where substr(ENAME,1,1) > to_number('S')`

    D. `and EMPNO > 02000`

    E. `order by EMPNO desc, ENAME asc;`

    F. No errors in this statement

Fill-in-the-Blank Answers

1. Schema

2. DUAL

3. decode( )

4. SQL*Plus

5. concat( )

6. RDBMS or relational database management system

7. SQL or structured query language

Answers to Chapter Questions

1. D. `select EMPNO where EMPNO = 56949 and ENAME = 'SMITH';`

Explanation There is no `from` clause in this statement. Although a `select` statement can be issued without a `where` clause, no `select` statement can be executed without a `from` clause specified. For that reason, the DUAL table exists to satisfy the `from` clause in situations in which you define all data needed within the statement.

2. B. Place the alias after each column, separated by a space, to describe the column.

Explanation Aliases do not describe tables; they describe columns, which eliminates choices A and D. Commas are needed between each column appearing in the column clause of the `select` statement. If a column alias appeared after a column, Oracle would either select the wrong column name, based on information provided in the alias, or return an error.

3. C. Allows you to specify alternate output for NULL column values

Explanation The `nvl( )` function is a simple `if-then` operation that tests column value output to see whether it is NULL. If it is, `nvl( )` substitutes the specified default value for the NULL value. Because this function only operates on one column per call to `nvl( )`, choice A is incorrect. Choice B is incorrect because it is the logical opposite of choice C. Choice D is incorrect because `nvl( )` is designed to substitute actual values for situations where NULL is present, not to nullify data.

4. D. select PLAY_NAME||', ' || AUTHOR play_table from PLAYS;

Explanation   This question illustrates the need to read carefully. Because the output specified for the question contains a column alias for the output of the statement, choice D is the only one that is correct, even though choice C also performs the correct calculation. Choice A is incorrect because it specifies an inaccurate concatenation method, and choice B is wrong because it doesn't specify concatenation at all.

5. A. The emacs editor will become the SQL*Plus default text editor.

Explanation   The define _editor statement is designed to define the default text editor in SQL*Plus. Changing the definition will not start or stop the editor specified from running, which eliminates choices B and D. Choice C is the logical opposite of choice A and is, therefore, incorrect.

6. B. decode( )

Explanation   The decode( ) function is a full-fledged if-then-else statement that can support manipulation of output values for several different cases, along with a default. The sqrt( ) statement simply calculates square roots, thus eliminating choice A. Choice C is incorrect because new_time( ) is a date function that converts a time in one time zone to a time in another time zone. Choice D is incorrect because it is a simple conversion operation.

7. A, C, and D. sinh( ), sqrt( ), and round( )

Explanation   The only nonnumber function in this list is the to_number( ) function, which is a conversion operation. Several questions of this type appear throughout the OCP exams, and for these types of questions you must choose multiple answers.

8. B. LOA

Explanation   The decode( ) statement has a provision in it that will return LOA if the employee number in the row matches the employee number specified for that case, which also eliminates choice D. Also, because a default value is specified by the decode( ) statement, there will never be an employee number returned by this query. Therefore, choice A is incorrect. Choice C is also eliminated because Terminated is only displayed when 38475 is the column value.

9. A. select to_char(nvl(sqrt(59483), '0')) from dual;

Explanation   Functions such as these can be used in conjunction with one another. Although usually the datatype of the value inserted if the column value is NULL and the column specified for `nvl( )` must match, Oracle performs many datatype conversions implicitly, such as this one.

    10. C. DUAL

Explanation   When all data to be processed by the query is present in the statement, and no data will be pulled from the database, users typically specify the DUAL table to fulfill the syntactic requirements of the `from` clause.

    11. B and C. `asc` and `desc`

Explanation   The `abs( )` function is the absolute value function, which eliminates choice A. The `disc( )` function is not an actual option either, thus eliminating choice D.

    12. B. Only one column can be used to define the sort order in an `order by` clause.

Explanation   Notice, first, that there is a logical difference between choices B and C, meaning you can eliminate one of them on principle. Multiple columns can be used to define order in `order by` statements, thereby eliminating choice C automatically. Choice A is incorrect because you can use `asc` or `desc` to specify ascending or descending order in your `order by` clause. Finally, choice D is incorrect because you can use numbers to represent the column you want to place an order on, based on how the columns are listed in the `select` statement.

    13. C. `where substr(ENAME,1,1) > to_number('S')`

Explanation   Characters that are alphabetic, such as *S*, cannot be converted into numbers. When this statement is run, it will produce an error on this line.

CHAPTER
2

Advanced Data
Selection in Oracle

n this chapter, you will learn about and demonstrate knowledge in the following areas:

- Displaying data from multiple tables

- Group functions and their uses

- Using subqueries

- Multiple-column subqueries

- Producing readable output from SQL*Plus

This chapter covers the advanced topics of Oracle data selection. First, we will cover how you can write `select` statements to access data from more than one table. You will also learn how to create joins that display data from different tables even when the information in the two tables does not correspond completely. The chapter discusses how to create and use table self-joins as well. After discussing table joins, the chapter introduces the `group by` clause used in `select` statements and group functions. This clause allows you to treat entire columns of data as a single unit for operations. You will also learn the use of the subquery. Finally, this chapter will cover how to specify special formatting in order to use SQL*Plus as a reporting tool. The material in this chapter will complete your knowledge of data selection and comprises 22 percent of OCP Exam 1.

NOTE
Like Chapter 1, this chapter uses the standard demo tables created by `utlsampl.sql` *or* `demobld.sql`*. However, this chapter also uses trivial and not-so-trivial examples from other tables. For nontrivial examples, I've included commands that will create and populate the table used. Because it's so important that you practice your use of Oracle as much as possible for OCP, I don't provide scripts to automatically generate the objects for you.*

Displaying Data from Multiple Tables

This section will cover the following areas related to displaying data from multiple tables:

- Using `select` statements to join data from more than one table

- Creating outer joins

- Joining a table to itself

The typical database contains many tables. Some smaller databases may have only a dozen or so tables, whereas other databases may have hundreds or even thousands. The common factor, however, is that very few databases have just one table containing everything you need. Therefore, you usually have to draw data from multiple tables together in a meaningful way. To show data from multiple tables in one query, Oracle allows you to perform *table joins*. Here are the two rules you need to remember for table joins. Data from two (or more) tables can be joined, if The same column (under the same or a different name) appears in *both* tables, and The column is the primary key (or part of that key) in *one* of the tables.

TIP
At least one column must be shared between two tables for you to join the two tables in a select *statement, and that column must be a primary key (or part of the key) in at least one of the tables.*

The Keys to Table Joins
Having a common column in two tables implies a relationship between the two tables. The nature of that relationship is determined by which table uses the column as a primary key. This begs the question, what is a primary key? A *primary key* is a column in a table used for identifying the uniqueness of each row in a table. The table in which the column appears as a primary key is referred to as the *parent table* in this relationship (sometimes also called the *master table*), whereas the column that references the other table in the relationship is often called the *child table* (sometimes also called the *detail table*). The common column appearing in the child table is referred to as a *foreign key*. Figure 2-1 demonstrates how the relationship may work in a database.

select Statements That Join Data from More Than One Table
Recall from Chapter 1 that a select statement can have three parts: the select clause, the from clause, and the where clause. That final clause, the where clause, contains comparison operations that will filter out the unwanted data from

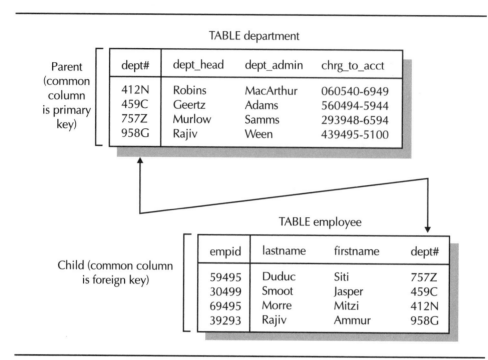

FIGURE 2-1. *Parent and child tables*

what you want to see. To join data from one table to another, you must compare the data in the common column from one table to that same column in the other table in the where clause. Let's look at an example:

```
SQL> select e.ename, e.deptno, d.dname
  2  from emp e, dept d
  3  where e.deptno = d.deptno;
ENAME         DEPTNO DNAME
---------- --------- --------------
SMITH            20 RESEARCH
ALLEN            30 SALES
WARD             30 SALES
JONES            20 RESEARCH
MARTIN           30 SALES
BLAKE            30 SALES
CLARK            10 ACCOUNTING
SCOTT            20 RESEARCH
KING             10 ACCOUNTING
TURNER           30 SALES
ADAMS            20 RESEARCH
```

```
JAMES              30 SALES
FORD               20 RESEARCH
MILLER             10 ACCOUNTING
```

Note the many important components in this table join. Listing two tables in the from clause clearly indicates that a table join is taking place. Note also that each table name is followed by a letter: E for emp or D for dept. This demonstrates an interesting concept—just as columns can have aliases, so, too, can tables. The aliases serve an important purpose—they prevent Oracle from getting confused about which table to use when listing the data in the DEPTNO column. Remember, emp and dept both have a column named DEPTNO. Look what happens when we don't use aliases:

```
SQL> select ename, deptno, dname
  2  from emp, dept
  3  where deptno = deptno;
where deptno = deptno
             *
ERROR at line 3:
ORA-00918: column ambiguously defined
```

You can also avoid ambiguity in table joins by prefixing references to the columns with the table names, but this often requires extra coding. You can also give the column two different names, but then you might forget that the relationship exists between the two tables. It's just better to use aliases! Notice something else, though. Neither the alias nor the full table name needs to be specified for columns appearing in only one table. Take a look at another example:

```
SQL> select ename, emp.deptno, dname
  2  from emp, dept
  3  where emp.deptno = dept.deptno;
ENAME           DEPTNO DNAME
---------- --------- --------------
SMITH              20 RESEARCH
ALLEN              30 SALES
WARD               30 SALES
JONES              20 RESEARCH
MARTIN             30 SALES
BLAKE              30 SALES
CLARK              10 ACCOUNTING
SCOTT              20 RESEARCH
KING               10 ACCOUNTING
TURNER             30 SALES
ADAMS              20 RESEARCH
JAMES              30 SALES
FORD               20 RESEARCH
MILLER             10 ACCOUNTING
```

where Clauses, Joins, and Cartesian Products

Notice also that our `where` clause includes a comparison on DEPTNO linking data in EMP to that of DEPT. Without this link, the output would have included all data from EMP and DEPT, jumbled together in a mess called a *Cartesian product*. Cartesian products are big, meaningless listings of output that are nearly never what you want. Let's look at a simple example in which we attempt to join two tables, each with three rows, using a `select` statement with no `where` clause, resulting in output with nine rows:

```
SQL> select a.col1, b.col_2
  2  from example_1 a, example_2 b;
     COL1 COL_2
--------- ------------------------------
        1 one
        2 one
        3 one
        1 two
        2 two
        3 two
        1 three
        2 three
        3 three
```

TIP
This table isn't created by utlsampl.sql *or* demobld.sql. *It's a trivial example, so unless you want to get some experience creating and populating tables, don't bother trying to execute the query on Oracle. If you want some experience on your own database, run the* select *statement on EMP and DEPT from the previous example, but leave off the* where *clause.*

Take note of another important fact. Although you learned in Chapter 1 that `where` clauses can contain comparison operations other than equality, to avoid Cartesian products, *you must always use equality operations in a comparison joining data from two tables.* If you want to use another comparison operation, you must first join the information using an equality comparison and then perform the other comparison somewhere else in the `where` clause. This is why table join operations are also sometimes referred to as *equijoins*. Take a look at the following example, which shows proper construction of a table join, where the information being joined is compared further using a non-equality operation to eliminate the employees from accounting:

```
SQL> select ename, emp.deptno, dname
  2  from emp, dept
  3  where emp.deptno = dept.deptno
  4  and dept.deptno > 10;
ENAME          DEPTNO DNAME
---------- --------- -------------
SMITH             20 RESEARCH
ALLEN             30 SALES
WARD              30 SALES
JONES             20 RESEARCH
MARTIN            30 SALES
BLAKE             30 SALES
SCOTT             20 RESEARCH
TURNER            30 SALES
ADAMS             20 RESEARCH
JAMES             30 SALES
FORD              20 RESEARCH
```

How Many Comparisons Do You Need?

A query on data from more than two tables must contain the right number of equality operations to avoid a Cartesian product. To avoid confusion, use this simple rule: If the number of tables to be joined equals N, include at least $N - 1$ equality conditions in the `select` statement so that each common column is referenced at least once.

TIP
For N joined tables, you need at least N – 1 equijoin conditions in the `where` clause of your `select` statement in order to avoid a Cartesian product.

For Review

1. A *table join* is a type of query that obtains data from two or more tables based on common information in both tables.

2. In order to join data from two tables, you must have a common column in both tables, and that column must be a primary key in *one* of the tables.

3. You must use equality comparison in the `where` clause joining data between two tables. Non-equality comparisons usually result in Cartesian products.

4. To know how many comparisons to include in a join statement, remember this formula: For N tables, use $N - 1$ equality comparisons.

Exercises

1. Two tables, PRODUCT and STORAGE_BOX, exist in a database. Individual products are listed in the table by unique ID number, product name, and the box a particular product is stored in. Individual storage boxes (identified by number) listed in the other table can contain many products, but each box can be found in only one location. Which of the following statements will correctly display the product ID, name, and box location of all widgets in this database?

   A. `select p.prod_id, p.prod_name, b.box_loc from product p, storage_box b where p.prod_id = b.prod_id and prod_name = 'WIDGET';`

   B. `select p.prod_id, p.prod_name, b.box_loc from product p, storage_box b where prod_name = 'WIDGET';`

   C. `select p.prod_id, p.prod_name, b.box_loc from product p, storage_box b where p.stor_box_num = b.stor_box_num and p.prod_name = 'WIDGET';`

   D. `select prod_id, prod_name, box_loc from product, storage_box where stor_box_num = stor_box_num and prod_name = 'WIDGET';`

2. You want to join information from three tables as part of developing a report. The tables are EMP, DEPT, and SALGRADE. Only records corresponding to employee, department location, and salary range are required for employees in grades 10 and higher for the organization. How many comparison operations are required for this query?

   A. Two

   B. Three

   C. Four

   D. Five

3. What is the name of the result when a join statement lacks a where clause (two words)? _____

Answer Key

1. C. **2.** B. Remember, you must include two equality comparisons to form the join properly, plus an additional filtering comparison to get only records where salary grade is greater than 10.
3. Cartesian product.

Creating Outer Joins

In some cases, you will want to see information from tables even when no corresponding records exist in the common column. For the purposes of this demonstration, let's issue the following statement in our SQL*Plus session:

```
SQL> update emp set deptno = NULL where ename = 'KING';
1 row updated.
```

TIP

We'll talk more about `update` statements in Chapter 3.

In effect, we're telling Oracle that because KING is the company president, he is no longer reporting to his old department number. Now look at what happens when we try to join the EMP table to the DEPT table using the common DEPTNO column:

```
SQL> select e.ename, e.deptno, d.dname
  2  from emp e, dept d
  3  where e.deptno = d.deptno;
ENAME         DEPTNO DNAME
---------- --------- --------------
SMITH             20 RESEARCH
ALLEN             30 SALES
WARD              30 SALES
JONES             20 RESEARCH
MARTIN            30 SALES
BLAKE             30 SALES
CLARK             10 ACCOUNTING
SCOTT             20 RESEARCH
TURNER            30 SALES
ADAMS             20 RESEARCH
JAMES             30 SALES
FORD              20 RESEARCH
MILLER            10 ACCOUNTING
```

Notice someone missing? KING does not appear in the output because he isn't assigned to a department anymore. When no corresponding information exists in the common column from either table, the join statement ignores the record from that table. To force the query to return data from EMP even when there is no corresponding record in DEPT, you must specify an *outer join* operation. Let's look at how such a join operation would be written:

```
SQL> select e.ename, e.deptno, d.dname
  2  from emp e, dept d
```

```
 3  where e.deptno = d.deptno (+);
ENAME           DEPTNO DNAME
---------- --------- --------------
SMITH              20 RESEARCH
ALLEN              30 SALES
WARD               30 SALES
JONES              20 RESEARCH
MARTIN             30 SALES
BLAKE              30 SALES
CLARK              10 ACCOUNTING
SCOTT              20 RESEARCH
KING
TURNER             30 SALES
ADAMS              20 RESEARCH
JAMES              30 SALES
FORD               20 RESEARCH
MILLER             10 ACCOUNTING
```

By using outer join statements, we can get KING listed in the result, even though he is "outside" the join criteria specified by the query. Notice the use of the (+) marker (in bold) at the end of the comparison joining the tables; this is called the *outer join operator*. This marker denotes which table can have NULL data corresponding to non-NULL values in the column values from the other table. The outer join marker is on the side of the DEPT table, meaning that data in the EMP table can correspond either to values in DEPT or to NULL if there is no corresponding value in the DEPT table. Had the order been reversed, such that the outer join operator appears next to the column reference in EMP, then values from DEPT with or without corresponding values in EMP would have been listed. Take a look at the following code block to see what I mean:

```
SQL> select e.ename, e.deptno, d.dname
  2  from emp e, dept d
  3  where e.deptno (+) = d.deptno;
ENAME           DEPTNO DNAME
---------- --------- --------------
CLARK              10 ACCOUNTING
MILLER             10 ACCOUNTING
SMITH              20 RESEARCH
SCOTT              20 RESEARCH
ADAMS              20 RESEARCH
FORD               20 RESEARCH
JONES              20 RESEARCH
ALLEN              30 SALES
JAMES              30 SALES
TURNER             30 SALES
BLAKE              30 SALES
```

```
MARTIN          30 SALES
WARD            30 SALES
                   OPERATIONS
```

TIP

Be careful where you place the (+) symbol for outer joins—if it appears next to the column reference for the wrong table in the join comparison, your result set will have unexpected results.

Concluding This Lesson

Because we have made a change to KING's record in the EMP table for our sample data, we will want to discard those changes using the following command:

```
SQL> rollback;
Rollback complete.
```

TIP

You'll learn more about the `rollback` command in Chapter 3.

For Review

1. Understand that an outer join accommodates the situation in which you want to display data in a join statement where records from one table don't necessarily all have corresponding records in the other.

2. Memorize the special character used to denote outer joins.

3. Remember the importance of where you place the outer join operator—it tells Oracle which table in the join can have NULL records corresponding to values from the other table.

Exercises

1. Identify the symbol used for outer join operations: _____

2. You are defining an outer join statement. Which of the following choices is true concerning outer join statements?

    A. Because outer join operations permit NULL values from one of the tables, you do not have to specify equality comparisons to join those tables.

B. In outer join statements, you place the outer join operator next to the column from the table that may or may not contain values corresponding to the column from the other table.

C. An outer join can display records from one table where there is no corresponding match of column information in the other table.

D. Even though outer join operations permit NULL values from one of the tables, you still need to specify equality comparisons to join those tables.

3. **Two tables, PRODUCT and STORAGE_BOX, exist in a database. Individual products are listed in the table by unique ID number, product name, and the box a particular product is stored in. Individual storage boxes (identified by number) listed in the other table can contain many products, but the box can be found in only one location. Which of the following statements will correctly display the product ID, name, and box location of all widgets in this database that have or have not been assigned to a storage box?**

A. `select p.prod_id, p.prod_name, b.box_loc from product p, storage_box b where p.stor_box_num = b.stor_box_num and p.prod_name = 'WIDGET'(+);`

B. `select p.prod_id, p.prod_name, b.box_loc from product p, storage_box b where p.stor_box_num = b.stor_box_num (+) and p.prod_name = 'WIDGET';`

C. `select p.prod_id, p.prod_name, b.box_loc from product p, storage_box b where b.stor_box_num = p.stor_box_num (+) and p.prod_name = 'WIDGET';`

D. `select p.prod_id, p.prod_name, b.box_loc from product p, storage_box b where p.stor_box_num = b.stor_box_num and or b.stor_box_num is NULL;`

Answer Key

1. (+). **2.** A. **3.** B.

Joining a Table to Itself

In special situations, it may be necessary for you to perform a join using only one table. What you are really doing is using two copies of the table to join the data in the table to itself. This SQL programming technique is known as a table *self-join*.

This task can be useful in cases where there is a possibility that some slight difference exists between two rows that would otherwise be duplicate records. If you want to perform a self-join on a table, utilize table aliases described earlier in the chapter to specify the same table so that Oracle understands that a self-join is being performed. This lesson will illustrate use of a self-join to show how to employ the technique properly. To follow along in your Oracle database, issue the following command:

```
SQL> insert into emp values (7903, 'FORD', 'ANALYST', '7566',
  2  '03-DEC-81', 3000, null, 10);
1 row created.
```

TIP

You'll see more examples of using the `insert`
command in Chapter 3.

In this case, we've added a new record to table EMP for employee FORD, who is already an employee of the company. Everything about this user is the same, except for her employee number. Once we realize our mistake, we can issue the following simple query to obtain the duplicate records:

```
SQL> select * from emp where ename = 'FORD';
EMPNO ENAME     JOB  MGR HIREDATE    SAL COMM DEPTNO
----- -----   ------- ---- --------- ---- ---- ------
 7902 FORD   ANALYST 7566 03-DEC-81 3000         20
 7903 FORD   ANALYST 7566 03-DEC-81 3000         20
```

This simple query works fine for this uncomplicated example, but let's make it more complex. Let's pretend that the EMP table stores values for a company with hundreds of employees named FORD, all working in different jobs and under different managers. In this case, we might use the following query to guarantee that the instances of FORD we get are the ones we want:

```
SQL> select e.empno, e.ename, e.job
  2  from emp e, emp e2
  3  where e.empno <> e2.empno
  4  and e.ename = e2.ename
  5  and e.job = e2.job
  6  and e.mgr = e2.mgr;
  EMPNO ENAME       JOB        MGR
--------- ---------- --------- ----
     7903 FORD       ANALYST   7566
     7902 FORD       ANALYST   7566
```

This query says, "OK, Oracle, give me the records for users named FORD who have different employee numbers, but filter out the FORDs working in different jobs for different managers." As you can see, self-joins can be useful for obtaining nearly duplicate records in the event some error occurs. Situations where this might be useful include the following:

- Batch jobs that incorrectly load lots of duplicate records

- Situations where users enter nearly duplicate records by mistake

- Any instance where a record nearly identical to a record already in the table may have been entered

Some Self-Join Caveats

Here's a final note of caution. Although very powerful and useful for identifying duplicate records, self-joins should be run with extreme caution because of two very important factors. First, self-joins often take a long time to process and can cause performance issues for other users on the database. This is because Oracle must read all table data twice sequentially. Second, because the required number of equality operations is at least *two* in the situation of self-joins (one to join the table to itself and the other to distinguish the duplication), Cartesian products can result when you don't formulate your where clause properly. Without a proper comparison operation set up in the where clause, you may wind up with many copies of every row in the table returned, which will certainly run for a long time and produce a lot of unnecessary output.

TIP
The number of equality operations usually needed in the where *clause of a self-join of a table to itself should be two or more—one to join the table to itself and the other to distinguish the duplicates.*

In Conclusion

To wrap up this lesson, let's once again make sure that the changes we made to the demo tables don't get saved. To do this, issue the following command:

```
SQL> rollback;
Rollback complete.
```

TIP
Once again, you'll learn more about the rollback *command in Chapter 3.*

For Review

  1. Know what a self-join is and how one is formulated and used.

  2. When using a self-join, remember that you need enough comparison operations in the `where` clause to join the table to itself and distinguish the duplicate records.

  3. Understand the slow performance and Cartesian product issues that may arise from the use of self-joins.

Exercises

  1. **A multinational Fortune 500 company uses internal testing to determine employee promotability and job placement. Tests are offered at multiple locations. Employees are permitted to take tests for any job they want to apply for, with one restriction: an employee may take a specific exam for a corresponding job position only once per year. Recently, Human Resources discovered that some employees were circumventing this restriction by taking the same exam in different test locations. Which of the following queries might be useful in identifying employees who have circumvented this restriction?**

     A.
```
select a.ename, a.test_name, a.test_date, a.location
b.test_date, b.location from tests a, tests b where
a.ename = b.ename and a.test_name = b.test_name and
a.location = b.location and trunc(a.test_date) >
trunc(sysdate-365) and trunc(b.test_date) >
trunc(sysdate-365);
```

     B.
```
select a.ename, a.test_name, a.test_date, a.location
b.test_date, b.location from tests a, tests b where
a.ename <> b.ename and a.test_name = b.test_name and
a.location = b.location and trunc(a.test_date) >
trunc(sysdate-365) and trunc(b.test_date) >
trunc(sysdate-365);
```

     C.
```
select a.ename, a.test_name, a.test_date, a.location
b.test_date, b.location from tests a, tests b where
a.ename = b.ename and a.test_name <> b.test_name and
a.location = b.location and trunc(a.test_date) >
trunc(sysdate-365) and trunc(b.test_date) >
trunc(sysdate-365);
```

    D. `select a.ename, a.test_name, a.test_date, a.location`
        `b.test_date, b.location from tests a, tests b where`
        `a.ename = b.ename and a.test_name = b.test_name and`
        `a.location <> b.location and a.test_date >`
        `trunc(sysdate-365) and b.test_date >`
        `trunc(sysdate-365);`

2. Identify a general concern related to the use of self-joins on the Oracle database: _____

3. Identify a problem with self-joins resulting from malformed **where** clauses (two words): _____

Answer Key

1. **D. 2.** Performance. **3.** Cartesian products.

Group Functions and Their Uses

This section will cover the following topics related to group functions and their uses:

- Identifying and using group functions

- Using the `group by` clause

- Excluding group data with the `having` clause

    A *group function* allows you to perform a data operation on several values in a column of data as though the column were one collective group of data. These functions are also called *group-by functions* because they are often used in a special clause of `select` statements, called the `group by` clause. A more complete discussion of the `group by` clause appears later in this section. This discussion also describes how to use the `having` clause in `group by` clauses, which can act as a `where` clause within a `where` clause.

Identifying and Using Group Functions

Sometimes, you may want to treat the data in a column as if it were a list of items to be manipulated as a group. Think about the contents of the EMP table. Let's say you want to obtain the average salary for employees in the company. The formula for averaging numbers is to add all the numbers in the list together and then divide by the number of elements in that list. Group functions are useful for this sort of activity because, unlike single-row functions, group functions can operate on column data in several rows at a time. Here's a list of the available group functions:

avg(x)	Averages all x column values returned by the select statement
count(x)	Counts the number of non-NULL values returned by the select statement for column x
max(x)	Determines the maximum value in column x for all rows returned by the select statement
min(x)	Determines the minimum value in column x for all rows returned by the select statement
stddev(x)	Calculates the standard deviation for all values in column x in all rows returned by the select statement
sum(x)	Calculates the sum of all values in column x in all rows returned by the select statement
variance(x)	Calculates the variance for all values in column x in all rows returned by the select statement

TIP
All group functions do not include NULL column values in their computations—an essential OCP fact! Also, the result is sorted implicitly by the Oracle RDBMS and will not alter the values stored in your columns in any way. The result of one group function can be passed as input into another group function.

Group Functions in Action

Let's take a closer look at the grouping functions. The avg( ) function takes the values for a single column on all rows returned by the query and calculates the average value for that column. Based on EMP, the avg( ) function on the SAL column produces the following result:

```
SQL> select avg(sal) from emp;
  AVG(SAL)
---------
2073.2143
```

The second grouping function listed is count( ). This function is bound to become the cornerstone of any Oracle professional's repertoire. The count( ) function returns a row count for the table, given certain column names, select criteria, or both. Note that the fastest way to execute count ( ) is to pass a value that resolves quickly in the SQL processing mechanism. Some values that resolve quickly are integers and the ROWID pseudocolumn. Here's an example:

```
SQL> SELECT COUNT(*), -- Slow
  2  COUNT(1), -- Fast
  3  COUNT(rowid) -- Fast
  4  FROM EMP;

COUNT(*)  COUNT(1) COUNT(rowid)
--------  -------- ------------
      14        14           14
```

TIP
The count (expr) function returns the number of rows in the table with a non-NULL value in the column you are counting. In other words, if you specify a column for the count ( ) function, and a row for that column contains a NULL value, then the row won't be counted. Many users of Oracle avoid this problem by using count (ROWID). It's faster than count (*), and every row in a table will have a ROWID value.

Oracle **8i** and higher | The asterisk (*) in the previous query is a wildcard variable that indicates all columns in the table. For better performance, this wildcard should not generally be used because the Oracle SQL processing mechanism must first resolve all column names in the table—a step that is unnecessary if you're simply trying to count rows. Notice that one of these examples uses the special pseudocolumn ROWID, which is a special value that uniquely identifies each row. Each row in a table has one unique ROWID.

TIP
Do not use count (*) to determine the number of rows in a table. Use count (1) or count (ROWID) instead. These options are faster because they bypass some unnecessary operations in Oracle's SQL processing mechanism.

The next pair of grouping functions to be covered are the max ( ) and min ( ) functions. The max ( ) function determines the largest value for the column passed, whereas min ( ) determines the smallest value for the column passed, as shown here:

```
SQL> select max(sal), min(sal) from emp;
  MAX(SAL)   MIN(SAL)
--------- ---------
     5000       800
```

The final group function, sum( ), is used commonly in simple accounting reports. The sum( ) function gives the total of all values in a column. Here's an example:

```
SQL> select sum(sal) from emp;
  SUM(SAL)
---------
     29025
```

In general, the group functions will operate on columns of datatypes NUMBER and DATE because many of the functions they represent in mathematics are numeric operations. It makes little sense to take the standard deviation for a set of 12 words, unless the user wants to take the standard deviation of the length of those words by combining the use of the length( ) function with the stddev( ) function. A few notable exceptions to this general rule exist, though. The first exception is the count( ) function. The count( ) function will operate on a column of any datatype. The other exceptions are max( ) and min( ), which operate on many different Oracle datatypes in addition to NUMBER and DATE.

For Review

1. Know what the group functions are and how they are used in simple select statements.

2. Understand specifically how to use the count( ) function and why using count(rowid) or count(1) might be a better idea than using count(*).

Exercises

1. A table containing all 1,232,432 customer orders for the previous year has a column, TOTAL, that lists the total amount spent by the customers on their orders. You issue the following command to obtain gross sales for the year: **select sum(total) from customers.** Which of the following choices identifies the number of rows that will appear in the output?

   A. 1

   B. 2

   C. 500

   D. 1,232,432

2. **The standard EMP table we have worked with so far in the chapter contains 14 records corresponding to employees of the corporation. You issue the following command on that table: `select count(mgr)` from `emp;`. Which of the following choices identifies the result Oracle will return?**

   A. 11

   B. 12

   C. 13

   D. 14

3. **Identify the type of value that group functions ignore by default:**

   _____

Answer Key
1. A. 2. C. 3. NULL.

Using the group by Clause

So far, you've seen examples of using group functions by themselves in the column clause of your query. This use is well and good, but sometimes it gives more meaning to the output of a `select` statement to collect data into logical groupings in combination with group functions. For example, let's say you want a listing of the different job roles in the corporation, along with the number of employees who fill those roles. For our small company, you could simply list all the information in the EMP table and count by hand. However, that process wouldn't work in a larger organization. Instead, you might want to use a `select` statement with a group function such as `count( )` to produce a meaningful listing of information. Let's try it out:

```
SQL> select job, count(job)
  2   from emp;
SQL> select job, count(job)
             *
ERROR at line 1:
ORA-00937: not a single-group group function
```

What happened? Well, we forgot something. Oracle expects group functions to produce one line of output for all rows in the table whose column you specify. In this case, Oracle became confused when we told it to list the individual values for the JOB column by including a reference to JOB in the column clause, too. The solution is to include a `group by` clause, which, in effect, tells Oracle to list each *distinct* value for JOB and then count the number of times that value appears in the EMP table. Let's take another look:

```
SQL> select job, count(job)
  2  from emp
  3  group by job;
JOB        COUNT(JOB)
---------  ----------
ANALYST             2
CLERK               4
MANAGER             3
PRESIDENT           1
SALESMAN            4
```

Perfect! The `group by` clause in this example saves you from performing a great deal of work by hand. Instead, Oracle shoulders most of the work and shows only the results you need. The `group by` clause works well in many situations in which you want to report calculations on data according to groups or categories.

Now let's consider a more complex example. Suppose you want a list of our company's highest paid employees, broken out by department and job position. You already saw what happens when the `group by` clause is left out entirely. But there's something else we need to be careful about. Take a look at a first stab for developing a `group by` query that satisfies our requirements:

```
SQL> select deptno, avg(sal), job
  2  from emp
  3  group by deptno;
select deptno, avg(sal), job
                         *
ERROR at line 1:
ORA-00979: not a GROUP BY expression
```

When you use a `group by` clause in your query, all the non-group expressions in the column clause of the query must appear before the grouped expression in the column clause. Put another way, *no non-group expression can appear after the group expression in the column clause.* To solve the problem, we can remove the JOB column from the column clause entirely. However, that won't give us the output we need. Instead, we must first rearrange the non-group expressions in the column clause to appear in front of the group function and then add the JOB column to the `group by` clause. This way, Oracle knows how to evaluate the aggregate columns in the `select` statement that are part of the grouping expression. The solution is shown here:

```
SQL> select deptno, job, avg(sal)
  2  from emp
```

```
3  group by deptno, job;
   DEPTNO JOB         AVG(SAL)
   --------- --------- ---------
       10 CLERK          1300
       10 MANAGER        2450
       10 PRESIDENT      5000
       20 ANALYST        3000
       20 CLERK           950
       20 MANAGER        2975
       30 CLERK           950
       30 MANAGER        2850
       30 SALESMAN       1400
```

Notice something else about this output—the records are listed in order based on the contents of the DEPTNO column. This is because DEPTNO appears first in the group by clause. If we listed JOB first, the output would be alphabetized by job, as shown here:

```
SQL> select deptno, job, avg(sal)
  2  from emp
  3  group by job, deptno;
   DEPTNO JOB         AVG(SAL)
   --------- --------- ---------
       20 ANALYST        3000
       10 CLERK          1300
       20 CLERK           950
       30 CLERK           950
       10 MANAGER        2450
       20 MANAGER        2975
       30 MANAGER        2850
       10 PRESIDENT      5000
       30 SALESMAN       1400
```

You can use order by clauses with group by clauses as well—it's actually fairly common to do so. Take a look at the following output, where we've created some additional meaning by ordering the output such that the highest average salaries are listed at the top, so we can figure out which departments and jobs pay the most:

```
SQL> select deptno, job, avg(sal)
  2  from emp
  3  group by deptno, job
  4  order by 3 desc;
   DEPTNO JOB         AVG(SAL)
   --------- --------- ---------
       10 PRESIDENT      5000
```

```
20 ANALYST        3000
20 MANAGER        2975
30 MANAGER        2850
10 MANAGER        2450
30 SALESMAN       1400
10 CLERK          1300
20 CLERK           950
30 CLERK           950
```

TIP

When you're using an order by *clause with a* group by *clause, the order in which you list columns in the* group by *clause doesn't matter— the order of output will be dictated by the* order by *clause.*

OLAP Features in Oracle8i

Oracle **8i** and higher

Some new features for query processing in Oracle8i include the use of online analytical processing (OLAP) operations in your database. These features are useful for data warehousing and data mart applications used for supporting business decision-making processes. The first of these new operations is a performance enhancement to a specific type of query, called a top-N query. We will discuss top-N queries more extensively later in the chapter. The other two new operations make it possible to perform certain OLAP operations in a group by clause. These two operations are cube and rollup. Let's look at each in more detail.

rollup   This group by operation is used to produce subtotals at any level of aggregation needed. These subtotals then "roll up" into a grand total, according to items listed in the group by expression. The totaling is based on a one-dimensional data hierarchy of grouped information. For example, let's say we wanted to get a payroll breakdown for our company by department and job position. The following code block would give us that information:

```
SQL> select deptno, job, sum(sal) as salary
  2  from emp
  3  group by rollup(deptno, job);
   DEPTNO JOB            SALARY
--------- --------- ---------
       10 CLERK          1300
       10 MANAGER        2450
       10 PRESIDENT      5000
       10                8750
       20 ANALYST        6000
```

```
20  CLERK          1900
20  MANAGER        2975
20                10875
30  CLERK           950
30  MANAGER        2850
30  SALESMAN       5600
30                 9400
                  29025
```

TIP

*Notice that NULL values in the output of `rollup`
operations typically mean that the row contains
subtotal or grand total information. If you want, you
can use the `nvl( )` function to substitute a more
meaningful value.*

cube   This is an extension, similar to `rollup`, that allows you to take a specified
set of grouping columns and create subtotals for all possible combinations of them.
The `cube` operation calculates all levels of subtotals on horizontal lines across
spreadsheets of output and creates cross-tab summaries on multiple vertical
columns in those spreadsheets. The result is a summary that shows subtotals for
every combination of columns or expressions in the `group by` clause, which is also
known as n-*dimensional cross-tabulation*. In the following example, notice how
`cube` not only gives us the payroll breakdown of our company by DEPTNO and
JOB, but it also gives us the breakdown of payroll by JOB across all departments:

```
SQL>  select deptno, job, sum(sal) as salary
   2  from emp
   3  group by cube(deptno, job);
DEPTNO JOB          SALARY
--------- --------- ---------
      10  CLERK         1300
      10  MANAGER       2450
      10  PRESIDENT     5000
      10                8750
      20  ANALYST       6000
      20  CLERK         1900
      20  MANAGER       2975
      20               10875
      30  CLERK          950
      30  MANAGER       2850
      30  SALESMAN      5600
      30                9400
          ANALYST       6000
          CLERK         4150
```

```
MANAGER         8275
PRESIDENT       5000
SALESMAN        5600
               29025
```

For Review

1. Know that the use of a group function in combination with a non-group expression in the column clause requires using the group by clause. All non-group expressions must be listed before the group expression.

2. Understand the relationship between the order in which columns are listed in the group by expression and the order in which Oracle will list records in the output. Also, know that when an order by clause is used, it overrides the order set by the group by clause.

3. Be sure you can identify the situations in which statements containing the group by clause return errors, as well as how to resolve those errors.

4. Know how to use OLAP functionality provided by cube and rollup in the group by clause. Also, know that without this functionality, you would have to develop very long multiple queries whose output is joined by union all operations (don't worry about what a union all operation is, just be sure you can identify it as an alternative to the OLAP functions described in this section).

Exercises

1. **You are developing a query on the PROFITS table, which stores profit information by company region, product type, and quarterly time period. Which of the following SQL statements will display a cross-tabulation of output showing profits by region, product type, and time period?**

   A. select region, prod_type, time, sum(profit) from profits group by region, prod_type, time;

   B. select region, prod_type, time from profits group by rollup (region, prod_type, time);

   C. select region, prod_type, time from profits group by cube (region, prod_type, time);

   D. select region, prod_type, time, sum(profit) from profits group by cube (region, prod_type, time);

2. Which of the following choices identifies a `group by` query that will not result in an error from Oracle when run against the database?

   A. `select deptno, job, sum(sal) from emp group by job, deptno;`

   B. `select sum(sal), deptno, job from emp group by job, deptno;`

   C. `select deptno, job, sum(sal) from emp;`

   D. `select deptno, sum(sal), job from emp group by job, deptno;`

3. Review the following SQL statement:

   ```
   SQL> select a.deptno, a.job, b.loc, sum(a.sal)
     2  from emp a, dept b
     3  where a.deptno = b.deptno
     4  group by a.deptno, a.job, b.loc
     5  order by sum(a.sal);
   ```

   Which of the following choices identifies the column upon which the order of output from this query will be returned?

   A. `a.deptno`

   B. `a.job`

   C. `b.loc`

   D. `sum(A.SAL)`

4. Without the OLAP functionality built into `group by` statements, you would need to develop multiple SQL queries whose output is joined by these types of statements (two words): _____

Answer Key

1. D. 2. A. 3. D. 4. `union all`.

Excluding group Data with having

Once the data is grouped using the `group by` statement, it is sometimes useful to *weed out* unwanted data. For example, let's say we want to list the average salary paid to employees in our company, broken down by department and job title. However, for this query, we only care about departments and job titles where the average salary is over $2000. In effect, we want to put a `where` clause on the `group by` clause to limit the results we see to departments and job titles where the average salary equals $2001 or higher. This effect can be achieved with the use of a special clause called the `having` clause, which is associated with `group by` statements. Take a look at an example of this clause:

```
SQL> select deptno, job, avg(sal)
  2  from emp
  3  group by deptno, job
  4  having avg(sal) > 2000;
  DEPTNO JOB         AVG(SAL)
--------- --------- ---------
       10 MANAGER       2450
       10 PRESIDENT     5000
       20 ANALYST       3000
       20 MANAGER       2975
       30 MANAGER       2850
```

Consider the output of this query for a moment. First, Oracle computes the average for every department and job title in the entire company. Then, the `having` clause eliminates departments and titles whose constituent employees' average salary is $2000 or less. This selectivity cannot easily be accomplished with an ordinary `where` clause, because the `where` clause selects individual rows, whereas this example requires that groups of rows be selected. In this query, you successfully limit output on the `group by` rows by using the `having` clause.

TIP
There is no specific order that the `having` and `group by` clauses must appear in. A `having` clause can appear before the `group by` clause in the query. However, it is logical that the `group by` appear first in the SQL statement.

For Review

1. Know what the `having` clause is and the function that it serves.

2. Know that referencing the group expression in the `having` clause allows Oracle to filter data based on known or derived criteria.

Exercises

1. You are developing a query on the PROFITS table, which stores profit information by company region, product type, and quarterly time period. Which of the following choices identifies a query that will obtain the average profits greater than $100,000 by product type, region, and time period?

   A. `select region, prod_type, period, avg(profit) from profits where avg(profit) > 100000 group by region, prod_type, period;`

   B. `select region, prod_type, period, avg(profit) from profits where avg(profit) > 100000 order by region, prod_type, period;`

   C. `select region, prod_type, period, avg(profit) from profits group by region, prod_type, period having avg(profit) > 100000;`

   D. `select region, prod_type, period, avg(profit) from profits group by region, prod_type, period having avg(profit) < 100000;`

2. A `having` clause can act like this type of clause inside `group by` expressions: _____

Answer Key

1. C. 2. `where`.

Using Subqueries

This section will cover the following topics related to using subqueries:

- ■ Understanding and defining subqueries
- ■ Listing and writing different types of subqueries

A *subquery* is a "query within a query." In other words, a subquery is a `select` statement nested within a `select` statement, designed to limit the selected output of the parent query by producing an intermediate result set of some sort. There are several different ways to include subqueries in SQL statements' where clauses.

We'll talk in this section about the types of problems subqueries can solve, how to develop subqueries, the different subquery types, and how to write single-row and multiple-row subqueries.

Understanding and Defining Subqueries

Subqueries can be used to obtain values for parent `select` statements when specific search criteria isn't known. To do so, the `where` clause in the parent `select` statement must have a comparison operation where the unknown value being compared is determined by the result of the subquery. Consider the following example, where we search for the name, department number, and salary information for employees working in New York. The known criterion is that the employees work in New York. However, without looking at the DEPT table, we won't know which department number corresponds to the New York office. Let's take a look at how a subquery can help us out:

```
SQL>  select ename, deptno, sal
  2    from emp
  3    where deptno =
  4      ( select deptno
  5        from dept
  6        where loc = 'NEW YORK' );
ENAME          DEPTNO         SAL
----------    ---------    ---------
CLARK              10         2450
KING               10         5000
MILLER             10         1300
```

TIP
Subqueries must appear inside parentheses, or else Oracle will have trouble distinguishing the subquery from the parent query.

The highlighted portion of the SQL statement is the subquery. Notice how the parent query requires the subquery to resolve itself for the DEPTNO value corresponding to the New York office. When this `select` statement is submitted, Oracle will process the subquery *first* in order to resolve all unknown search criteria and then feed that resolved criteria to the outer query. The outer query then can resolve the dataset it is supposed to return.

Consider also that the preceding example uses an equality comparison to connect the parent query to the subquery. This is the most commonly used method for connecting subqueries to their parents, but it isn't the only one. You could use many of the other comparison operations, such as <, >, <=, and >=. You can also use the `in` comparison, which is similar to the `case` statement offered in many programming languages, because resolution can be established based on the parent column's equality with any element in the group. Let's take a look at an example:

```
SQL> select ename, job, sal
  2  from emp
  3  where deptno in
  4    ( select deptno
  5      from dept
  6      where dname in
  7      ('ACCOUNTING', 'SALES'));
ENAME      JOB            SAL
---------- --------- ---------
ALLEN      SALESMAN      1600
WARD       SALESMAN      1250
MARTIN     SALESMAN      1250
BLAKE      MANAGER       2850
CLARK      MANAGER       2450
KING       PRESIDENT     5000
TURNER     SALESMAN      1500
JAMES      CLERK          950
MILLER     CLERK         1300
```

Another way of including a subquery in the `where` clause of a `select` statement is to use the `exists` clause. When you specify the `exists` operation in a `where` clause, you must include a subquery that satisfies the `exists` operation. If the subquery returns data, the `exists` operation returns TRUE, and a record from the parent query will be returned. If not, the `exists` operation returns FALSE, and no record for the parent query will be returned. Let's look at an example in which we obtain the same listing of employees working in the New York office, only this time, we use the `exists` operation:

```
SQL> select e.ename, e.job, e.sal
  2  from emp e
  3  where exists
  4      ( select d.deptno
  5        from dept d
  6        where d.loc = 'NEW YORK'
  7        and d.deptno = e.deptno);
ENAME      JOB            SAL
---------- --------- ---------
CLARK      MANAGER       2450
KING       PRESIDENT     5000
MILLER     CLERK         1300
```

Notice something very interesting about this subquery example. We used table aliases in both the parent query and the subquery to create a *correlated subquery*. This technique allows us to "jump" from the subquery to the parent level in order to perform incredibly complex, almost counterintuitive, processing that necessarily must involve some discussion of a programming concept known as *variable scope*.

Variable scope refers to the availability or "viewability" of data in certain variables at certain times. Sometimes a variable has a *local* scope. That is to say that the variable can only be seen when the current block of code is being executed. You can consider the columns in subquery comparison operations to be variables whose scope is *local* to the query. There is also *global* scope. In addition to a variable having local scope within the subquery in which it appears, the variable also has *global* scope, meaning that it is available in all subqueries to that query. In the previous example, all variables or columns named in comparison operations in the outermost `select` operation are local to that operation and global to all the nested subqueries.

TIP
You've only seen some simple examples, but you should know that subqueries can be nested inside other subqueries up to 225 levels deep. Subqueries are also the topic of many OCP questions, so you should make sure you have plenty of experience writing them before taking the exam—and make sure you know the subquery discussions in this book cold!

For Review

1. Know what a subquery is, as well as when you might want to incorporate a subquery into a database `select` statement.

2. Be sure you can identify and give examples of how to write subqueries that are linked to their parent query by means of equality comparison, the `in` comparison, and the `exists` comparison.

Exercises

1. **The company has an employee expense application with two tables. One table, called EMP, contains all employee data. The other, called EXPENSE, contains expense vouchers submitted by every employee in the company. Which of the following queries will obtain the employee ID and name for**

those employees who have submitted expenses whose total value exceeds their salary?

A. `select e.empno, e.ename from emp e where e.sal < (select sum(x.vouch_amt) from expense x) and x.empno = e.empno;`

B. `select e.empno, e.ename from emp e where e.sal < (select x.vouch_amt from expense x where x.empno = e.empno);`

C. `select e.empno, e.ename from emp e where sal < (select sum(x.vouch_amt) from expense x where x.empno = e.empno);`

D. `select e.empno, e.ename from emp e where exists (select sum(x.vouch_amt) from expense x where x.empno = e.empno);`

2. **Take a look at the following statement:**

```
SQL>  select ename
2     from emp
3     where empno in
4       ( select empno
5         from expense
6         where vouch_amt > 10000 );
```

Which of the following choices identifies a SQL statement that will produce the same output as the preceding, rewritten to use the `exists` operator?

A. `select e.ename from emp e where exists (select x.empno from expense x where x.vouch_amt > 10000) and x.empno = e.empno;`

B. `select e.ename from emp e where exists (select x.empno from expense x where x.vouch_amt > 10000 and x.empno = e.empno);`

C. `select e.ename from emp e where x.empno = e.empno and exists (select x.empno from expense x where x.vouch_amt > 10000);`

D. `select e.ename from emp e, expense x where x.empno = e.empno and x.vouch_amt > 10000 and exists (select x.empno from expense x where x.vouch_amt > 10000);`

3. **In order to jump levels in nested subqueries, the availability of data from the parent query is often useful. Therefore, the variables from the parent query are said to be _____ in scope.**

Answer Key

1. C. **2.** B. **3.** global.

Listing and Writing Different Types of Subqueries

The following list identifies several different types of subqueries you may need to understand and use on the OCP exam:

- **Single-row subqueries**   The main query expects the subquery to return only one value.

- **Multirow subqueries**   The main query can handle situations where the subquery returns more than one value.

- **Inline views**   A subquery in a `from` clause used for defining an intermediate result set to query from. These types of subqueries will be discussed later in the chapter.

- **Multiple-column subqueries**   A subquery that contains more than one column of return data in addition to however many rows are given in the output. These types of subqueries will be discussed later in the chapter.

Writing Single-Row Subqueries

Check out the following example, which should look familiar:

```
SQL>  select ename, deptno, sal
  2   from emp
  3   where deptno =
  4    ( select deptno
  5      from dept
  6      where loc = 'NEW YORK' );
ENAME          DEPTNO        SAL
----------  ---------  ---------
CLARK             10       2450
KING              10       5000
MILLER            10       1300
```

Believe it or not, this is a single-row subquery. Why, you ask? Because, although the resulting set of data contains multiple rows of output from the EMP table, the subquery on the DEPT table to derive the output from EMP returns only one row of data. If you don't believe me, check out the following code block and see for yourself:

```
SQL> select deptno
  2  from dept
  3  where loc = 'NEW YORK';
   DEPTNO
---------
       10
```

Sure enough, there's only one row of data returned by this query. What makes the difference between whether a subquery can handle a single value or multiple values has to do with the comparison operation used for linking the parent query to the subquery. Notice in this situation that we used an equal sign. Therefore, we can generalize a simple rule: *When subqueries are linked to the parent by equality comparisons, the parent query expects only one row of data from the subquery.* Therefore, parent queries with subqueries linked by equality comparison operations are single-row subqueries.

TIP
Other comparison operations that indicate single-row subqueries include <, >, <=, >, and <>.

Writing Multirow Subqueries
Check out what happens when a parent query gets more than it bargained for:

```
SQL> select ename, job, sal
  2  from emp
  3  where deptno =
  4  (select deptno
  5  from dept
  6  where dname in ('ACCOUNTING','SALES'));
     (select deptno
      *
ERROR at line 4:
ORA-01427: single-row subquery returns more than one row
```

To solve the problem that arises in this example, you must transform the single-row subquery into a multirow subquery. How, you ask? Well, you could remove the second value that DNAME can be equal to in the subquery, but that will change the expected output. Instead, you should transform the equality comparison that links the subquery to its parent into a comparison operation that handles multiple rows of output from the subquery—an operation such as `in` (shown in bold in the following example):

```
SQL> select ename, job, sal
  2  from emp
  3  where deptno in
  4  (select deptno
  5  from dept
  6  where dname in ('ACCOUNTING','SALES'));
ENAME       JOB            SAL
----------  ---------  ---------
ALLEN       SALESMAN      1600
WARD        SALESMAN      1250
MARTIN      SALESMAN      1250
BLAKE       MANAGER       2850
CLARK       MANAGER       2450
KING        PRESIDENT     5000
TURNER      SALESMAN      1500
JAMES       CLERK          950
MILLER      CLERK         1300
```

TIP
The `exists` operator is something of an anomaly, because it can mask the complexity of dealing with multiple rows returned in subqueries by correlating the records in the subquery to those of the parent query.

having Clauses and Subqueries

The `having` clause can use subqueries, too. Let's say you want to look at the average salaries of people in the company, broken out by department and job title again. This time, however, you only want to see departments and job titles where the average salary is higher than what the company is paying MARTIN, a salesman. There's just one small problem—you don't remember what MARTIN's salary is. We know that subqueries are useful when you need valid data that you don't know the value of, but you do know how to obtain it. You'll see how to use subqueries with the `having` clause in the following example:

```
SQL> select deptno, job, avg(sal)
  2  from emp
  3  group by deptno, job
  4  having avg(sal) >
  5    ( select sal
  6      from emp
  7      where ename = 'MARTIN');
```

```
DEPTNO JOB        AVG(SAL)
--------- --------- ---------
     10 CLERK        1300
     10 MANAGER      2450
     10 PRESIDENT    5000
     20 ANALYST      3000
     20 MANAGER      2975
     30 MANAGER      2850
     30 SALESMAN     1400
```

TIP
The order by *clause can be used in a query that uses subqueries, but this clause must appear in the outermost query only. The subquery cannot have the* order by *clause defined for it.*

For Review

1. Know what the four different types of subqueries are. Also, be sure you can write and understand examples of single-row and multirow subqueries.

2. Know what happens when a parent query expecting a subquery to return only one row receives more than one row from the subquery.

3. Know that you can substitute the in operator for equality or other single-row comparison operations in order to let the parent query support multiple rows returned.

Exercises

1. **Use the following code block to answer the question:**

```
SQL> select deptno, job, avg(sal)
  2  from emp
  3  group by deptno, job
  4  having avg(sal) >
  5    ( select sal
  6      from emp
  7      where ename = 'MARTIN');
```

Which of the following choices identifies the type of subquery used in the preceding statement?

A. A single-row subquery

B. A multirow subquery

    C. A `from` clause subquery

    D. A multicolumn subquery

2. **The company's sales database has two tables. The first, PROFITS, stores the amount of profit made on products sold by the different corporate regions in different quarters. The second, REGIONS, stores the name of each departmental region, the headquarters location for that region, and the name of the region's vice president. Which of the following queries will obtain total profits on toys for regions headed by SMITHERS, FUJIMORI, and LAKKARAJU?**

    A. `select sum(profit) from profits where region in ( select region from regions where reg_head in ('SMITHERS', 'FUJIMORI', 'LAKKARAJU')) and product = 'TOYS';`

    B. `select sum(profit) from profits where region in ( select region from regions where reg_head in ('SMITHERS', 'FUJIMORI', 'LAKKARAJU') and product = 'TOYS');`

    C. `select sum(profit) from profits where region = ( select region from regions where reg_head in ('SMITHERS', 'FUJIMORI', 'LAKKARAJU')) and product = 'TOYS';`

    D. `select sum(profit) from profits where region in ( select region from regions where reg_head in ('SMITHERS', 'FUJIMORI', 'LAKKARAJU') and product = 'TOYS';`

3. **Provide the name of the operator used for transforming single-row subqueries into multirow subqueries:** _____

Answer Key

1. A. 2. A. 3. `in`.

Multiple-Column Subqueries

This section will cover the following topics:

- Writing multiple-column subqueries
- NULL values and subqueries
- Subqueries in a `from` clause

Subqueries can get pretty complex. This section covers a few aspects of subqueries to help clarify your understanding for the OCP exam. This section covers how to write multiple-column subqueries against the Oracle database. The section also covers what Oracle does in situations in which subqueries encounter NULL values in columns. Finally, this section covers the construction and use of inline views, or *subqueries*, in a from clause.

Writing Multiple-Column Subqueries

Notice that in all the prior examples, regardless of whether one row or multiple rows were returned from the subquery, each of those rows contained only one column's worth of data to compare at the main query level. The main query can be set up to handle multiple columns in each row returned, too. To evaluate how to use multiple-column subqueries, let's consider an example. Let's say we want to find out the highest paid employee in each department. Check out the following code block to see how we might perform this task:

```
SQL> select deptno, ename, job, sal
  2  from emp
  3  where (deptno, sal) in
  4    (select deptno, max(sal)
  5     from emp
  6     group by deptno);
   DEPTNO ENAME      JOB           SAL
--------- ---------- --------- ---------
       10 KING       PRESIDENT    5000
       20 SCOTT      ANALYST      3000
       20 FORD       ANALYST      3000
       30 BLAKE      MANAGER      2850
```

A couple of noteworthy points need to be made concerning multiple-column subqueries and syntax. For multiple-column subqueries only, you must enclose the multiple columns requested in the main query in parentheses; otherwise, the query will result in an "invalid relational operator" error. Also, your column references in both the main query's where clause and the subquery must match positionally—in other words, because DEPTNO is referenced first in the main query, it must be selected first in the subquery.

For Review

Be sure you understand the syntax and semantics of multiple-column subqueries.

Exercises

1. **The database for an international athletic competition consists of one table, ATHLETES, containing contestant name, age, and represented country. To determine the youngest athlete representing each country, which of the following queries could be used?**

   A. `select name, country, age from athletes where (country, age) in (select min(age), country from athletes group by country);`

   B. `select name, country, age from athletes where (country, age) in (select country, min(age) from athletes) group by country;`

   C. `select name, country, age from athletes where age in (select country, min(age) from athletes group by country);`

   D. `select name, country, age from athletes where (country, age) in (select country, min(age) from athletes group by country);`

2. **You are developing a multiple-column subquery on an Oracle database. Which of the following statements is true about SQL statements containing multiple-column subqueries?**

   A. The parent query must use a single-column subquery.

   B. The order of multiple columns being referenced in the `where` clause must match the column order in the subquery.

   C. The parent query must use an inline view, or else the query must be rewritten.

   D. The parent query must contain a `group by` expression in order to obtain the correct result.

Answer Key

1. D. 2. B.

NULL Values and Subqueries

If you're planning to follow along on your own EMP table built by `utlsampl.sql` or `demobld.sql`, you need to execute the following statement for this lesson to flow properly:

```
SQL> update emp set deptno = null where ename = 'KING';
1 row updated.
```

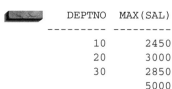

TIP
You'll learn more about update *statements in Chapter 3.*

Now, review the following code block, where we rerun the multiple-column subquery from the previous example:

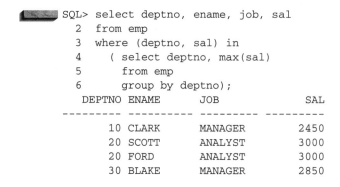

```
SQL> select deptno, ename, job, sal
  2  from emp
  3  where (deptno, sal) in
  4    ( select deptno, max(sal)
  5      from emp
  6      group by deptno);
    DEPTNO ENAME      JOB            SAL
--------- ---------- --------- ---------
        10 CLARK      MANAGER       2450
        20 SCOTT      ANALYST       3000
        20 FORD       ANALYST       3000
        30 BLAKE      MANAGER       2850
```

Notice someone missing from the output? Even though KING is still listed in the EMP table, he is no longer the highest paid employee in his department. That's strange, especially when we review the output from the subquery in our example:

```
    DEPTNO   MAX(SAL)
--------- ---------
        10      2450
        20      3000
        30      2850
                5000
```

You can see that KING was listed among the highest paid in his respective department. However, notice that his department is set to NULL. If you're thinking that the problem must have something to do with how subqueries handle NULL values, you're right. Unfortunately, the subquery only returns non-NULL values to the parent query. Therefore, we don't see KING listed in the output from that main query. In order to ensure that your queries don't miss any NULL values, you should rewrite them in such a way that they don't use the `group by` expression. This step can be done using a correlated subquery, as demonstrated in the following code block:

```
SQL> select e.deptno, e.ename, e.job, e.sal
  2  from emp e
  3  where e.sal =
  4  (select max(e2.sal)
  5   from emp e2
  6* where nvl(e.deptno,99) = nvl(e2.deptno,99));
DEPTNO ENAME       JOB         SAL
------ ---------   ---------   ---------
    30 BLAKE       MANAGER        2850
    10 CLARK       MANAGER        2450
    20 SCOTT       ANALYST        3000
       KING        PRESIDENT      5000
    20 FORD        ANALYST        3000
```

Notice something interesting about this query? The use of the `nvl( )` function in the subquery substitutes the value 99 for NULL on KING's record. This is an arbitrary value I picked simply because it wasn't already in use as a department number. However, you're probably wondering why the output doesn't display 99 in the DEPTNO column for KING. The reason is that the subquery is not actually returning a value for DEPTNO to the parent query—it only returns the maximum salary for that department! We use `nvl( )` in the subquery only so we have a non-NULL value to compare E.DEPTNO and E2.DEPTNO in the subquery. Because the department number for KING's record is still NULL, that is what the parent query displays.

TIP
When writing queries that use subqueries, remember that certain operations, such as `group by`*, may return NULL values and that NULL values are ignored by subqueries when the subquery returns its dataset to the main query. If you need to include NULL values in your output, experiment with rewriting the query in other ways.*

In Conclusion
Remember to discard the change to KING's record in the EMP table when you're done:

```
SQL> rollback;
Rollback complete.
```

For Review

Be sure you understand that certain operations, such as group by, may generate NULL values, which are ignored by subqueries when the dataset is returned to the main query. Know how to rewrite a subquery if you need to handle NULL values.

Exercises

1. Subqueries ignore this value by default: _____

2. Use the output in the code block to answer the following question:

```
SQL> select e.deptno, e.ename, e.job, e.sal
  2  from emp e
  3  where e.sal =
  4  (select max(e2.sal)
  5    from emp e2
  6*  where nvl(e.deptno,99) = nvl(e2.deptno,99));
DEPTNO ENAME      JOB             SAL
--------- ---------- --------- ---------
    30 BLAKE      MANAGER        2850
    10 CLARK      MANAGER        2450
    20 SCOTT      ANALYST        3000
       KING       PRESIDENT      5000
    20 FORD       ANALYST        3000
```

In order to display a value of 99 in the DEPTNO column in the preceding return set, which of the following SQL statements might be appropriate?

A. select nvl(e.deptno,99), e.ename, e.job, e.sal from emp e where (e.deptno, e.sal) =(select max(e2.sal) from emp e2 where nvl(e.deptno,99) = nvl(e2.deptno,99));

B. select nvl(e.deptno,99), e.ename, e.job, e.sal from emp e where e.sal =(select max(e2.sal) from emp e2 where nvl(e.deptno,99) = nvl(e2.deptno,99));

C. select nvl(e.deptno,99), e.ename, e.job, e.sal from emp e where (e.deptno, e.sal) =(select e2.deptno, max(e2.sal) from emp e2 where nvl(e.deptno,99) = nvl(e2.deptno,99));

D. select nvl(e.deptno,99), e.ename, e.job, e.sal from emp e where (e.deptno, e.sal) =(select e2.deptno,

```
max(e2.sal) from emp e2 where nvl(e.deptno,99) =
nvl(e2.deptno,99) group by e2.deptno);
```

Answer Key

1. NULL. **2.** B.

Subqueries in a from Clause

If you're planning to follow along on your own EMP table built by `utlsampl.sql` or `demobld.sql`, you need to execute the following statement for this lesson to flow properly:

```
SQL> update emp set deptno = null where ename = 'KING';
1 row updated.
```

TIP

You'll learn more about `update` *statements in Chapter 3.*

You can also write subqueries that appear in your `from` clause. Writing subqueries in the `from` clause of the main query can be a handy way to collect an intermediate set of data that the main query treats as a table for its own query-access purposes. This subquery in the `from` clause of your main query is called an *inline view*. You must enclose the query text for the inline view in parentheses and also give a label for the inline view so that columns in it can be referenced later. The subquery can be a `select` statement that utilizes joins, the `group by` clause, or the `order by` clause. The following code block shows you a very simple example of using an inline view that accomplishes the same result as a regular table join:

```
SQL> select e.ename, subq.loc
  2  from emp e,
  3    ( select deptno, loc
  4      from dept
  5      where loc in ('NEW YORK', 'DALLAS')) subq
  6  where e.deptno = subq.deptno;
ENAME       LOC
----------  -------------
SMITH       DALLAS
JONES       DALLAS
CLARK       NEW YORK
SCOTT       DALLAS
ADAMS       DALLAS
```

```
FORD        DALLAS
MILLER      NEW YORK
```

TIP

In some cases, the columns referenced in your inline view might call single-row or group functions. This is permitted; however, if you want to refer to those columns in the main query's where clause, you will need to supply column aliases for that column in the inline view, in addition to supplying a table alias for the entire inline view.

Inline Views and Top-N Queries

Top-N queries use inline views and are handy for displaying a short list of table data, based on "greatest" or "least" criteria. For example, let's say that profits for our company were exceptionally strong this year, and we want a list of the three lowest paid employees in our company so that we can give them a raise. A top-N query would be useful for this purpose. Take a look at a top-N query that satisfies this business scenario:

```
SQL> select ename, job, sal, rownum
  2  from (select ename, job, sal from emp
  3        order by sal)
  4  where rownum <=3;
ENAME       JOB             SAL    ROWNUM
---------- --------- --------- ---------
SMITH       CLERK           800         1
JAMES       CLERK           950         2
ADAMS       CLERK          1100         3
```

There are two important things you need to know about top-N queries for OCP. The first is their use of the inline view to list all data in the table in sorted order. The second is their use of ROWNUM—a virtual column identifying the row number in the table—to determine the top number of rows to return as output. Conversely, if we have to cut salaries based on poor company performance and want to obtain a listing of the highest paid employees, whose salaries will be cut, we would reverse the sort order inside the inline view, as shown here:

```
SQL> select ename, job, sal, rownum
  2  from (select ename, job, sal from emp
  3        order by sal desc)
  4  where rownum <=3;
ENAME       JOB             SAL    ROWNUM
```

```
---------- --------- --------- ---------
KING       PRESIDENT      5000          1
SCOTT      ANALYST        3000          2
FORD       ANALYST        3000          3
```

TIP
Inline views support the use of the `order`
by clause.

In Conclusion
Remember to discard the change to KING's record in the EMP table when
you're done:

```
SQL> rollback;
Rollback complete.
```

For Review

1. Understand the syntax and semantics of creating basic inline views.
   Be able to remember that inline views are the only views in Oracle
   that support the use of the `order by` clause.

2. Know what a top-N query is and how to use an inline view to create
   one. Also, be sure you understand the use of ROWNUM in these types
   of queries.

Exercises

1. This is the name of the pseudocolumn often utilized for obtaining
   information for top-N queries: _____

2. Your company's sales database contains one table, PROFITS, which stores
   profits listed by product name, sales region, and quarterly time period. If
   you wanted to obtain a listing of the five best-selling products in company
   history, which of the following SQL statements would you use?

   A. `select p.prod_name, p.profit from (select prod_name,`
      `profit from profits order by profit desc) where rownum`
      `<= 5;`

    B. `select p.prod_name, p.profit from (select prod_name, sum(profit) from profits group by prod_name order by sum(profit) desc) subq where p.prod_name = subq.prod_name;`

    C. `select prod_name, profit from (select prod_name, sum(profit) from profits group by prod_name order by sum(profit) desc) where rownum <=5;`

    D. `select prod_name, profit from (select prod_name, sum(profit) from profits order by sum(profit) desc) where rownum <=5;`

Answer Key

1. ROWNUM. **2.** C. Remember, you must account for the fact that the profits for the same products will appear once for each quarter.

Producing Readable Output with SQL*Plus

This section will cover the following topics related to using runtime variables:

- Entering variables

- Customizing SQL*Plus environments

- Producing readable output

- Creating and executing scripts

- Saving customizations

    SQL*Plus is a powerful tool that can be used interactively to enter commands, as I have demonstrated so far throughout the book, or silently through batch processing and reporting. It is on this second topic that I will focus considerable attention in the next section. In this section, you will learn more about entering variables into statements in SQL*Plus; customizing your work environment; producing readable output for reporting; creating and executing scripts; and saving your environment customizations.

TIP
*At any point in a SQL*Plus operation, you can enter
the* help SQLPLUS_command *command, and
SQL*Plus will give you more information about use
of that command.*

Entering Variables

Let's say you have to pull up data for several different employees manually for the
purpose of reviewing some aspect of their data. The following example shows how
you've learned to do it so far:

```
SQL> select ename, job, deptno, sal
  2  from emp
  3  where empno = 7844;
ENAME       JOB          DEPTNO       SAL
----------  ---------    ---------  ---------
TURNER      SALESMAN         30      1500
```

Now, let's say you wanted to pull up the same data for KING, whose employee
number is 7839. You've seen how to edit SQL commands in SQL*Plus and how to
reexecute them using the slash (/) command. In light of these facts, you could edit the
SQL statement with either the change or edit command to change the EMPNO
information and then reissue the command. But let's face it, you'll have to do a lot of
typing and mouse clicking, and all that work is tedious. First, you have to open the
text editor; then you have to find the text to change, modify it, and then save it to the
SQL*Plus buffer—all before you reexecute the command. There is an easier way. Take
a look at the following code block:

```
SQL> select ename, job, deptno, sal
  2  from emp
  3  where empno = &empno;
Enter value for empno: 7844
old   3: where empno = &empno
new   3: where empno = 7844
ENAME       JOB          DEPTNO       SAL
----------  ---------    ---------  ---------
TURNER      SALESMAN         30      1500
```

Now, all you have to do is issue the slash command and then enter a new
employee number every time you want to see this information from the EMP table,
as shown here:

```
SQL> /
Enter value for empno: 7839
```

```
old    3: where empno = &empno
new    3: where empno = 7839
ENAME       JOB           DEPTNO      SAL
---------- --------- --------- ---------
KING         PRESIDENT        10       5000
```

You can repeat this activity as often as you want until you enter a new SQL statement, which is great when you have repetitive SQL operations that you need to execute. Notice two important things about this output. First, notice the ampersand (&) preceding the reference to EMPNO in the `where` clause. This ampersand indicates to Oracle that you want to specify a value for that column before Oracle processes the query. This combination of ampersand and column identifier creates a *lexical substitution variable*. Second, Oracle shows you the line as it appeared in the buffer and then shows you the value you substituted. This presentation lets you know what data was changed by your input.

TIP
*You can also use the double-ampersand (&&) keyword in Oracle to define variable values in SQL*Plus. The && keyword has an advantage over & in that && will preserve the value you define for the variable, whereas & will prompt you to specify a value every time you execute the statement.*

If you don't want to use the ampersand to create the substitution variable, the input can be changed with the `set define` command at the SQL prompt in SQL*Plus. You can reexecute the statement containing a runtime variable declaration by using the slash (/) command at the prompt in SQL*Plus. The following code block illustrates this:

```
SQL> set define ?
SQL> select ename, job, deptno, sal
  2  from emp
  3  where empno = ?empno;
Enter value for empno: 7839
old    3: where empno = ?empno
new    3: where empno = 7839
ENAME       JOB           DEPTNO      SAL
---------- --------- --------- ---------
KING         PRESIDENT        10       5000
SQL> /
Enter value for empno: 7844
old    3: where empno = ?empno
new    3: where empno = 7844
```

```
ENAME       JOB        DEPTNO       SAL
----------  ---------  ----------  ---------
TURNER      SALESMAN         30       1500
```

Automatic Definition of Runtime Variables

In some cases, it may not be useful to enter new values for a runtime variable every time the statement executes. For example, assume there is some onerous reporting process that you must perform weekly for every person in a company. A great deal of value is added to the process by having a variable that can be specified at runtime because you can then simply execute the same statement over and over again, with new EMPNO values each time. However, even this improvement does not streamline the process as much as one might like. Instead of running the statement over and over again with new values specified each time, you could create a script similar to the following:

```
-------------------------
--  empinfo.sql -
--  This script selects information
--  from EMP and returns it to
--  the user
-------------------------
define var_empno = 7844
select ename, job, deptno, sal
from emp
where empno = ?var_empno;
undefine var_empno
define var_empno = 7839
select ename, job, deptno, sal
from emp
where empno = ?var_empno;
```

TIP
You'll get the most out of your preparation time for OCP if you teach yourself by example. Therefore, spend the extra time coding in these scripts by hand to test them on your system. The more experience you have with Oracle, the better you will do on your OCP exam.

When you use the @ command to run this script in SQL*Plus, the following output is produced:

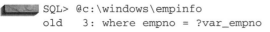

```
SQL> @c:\windows\empinfo
old   3: where empno = ?var_empno
```

```
new    3: where empno = 7844
ENAME       JOB          DEPTNO      SAL
----------  ---------  ---------  ---------
TURNER      SALESMAN          30       1500
old    3: where empno = ?var_empno
new    3: where empno = 7839
ENAME       JOB          DEPTNO      SAL
----------  ---------  ---------  ---------
KING        PRESIDENT         10       5000
```

TIP

The @@ command can also be used to execute scripts in SQL*Plus when the contents of one script call for execution of another script. When used, @@ tells SQL*Plus to look for the script in the same path where it found the currently executing script.

The time spent actually keying in values for the variables named in the SQL select statement is eliminated with the define statement. Notice, however, that in between each execution of the SQL statement is a special statement using a command called undefine. In Oracle, the data that is defined with the define statement will remain defined for the variable for the entire session, unless the variable is undefined. By *undefining* a variable, you allow another define statement to reuse the variable in another execution of the same or a different statement.

TIP

You can also use the define command if you want to reuse substitution variables over different SQL statements, allowing you to pass a value from one statement to another.

accept: Another Way to Define Variables

You may have noticed that Oracle's method for identifying input, though not exactly cryptic, is fairly nonexpressive. You need not stick with Oracle's default messaging to identify the need for input. Instead, you can define a more expressive message that Oracle will use to prompt for input data. The name of the command that provides this functionality is the accept command. Check out the following code block, where I show a slight modification to empinfo.sql that uses the accept command:

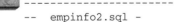

```
-- ------------------------
--  empinfo2.sql -
```

```
--   This script selects information
--   from EMP and returns it to
--   the user
-------------------------
accept var_empno prompt 'Enter EMPNO now => '
select ename, job, deptno, sal
from emp
where empno = ?var_empno;
```

TIP

You'll get the most out of your preparation time for OCP if you teach yourself by example. Therefore, spend the extra time coding in these scripts by hand to test them on your system. The more experience you have with Oracle, the better you will do on your OCP exam. Also, notice the use of two dashes next to each other in the first few lines of this code block. That usage indicates a comment.

We can then run the script, as follows:

```
SQL> @c:\windows\empinfo2
Enter EMPNO now => 7844
old    3: where empno = ?var_empno
new    3: where empno = 7844
ENAME      JOB         DEPTNO      SAL
---------- --------- --------- ---------
TURNER     SALESMAN         30      1500
```

Using the `accept` command can be preferable to Oracle's default output message in situations in which you want to define a more accurate or specific prompt or when you want more output to display as the values are defined.

TIP

By default, the datatype for a variable defined with the `accept` command is CHAR. Fortunately, Oracle can execute implicit type conversions from CHAR to the datatype required for the input variable, so usually you won't have a problem. You can also explicitly specify the datatype in the `accept` command.

For Review

1. Know the special character used to specify a lexical substitution variable (it's the ampersand).

2. Understand how to use the `accept` command and the benefits offered by the `accept` command.

3. Be sure you can tell how variables are defined within the SQL*Plus session using the `define` and `undefine` commands.

4. Know that two dashes next to each other («--) in a script indicates to SQL*Plus that everything else on that line is a comment.

Exercises

1. **Your sales database consists of one table, PROFITS, which lists profits for every product type the company sells, listed by quarter and by sales region. You need to develop a report that users can run interactively to show them the profits on toys for a given quarter. You have concerns about the users of this report because they have frequently complained about the readability and usability of your reports. Which of the following choices shows the contents of the script you should use for your report?**

   A.
   ```
   select profit from profits
   where prod_type = 'TOYS'
   and time_period = "&v_period";
   ```

   B.
   ```
   define v_period
   select profit from profits
   where prod_type = 'TOYS'
   and time_period = "&v_period";
   ```

   C.
   ```
   accept v_period prompt "Enter the time period => "
   select profit from profits
   where prod_type = 'TOYS'
   and time_period = "&v_period";
   ```

   D.
   ```
   accept v_period
   select profit from profits
   where prod_type = 'TOYS'
   and time_period = "&v_period";
   ```

2. **Review the following code block containing the contents of a script called `dates.sql`:**

```
accept v_hiredate prompt 'enter hire date => '
select empno, ename, job
from emp
where trunc(hiredate) = trunc('&v_hiredate');
```

Which of the following aspects of the script must be changed in order for the script to function properly?

A. Variable `v_hiredate` must be changed to accept DATE information.

B. The `trunc( )` function in the query should be eliminated.

C. The `prompt` clause in the `accept` command is unnecessary.

D. Nothing, the script will work fine as is.

3. **This is the string that must prefix lexical substitution variables if you want the value saved between statement executions:** _____

Answer Key

1. C. Remember, part of your goal is pleasing the users. **2.** A. **3.** &&.

Customizing SQL*Plus Environments

You can customize your SQL*Plus operating environment with the set *system_variable value* command, where *system_variable* is the name of a system variable you can set in SQL*Plus and *value* is the value you would like to set that system variable to. We'll cover some common system variables and their acceptable values in this discussion. Each of the headers for the following subtopics contains the full name of the system variable, followed by its abbreviation in brackets ([ ]), followed by its valid values in curly braces ({ }).

NOTE
*This section is provided primarily for reference purposes and for your OCP study. No examples are provided, but it is assumed that you will practice using each of these commands on your own. Recognizing that this list of SQL*Plus commands is extensive, you may want to focus mainly on ARRAYSIZE, COLSEP, FEEDBACK, HEADING, LINESIZE, LONG, PAGESIZE, PAUSE, and TERMOUT for OCP and use the rest of this information as a reference.*

ARRAYSIZE [ARRAY] {15|n}   Sets the number of rows that SQL*Plus fetches from the database at one time. Valid values are 1 to 5000. A large value increases the efficiency of queries and subqueries that fetch many rows, but it requires more memory.

AUTOCOMMIT [AUTO] {OFF|ON|IMMEDIATE|n}   Controls when Oracle commits pending changes to the database. ON commits pending changes to the database after Oracle executes each successful data change command or PL/SQL block. OFF suppresses automatic committing so that you must commit changes manually. IMMEDIATE functions in the same manner as the ON option. The value n commits pending changes to the database after Oracle executes n successful data change commands or PL/SQL blocks, where n cannot be less than zero or greater than 2,000,000,000.

AUTOTRACE [AUTOT] {OFF|ON|TRACEONLY}   Displays a report on the execution of successful SQL statements. The report can include execution statistics and the query execution path. OFF does not display a trace report. ON displays a trace report. TRACEONLY displays a trace report but does not print query data, if any. Before using autotrace, you must run the plustrce.sql script found in the sqlplus/admin directory under your Oracle software home directory.

CMDSEP [CMDS] {;|c|OFF|ON}   Sets the nonalphanumeric character used to separate multiple SQL*Plus commands entered on one line to c. ON or OFF controls whether you can enter multiple commands on a line; ON automatically sets the command separator character to a semicolon (;).

COLSEP [COLSEP] { |text}   Sets the text to be printed between selected columns. If the colsep variable contains blanks or punctuation characters, you must enclose it with single quotes. The default value for text is a single space. In multiline rows, the column separator does not print between columns that begin on different lines.

COMPATIBILITY [COM] {V7|V8|NATIVE}   Specifies the version of Oracle to which you are currently connected. Set compatibility to V7 for Oracle7 or V8 for Oracle8 and Oracle8i. Set compatibility to NATIVE if you want the database to determine the setting (for example, if you're connected to Oracle8 or Oracle8i, compatibility would default to V8). The compatibility variable must be correctly set for the version of Oracle to which you are connected; otherwise, you will be unable to run any SQL commands. However, you can set compatibility to V7 when connected to Oracle8i. This enables you to run Oracle7 SQL against Oracle8i.

CONCAT [CON] {.|c|OFF|ON}   Sets the character you can use to terminate a substitution variable reference if you want to immediately follow the variable with a character that SQL*Plus would otherwise interpret as a part of the substitution variable name. SQL*Plus resets the value of concat to a period when you switch concat on.

COPYCOMMIT [COPYC] {0|*n*}   Controls the number of batches after which the copy command commits changes to the database. copy commits rows to the destination database each time it copies *n* row batches. Valid values are 0 to 5000. You can set the size of a batch with the arraysize variable. If you set copycommit to 0, copy performs a commit operation only at the end of a copy operation.

COPYTYPECHECK [COPYTYPECHECK] {OFF|ON}   Sets the suppression of the comparison of datatypes while inserting or appending to tables with the copy command. This is to facilitate copying to DB2, which requires that a CHAR be copied to a DB2 DATE.

DESCRIBE [DESCRIBE] DEPTH {1|n|ALL} LINENUM {ON|OFF} INDENT {ON|OFF}   Sets the depth of the level to which you can recursively describe an object. The valid range of the depth clause is from 1 to 50. If you issue the set describe depth ALL command, the depth will be set to 50, which is the maximum level allowed. You can also display the line number and indentation of the attribute or column name when an object contains multiple object types. Use the set linesize command to control the width of the data displayed.

ECHO [ECHO] {OFF|ON}   Controls whether the start command lists each command in a command file as the command is executed. ON lists the commands; OFF suppresses the listing.

EDITFILE [EDITF] { file_name[.ext]}   Sets the default filename for the edit command. You can include a path and/or file extension. For information on changing the default extension, see the suffix variable of this command. The default filename and maximum filename length are operating system specific.

EMBEDDED [EMB] {OFF|ON}   Controls where on a page each report begins. OFF forces each report to start at the top of a new page. ON allows a report to begin anywhere on a page. Set embedded to ON when you want a report to begin printing immediately following the end of the previously run report.

ESCAPE [ESC] {\|c|OFF|ON}   Defines the character you enter as the escape character. OFF undefines the escape character. ON enables the escape character. ON also changes the value of *c* back to the default (\). You can use the escape character before the substitution character (set through set define) to indicate that SQL* Plus should treat the substitution character as an ordinary character rather than as a request for variable substitution.

FEEDBACK [FEED] {6|n|OFF|ON}   Displays the number of records returned by a query when a query selects at least *n* records. ON or OFF turns this display on or off. Turning feedback ON sets *n* to 1. Setting feedback to 0 is equivalent to turning it OFF.

FLAGGER [FLAGGER] {OFF|ENTRY |INTERMEDIATE|FULL}   Checks to make sure that SQL statements conform to the ANSI/ISO SQL92 standard. If any nonstandard constructs are found, the Oracle server flags them as errors and displays the violating syntax. This is the equivalent of the SQL language alter session set flagger command. You may execute set flagger even if you are not connected to a database. Flagging will remain in effect across SQL*Plus sessions until a set flagger OFF (or alter session set flagger = OFF) command is successful or you exit SQL*Plus.

FLUSH [FLU] {OFF|ON}   Controls when output is sent to the user's display device. OFF allows the host operating system to buffer output. ON disables buffering. Use OFF only when you run a command file noninteractively. The use of flush OFF may improve performance by reducing the amount of program I/O.

HEADING [HEA] {OFF|ON}   Controls the printing of column headings in reports. ON prints column headings in reports; OFF suppresses column headings. The set heading OFF command will not affect the column width displayed; it only suppresses the printing of the column header itself.

HEADSEP [HEADS] {||c|OFF|ON}   Defines the character you enter as the heading separator character. The heading separator character cannot be alphanumeric or whitespace. ON or OFF turns heading separation on or off. When heading separation is OFF, SQL*Plus prints a heading separator character like any other character. ON changes the value of *c* back to the default (|).

LINESIZE [LIN] {80|n}   Sets the total number of characters that SQL*Plus displays on one line before beginning a new line. You can define linesize as a value from 1 to a system-dependent maximum.

LOBOFFSET [LOBOF] {n|1}   Sets the starting position from which large object (LOB) data is retrieved and displayed.

LONG [LONG] {80|n}   Sets the maximum width (in bytes) for displaying LONG, CLOB, and NCLOB values, as well as for copying LONG values. The maximum value of n is 2GB.

LONGCHUNKSIZE [LONGC] {80|n}   Sets the size (in bytes) of the increments in which SQL*Plus retrieves a LONG, CLOB, or NCLOB value.

NEWPAGE [NEWP] {1|n|NONE}   Sets the number of blank lines to be printed from the top of each page to the top title. A value of 0 places a formfeed at the beginning of each page (including the first page) and clears the screen on most terminals. If you set newpage to NONE, SQL*Plus does not print a blank line or formfeed between the report pages.

NULL [NULL] {text}   Sets the text that represents a NULL value in the result of a select command.

NUMFORMAT [NUMF] {format}   Sets the default format for displaying numbers. Enter a number format for format.

NUMWIDTH [NUM] {10|n}   Sets the default width for displaying numbers.

TIP
*More information about formatting numbers as output in SQL*Plus is offered in the next discussion.*

PAGESIZE [PAGES] {24|n}   Sets the number of lines in each page. You can set pagesize to 0 to suppress all headings, page breaks, titles, the initial blank line, and other formatting information.

PAUSE [PAU] {OFF|ON|text}   Allows you to control scrolling of your terminal when running reports. ON causes SQL*Plus to pause at the beginning of each page of report output. You must press ENTER after each pause. The text you enter specifies the text to be displayed each time SQL*Plus pauses. If you enter multiple words, you must enclose the text in single quotes. You can embed terminal-dependent escape sequences in the pause command. These sequences allow you to create inverse video messages or other effects on terminals that support such characteristics.

RECSEP [RECSEP] {WRAPPED|EACH|OFF}   Tells SQL*Plus where to make the record separation. For example, if you set `recsep` to WRAPPED, SQL*Plus prints a record separator only after wrapped lines. If you set `recsep` to EACH, SQL*Plus prints a record separator following every row. If you set `recsep` to OFF, SQL*Plus does not print a record separator.

RECSEPCHAR [RECSEPCHAR] { |c}   Displays or prints record separators. A record separator consists of a single line of the record-separating character (`recsepchar`) repeated `linesize` times. The `recsepchar` command defines the record-separating character. A single space is the default.

SERVEROUTPUT [SERVEROUT] {OFF|ON} SIZE {n}   Controls whether to display the output from `DBMS_OUTPUT.put_line( )` calls in PL/SQL blocks in SQL*Plus. OFF suppresses the output of `DBMS_OUTPUT.put_line( )`; ON displays the output. The `size` clause sets the number of bytes of the output that can be buffered within Oracle8i. The default for n is 2,000, and it cannot be less than 2,000 or greater than 1,000,000.

SHIFTINOUT [SHIFT] {VISIBLE]|INVISIBLE]}   Allows correct alignment for terminals that display shift characters. The `set shiftinout` command is useful for terminals that display shift characters together with data (for example, IBM 3270 terminals). You can only use this command with shift-sensitive character sets (for example, JA16DBCS). Use VISIBLE for terminals that display shift characters as a visible character (for example, a space or a colon). INVISIBLE is the opposite and does not display any shift characters.

SHOWMODE [SHOW] {OFF|ON}   Controls whether SQL*Plus lists the old and new settings of a SQL*Plus system variable when you change the setting with `set`. ON lists the settings; OFF suppresses the listing.

SQLBLANKLINES [SQLBL] {ON|OFF}   Controls whether SQL*Plus allows blank lines within a SQL command. ON interprets blank lines and new lines as part of a SQL command. OFF, the default value, does not allow blank lines or new lines in a SQL command. SQL*Plus returns to the default behavior when a SQL statement terminator or PL/SQL block terminator is encountered.

SQLCASE [SQLC] {MIXED|LOWER|UPPER}   Converts the case of SQL commands and PL/SQL blocks just prior to execution. SQL*Plus converts all text within the command, including quoted literals and identifiers, as follows:

- Uppercase if `sqlcase` equals UPPER

- Lowercase if `sqlcase` equals LOWER

- Unchanged if `sqlcase` equals MIXED

TIP
The `sqlcase` keyword does not change the SQL buffer itself.

SQLCONTINUE [SQLCO] {> |text}   Sets the character sequence SQL*Plus displays as a prompt after you continue a SQL*Plus command on an additional line using a hyphen (-).

SQLNUMBER [SQLN] {OFF|ON}   Sets the prompt for the second and subsequent lines of a SQL command or PL/SQL block. ON sets the prompt to be the line number. OFF sets the prompt to the value of `sqlprompt`.

SQLPREFIX [SQLPRE] {#|c}   Sets the SQL*Plus prefix character. While you are entering a SQL command or PL/SQL block, you can enter a SQL*Plus command on a separate line, prefixed by the SQL*Plus prefix character. SQL*Plus will execute this command immediately without affecting the SQL command or PL/SQL block that you are entering. The prefix character must be a nonalphanumeric character.

SQLPROMPT [SQLP] {SQL>|text}   Sets the SQL*Plus command prompt.

SQLTERMINATOR [SQLT] {;|c|OFF|ON}   Sets the character used to end and execute SQL commands to c. OFF means that SQL*Plus recognizes no command terminator; you terminate a SQL command by entering an empty line. ON resets the terminator to the default—a semicolon (;).

SUFFIX [SUF] {SQL|text}   Sets the default file extension that SQL*Plus uses in commands that refer to command files. The value for `suffix` does not control extensions for spool files.

TAB [TAB] {OFF|ON}   Determines how SQL*Plus formats whitespace in terminal output. OFF uses spaces to format whitespace in the output. ON uses the `tab` character. The `tab` character creates a space setting of eight blank characters. The default value for `tab` is system dependent.

TERMOUT [TERM] {OFF|ON}   Controls the display of output generated by commands executed from a command file. OFF suppresses the display so that you can spool output from a command file without seeing the output on the screen. ON displays the output. Setting `termout` OFF does not affect output from commands you enter interactively.

TIME [TI] {OFF|ON}   Controls the display of the current time. ON displays the current time before each command prompt. OFF suppresses the time display.

TIMING [TIMI] {OFF|ON}   Controls the display of timing statistics. ON displays timing statistics on each SQL command or PL/SQL block run. OFF suppresses timing of each command.

TRIMOUT [TRIM] {OFF|ON}   Determines whether SQL*Plus allows trailing blanks at the end of each displayed line. ON removes blanks at the end of each line, thus improving performance, especially when you access SQL*Plus from a slow communications device. OFF allows SQL*Plus to display trailing blanks. Setting `trimout` ON does not affect spooled output.

TRIMSPOOL [TRIMS] {ON|OFF}   Determines whether SQL*Plus allows trailing blanks at the end of each spooled line. ON removes blanks at the end of each line. OFF allows SQL*Plus to include trailing blanks. Using `trimspool` ON does not affect terminal output.

VERIFY [VER] {OFF|ON}   Controls whether SQL*Plus lists the text of a SQL statement or PL/SQL command before and after SQL*Plus replaces substitution variables with values. ON lists the text; OFF suppresses the listing.

TIP
*In most cases, if you want to see the value set for a particular SQL*Plus attribute, you can precede that attribute with the `show` command. For example, to see the value set for `linesize`, use the `show` `linesize` command.*

For Review

Be sure you know how to customize the SQL*Plus running environment using the `set` command, including the use of common system variables such as `pagesize`, `linesize`, `termout`, `feedback`, `sqlprompt`, and `echo`.

Exercises

1. **This SQL*Plus command is useful for determining whether the "*N* rows selected" message will appear:** _____

2. **This SQL*Plus command is useful for determining what extension SQL*Plus expects for files containing SQL commands:**

   _____

3. **Use of this command requires that you first run the `plustrce.sql` script:** _____

Answer Key

1. `feedback`. **2.** `suffix`. **3.** `autotrace`.

Producing Readable Output

Certain commands are also available to improve the look of your SQL*Plus output. These commands are explained in the following subtopics. If an abbreviation is available for the command, the abbreviation will be given inside brackets ([ ]). The valid values for this command will be given inside curly braces ({ }).

COLUMN {col} FORMAT {fmt} HEADING {string}   The most commonly used command for injecting readability into your SQL*Plus output is the `column col` command, where `col` is the name of your column in the SQL query. You can turn formatting on and off by specifying `column col` on or `column col` off, respectively. You can also clear any setting by issuing `column col clear`. You can change the heading used for a column by using the `heading 'string'` clause. You can also refine the format of output appearing in that column using the `format fmt` clause. For alphanumeric information appearing in a column, `fmt` is specified in the form `anum`, where `num` is a number representing how many characters wide the column should be. For numbers, `fmt` can be specified as a series of 9's representing the number of digits you want to see, optionally with currency symbols (L for local currency), commas, and/or periods. For example, `column sal format $9,999.99` would display all numbers in the salary column of a query as follows:

```
SQL> column sal format $9,999.99
SQL> select sal from emp;
       SAL
----------
    $800.00
  $1,600.00
  $1,250.00
  $2,975.00
  $1,250.00
  $2,850.00
  $2,450.00
  $3,000.00
  $5,000.00
  $1,500.00
```

```
$1,100.00
  $950.00
$3,000.00
$1,300.00
```

UNDERLINE [UND] {-|c|ON|OFF}   This command sets the character used to underline column headings in SQL*Plus reports to *c*. Note, *c* cannot be an alphanumeric character or a whitespace character. ON or OFF turns underlining on or off. ON changes the value of *c* back to the default (-). For example, you can use asterisks to underline column headings in the following way:

```
SQL> column empno format 99999
SQL> column ename format a12
SQL> set underline *
SQL> select empno, ename, sal
  2  from emp;
EMPNO ENAME              SAL
****** ************ **********
  7369 SMITH          $800.00
  7499 ALLEN        $1,600.00
  7521 WARD         $1,250.00
  7566 JONES        $2,975.00
  7654 MARTIN       $1,250.00
  7698 BLAKE        $2,850.00
  7782 CLARK        $2,450.00
  7788 SCOTT        $3,000.00
  7839 KING         $5,000.00
  7844 TURNER       $1,500.00
  7876 ADAMS        $1,100.00
  7900 JAMES          $950.00
  7902 FORD         $3,000.00
  7934 MILLER       $1,300.00
```

WRAP [WRA] {OFF|ON}   The heading string specified for column can also contain a pipe character (|). For example, column dname heading 'd|name' denotes that you would like to split the heading into two separate lines. In some cases when you format column output in this way, the value for the column may not fit in the space allotted. The wrap variable controls whether SQL*Plus truncates the display of a selected row if it is too long for the current line width. OFF truncates the selected row; ON allows the selected row to wrap to the next line. If you want, you can also specify recsep and recsepchar to print separators between word-wrapped lines to make output clearer. Here's an example:

```
SQL> column dname heading d|name format a4
SQL> set recsep wrapped
SQL> set recsepchar '-'
SQL> select * from dept;
            d
    DEPTNO name LOC
--------- ---- -------------
       10 ACCO NEW YORK
          UNTI
          NG
--------------------------------------------------
       20 RESE DALLAS
          ARCH
--------------------------------------------------
       30 SALE CHICAGO
          S
--------------------------------------------------
       40 OPER BOSTON
          ATIO
          NS
--------------------------------------------------
```

BREAK   Sometimes when the information returned by your SQL query is ordered
on a column, you may have multiple rows of data, each with the same value in the
ordered column. The output can be changed so that only the first in a series of rows,
where the ordered column value is the same, will show the column value. Observe
how this is accomplished in the following code block using the break command:

```
SQL> break on deptno
SQL> select deptno, ename from emp
  2  order by deptno;
    DEPTNO ENAME
--------- ----------
       10 CLARK
          KING
          MILLER
       20 SMITH
          ADAMS
          FORD
          SCOTT
          JONES
       30 ALLEN
          BLAKE
          MARTIN
          JAMES
```

```
          TURNER
          WARD
```

TIP
You can also use the `skip` n *or* `skip page` *clauses in the* `break` *command to insert* n *blank lines or page breaks, respectively.*

COMPUTE   You can also generate simple reports in SQL*Plus using the `compute` command in conjunction with the `break` command. The `compute` command performs one of several grouping functions on the column you are breaking on, including `sum`, `minimum`, `maximum`, `avg` (average), `std` (standard deviation), `variance`, `count`, and `number` (number of rows in the column). The following block illustrates a couple of uses for this command, in conjunction with `break`:

```
SQL> -- example 1
SQL> break on deptno skip 1
SQL> compute sum of sal on deptno
SQL> select deptno, ename, sal
  2  from emp order by deptno;
    DEPTNO ENAME           SAL
--------- ---------- ---------
       10 CLARK          2450
          KING           5000
          MILLER         1300
********* ---------
sum                      8750

       20 SMITH           800
          ADAMS          1100
          FORD           3000
          SCOTT          3000
          JONES          2975
********* ---------
sum                     10875

       30 ALLEN          1600
          BLAKE          2850
          MARTIN         1250
          JAMES           950
          TURNER         1500
          WARD           1250
********* ---------
sum                      9400
```

```
SQL> -- example 2
SQL> clear breaks
breaks cleared
SQL> clear computes
computes cleared
SQL> break on report
SQL> compute sum of sal on report
SQL> /
    DEPTNO ENAME            SAL
 --------- ---------- ---------
        10 CLARK           2450
        10 KING            5000
        10 MILLER          1300
        20 SMITH            800
        20 ADAMS           1100
        20 FORD            3000
        20 SCOTT           3000
        20 JONES           2975
        30 ALLEN           1600
        30 BLAKE           2850
        30 MARTIN          1250
        30 JAMES            950
        30 TURNER          1500
                     ---------
sum                      29025
```

TTITLE and BTITLE   The use of break and compute segues into a larger discussion of using SQL*Plus to write reports. If you want a top or bottom title to appear on each page of a report, you can place one through the use of the ttitle and btitle commands, respectively. The syntax is [btitle | ttitle] *position* 'title_text', where *position* can be LEFT, CENTER, RIGHT, or COL *n* to indicate a fixed number of characters from the left to start the title line.

TIP
Using linesize and pagesize to determine page width and how many lines of text appear on a page will also determine where btitle and ttitle place your top and bottom title lines, respectively.

For Review

Practice writing SQL*Plus reports using the commands covered in this and the previous discussion.

Exercises

1. This SQL*Plus command can be used for calculating sums of data on columns in the same way as a group function: _____

2. This SQL*Plus command can be used to enhance report readability by reducing the number of times a duplicate value appears in a sorted column: _____

3. This SQL*Plus command can be used for placing a footer title on the bottom of a report page: _____

Answer Key

1. compute. 2. break. 3. btitle.

Creating and Executing Scripts

Each time you execute a SQL statement in SQL*Plus, that statement gets saved to a buffer used by SQL*Plus for repeat execution. One thing you might want to do when you have SQL statements you execute routinely in SQL*Plus is save those statements as scripts. You can do this in a few different ways, one of which is to simply open up a text editor available on your operating system, enter the statements you want to execute routinely, and save the script to your host machine as a plain-text file. Another method available to you within SQL*Plus is to use the save command, as follows:

```
SQL> select empno, ename, sal, deptno, hiredate
  2  from emp;
    EMPNO ENAME            SAL    DEPTNO HIREDATE
--------- ---------- --------- --------- ---------
     7369 SMITH            800        20 17-DEC-80
     7499 ALLEN           1600        30 20-FEB-81
     7521 WARD            1250        30 22-FEB-81
     7566 JONES           2975        20 02-APR-81
     7654 MARTIN          1250        30 28-SEP-81
     7698 BLAKE           2850        30 01-MAY-81
     7782 CLARK           2450        10 09-JUN-81
     7788 SCOTT           3000        20 19-APR-87
     7839 KING            5000        10 17-NOV-81
     7844 TURNER          1500        30 08-SEP-81
     7876 ADAMS           1100        20 23-MAY-87
     7900 JAMES            950        30 03-DEC-81
```

```
    7902 FORD                   3000          20 03-DEC-81
    7934 MILLER                 1300          10 23-JAN-82
SQL> save employee.sql
Created file employee.sql
```

You have already seen that, when you want to execute the script again, you can use the @ command within SQL*Plus. Let's take one more look for review:

```
SQL> @employee.sql
SQL> @employee.sql
    EMPNO ENAME                  SAL    DEPTNO HIREDATE
--------- ---------- --------- --------- ---------
    7369 SMITH                   800          20 17-DEC-80
    7499 ALLEN                  1600          30 20-FEB-81
    7521 WARD                   1250          30 22-FEB-81
    7566 JONES                  2975          20 02-APR-81
    7654 MARTIN                 1250          30 28-SEP-81
    7698 BLAKE                  2850          30 01-MAY-81
    7782 CLARK                  2450          10 09-JUN-81
    7788 SCOTT                  3000          20 19-APR-87
    7839 KING                   5000          10 17-NOV-81
    7844 TURNER                 1500          30 08-SEP-81
    7876 ADAMS                  1100          20 23-MAY-87
    7900 JAMES                   950          30 03-DEC-81
    7902 FORD                   3000          20 03-DEC-81
    7934 MILLER                 1300          10 23-JAN-82
```

For Review

Be sure you understand which commands to use for saving and executing your scripts in SQL*Plus.

Exercises

1. This is the command for storing the contents of your SQL*Plus buffer as a command file: _____

2. This is a command for loading a SQL command file into the operating buffer and executing it: _____

Answer Key

1. save. 2. @.

Saving Customizations

To save customizations to a file, you should use the `store` command, which accepts the `set` keyword along with a filename to save the environment settings to. The following code block illustrates this principle:

```
SQL> set termout on
SQL> set pagesize 132
SQL> store set myfile.out
Created file myfile.out
SQL>
```

Once your settings are saved, you can look at them in the file SQL*Plus created. To restore your settings, you must execute the contents of the file in SQL*Plus. Both these points are demonstrated in the following code block:

```
SQL> get myfile.out
  1   set appinfo ON
  2   set appinfo "SQL*Plus"
  3   set arraysize 15
  4   set autocommit OFF
  5   set autoprint OFF
  6   set autotrace OFF
  7   set shiftinout invisible
  8   set blockterminator "."
  9   set cmdsep OFF
 10   set colsep " "
 11   set compatibility NATIVE
 12   set concat "."
 13   set copycommit 0
 14   set copytypecheck ON
 15   set define "&"
 16   set echo OFF
 17   set editfile "afiedt.buf"
 18   set embedded OFF
 19   set escape OFF
 20   set feedback 6
 21   set flagger OFF
 22   set flush ON
 23   set heading ON
 24   set headsep "|"
 25   set linesize 100
 26   set long 80
 27   set longchunksize 80
 28   set newpage 1
 29   set null ""
 30   set numformat ""
 31   set numwidth 9
```

```
32   set pagesize 132
33   set pause OFF
34   set recsep WRAP
35   set recsepchar " "
36   set serveroutput OFF
37   set showmode OFF
38   set sqlcase MIXED
39   set sqlcontinue "> "
40   set sqlnumber ON
41   set sqlprefix "#"
42   set sqlprompt "SQL> "
43   set sqlterminator ";"
44   set suffix "sql"
45   set tab ON
46   set termout ON
47   set time OFF
48   set timing OFF
49   set trimout ON
50   set trimspool OFF
51   set underline "-"
52   set verify ON
53*  set wrap ON
SQL> @myfile.out
SQL>
```

NOTE
Your settings for column, break, compute,
btitle, *and* ttitle *will not be included in the*
output file.

Alternately, if your environment file is stored in a file called login.sql,
SQL*Plus can automatically execute the contents of the file so that the next time
you log into SQL*Plus, your environment will be exactly the way you want it. This
file must be stored either in the local directory from where you start SQL*Plus or
on an operating system–specific path.

For Review

Be sure you understand how to store your environment settings and what the
use of the login.sql file is.

Exercises

**1. This is the command for writing all SQL*Plus environment data to a script
for executing later: _____**

2. This is the name of the script that will run whenever you start SQL*Plus to configure your environment settings: _____

Answer Key

1. `store`. 2. `login.sql`.

Chapter Summary

This chapter covered a lot of territory. You learned a great deal about advanced selection of data in SQL*Plus, including table joins, group functions, ordering output, and so on. We discussed subqueries in some detail as well. The text covered important facts such as how to structure single-row, multiple-row, and correlated subqueries, as well as how to identify all those different types of queries. You also learned that subqueries ignore NULL results—a crucial fact to remember for OCP. After that, we discussed the many commands in SQL*Plus for formatting output for reports, how to write scripts, and how to enter variables into SQL queries for ease of use.

Two-Minute Drill

- `select` statements that obtain data from more than one table and merge the data together are called *joins*.

- In order to join data from two tables, a common column must exist.

- A common column between two tables can create a foreign key, or *link*, from one table to another. This condition is especially true if the data in one of the tables is part of the primary key—the column that defines uniqueness for rows on a table.

- A foreign key can create a parent/child relationship between two tables.

- One type of join is the inner join, or *equijoin*. An equijoin operation is based on an equality operation linking the data in common columns of two tables.

- Another type of join is the outer join. An outer join returns data in one table even when there is no data in the other table. The "other" table in the outer join operation is called the *outer table*.

- The common column that appears in the outer table of the join must have a special marker next to it in the comparison operation of the `select` statement that creates the table.

■   The outer join marker is (+).

■   If the column name is the same in both tables, the common column in both tables used in join operations must be preceded either with a table alias that denotes the table in which the column appears or the entire table name.

■   The data from a table can be joined to itself. This technique is useful in determining whether there are rows in the table that have slightly different values but are otherwise duplicate rows. This is called a *self-join* operation.

■   Table aliases must be used in self-join `select` statements.

■   Data output from table `select` statements can be grouped together according to criteria set by the query.

■   The `group by` clause assists you in grouping data together.

■   Several grouping functions are available that allow you to perform operations on data in a column as though the data were logically one variable.

■   The grouping functions are `max( )`, `min( )`, `sum( )`, `avg( )`, `stddev( )`, `variance( )`, and `count( )`.

■   These grouping functions can be applied to the column values for a table as a whole or for subsets of column data for rows returned in `group by` statements.

■   Data in a `group by` statement can be excluded or included based on a special set of `where` criteria defined specifically for the group in a `having` clause.

■   The data used to determine the `having` clause can either be specified at runtime by the query or by a special embedded query, called a *subquery*, which obtains unknown search criteria based on known search methods.

■   Subqueries can be used in other parts of the `select` statement to determine unknown search criteria, as well. Subqueries are generally included in this fashion in the `where` clause.

■   Subqueries can use columns in comparison operations that are local to the table specified in the subquery, or they can use columns that are specified in tables named in any parent query to the subquery. This use is based on the principles of variable scope, as presented in this chapter.

■   Various types of subqueries you might encounter when using Oracle include the following:

   ■   **Single-row subqueries**   The main query expects the subquery to return only one value.

- ■ **Multiple-row subqueries**   The main query can handle situations where the subquery returns more than one value.

- ■ **Inline views**   A subquery in a `from` clause used for defining an intermediate result set to query from.

- ■ **Multiple-column subqueries**   A subquery that contains more than one column of return data in addition to however many rows are given in the output.

■ Be sure you understand how to set up and use a correlated subquery in Oracle to retrieve data.

■ Recall that most subqueries (even those returning multiple rows) generally only return one column of output per row. However, you can construct subqueries that return multiple columns. Review the chapter to refresh your understanding of the syntax and semantics involved.

■ Subqueries that contain `group by` expression-s will ignore rows if the `group by` column contains NULL values for those rows. Be sure you understand how to rewrite such queries, if necessary, to obtain those NULL values.

■ A subquery found in a `from` clause of the parent SQL query is called an *inline view*. Be sure you recall the syntax and semantics involved in using inline views, especially if you want to refer directly to columns in an inline view. Recall the use of inline views for top-N queries as well.

■ Review the SQL*Plus environment characteristics that can be configured using the `set` command.

■ In addition, be sure you understand completely how to use the following SQL*Plus commands for enhancing output readability:

- ■ `format`
- ■ `btitle`
- ■ `ttitle`
- ■ `break`
- ■ `compute`

■ Variables can be set in a `select` statement at runtime with use of runtime variables. A runtime variable is designated with the ampersand character (&) preceding the variable name.

■ The special character that designates a runtime variable can be changed using the `set define` command.

■ The `define` command can identify a runtime variable value to be picked up by the `select` statement automatically.

■ Once defined, the variable remains defined for the rest of the session or until it is undefined by the user or process with the `undefine` command.

■ You can modify the message that prompts the user to input a variable value. This activity is performed with the `accept` command.

Fill-in-the-Blank Questions

1. In order to generate reports that display sums of information by report, you might use this SQL*Plus command: _____

2. After assigning a value to a variable in a SQL*Plus command, you can reassign that variable a value using this SQL*Plus command:
   _____

3. This SQL command allows you to aggregate data using column functions (two words): _____

4. This phrase describes the result of a join operation on two or more tables when the where clause is poorly defined:
   _____

5. This SQL keyword extends the functionality of a grouping expression to act as a where clause within a where clause:
   _____

6. This SQL*Plus keyword is used for defining formats for how SQL*Plus displays column information: _____

7. This phrase describes a query that feeds one row of results to a parent query for the purpose of selection when the exact where clause criteria is not known: _____

8. This type of constraint in Oracle is used for defining a relationship between two tables so that join operations can be executed:
   _____

Chapter Questions

1. **Which of the following is not a group function?**

   A. avg ( )

   B. sqrt ( )

   C. sum ( )

   D. max ( )

2. **In order to perform an inner join, which criteria must be true?**

   A. The common columns in the join do not need to have shared values.

B. The tables in the join need to have common columns.

C. The common columns in the join may or may not have shared values.

D. The common columns in the join must have shared values.

3. **Once a variable is defined, how long will it remain defined in SQL*Plus?**

   A. Until the database is shut down

   B. Until the instance is shut down

   C. Until the statement completes

   D. Until the session completes

4. **You want to change the prompt Oracle uses to obtain input from a user. Which of the following choices are used for this purpose? (Choose two.)**

   A. Change the prompt in the `config.ora` file.

   B. Alter the `prompt` clause of the `accept` command.

   C. Enter a new prompt in the `login.sql` file.

   D. There is no way to change a prompt in Oracle.

5. **No search criteria for the EMPLOYEE table is known. Which of the following options are appropriate for use when search criteria is unknown for comparison operations in a `select` statement? (Choose two.)**

   A. `select * from EMPLOYEE where empid = &empid;`

   B. `select * from EMPLOYEE where empid = 69494;`

   C. `select * from EMPLOYEE where empid =`
      `(select empid from invoice where invoice_no = 4399485);`

   D. `select * from EMPLOYEE;`

6. **What is the default character for specifying substitution variables in `select` statements?**

   A. Ampersand

   B. Ellipses

   C. Quotation marks

   D. Asterisk

7. **A user is setting up a join operation between tables EMPLOYEE and DEPT. There are some employees in the EMPLOYEE table that the user wants**

returned by the query, but the employees are not assigned to department heads yet. Which `select` statement is most appropriate for this user?

A. `select e.empid, d.head from EMPLOYEE e, dept d;`

B. `select e.empid, d.head from EMPLOYEE e, dept d where`
`e.dept# = d.dept#;`

C. `select e.empid, d.head from EMPLOYEE e, dept d where`
`e.dept# = d.dept# (+);`

D. `select e.empid, d.head from EMPLOYEE e, dept d where`
`e.dept# (+) = d.dept#;`

8. **Which of the following uses of the `having` clause are appropriate? (Choose three.)**

A. To put returned data into sorted order

B. To exclude certain data groups based on known criteria

C. To include certain data groups based on unknown criteria

D. To include certain data groups based on known criteria

9. **What is a Cartesian product?**

A. A group function

B. The result of a join `select` statement with no `where` clause

C. The result of fuzzy logic

D. A special feature of Oracle server

10. **The default character that identifies runtime variables is changed by which of the following?**

A. Modifying the `initsid.ora` file

B. Modifying the `login.sql` file

C. Issuing the `define variablename` command

D. Issuing the `set define` command

11. **Which line in the following `select` statement will produce an error?**

```
select deptno, avg(sal) from emp
group by empno
```

A. `select deptno, avg(sal)`

B. `from emp`

C. `group by empno;`

D. There are no errors in this statement.

12. **You are developing a multiple-row query to handle a complex and dynamic comparison operation for the Olympics. Two tables are involved. CONTESTANT lists all contestants from every country, and MEDALS lists every country and the number of gold, silver, and bronze medals they have. If a country has not received one of the three types of medals, a zero appears in the column. Therefore, a query will always return data, even for countries that haven't won a medal. Which of the following queries shows only the contestants from countries with more than ten medallists of any type?**

    A. `select name from contestant c, medals m where c.country`
        `= m.country;`

    B. `select name from contestant where country c in (select`
        `country from medals m where c.country = m.county)`

    C. `select name from contestant where country c = (select`
        `country from medals m where c.country = m.county)`

    D. `select name from contestant where country in (select`
        `country from medals where num_gold + num_silver +`
        `num_bronze > 10)`

13. **You issue the following query in a SQL*Plus session:**

```
SELECT NAME, AGE, COUNTRY FROM CONTESTANT
WHERE (COUNTRY, AGE) IN ( SELECT COUNTRY, MIN(AGE)
FROM CONTESTANT GROUP BY COUNTRY);
```

    Which of the following choices identifies both the type of query and the expected result from the Oracle database?

    A. Single-row subquery; the youngest contestant from one country.

    B. Multiple-row subquery; the youngest contestant from all countries.

    C. Multiple-column subquery; the youngest contestant from all countries.

    D. Multiple-column subquery; Oracle will return an error because = should replace `IN`.

14. **The contents of the CONTESTANT table are listed as follows:**

```
NAME                      AGE COUNTRY
-------------    -------------- ---------------
BERTRAND                   24 FRANCE
GONZALEZ                   29 SPAIN
HEINRICH                   22 GERMANY
```

```
TAN                              39 CHINA
SVENSKY                          30 RUSSIA
SOO                              21
```

You issue the following query against this table:

```
select name from contestant
where (country, age) in ( select country, min(age)
from contestant  country);
```

What is the result?

A. SOO

B. HEINRICH

C. BERTRAND

D. GONZALEZ

Fill-in-the-Blank Answers

1. compute

2. undefine

3. group by

4. Cartesian product

5. having

6. set

7. Single-row subquery

8. Foreign key

Answers to Chapter Questions

1. B. sqrt( )

Explanation Square root operations are performed on one column value. Review the discussion of available group functions.

2. B. The tables in the join need to have common columns.

Explanation It is possible that a join operation will produce no return data, just as it is possible for any select statement not to return any data. Choices A, C, and D represent the spectrum of possibilities for shared values that may or may not be present in common columns. However, joins themselves are not possible without two tables having common columns. Refer to the discussion of table joins.

3. D. Until the session completes

Explanation A variable defined by the user during a session with SQL*Plus will remain defined until the session ends or until the user explicitly undefines the variable. Refer to the discussion of defining variables earlier in the chapter.

4. B and C. Alter the prompt clause of the accept command *and* enter a new prompt in the login.sql file.

Explanation Choice D should be eliminated immediately, leaving choices A, B, and C. Choice A is incorrect because config.ora is a feature associated with Oracle's client/server network communications product. Choice C is correct because you can use the set sqlprompt command within your login.sql file.

This is a special file Oracle users can incorporate into their use of Oracle that will automatically configure aspects of the SQL*Plus session, such as the default text editor, column and NLS data formats, and other items.

5. A and C.

Explanation Choice A details the use of a runtime variable that can be used to have the user input appropriate search criteria after the statement has begun processing. Choice C details the use of a subquery that allows the user to select unknown search criteria from the database using known methods for obtaining the data. Choice B is incorrect because the statement simply provides a known search criterion; choice D is incorrect because it provides no search criteria at all. Review the discussion of defining runtime variables and subqueries.

6. A. Ampersand

Explanation The ampersand (&) character is used by default to define runtime variables in SQL*Plus. Review the discussion of the definition of runtime variables and the set define command.

7. C. select e.empid, d.head from EMPLOYEE e, dept d where e.dept# = d.dept# (+);

Explanation Choice C details the outer join operation most appropriate to this user's needs. The outer table in this join is the DEPT table, as identified by the (+) marker next to the DEPT# column in the comparison operation that defines the join.

8. B, C, and D. To exclude certain data groups based on known criteria, to include certain data groups based on unknown criteria, *and* to include certain data groups based on known criteria

Explanation All exclusion or inclusion of grouped rows is handled by the having clause of a select statement. Choice A is not an appropriate answer because sort order is given in a select statement by the order by clause.

9. B. The result of a join select statement with no where clause

Explanation A Cartesian product is the resultant dataset from a select statement in which all data from both tables is returned. Some potential causes of a Cartesian product include not specifying a where clause for the join select statement. Review the discussion of performing join select statements.

10. D. Issuing the `set define` command

Explanation   Choice A is incorrect because a change to the `initsid.ora` file will alter the parameters Oracle uses to start the database instance. Use of this feature will be covered in the next unit. Choice B is incorrect because although the `login.sql` file can define many properties in a SQL*Plus session, the character that denotes runtime variables is not one of them. Choice C is incorrect because the `define` command is used to define variables used in a session, not an individual statement. Review the discussion of defining runtime variables in `select` statements.

11. C. `group by empno;`

Explanation   Because the EMPNO column does not appear in the original list of columns to be displayed by the query, it cannot be used in a `group by` statement. Review the discussion of using `group by` in `select` statements.

12. D. SELECT NAME FROM CONTESTANT WHERE COUNTRY IN (SELECT COUNTRY FROM MEDALS WHERE NUM_GOLD + NUM_SILVER + NUM_BRONZE > 10)

Explanation   The SELECT NAME FROM CONTESTANT WHERE COUNTRY IN (SELECT COUNTRY FROM MEDALS WHERE NUM_GOLD + NUM_SILVER + NUM_BRONZE > 10) query is correct because it contains the subquery that correctly returns a subset of countries that have contestants who won ten or more medals of any type. Choice A is incorrect because it contains a join operation, not a subquery. Choice B is simply a rewrite of choice A to use a multiple-row subquery; however, it does not go far enough to restrict return data and is, therefore, incorrect. Choice C is a single-row subquery that does essentially the same thing as choice B and is, therefore, incorrect.

13. C. Multiple-column subquery; the youngest contestant from all countries.

Explanation   Because the main query compares against the results of two columns returned in the subquery, this is a multiple-column subquery that will return the youngest contestant from all countries in the table. This multiple-column subquery is also a multiple-row subquery; but because the defining factor is the fact that two columns are present, you should focus more on that fact than on the rows being returned. This fact eliminates choices A and B. The subquery does return multiple rows, however. You should also be sensitive to the fact that the main query must use an IN clause, not the equal sign (=), thus making choice D incorrect as well.

14. A. SOO

Explanation If you guessed SOO, great job! The correct answer is SOO because the subquery operation specified by the `IN` clause ignores NULL values implicitly. Therefore, because SOO has no country defined, that row is not selected as part of the subquery. As a result, the output lists each of the youngest contestants from the named countries, so choices B, C, and D will all appear in the result set.

CHAPTER
3

Creating Oracle
Database Objects

n this chapter, you will learn about and demonstrate knowledge in the following topics:

- Creating the tables of an Oracle database
- Including constraints
- The Oracle data dictionary
- Manipulating Oracle data

The topics covered in this chapter include creating tables, including constraints, using the data dictionary, and manipulating data. With mastery of these topics, your experience with Oracle moves from the level of casual user to the world of application development. Application developers usually create database objects and determine how casual users will access those objects in production environments. The database administrator (DBA) is the person who is responsible for migrating developed objects into production and then managing the needs of production systems. This chapter will lay the foundation for discussion of Oracle database object creation and other advanced topics, which is important for both developers and DBAs, so pay close attention to this material. The OCP Exam 1 test questions in this subject area are worth 15 percent of the final score.

Creating the Tables of an Oracle Database

This section covers the following topics related to creating tables:

- Describing tables
- Creating tables
- Datatypes and column definitions
- Altering table definitions
- Dropping, renaming, and truncating tables

This section will explain the basic syntax required of developers and DBAs in order to produce the logical database objects in Oracle known as *tables*. You will learn the syntax and semantics of creating tables and related database objects.

You will also learn how to identify characteristics of tables already created. The section will cover how to change the definition of existing tables and other advanced types of table manipulation in the database as well. Finally, you will see a fast, neat way for deleting records from tables while leaving the definition of the table intact.

Describing Tables

The best way to think of a table for most Oracle beginners is to envision an Excel spreadsheet containing several records of data. Across the top, try to envision a horizontal list of column names that label the values in these columns. Each record listed across the table is called a *row*. In SQL*Plus, the command `describe` allows you to obtain a basic listing of characteristics about the table. We've already seen this command earlier in the book, but let's take another look at it using our trusty standby demo table, EMP, owned by SCOTT:

```
SQL> describe scott.emp
 Name                    Null?    Type
 --------------------    -------- --------------
 EMPNO                   NOT NULL NUMBER(4)
 ENAME                            VARCHAR2(10)
 JOB                              VARCHAR2(9)
 MGR                              NUMBER(4)
 HIREDATE                         DATE
 SAL                              NUMBER(7,2)
 COMM                             NUMBER(7,2)
 DEPTNO                           NUMBER(2)
```

TIP
The `describe` command can be abbreviated as `desc` to obtain the same result with fewer keystrokes.

Note some interesting characteristics about the output in the preceding code block. First, the `describe` command lists the columns in the EMP table by name. We prefixed table EMP with its schema owner, SCOTT. If we didn't, Oracle would assume we wanted to see a description of the EMP table in our own schema, if one existed. Second, notice the column with the heading NULL?. This information indicates whether the column listed allows NULL information. A listing of not NULL for the table column usually (although not always) indicates that the table column is the primary key for identifying unique rows in the table. Finally, notice that the output shows detailed information about the datatype for that table column.

TIP
You've progressed quite a bit in your knowledge of Oracle. Therefore, the demo tables we used in Chapters 1 and 2 are of less and less use to you. From here on out in the book, we're going to work with our own database objects, creating them first, then populating them, and then selecting information from them if necessary. You'll probably want to continue using the SCOTT user ID, however, because it has the privileges you need to execute these examples!

For Review

Know how to use the `describe` command and what its abbreviation is. Understand what three pieces of information are listed in the output for this command, as well as what that information means.

Exercises

1. You issue the following command in SQL*Plus: `describe PROFITS`. Which of the following choices identifies information that will not be shown in the results listed by this command?

   A. Columns in the table

   B. Foreign keys from this table to other tables

   C. Datatypes of columns in the table

   D. The primary key of the table

2. You issue the following command in SQL*Plus: `describe PROFITS`. Potential primary key information given in the output of the `describe` command will be listed under which of the following headings?

   A. NAME

   B. NULL?

   C. TYPE

   D. None of the above

3. **This is the keyword you can enter as an abbreviation for the `describe` command:** _____

Answer Key

1. B. **2.** D. **3.** `desc.`

Creating Tables

To create a table in Oracle, you use the `create table` command. This statement is one of many database object creation statements known in Oracle as the *data definition language (DDL)*. In the next several examples, you're going to create your own table of employees in a company of your own making. The following code block provides the basic `create table` statement that will create your new EMPLOYEE table:

```
SQL>  create table employee
  2  (empid varchar2(5),
  3    firstname varchar2(10),
  4    lastname varchar2(10),
  5    salary number(7));
Table created.
```

TIP
In order to create tables in the Oracle database, you need the `create table` privilege. User SCOTT has this privilege. You can find information for granting the needed privileges to other users in Chapter 4. Alternatively, you can ask your DBA at work to grant the `create table` privilege to the user ID you intend to use for working through the examples in this chapter.

Notice the important aspects of this basic `create table` statement. You define the table's name and then define all the columns you want in your table (inside parentheses and separated by commas). The absolute maximum number of columns that a table may have is 1000. Each column has an associated datatype that the information stored in that column must conform to. Make sure to close off the parentheses properly, so that Oracle will create your table for you. If a table called

EMPLOYEE already existed in our user schema, Oracle would give the following error and no table would be created:

```
SQL> create table employee
  2  (empid varchar2(5));
create table employee
       *
ERROR at line 1:
ORA-00955: name is already used by an existing object
```

TIP

In a case in which a table name you select is in use by an existing object in your schema, you can create the object in a different user schema, rename the object you want to create, rename the object that already exists, or remove the object that already exists.

Creating Temporary Tables

Most of the time, when you create a table in Oracle, the records that eventually populate that table will live inside your database forever (or until someone removes them). However, there might be situations in which you only want records in a table to live inside the database for a short while. In this case, you can create temporary tables in Oracle, where the data placed into the tables persists for only the duration of the user session, or for the length of your current transaction. A *transaction* is a span of time during which all data changes made are treated as one logical unit of work. You'll learn more about transactions later in this chapter.

A temporary table is created using the `create global temporary table` command. Why does a temporary table have to be global? So that the temporary table's definition can be made available to every user on the system. However, the contents of a temporary table are visible only to the user session that added information to the temporary table, even though everyone can see the definition. Temporary tables are a relatively new feature in Oracle, and Oracle hasn't had enough time yet to implement "local" temporary tables (that is, temporary tables that are only available to the user who owns them). Look for this functionality in later database releases. The appropriate `create global temporary table` command is shown in the following code block:

```
SQL> create global temporary table temp_emp
  2  (empno number,
  3   ename varchar2(10));
Table created.
```

Creating One Table with Data from Another

In most cases, when a developer creates a table in Oracle, the table is empty—it has no data in it. Once the table is created, the users or developers are then free to populate it as long as proper access has been granted. However, in some cases, the developer can create a table that already has data in it. The general statement used to create tables with data built in is the `create table as select` statement, as shown here:

```
SQL> create table emp_copy
  2  as select * from emp
  3  where deptno = 10;
Table created.
```

Two things are worthy of note about the `create table as select` statement. First, notice we didn't have to define any column names in table EMP_COPY. This is because we used a wildcard in the column clause to obtain data from the EMP table, telling Oracle to create the columns in EMP_COPY just as they appear in EMP—same names, same datatype definitions. The second thing is that any `select` statement you can issue from SQL*Plus can also be included in the `create table as select` statement. Oracle then automatically obtains whatever data you selected from EMP and populates EMP_COPY with that data. However, if the `select` statement includes a specific list of columns named in the column clause, your `create table` clause must list the columns you want the table to include, enclosed in parentheses. Here's an example of what I mean:

```
SQL> create table emp_copy_2
  2  (empno, sal) as
  3  select empno, sal from emp
  4  where deptno = 10;
Table created.
```

Table-Naming Conventions

Many philosophies about the naming of variables, tables, columns, and other items in software come from the early days of computing. Available memory and disk space was limited on those early machines, so the names of tables and columns in those environments were often small and cryptic. In systems today, however, developers are not faced with that restriction. The names of columns and tables need not be bound by the naming rules of yesteryear. However, standards for naming tables and columns still have value, if only for the sake of readability. There are also some hard-and-fast rules about table and column names in Oracle. For our purposes, we'll divide our rules into two categories: hard-n-fast and soft-n-stylish.

Keep Names Short and Descriptive   Your table- and column-naming conventions in your Oracle database may be compact, but someone viewing the tables and columns in your database for the first time should also have some idea of what the tables and columns represent.

■ **Hard-n-fast**   Oracle database object names must begin with a letter and can usually be between 1 and 30 characters long, except for databases (which have a maximum of eight characters) and database links (with a maximum of 128 characters). Names are not case sensitive.

■ **Soft-n-stylish**   Calling a table EMP_LN_FN_SAL might not be as easily understood as simply calling the table EMPLOYEE, or even EMP.

Relate Names for Child Tables to Their Parent   In certain situations, the developers of an application may find themselves creating multiple tables to define a logical entity representing a parent-child relationship. Consider an example where an employee expense application contains two tables—one called EXPENSE, listing information such as total invoiced amount and employee name, and the other called EXPENSE_DETAIL, containing individual entries for airfare, car rental, hotel, and so on. Both are descriptive names, and it is obvious from those names that there is some relationship between the tables.

■ **Hard-n-fast**   A user cannot own or refer to two objects with the same name; so if both you and SCOTT own a table called EMPLOYEE, you must prefix references to EMPLOYEE with the schema owner.

■ **Soft-n-stylish**   Tables related by foreign key (that is, parent/child relationships) should share part of the same table name.

Foreign-Key Columns Should Have the Same Name in Both Tables   If you are creating foreign-key relationships between columns in two different tables, it also helps if the column appearing in both tables has the same name in both places, implying the potential existence of a foreign key a bit more obvious. Remember, you can use table aliases in your join statements when you reference columns that have the same name in both tables in order to avoid ambiguity.

■ **Hard-n-fast**   Don't name a table DUAL, because, as you know, Oracle already has a table called DUAL that is accessible by everyone.

■ **Soft-n-stylish**   Give columns shared in multiple tables for parent-child relationships the same name.

Names of Associated Objects Should Relate to the Table   Sometimes other objects exist in conjunction with tables in Oracle. These objects include integrity constraints, triggers, and indexes. You'll learn what all these objects are later. For now, just know that they exist, and that it is useful to give these objects meaningful names that relate back to the table.

- ■ **Soft-n-stylish**   Give objects that are associated with tables meaningful names that relate back to the table: for example, PK_EMP_01 (primary key for EMP table), IDX_EMP_01 (index on EMP table), and TRIG_EMP_01 (trigger on EMP table).

Avoid Quotes, Keywords, and Nonalphanumeric Characters   You can't use quotes in the name of a table or column. Nor can you use most nonalphanumeric characters, with three exceptions: the dollar sign ($), the underscore (_), and the hash mark (#)—sometimes also called the *pound sign*. The dollar sign is most notable in naming dynamic performance views, whereas the hash mark is used in some data dictionary tables owned by a privileged user called SYS in Oracle. In general, you should steer clear of using $ or #. The underscore is useful for separating two words or abbreviations.

- ■ **Hard-n-fast**   Don't use table names beginning with "SYS."

- ■ **Hard-n-fast**   You can only use the following three special characters in table and column names: #, $, and _.

- ■ **Hard-n-fast**   Don't use special characters from European or Asian character sets in a database name, global database name, or database link names.

- ■ **Hard-n-fast**   An object name cannot be an Oracle reserved word, such as `select` or `from`; a datatype, such as NUMBER; or a built-in function, such as `decode( )`. Oracle may not complain when you create the object, but it may give you an unpleasant surprise when you refer to the object in your SQL statement.

- ■ **Hard-n-fast**   Depending on the product you plan to use to access a database object (for example, WebDB, JDeveloper, or Developer), names might be further restricted by other reserved words. For a list of a product's reserved words, see the manual for that specific product.

For Review

1. Know how to use the statements for creating tables, temporary tables, and tables with data already populated in them. Know that the maximum number of columns a table may have is 1000.

2. Be sure you can identify some table-naming conventions for descriptiveness, syntactic and semantic correctness, and relatedness to other objects.

Exercises

1. You are defining database tables in Oracle. Which of the following choices identifies a table name that is not valid for use?

    A. TEST_NUMBER

    B. P$$#_LOC

    C. 1_COPY_OF_EMP

    D. FLOP_TEST_#3

2. You are creating tables in the Oracle database. Which of the following statements identifies a table-creation statement that is not valid?

    A. `create table cats (c_name varchar2(10), c_weight number, c_owner varchar2(10));`

    B. `create table my_cats as select * from cats where owner = 'ME';`

    C. `create global temporary table temp_cats (c_name varchar2(10), c_weight number, c_owner varchar2(10));`

    D. `create table cats_over_5_lbs as select c_name, c_weight from cats where c_weight > 5;`

3. Your attempt to create a table in Oracle results in the following error: `ORA-00955 - name is already used by existing object.` Which of the following choices does not identify an appropriate correction for this situation?

    A. Create the object as a different user.

    B. Drop the existing object with the same name.

    C. Change the column names in the object being created.

    D. Rename the existing object.

4. In Oracle8i, all temporary tables are available to all users, implying the need for this keyword: _____

Answer Key

1. C. 2. D. 3. C. 4. `global.`

Datatypes and Column Definitions

The need for and use of datatypes when identifying the type of data columns a table can hold has already been mentioned in Chapter 1. When we initially discussed it, we limited our discussion to only the datatypes used in the EMP table (VARCHAR2, DATE, and NUMBER) so that we could get busy learning how to develop queries. However, it is now necessary for us to discuss all the available datatypes in the Oracle database so that you know about all the datatypes available in order to pass the OCP exam. Here is a list of all the datatypes in Oracle, along with their descriptions:

Datatype	Description
VARCHAR2(n)	Contains variable-length text strings of length n bytes, where n can be of up to 4,000 bytes in Oracle8i.
NVARCHAR2(n)	Contains single-byte or multibyte variable-length text strings of n bytes, where n can be up to 4,000 bytes in Oracle8i.
CHAR(n)	Contains fixed text strings of n bytes, where n can be up to 2,000 bytes in Oracle8i.
NCHAR(n)	Contains single-byte or multibyte fixed-length text strings of n bytes, where n can be up to 2,000 bytes in Oracle8i.
NUMBER(n[,m])	Contains numeric data up to n digits in length, where n can be up to 38 digits in Oracle8i. A NUMBER can also have an optional m number of digits to the right of the decimal point. This collection of digits is called a *mantissa*. The mantissa can have up to 38 digits as well. If no value is specified for n, Oracle defaults to 38.
DATE	Contains date information. DATE columns are 7 bytes in length.
RAW	Contains binary data of up to 2,000 bytes in Oracle8i.
LONG	Contains text data of up to 2GB.
LONG RAW	Contains binary data of up to 2BG.
ROWID	Contains the address for rows in your table.
BLOB	Large binary object (available in Oracle8 and later versions only) of up to 4GB.
CLOB	Large character-based object (available in Oracle8 and later versions only) of up to 4GB.

Datatype	Description
NCLOB	Large single-byte or multibyte character-based object (available in Oracle8 and later versions only) of up to 4GB.
BFILE	Large external file (available in Oracle8 and later versions only).

Text Datatypes Explained

There are two text datatypes that can contain alphanumeric information—CHAR and VARCHAR2. Although both CHAR and VARCHAR2 hold character strings, some subtle differences exist. First, the CHAR datatype only supports character strings up to a length of 2,000 bytes for Oracle8i, whereas the VARCHAR2 datatype supports character strings up to a length of 4,000 bytes for Oracle8i. The more important difference is demonstrated in the following code block:

```
SQL> create table tester
  2  (col1 char(10),
  3    col2 varchar2(10));
Table created.
SQL> insert into tester values ('BRADY','BRADY');
1 row created.
SQL> select vsize(col1), vsize(col2) from tester;
VSIZE(COL1) VSIZE(COL2)
----------- -----------
         10           5
```

TIP

We'll discuss data manipulation statements such as `insert` *later in the chapter in the section "Manipulating Oracle Data." For now, simply understand that* `insert` *is used for adding rows to a table in Oracle. Otherwise, nothing issued in this code block should be unfamiliar to you. If you don't remember what the* `vsize( )` *function tells us, review its explanation in Chapter 1.*

Notice that in our TESTER table, the value BRADY that we stored in COL1 takes up 10 bytes. This is because Oracle pads the value stored in CHAR columns with blanks up to the declared length of the column. In contrast, Oracle does not store padded blank spaces if the same value is stored in a column defined as datatype VARCHAR2.

TIP
VARCHAR2 has the "2" on the end of its name because there may be a VARCHAR datatype defined in future releases of Oracle. Although VARCHAR and VARCHAR2 are currently synonymous, they may not be in the future, so Oracle recommends using VARCHAR2. VARCHAR is a valid data type due to the ANSI standard and Oracle includes that data type so they can say they are ANSI compliant.

The NUMBER Datatype

The NUMBER datatype stores number data and can be specified to store integers or real numbers. In order to understand how to define NUMBER columns, let's say you were defining a column as shown in the following code block:

```
SQL> create table tester2
  2  (col1 number(15,2));
Table created.
```

The overall number of digits that this NUMBER column will store is 15 in this case. Thirteen digits can appear in front of the decimal point, whereas two digits are reserved for the mantissa. Therefore, 1234567891011 can be stored in this column as shown here:

```
SQL> insert into tester2 values (1234567891011);
1 row created.
```

However, 12345678910111 cannot fit into this column, as you see here:

```
SQL> insert into tester2 values (12345678910111);
insert into tester2 values (12345678910111)
                            *
ERROR at line 1:
ORA-01438: value larger than specified precision allows
 for this column
```

Interesting things happen when we try to insert values in this column that exceed the mantissa's specified length of two digits, as you see here:

```
SQL> insert into tester2 values (1234567891011.121)
1 row created.
```

Wait a minute, you say. When we tried to add a number to this column that was more than 13 digits to the left of the decimal point, Oracle gave us an error. Yet, when we add a value with more than 15 digits, where the overflow digits appear after the decimal point, Oracle accepts the value. Well, that's only partially true. To better understand what happened, let's take a look at the contents of TESTER2:

```
SQL> column col1 format 9999999999999.99
SQL> select * from tester2;
              COL1
-----------------
 1234567891011.00
 1234567891011.12
```

The first command in the code block formats the output from COL1 so that we can read it more easily. Had we omitted that formatting command, Oracle would have returned the data in scientific notation. Second, notice in the second row of values from COL1 that Oracle changed our inserted value 1234567891011.121 to 1234567891011.12! Therefore, we can extrapolate two simple rules:

- Oracle always rounds off when you try to insert values that exceed the number of digits allowed, so long as those extra digits appear after the decimal point.

- If the extra digits appear in front of the decimal point, Oracle returns an error.

Other Datatypes in Oracle

Let's briefly cover the remaining datatypes in Oracle. We've seen the DATE datatype in action, which stores date values in a special Oracle format represented as the number of days since December 31, 4713 B.C.E. This datatype offers a great deal of flexibility when you want to perform date-manipulation operations, such as adding 30 days to a given date. Recall also that there are many functions that handle complex date operations. Another nice feature of Oracle's method for date storage is that it is inherently millennium compliant.

Beyond the DATE datatype, there is an entire set of important type declaration options dedicated to the storage of small and large amounts of text and unformatted binary data. These datatypes include LONG, RAW, and LONG RAW. RAW datatypes in Oracle store data in binary format up to 2,000 bytes. It is useful to store graphics and sound files, used in conjunction with LONG, to form the LONG RAW datatype, which can accommodate up to 2GB of data. You can also declare columns as type LONG, which stores up to 2GB of alphanumeric text data. However, because data in a LONG or LONG RAW column is stored contiguously or *inline* with the rest of the table data, there can be only one column declared to be of type LONG in a table.

Storing large blocks of data has been enhanced significantly in Oracle8 and Oracle8i with the introduction of the BLOB, CLOB, and NCLOB datatypes. These four types can each contain up to 4GB of binary, single-byte, and multibyte character-based data, respectively. Data in a BLOB, CLOB, or NCLOB column is stored in the following way. If the value is less than 4KB, the information can also be stored contiguously (inline) with the rest of table data. Otherwise, a pointer to where Oracle8i has stored this data outside of the table is stored inline with the rest of the table. This is in contrast to earlier versions of Oracle, where the actual LONG or LONG RAW data must *always* be stored inline with the rest of the table information. As a result of this new way for storing large blocks of data, Oracle allows more than one BLOB, CLOB, or NCLOB column per table.

TIP

Storing data "inline" means that the data in a LONG datatype column is stored literally "in line" with the rest of the data in the row, as opposed to Oracle storing a pointer inline with row data, pointing to LONG column data stored somewhere else.

Finally, the ROWID datatype stores information related to the disk location of table rows. Generally, no column should be created to store data using type ROWID, but this datatype supports the ROWID pseudocolumn associated with every table. A *pseudocolumn* can be thought of as a virtual column in a table. Every table has several pseudocolumns, including one called ROWID. ROWIDs are critical to your ability to store information in tables because they identify how Oracle can locate the rows. They also uniquely identify the rows in your table. Every table contains a ROWID pseudocolumn that contains the ROWID for the rows of the table. The following code block illustrates that we can query data in the ROWID column of a table, just as if it were any other column:

```
SQL> select rowid from emp;
ROWID
------------------
AAACwdAABAAAJGdAAA
AAACwdAABAAAJGdAAB
AAACwdAABAAAJGdAAC
AAACwdAABAAAJGdAAD
AAACwdAABAAAJGdAAE
AAACwdAABAAAJGdAAF
AAACwdAABAAAJGdAAG
AAACwdAABAAAJGdAAH
AAACwdAABAAAJGdAAI
AAACwdAABAAAJGdAAJ
AAACwdAABAAAJGdAAK
AAACwdAABAAAJGdAAL
AAACwdAABAAAJGdAAM
AAACwdAABAAAJGdAAN
```

TIP
Although ROWIDs are essential for Oracle database processing, you don't need to know too much about how they work. ROWIDs are tested more extensively on the OCP Database and Administration exam.

For Review

1. Be sure you can name all the datatypes available in Oracle. Know the format of data stored in the DATE datatype and what the ROWID datatype is.

2. Know how to define NUMBER columns and know the significance of the value specified both for overall length and for the mantissa. Know what may happen when the value added to a NUMBER column exceeds the specified length both before and after the mantissa.

3. Understand the difference between the LONG and CLOB datatypes with respect to where data is stored in relation to the overall table.

4. Be able to describe the differences between the CHAR and the VARCHAR2 datatypes—particularly with respect to CHAR's use of additional padding when storing text strings.

Exercises

1. **The PROFITS column inside the SALES table is declared as NUMBER(10,2). Which of the following values cannot be stored in that column?**

   A. 5392845.324

   B. 871039453.1

   C. 75439289.34

   D. 60079829.25

2. **Employee KING was hired on November 17, 1981. You issue the following query on your Oracle database: `select vsize(hiredate) from emp where ename = 'KING';`. Which of the following choices identifies the value returned?**

   A. 4

B. 7

C. 9

D. 17

3. **You define the PRODUCT_NAME column in your SALES table to be CHAR(40). Later, you add one row to this table with the value "CAT_TOYS" for PRODUCT_NAME. You then issue the following command:** `select vsize(product_name) from sales.` **Which of the following choices best identifies the value returned?**

   A. 8

   B. 12

   C. 40

   D. 4000

4. **Data in LONG RAW columns over 4KB in size is stored _____ with respect to the rest of the data in the table.**

Answer Key

1. B. **2.** B. **3.** C. **4.** inline.

Altering Table Definitions

Suppose that, after you create a table in Oracle, you discover there is some fact that the table needs to store that you forgot to include. Is this a problem? Absolutely not! You can modify existing Oracle tables with ease using the `alter table` statement. There are several basic changes you might want to make using this statement, as listed here:

- You can add more columns to a table.

- You can modify the size of existing columns in a table.

- You can remove columns from a table (but only in Oracle8i and later versions).

- You can add or modify constraints on columns in the table. We'll defer most of the discussion of this topic until later in the chapter.

TIP
A third type of change you can make with the `alter table` *statement has to do with the way tables are stored inside the Oracle database. This is a big topic on OCP Exam 2 in the DBA track. You don't need to worry about this type of modification for OCP Exam 1.*

Adding New Columns to a Table

You can use the `alter table` statement to add new columns to a table in Oracle. However, there are some restrictions on doing so. First, no two columns can have the same name in an Oracle table. Second, only one column of the LONG or LONG RAW datatype can appear in a table in Oracle. Third, the maximum number of columns a table may have is 1000. The following code block shows an example of the `alter table` statement:

```
SQL> alter table employee add (hire_date date);
Table altered.
```

As mentioned, only one column in the table may be of type LONG within a table. That restriction includes the LONG RAW datatype. However, many columns of datatype BLOB, CLOB, NCLOB, and BFILE can appear in one table, in both Oracle8 and Oracle8i. It is sometimes useful to emulate Oracle8i in Oracle7 databases as well, by having a special table that contains the LONG column and a foreign key to the table that would have contained the column; this reduces the amount of data migration and row chaining on the database.

TIP
Row chaining *and* row migration *occurs when the Oracle RDBMS has to move row data around or break it up and save it in pieces inside the files on disk that comprise an Oracle database. This activity is a concern to DBAs because it hurts database performance.*

Modifying Column Datatypes

Another important aspect of table columns that can be modified using the `alter table` statement is the configuration of the column's datatype. Suppose that our newly formed company using our new EMPLOYEE table has just hired a woman named Martha Paravasini-Clark. Recall at the beginning of the chapter that we created our EMPLOYEE table with a LASTNAME column of type VARCHAR2(10).

Unfortunately, Ms. Paravasini-Clark's last name has 16 characters, so we need to change the LASTNAME column to accept larger text strings. To resolve the issue, you can issue the following statement, making the LASTNAME column length longer:

```
SQL> alter table products modify (lastname varchar2(25));
Table altered.
```

When you're modifying existing columns' datatypes, the general rule of thumb is that increases are generally okay, but decreases are usually a little trickier. Here are some examples of operations that are generally acceptable:

- Increasing the size of a VARCHAR2 or CHAR column

- Increasing the size of a NUMBER column

However, decreasing the size of column datatypes usually requires special steps. Take a look at the following code block, in which we reduce the size of COL2 from our TESTER table:

```
SQL> desc tester
 Name                          Null? Type
 ---------------------- -------- ------------
 COL1                                CHAR(10)
 COL2                                VARCHAR2(10)
SQL> alter table tester modify (col2 varchar2(5));
alter table tester modify (col2 varchar2(5))
                            *
ERROR at line 1:
ORA-01441: column to be modified must be empty to decrease length
SQL> create table tester_col2
  2  (col2) as select col2 from tester;
Table created.
SQL> update tester set col2 = null;
1 row updated.
SQL> alter table tester modify (col2 varchar2(5));
Table altered.
SQL> update tester set col2 = (select col2 from tester_col2);
1 row updated.
```

TIP

You've already seen examples of every statement used in the code block, and you know what a subquery is, so there shouldn't be anything confusing going on here. You'll learn more about the update *statement later in the chapter.*

Let's walk through the statements in the preceding code block. First, we described the TESTER table to see how large COL2 was. Then, we attempted to reduce it from 10 bytes to 5. Oracle didn't like that, because COL2 contained data. Therefore, we had to copy all the data in COL2 to a temporary location using the `create table as select` command. We then changed the column values to NULL on the column we want to reduce the size of, and we made the actual change to the datatype size. Finally, we added the data back into the TESTER table using an `update` statement containing a subquery. Here are some other allowable operations that follow this principle:

- Reducing the size of a NUMBER column (empty column for all rows only)

- Reducing the length of a VARCHAR2 or CHAR column (empty column for all rows only)

- Changing the datatype of a column (empty column for all rows only)

Dropping Columns in Oracle8i

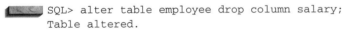

You can also drop columns in Oracle8i using the `alter table` statement. There are two ways to do so. The first is to instruct Oracle to ignore the column by using the `set unused column` clause. In this situation, no information is removed from the table column. Oracle simply pretends the column isn't there. Later, we can remove the column using the `drop unused columns` clause. Both steps are shown in the following block:

```
SQL> alter table employee set unused column salary;
Table altered.
SQL> alter table employee drop unused columns;
Table altered.
```

The second option is to remove the column and all contents entirely from the table immediately. This statement is shown in the following block:

```
SQL> alter table employee drop column salary;
Table altered.
```

TIP
If you're following along in your Oracle database, make sure you add the SALARY column back to the EMPLOYEE table when you've finished practicing both methods for dropping columns. We refer back to the EMPLOYEE table quite often later.

For Review

1. Be sure you know how to add columns using the `alter table` statement with the `add` clause.

2. Know how to modify column datatype definitions using the `alter table` statement with the `modify` clause.

3. Understand both uses of the `alter table` command for dropping columns—one using the `set unused column` and `drop unused columns` syntax, and the other with the `drop column` syntax.

Exercises

1. **You want to reduce the size of a non-NULL NUMBER(10) column to NUMBER(6). Which of the following steps must be completed after the appropriate `alter table` command is issued?**

   A. Copy column records to a temporary storage location.

   B. Set the NUMBER column to NULL for all rows.

   C. Create a temporary location for NUMBER data.

   D. Copy column records from the temporary location back to the main table.

2. **You just issued the following statement: `alter table sales drop column profit;`. Which of the following choices identifies when the column will actually be removed from Oracle?**

   A. Immediately following statement execution

   B. After the `alter table drop unused columns` command is issued

   C. After the `alter table set unused column` command is issued

   D. After the `alter table modify` command is issued

3. **You want to increase the size of a non-NULL VARCHAR2(5) column to VARCHAR2(10). Which of the following steps must be accomplished after executing the appropriate `alter table` command?**

   A. Set the VARCHAR2 column to NULL for all rows.

   B. Create a temporary location for VARCHAR2 data.

C. Copy the column records from the temporary location back to the main table.

D. Nothing. The statement is executed automatically.

4. **You want to increase the size of the PRODUCT_TYPE column, declared as a VARCHAR(5) column, to VARCHAR2(10) in the SALES table. Which of the following commands is useful for this purpose?**

A. `alter table sales add (product_type varchar2(10));`

B. `alter table sales modify product_type varchar2(10));`

C. `alter table sales set unused column product_type varchar2(10));`

D. `alter table sales drop column product_type;`

Answer Key
1. D. 2. A. 3. D. 4. B.

Dropping, Renaming, and Truncating Tables

Some additional operations are available for the modification of tables; they are designed for handling various situations, such as removing a table, changing the name of a table, and removing all the data from a table while still leaving the definition of the table intact. Let's talk about each of these operations in detail.

Dropping Tables

First, let's talk about how to eliminate a table. In order for a table to be deleted from the database, the `drop table` command must be executed:

```
SQL> drop table emp_copy_2;
Table dropped.
```

As mentioned earlier, sometimes objects are associated with a table that exist in a database along with the table. These objects may include indexes, constraints, and triggers. If the table is dropped, Oracle automatically drops any index, trigger, or constraint associated with the table as well.

Truncating Tables

Let's move on to discuss how you can remove all data from a table quickly using a special option available in Oracle. In this situation, the DBA or developer may use the `truncate table` statement. This statement is a part of the data definition language (DDL) of Oracle, much like the `create table` statement and completely unlike the `delete` statement. Truncating a table removes all row data from a table quickly, while leaving the definition of the table intact, including the definition of constraints and any associated database objects such as indexes, constraints, and triggers on the table. The `truncate` statement is a high-speed data-deletion statement that bypasses the transaction controls available in Oracle for recoverability in data changes. Truncating a table is almost always faster than executing the `delete` statement without a `where` clause; but once this operation has been completed, the data cannot be recovered unless you have a backed up copy of the data. Here's an example:

```
SQL> truncate table tester;
Table truncated.
```

TIP
Truncating tables affects a characteristic about them that Oracle calls the high-water mark. This characteristic is a value Oracle uses to keep track of the largest size the table has ever grown to. When you truncate the table, Oracle resets the high-water mark to zero.

Renaming Tables

You can rename a table in Oracle by using either the `rename` command or the `alter table rename` command. These commands allow you to change the name of a table without actually moving any data physically within the database. The following code block demonstrates the use of these commands:

```
SQL> rename tester to tester2;
Table renamed.
SQL> alter table tester3 rename to tester;
Table altered.
```

Commenting Objects

You can also add comments to a table or column using the `comment` command. This is useful especially for large databases where you want others to understand some specific bits of information about a table, such as the type of information stored in the table. An example of using this command to add comments to a table appears in the following block:

```
SQL> comment on table employee is
  2  'This is a table containing employees';
Comment created.
```

You can see how to use the comment command for adding comments on table columns in the following code block:

```
SQL> comment on column employee.empid is
  2  'unique text identifier for employees';
Comment created.
```

TIP
Comment information on tables is stored in an object called USER_TAB_COMMENTS, whereas comment information for columns is stored in a different database object, called USER_COL_COMMENTS. These objects are part of the Oracle data dictionary. You'll find out more about the Oracle data dictionary later in this chapter.

For Review

1. Understand how to remove a table from your database. Be sure you can describe what happens to any objects associated with the dropped table, such as indexes, constraints, and triggers.

2. Be sure you know how to rename and truncate tables. Understand what is meant by a table's *high-water mark* and how it is affected by the truncate command. Know how to add comments to a table as well.

Exercises

1. **You want to change the name of an existing database table. Which of the following choices does not identify a practical method for doing so?**

    A. Use the `create table as select` statement; then drop the original table.

    B. Use the `rename` command.

    C. Drop the table; then re-create it with its new name.

    D. Use the `alter table rename` command.

2. **You drop a table in an Oracle database that is the parent table in a parent-child data relationship. Which of the following objects will not be dropped when you drop the parent table?**

    A. Associated constraints

    B. The child column

    C. Associated triggers

    D. Associated indexes

3. **This is the name of the database object containing all comment information on tables: _____**

Answer Key

1. C. **2.** B. In fact, you will have trouble dropping the parent table if there is a child table due to Oracle's enforcement of existing foreign key constraints. **3.** USER_TAB_COMMENTS.

Including Constraints

This section covers the following topics related to including constraints in your database:

■ Describing constraints

■ Creating and maintaining constraints

Constraints have already been mentioned in some earlier discussions. This section will expand your understanding of constraints—those rules you can define in your Oracle tables that restrict the type of data you can place in the tables. In this section, you will learn more about the different types of constraints available in an Oracle system. You will also learn how to create and maintain the constraints you define in your Oracle database. This section also covers the different things you can do to modify, redefine, and manipulate your constraints. A note of caution: Constraints are one of the hardest areas to understand if you haven't used Oracle before. Proceed at your own pace.

Describing Constraints

Constraints accomplish two goals in an Oracle database. First, they create real and tangible relationships between the many tables that comprise the typical database application. We've already seen this to be the case in parent-child table relationships. Second, constraints prevent "unwanted" data from making its way into the database against your wishes. I put "unwanted" in quotes because ultimately, the definition of what constitutes unwanted data is entirely arbitrary and up to you as the developer of your system. But the point should be clear: *Constraints hold your database together and keep the bad data out.* Five basic types of constraints are available in Oracle. The types of constraints are described in the following subsections.

Primary Key A constraint of this type identifies the column or columns whose singular or combined values identify uniqueness in the rows of your Oracle table. Every row in the table must have a value specified for the primary key column(s). Recall the EMP table used in earlier chapters. In it, EMPNO is a unique identifier for every row in the table. EMPNO, then, is the primary key because no two employees have the same number assigned to them in the EMPNO column. In relational database parlance, other columns in the EMP table are said to be *functionally dependent* on the primary key, EMPNO. This simply means that every other column describes a potentially non-unique attribute of this unique row. In other words, many employees could be named SMITH, but only one can be the employee named SMITH who has an EMPNO of 7369. Figure 3-1 diagrams this relationship in more detail.

Foreign Key A constraint of this type signifies a parent-child relationship between two tables based on a shared column. The foreign key constraint is enforced on the shared column in the child table, whereas the shared column in the parent table must be enforced by a primary key constraint. When a foreign key constraint exists on a shared column in the child table, Oracle checks to make sure that there is a corresponding value in the shared column of the parent table for every value placed in the shared column of the child table. Note that potentially

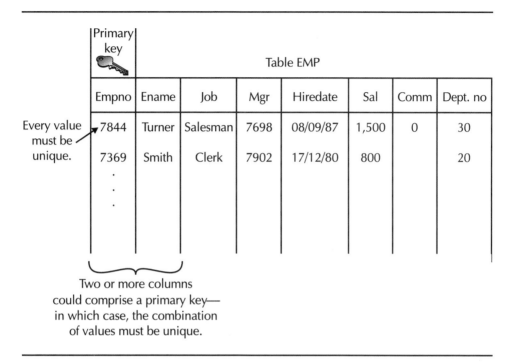

FIGURE 3-1. *Primary key constraints in Oracle*

many values in the parent table may not appear in the child table, but every value in the child table must have an associated value in the parent. Figure 3-2 diagrams this relationship in more detail.

Unique Constraint A constraint of this type enforces uniqueness on the values placed in this column. A good example of data requiring a unique constraint would be social security or government ID number. Every employee will need a unique one for tax purposes, so we will want to store it in a table of employee information. However, it isn't an appropriate number to use as the primary key for that table of employee information, because many people want to keep their government ID number a secret from others. Therefore, you might store social security or government ID numbers, but apply a unique constraint to prevent duplicated entries rather than use them as a primary key.

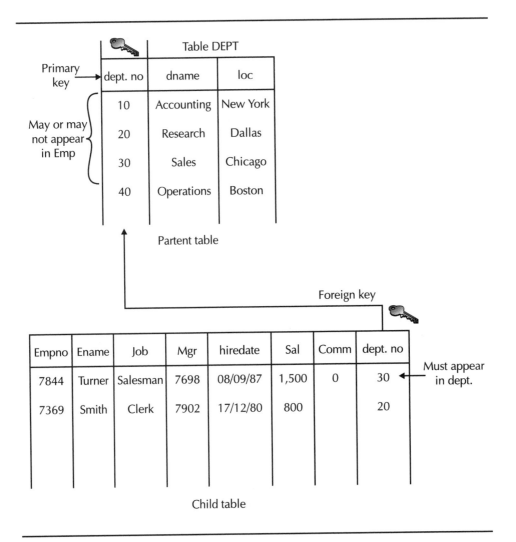

FIGURE 3-2. *Foreign key relationships in Oracle*

Check Constraint   A constraint of this type enforces that values placed in this column will meet specified static criteria. For example, a company may use check constraints to make sure that the salary entry for employees does not list an employee's salary as being over $250,000 per year. This is a static value that can easily be measured against an entered column value. Notice the repeated emphasis on *static* criteria. In the next discussion, you'll see what I mean by this.

TIP
Unique constraints, foreign keys, and check constraints usually allow NULL values to be placed in the column.

Not NULL Constraint   A constraint of this type enforces that values placed in the column will not be NULL. This is actually a very specific type of check constraint that only checks to see whether the value being entered into the column is NULL.

For Review

Be sure you can identify the five types of constraints in Oracle. With respect to primary key constraints, be sure you can identify what is meant by functional dependency between columns in a table and the primary key as well.

Exercises

1. This type of constraint enforces uniqueness on column values and prevents NULL data from being entered for the column: _____

2. This type of constraint indicates a parent-child relationship between this child table and another table: _____

3. This type of constraint enforces that values entered for the column meet some predefined static criteria: _____

Answer Key

1. Primary key. Remember, the constraint enforces uniqueness *and* does not allow NULL values to be entered. **2.** Foreign key. **3.** Check.

Creating and Maintaining Constraints

So much for the easy part, now let's get down to the tough stuff. Two methods exist for defining constraints: the *table constraint method* and the *column constraint method*. How can you tell the difference between the two? Well, here's how. The constraint is defined as a table constraint if the `constraint` clause syntax appears after the column and datatype definitions. The constraint is defined as a column constraint if the constraint definition syntax appears as part of an individual column's definition. All constraints can be defined either as table constraints or as column constraints, with two exceptions:

- not NULL constraints can only be defined as column constraints.

- Primary keys consisting of two or more columns (known also as *composite primary keys*) can only be defined as table constraints. However, single-column primary keys can be defined either as column or table constraints.

Creating Primary Key Constraints

Enough with the definitions, already. Let's start by taking a look at some examples for defining primary key constraints. Take a look at the following code listing, which displays a create table statement for creating our own EMPLOYEE table using constraints defined as table constraints (note that the constraint clause appears in bold):

```
SQL>  create table employee
  2   (empid varchar2(5),
  3    lastname varchar2(25),
  4    firstname varchar2(25),
  5    salary number(10,4),
  6    constraint pk_employee_01
  7    primary key (empid));
Table created.
```

TIP
If we wanted to create a composite primary key consisting of two or more columns, we would include the names of two (or more) columns inside the parentheses appearing after the keywords primary key.

Now, take a look at a create table statement for generating the same EMPLOYEE table. This time, the code listing shows the definition of the primary key as a column constraint. The constraint clause appears in bold in the following example:

```
SQL> create table employee
  2   (empid varchar2(5)
  3    constraint pk_employee_01 primary key,
  4    lastname varchar2(25),
  5    firstname varchar2(25),
  6    salary number(10,4));
Table created.
```

TIP
Both constraint declaration methods allow you to define your own names for your constraints. Remember that this feature is useful because constraints are database objects associated with tables, and from our earlier discussion, you know it's helpful to give associated database objects similar names.

With so many similarities between table and column constraint declarations, you may ask, are there any differences between constraints declared as table constraints and those declared as column constraints? Absolutely! Remember, *you can declare composite primary keys only by using the table constraint syntax, and you can declare not NULL constraints only using the column constraint syntax.* Another difference is that you can simplify the constraint declaration by merely indicating to Oracle that you want a constraint on the column (shown in bold), as you can see in the following block:

```
SQL> create table department
  2  (department_num number(5) primary key,
  3    department_name varchar2(25),
  4    location varchar2(25));
Table created.
```

TIP
When you simplify your column constraint definition in this way, Oracle names the constraint for you. When Oracle names the constraint for you, the naming convention is SYS_Cnnnnn.

Defining Foreign Key Constraints

To help you understand how to define foreign key constraints, let's think in terms of an example. Let's say we have our own table called DEPARTMENT, which we just created in the last code block. It lists the department number, name, and location for all departments in our own little company. Let's also say that we want to create our EMPLOYEE table with another column, called DEPARTMENT_NUM. Because there is an implied parent-child relationship between these two tables with the shared column, let's make that relationship official by using a foreign key constraint, shown in bold in the following block:

```
SQL>   create table employee
  2    (empid varchar2(5) primary key,
  3     lastname varchar2(25),
  4     firstname varchar2(25),
  5     salary number(10,4),
  6     department_num number(5)
  7       references department (department_num)
  8       on delete set null);
Table created.
```

For a foreign key constraint to be valid, the same column appearing in both tables must have exactly the same datatype. You needn't give the columns the same names, but it's a good idea to do so. The foreign key constraint prevents the DEPARTMENT_ NUM column in the EMP table from ever storing a value that can't also be found in the DEPT table. The final clause, on delete set null, is an option relating to the deletion of data from the parent table. If someone attempts to remove a row from the parent table that contains a referenced value from the child table, Oracle will set all corresponding values in the child to NULL. The other option is on delete cascade, where Oracle will remove all corresponding records from the child table when a referenced record from the parent table is removed.

Let's also test your eyes for distinguishing table and column constraints. Is the foreign key in the previous example a table or column constraint? At first, it might seem like a table constraint because the constraint definition appears after all the columns. However, close examination yields two important features. For one, there is no constraint clause. Table constraints must have a constraint clause; otherwise, Oracle returns an error. For another, there is no comma separating the constraint definition from the rest of the columns defined. If you flip back to our other constraint definition examples and look again carefully, you'll realize that this example shows the foreign key defined as a column constraint, not a table constraint.

TIP
A foreign key constraint cannot be created on the child table until the parent table is created and the primary key is defined on that parent table.

Defining Unique Key Constraints

Let's say we also want our employee table to store social security or government ID information. The definition of a UNIQUE constraint on the GOVT_ID column prevents anyone from defining a duplicate government ID for any two employees in the table. Take a look at the following example, where the unique constraint definition is shown in bold:

```
SQL>  create table employee
  2  (empid varchar2(5) primary key,
  3   lastname varchar2(25),
  4   firstname varchar2(25),
  5   salary number(10,4),
  6   department_num number(5)
  7     references department (department_num),
  8   govt_id number(10) unique);
Table created.
```

Defining Other Types of Constraints

The last two types of constraints are NOT NULL and CHECK constraints. The NOT NULL constraint prevents the data value defined by any row for the column from being NULL. By default, primary keys are defined to be NOT NULL. All other columns can contain NULL data, unless you explicitly define the column to be NOT NULL. CHECK constraints allow Oracle to verify the validity of data being entered on a table against static criteria. For example, you could specify that the SALARY column cannot contain values over $250,000. If someone tries to create an employee row with a salary of $1,000,000 per year, Oracle would return an error message saying that the record data defined for the SALARY column has violated the CHECK constraint for that column. Let's look at a code example where both not NULL and check constraints are defined in bold:

```
SQL> create table employee
  2  (empid varchar2(5) primary key,
  3   lastname varchar2(25) not null,
  4   firstname varchar2(25),
  5   salary number(10,4) check (salary <=250000),
  6   department_num number(5)
  7     references department (department_num),
  8   govt_id number(10) unique);
Table created.
```

Here's what is meant by static criteria for **CHECK** constraints: *CHECK constraints can only compare data in that column to a specific set of constant values or operations on those values.* A **CHECK** constraint cannot refer to any other column or row in this or any other table. It also cannot refer to special keywords, such as **user, sysdate, currval, nextval, level, uid, userenv, rownum,** and **rowid.**

Indexes Created by Constraints

Indexes are created automatically by Oracle to support integrity constraints that enforce uniqueness. The two types of integrity constraints that enforce uniqueness are PRIMARY KEY and UNIQUE constraints. When the primary-key or UNIQUE constraint is declared, a unique index to support the column's uniqueness is also created, and all values in all columns that were defined as part of the primary-key or UNIQUE constraint are placed into the index.

The name of the unique index created automatically to support unique and primary key constraints is the same name as the one given to the constraint. Therefore, if you were to explicitly name the primary key on your EMP table PK_EMPLOYEE_01, Oracle calls the unique index PK_EMPLOYEE_01 as well. If, however, you choose not to name your unique or primary key constraint, Oracle generates the name of your constraint for you. In this case, Oracle also gives the unique index the same name it gives the constraint.

TIP
When a primary key or unique constraint is created, a unique index corresponding to that constraint of the table is created to enforce uniqueness.

Adding Integrity Constraints to Existing Tables

Another constraint-related activity that you may need to do involves adding new constraints to an existing table. This can be easy if there is no data in the table already, but it can be a nightmare if data already exists in the table that doesn't conform to the constraint criteria. The simplest scenario for adding the constraint is to add it to the database before data is inserted. Take a look at the following code block:

```
SQL> create table employee
  2  (empid varchar2(5),
  3   lastname varchar2(25),
  4   firstname varchar2(25),
  5   salary number(10,4),
  6   department_num number(5),
  7   govt_id number(10));
Table created.
SQL> alter table employee add constraint
  2  pk_employee_01 primary key (empid);
Table altered.
SQL> alter table employee add constraint
  2  fk_employee_01 foreign key (department_num)
  3  references department (department_num);
Table altered.
```

```
SQL> alter table employee add constraint
  2   ck_employee_01 check (salary <=250000);
Table altered.
SQL> alter table employee add constraint
  2   uk_employee_01 unique (govt_id);
Table altered.
SQL> alter table employee modify
  2   (lastname not null);
Table altered.
```

Notice that all the examples follow a general pattern of `alter table` *table_name* add constraint *constraint_name type* (*definition*), except for NOT NULL constraints, which use the `alter table modify` statement we saw in earlier discussions. The column on which the constraint is added must already exist in the database table; no constraint can be created for a column that does not exist in the table. Some of the other restrictions on creating constraints when data already exists in the table are listed here:

- **Primary keys**   Columns cannot contain NULL values, and all values must be unique.

- **Foreign keys**   Referenced columns in the other table must contain all values found in this one; otherwise, this column's value must be NULL.

- **UNIQUE constraints**   Columns must contain all unique values or NULL values, or a combination of the two.

- **CHECK constraints**   The new constraint will only be applied to data added or modified after the constraint is created.

- **NOT NULL**   Columns cannot contain NULL values. If you want to add a column with a not NULL constraint to a table, you should use a `default` clause to identify a value Oracle can populate in this column for existing rows.

Disabling Constraints

A constraint can be turned on and off. When the constraint is disabled, it will no longer do its job of enforcing rules on the data entered into the table. The following code block demonstrates some sample statements for disabling constraints:

```
SQL> alter table employee disable primary key;
Table altered.
SQL> alter table employee disable constraint uk_employee_01;
Table altered.
```

You may experience a problem if you attempt to disable a primary key when existing foreign keys depend on that primary key. This problem is shown in the following situation:

```
SQL> alter table department disable primary key;
alter table department disable primary key
*
ERROR at line 1:
ORA-02297: cannot disable constraint (SCOTT.SYS_C001913) -
dependencies exist
```

If you try to drop a primary key when there are foreign keys depending on it, the cascade option is required as part of alter table disable *constraint*, as shown in the following code block:

```
SQL> alter table department disable primary key cascade;
Table altered.
```

TIP

Disabling a constraint leaves the table vulnerable to inappropriate data being entered! Care should be taken to ensure that the data loaded during the period the constraint is disabled will not interfere with your ability to enable the constraint later.

Enabling a Disabled Constraint

When the constraint is later enabled, the rules defined for the constraint are once again enforced, rendering the constraint as effective as it was when it was first added to the table. You can enable a disabled constraint as follows:

```
SQL> alter table department enable primary key;
Table altered.
SQL> alter table employee enable uk_employee_01;
Table altered.
```

TIP

Only constraints that have been successfully defined and are currently disabled can be enabled by this code. A constraint that fails on creation will not exist in the disabled state, waiting for you to correct the problem and reenable it.

When Existing Data in a Column Violates a Disabled Constraint

This topic is a bit advanced, so be forewarned. There are situations in which you may want to disable a constraint for some general purpose, such as disabling a primary key in order to speed up a large number of `insert` statements. *Be careful when using this approach!* If you disable a constraint and then load data into the table column that violates the integrity constraint while the constraint is disabled, your attempt to enable the constraint later with the `alter table enable constraint` statement will fail. You will need to use a special table called EXCEPTIONS (created by running the `utlexcpt.sql` script in `rdbms/admin` under the Oracle software home directory) to identify and correct the offending records. The following example involving a primary-key constraint should give you an idea of how this works:

```
SQL> @@C:\ORACLE\ORA81\RDBMS\ADMIN\UTLEXCPT
Table created.
SQL> create table example_1 (col1 number);
Table created.
SQL> insert into example_1 values (10);
1 row created.
SQL> insert into example_1 values (1);
1 row created.
SQL> alter table example_1 add (constraint pk_01 primary key (col1));
Table altered.
SQL> select * from example_1;
COL1
---------
       10
        1
SQL> alter table example_1 disable constraint pk_01;
Table altered.
SQL> insert into example_1 values (1);
1 row created.
SQL> alter table example_1 enable constraint pk_01
  2  exceptions into exceptions;
alter table example_1 enable constraint pk_01
*
ERROR at line 1:
ORA-02437: cannot enable (SCOTT.PK_01) - primary key violated
SQL> desc exceptions
 Name                            Null?    Type
 ------------------------------- -------- ----
 ROW_ID                                   ROWID
 OWNER                                    VARCHAR2(30)
 TABLE_NAME                               VARCHAR2(30)
 CONSTRAINT                               VARCHAR2(30)
```

```
SQL> select e.row_id, a.col1
  2  from exceptions e, example_1 a
  3  where e.row_id = a.rowid;
ROW_ID                COL1
------------------ --------
AAAAvGAAGAAAAPWAAB        1
AAAAvGAAGAAAAPWAAD        1
```

At this point, you have identified the ROWIDs of the offending rows in EXAMPLE_1 that break the rules of the primary key, which you can use either to modify the value of one of these rows or to remove one of the rows so the primary key can be unique. In the future, to ensure that enabling the constraint will be a smooth process, try not to load any data into columns with disabled constraints that would violate the constraint rules.

Removing Constraints

Usually, there is little about a constraint that will interfere with your ability to remove it, so long as you either own the table or have been granted appropriate privileges to do so. When a constraint is dropped, any index associated with that constraint (if there is one) is also dropped. Here is an example:

```
SQL> alter table employee drop unique (govt_id);
Table altered.
SQL> alter table employee drop primary key cascade;
Table altered.
SQL> alter table employee drop constraint ck_employee_01;
Table altered.
```

An anomaly can be found when disabling or dropping NOT NULL constraints. You cannot "disable" a not NULL constraint, per se—a column either accepts NULL values or it doesn't. Therefore, you must use the alter table modify clause when the not NULL constraints on a table must be added or removed. Here's an example:

```
SQL> alter table employee modify (lastname null);
Table altered.
SQL> alter table employee modify (lastname not null);
Table altered.
```

Dropping Parent Tables with Foreign Key Constraint References

In the same way that disabling a primary key constraint can be a problem when the primary key is referenced by a foreign key in a child table, dropping parent tables can also pose a problem when a child table is involved. If we wanted to drop the parent table DEPARTMENT in our parent-child relationship, the foreign key in the child table EMPLOYEE may interfere with our doing so. Let's take a look at what happens:

```
SQL> drop table department;
drop table department
             *
ERROR at line 1:
ORA-02449: unique/primary keys in table referenced by foreign keys
```

When there are constraints on other tables that reference the table to be dropped, you can use the `cascade constraints` clause in your `drop table` statement. The constraints in other tables that refer to the table being dropped are also dropped with `cascade constraints`:

```
SQL> drop table department cascade constraints;
Table dropped.
```

TIP
Alternately, you can disable or drop the foreign key in the child table before dropping the parent table by using the `alter table drop constraint` statement from earlier in the chapter.

Constraint Deferability in Oracle8i

Oracle **8i** and higher

When records are added to a database table, Oracle immediately validates the incoming records against any constraints that may exist on the columns in the table. If the data doesn't conform to the constraint criteria, Oracle returns an error immediately. However, you can modify this default behavior so that Oracle will not return an error immediately. Instead, you can force Oracle not to return an error until you are ready to end your transaction. Remember from an earlier discussion that a *transaction* is a series of data-change statements issued in a user session that comprise a logical unit of work. You will learn more about transaction processing later in the chapter. The concept of forcing Oracle not to return constraint violation errors until the end of your transaction is called *constraint deferability*.

In order for constraint deferability to work, you must define your constraint to be deferrable using the `deferrable initially deferred` syntax. For primary keys and unique constraints, this means that Oracle will use a non-unique index to store primary key values rather than a unique index. The non-unique index will allow for temporary storage of data in the primary key column until the transaction is completed and constraint violation errors can be reported. If you use the other deferability option, `deferrable initially immediate`, Oracle still creates a non-unique index to support the primary key, but it will enforce the primary key when data is entered, not when the transaction ends. If you omit either of these clauses entirely, Oracle will also enforce the constraint when data is entered, not when the transaction ends. Finally, remember that the keyword `deferrable` contains two R's, not one.

The options you have for enabling or disabling deferrable constraints include `enable validate` and `enable novalidate`. If you try to enable your constraint without specifying one of these options, Oracle will use `enable validate` by default. Using the `enable validate` option when you're enabling constraints forces Oracle to validate all the data in the constrained column to ensure that it meets the constraint criteria. This is the default behavior unless otherwise specified. The `enable validate` command is the same as simply using the `enable` keyword—`validate` is the default behavior of Oracle. However, Oracle also allows you to use the `enable novalidate` option when you want to enforce the constraint for new data entering the table but don't care about data that already exists in the table.

Let's look at an example. Assume that a table called PRODUCTS is used for storing products our company sells. The following code block illustrates how to create, disable, and enable a deferrable primary key constraint using appropriate syntax, which is shown in bold:

```
SQL> create table products
  2  (product# number,
  3   product_name varchar2(15),
  4   quantity number,
  5   color varchar2(10),
  6   prod_size varchar2(10));
Table created.
SQL> insert into products values
  2  (1, 'FLIBBER', 34, 'GREEN', 'XXL');
1 row created.
SQL> insert into products values
  2  (2, 'blobber', 4, 'GREEN', 'P');
1 row created.
SQL> select * from products;
PRODUCT# PRODUCT_NAME    QUANTITY COLOR      PROD_SIZE
-------- -------------  --------- ---------- ----------
       1 FLIBBER              34 GREEN       XXL
       2 blobber               4 GREEN       P
SQL> alter table products add
  2  (constraint pk_products_01 primary key (product#)
  3  deferrable initially deferred);
Table altered.
SQL> alter table products disable primary key;
```

```
Table altered.
SQL> update products set product# = 1
  2  where product_name = 'blobber';
1 row updated.
SQL> commit;
Commit complete.
SQL> alter table products enable validate primary key;
alter table products enable validate primary key
*
ERROR at line 1:
ORA-02437: cannot enable (SCOTT.PK_PRODUCTS_01) - primary
key violated
SQL> alter table products enable novalidate primary key;
Table altered.
SQL> select * from products;
PRODUCT# PRODUCT_NAME    QUANTITY COLOR      PROD_SIZE
-------- -------------  --------- ---------- ----------
       1 FLIBBER              34 GREEN       XXL
       1 blobber               4 GREEN       P
SQL> insert into products
  2  (product#, product_name, quantity, color, prod_size)
  3  values (1,'FLOBBER',23,'GREEN','L')
insert into products
*
ERROR at line 1:
ORA-00001: unique constraint (SCOTT.PK_PRODUCTS_01) violated
```

TIP
*disable novalidate is the same as disable;
however, new in Oracle8i is disable validate,
which disables the constraints, drops the index,
and disallows any modification on the constrained
columns.*

For Review

1. Be sure you can identify some differences between defining constraints as
   table constraints and as column constraints. Know how to define all five
   constraints on existing tables and as part of new table definitions. Know why
   defining a not NULL constraint is not like defining other types of constraints.

2. Know how to enable a disabled constraint. Be sure you know the
   restrictions on enabling constraints and how to create and use the
   EXCEPTIONS table for enabling constraints when data that violates these
   constraints exists in the table.

3. Be sure you can explain the concept of constraint deferability and the use of appropriate syntax for defining, enabling, and disabling deferrable constraints.

4. Understand that Oracle creates unique indexes in support of unique and primary key constraints. Know what determines the name given to an index created automatically.

Exercises

1. **The PROFITS table in your database has a primary key on the PRODUCT_NAME and SALE_PERIOD columns. Which of the following statements could *not* have been used to define this primary key?**

   A. `create table profits ( product_name varchar2 (10),`
   `sale_period varchar2 (10), profit number, constraint`
   `pk_profits_01 primary key (product_name, sale_period));`

   B. `alter table profits add constraint pk_profits_01`
   `primary key (product_name, sale_period) deferrable`
   `initially immediate;`

   C. `alter table profits add (constraint pk_profits_01`
   `primary key (product_name, sale_period));`

   D. `create table profits ( product_name varchar2 (10)`
   `primary key, sale_period varchar2 (10) primary key,`
   `profit number);`

2. **You are defining check constraints on your SALES table, which contains two columns, PRODUCT_TYPE and UNIT_SALES. Which of the following choices identify a properly defined check constraint? (Choose two.)**

   A. `alter table sales add constraint ck_sales_01 check`
   `(product_type in ('TOYS', 'HOT DOGS', 'PALM PILOTS'));`

   B. `alter table sales add constraint ck_sales_01 check`
   `(product_type in (select product_type from`
   `valid_products));`

   C. `alter table sales modify (product_type varchar2 (30)`
   `check (product_type in ('TOYS', 'HOT DOGS', 'PALM`
   `PILOTS')));`

   D. `alter table sales add (product_name varchar2 (30) check`
   `(product_name <> 'AK-47'));`

3. Use the following code block to answer the question:

```
SQL> create table prices
  2  ( product_name varchar2(30),
  3    price number(10,4));
Table created.
SQL> alter table prices add constraint pk_prices_01
  2  primary key (product_name);
Table altered.
SQL> insert into prices values ('DOGGY', 499.99);
1 row created.
SQL> alter table prices disable constraint pk_prices_01;
Table altered.
SQL> insert into prices values ('DOGGY', 449.99);
1 row created.
SQL> alter table prices enable novalidate pk_prices_01;
Table altered.
```

What happens next?

A. Existing entries are checked for violations, PK_PRICES_01 is enabled, and Oracle checks subsequent entries for violations immediately.

B. Existing entries are checked for violations, PK_PRICES_01 is not enabled, and Oracle does not check subsequent entries for violations immediately.

C. Existing entries are not checked for violations, PK_PRICES_01 is enabled, and Oracle checks subsequent entries for violations immediately.

D. Existing entries are checked for violations, PK_PRICES_01 is not enabled, and Oracle checks subsequent entries for violations immediately.

4. Your attempt to disable a constraint yields the following error:
`ORA-02297: cannot disable constraint - dependencies exist.`
Which of the following types of constraints is likely causing interference with your disablement of this one?

A. Check constraint

B. not NULL constraint

C. Foreign key constraint

D. Unique constraint

5. **You are disabling a not NULL constraint on the UNIT_PRICE column in the SALES table. Which of the following choices identifies the correct statement for performing this action?**

   A. `alter table sales modify (unit_prices null);`

   B. `alter table sales modify (unit_prices not null);`

   C. `alter table sales add (unit_prices null);`

   D. `alter table sales add (unit_prices not null);`

Answer Key

1. D. **2.** A and D. Nothing in the question said you can't add a new column. **3.** B. Remember, when a constraint cannot be enabled, it does not perform its job. **4.** C. **5.** A.

The Oracle Data Dictionary

In this section, we will cover the following topics related to the Oracle data dictionary:

- Available dictionary views
- Querying the data dictionary

Few resources in the Oracle database are as useful as the Oracle data dictionary. Developers, DBAs, and users will find themselves referring to the data dictionary time and time again to resolve questions about object availability, roles and privileges, and performance. Whatever the information, Oracle has it all stored in the data dictionary. This section will introduce the major components of the data dictionary in the Oracle database, pointing out its features and highlights in order to set the groundwork for fuller discussions on the data dictionary in later chapters. It is important to understand the major data dictionary concepts before moving on, because data dictionary views will be referred to in many other areas throughout the rest of the book.

Available Dictionary Views

A wealth of information about objects and data in your database can be found in a relatively small number of tables owned by a special privileged user in Oracle called SYS. Although Oracle prevents you from looking at these tables directly, several views are available for you to access this information. These views comprise the feature in Oracle known as the *data dictionary*.

TIP
A view can be thought of as a virtual table that can display data found in the actual table in the database. You'll learn more about views in Chapter 4.

As I said, data dictionary views help you avoid referring to the tables of the data dictionary directly. This safeguard is important for two reasons. First, it underscores the sensitivity of the SYS-owned tables that store dictionary data. If something happens to those tables, causing either data to be lost or a table to be removed, the effects could seriously damage your Oracle database—possibly even rendering it completely unusable! Second, the dictionary views distill the information in the data dictionary into highly understandable and useful formats.

What's in a Name?
Let's start by considering an example. Take a look at the following code block. In it, we can see the contents of a dictionary view called USER_TABLES:

```
SQL> select table_name from user_tables;
TABLE_NAME
------------------------------
BONUS
DEPARTMENT
DEPT
DUMMY
EMP
EMPLOYEE
EXAMPLE_1
PRICES
SALGRADE
TESTER
```

TIP
You can select data from dictionary views just as if they were tables. Any query technique you learned in Chapters 1 and 2 can be applied to dictionary views. You can also use the describe *command to obtain a listing of the columns in the view.*

I logged into Oracle as user SCOTT to obtain this output while generating the content for the previous chapters, so you can see that the output of this query displays the name of almost every table we've worked with. Look more carefully for a moment at the name of the view I used: USER_TABLES. Its very name implies two vitally important aspects of this (and indeed every) view in the data dictionary:

- The view's *topic* (in this case, tables)

- The view's *scope* (in this case, tables owned by the user, SCOTT)

TIP
The scope and topic of the dictionary view are separated by an underscore.

Discerning a Dictionary View's Scope
Let's discuss the view's scope first. Dictionary views are divided into three general categories corresponding to how much of the related topic the database user querying the view is permitted to see. The categories are discussed in the following subsections.

USER   These views allow you to see relevant database objects owned by you. These views have the narrowest scope because they only display the database objects that are in your schema. Therefore, if SCOTT owns a table called EMP and I log into Oracle as user JASON to issue `select * from USER_TABLES`, I'm not going to see EMP listed among the output. Why? Because the table belongs to SCOTT.

ALL   These views allow you to see relevant database objects that you may or may not own but that nevertheless are accessible to you. These views have a wider scope than the USER views because they include every relevant object that you can access, regardless of ownership. However, the scope is still limited to you, the user. In order to be able to access a database object, one of three conditions must be true:

- You created the object.

- You were granted access to the object by the object owner.

- The PUBLIC user was granted access privileges on the object by the owner.

TIP
The PUBLIC user in the database is a special user who represents the access privileges every user has. Therefore, when an object owner creates a table and grants access to the table to user PUBLIC, every user in the database has access privileges to the table created.

DBA   These powerful views allow you to see all relevant database objects in the entire database, whether or not they are owned by or accessible to you. These views are incredibly handy for DBAs (and sometimes also for developers) needing information about every database object.

NOTE
You can grant a special role to users called SELECT_ CATALOG_ROLE in order to let them look at the DBA views. We'll discuss roles further in Chapter 4. For now, focus for the most part on the USER and ALL views throughout the rest of this book.

Identifying a Dictionary View's Topic

The second part of any dictionary view's name identifies the topic of that view. Based on this fact, we know that the topic of the USER_TABLES view is tables, whereas the topic for the ALL_INDEXES view is all indexes. The views that correspond to areas that have been or will be discussed are listed here:

- **USER_OBJECTS, ALL_OBJECTS**   Gives information about various database objects owned by or available to the current user, respectively

- **USER_TABLES, ALL_TABLES**   Displays information about tables owned by or available to the current user, respectively

- **USER_INDEXES, ALL_INDEXES**   Displays information about indexes owned by or available to the current user, respectively

TIP
An index *is an object that improves performance on table queries. You'll learn more about indexes in Chapter 4.*

- **USER_VIEWS, ALL_VIEWS**   Displays information about views owned by or available to the current user, respectively

- **USER_SEQUENCES, ALL_SEQUENCES**   Displays information about sequences owned by or available to the current user, respectively

TIP
A sequence *is a database object that generates numbers in sequential order. You'll learn more about sequences in Chapter 4.*

- **USER_USERS, ALL_USERS** Displays information about the current user or about all users in Oracle, respectively

- **USER_CONSTRAINTS, ALL_CONSTRAINTS** Displays information about constraints owned by or available to the current user, respectively

- **USER_CONS_COLUMNS, ALL_CONS_COLUMNS** Displays information about table columns that have constraints owned by or available to the current user, respectively

- **USER_IND_COLUMNS, ALL_IND_COLUMNS** Displays information about table columns that have indexes owned by or available to the current user, respectively

- **USER_TAB_COLUMNS, ALL_TAB_COLUMNS** Displays information about columns in tables owned by or available to the current user, respectively

- **USER_ROLES, ALL_ROLES** Displays information about roles owned by or available to the current user, respectively

TIP
A role is a database object that can be used for privilege management. You'll learn more about roles in Chapter 4.

- **USER_TAB_PRIVS, ALL_TAB_PRIVS** Displays information about object privileges on objects owned by the user or available to the current user, respectively

- **USER_SYS_PRIVS, ALL_SYS_PRIVILEGES** Displays information about object privileges on objects owned by the user or available to the current user, respectively

TIP
Object and system privileges govern your ability to perform every activity in the Oracle database. You'll learn more about these privileges in Chapter 4.

- **USER_SOURCE, ALL_SOURCE** Displays the source code for PL/SQL programs owned by the user or available to the current user, respectively

TIP
You'll learn more about PL/SQL programming in Chapter 5.

- **USER_TRIGGERS, ALL_TRIGGERS**   Displays information about triggers owned by the user or available to the current user, respectively

TIP
Triggers are special objects containing PL/SQL code that executes whenever a specified action takes place. You'll learn more about triggers in Chapter 5.

- **ROLE_TAB_PRIVS, ROLE_SYS_PRIVS, ROLE_ROLE_PRIVS**   Displays information about object privileges, system privileges, or roles granted to roles in the database, respectively.

TIP
These role-related views bend the general rule on dictionary view names somewhat. We'll discuss roles in more detail in Chapter 4.

A Look at the Views Themselves

Views do not actually contain any data—they are merely `select` statements stored as objects in Oracle. Every time you refer to a view in your own queries, Oracle dynamically executes the view's underlying `select` statement to obtain the contents of that view. Dictionary view definitions can be quite complex. So that you can appreciate this hidden complexity, the following code block shows you the definition of the ALL_TABLES view in Oracle. Because this view contains a column called TEXT that is defined as the LONG datatype, we have to do a little extra formatting via the `set long 9999` command to ensure that we'll see the output appropriately. Don't worry if you don't understand the structure of this view—you won't need to know the meanings of these columns for OCP Exam 1:

```
SQL> SET LONG 9999;
SQL> SELECT text FROM all_views WHERE view_name = 'ALL_TABLES';
TEXT
----------------------------------------
select u.name, o.name, ts.name, co.name,
t.pctfree$, t.pctused$,
t.initrans, t.maxtrans,
s.iniexts * ts.blocksize, s.extsize * ts.blocksize,
s.minexts, s.maxexts, s.extpct,
decode(s.lists, 0, 1, s.lists), decode(s.groups, 0, 1, s.groups),
decode(bitand(t.modified,1), 0, 'Y', 1, 'N', '?'),
t.rowcnt, t.blkcnt, t.empcnt, t.avgspc, t.chncnt, t.avgrln,
lpad(decode(t.spare1, 0, '1', 1, 'DEFAULT', to_char(t.spare1)), 10),
```

```
lpad(decode(mod(t.spare2, 65536), 0, '1', 1, 'DEFAULT',
to_char(mod(t.spare2, 65536))), 10),
lpad(decode(floor(t.spare2 / 65536), 0, 'N', 1, 'Y', '?'), 5),
decode(bitand(t.modified, 6), 0, 'ENABLED', 'DISABLED')
from sys.user$ u, sys.ts$ ts, sys.seg$ s,
 sys.obj$ co, sys.tab$ t, sys.obj$ o
where o.owner# = u.user#
and o.obj# = t.obj#
and t.clu# = co.obj# (+)
and t.ts# = ts.ts#
and t.file# = s.file# (+)
and t.block# = s.block# (+)
and (o.owner# = userenv('SCHEMAID')
or o.obj# in
(select oa.obj#
from sys.objauth$ oa
where grantee# in ( select kzsrorol from x$kzsro))
or /* user has system privileges */
exists (select null from v$enabledprivs
where priv_number in (-45 /* LOCK ANY TABLE */,
-47 /* SELECT ANY TABLE */,
-48 /* INSERT ANY TABLE */,
-49 /* UPDATE ANY TABLE */,
-50 /* DELETE ANY TABLE */)))
```

TIP
If you want to obtain a full listing of all data dictionary views available in Oracle, you can execute select * from DICTIONARY, *and Oracle will list all the dictionary views for you. Comments on the use of each dictionary view are offered in DICTIONARY as well. Some objects in Oracle that are synonymous with DICTIONARY are DICT, CATALOG, and CAT.*

For Review

1. Know what the data dictionary is. Be sure you can distinguish between dictionary views and the SYS-owned tables underlying those views.

2. Understand how to identify the topic and scope of a dictionary view based on the name of that view. Also, be sure you can identify all the views defined in this discussion.

3. Be sure you can identify the data dictionary views that will list all the dictionary views available in the Oracle database.

Exercises

1. **You want to list all the indexed columns for objects you own in the Oracle database. Which of the following views would you use?**

   A. USER_TAB_COLUMNS

   B. ALL_TAB_COLUMNS

   C. USER_IND_COLUMNS

   D. ALL_IND_COLUMNS

2. **You are identifying dictionary objects in the Oracle database. Which of the following is a view in the data dictionary?**

   A. V$DATABASE

   B. DBA_TABLES

   C. SYS.AUD$

   D. EMP

3. **This is the user who owns all the data dictionary objects in Oracle:**

   _____

4. **This is an object you can query to obtain a listing of all data dictionary objects in Oracle:** _____

Answer Key

1. C. 2. B. 3. SYS. 4. CATALOG, CAT, DICTIONARY, or DICT.

Querying the Data Dictionary

We'll now look at some examples of querying the dictionary so you can better understand how useful the data dictionary is in Oracle. (For the purposes of this section, the ALL_ views will be used, except where noted.) Recall that you can use the describe command on data dictionary views, just as if they were tables. The following code block shows what happens when you do so:

```
SQL> describe all_source
 Name                       Null?    Type
 ----------------------     -------- ----------------
 OWNER                      NOT NULL VARCHAR2(30)
```

```
NAME                       NOT NULL VARCHAR2(30)
TYPE                                VARCHAR2(12)
LINE                       NOT NULL NUMBER
TEXT                                VARCHAR2(4000)
```

The ALL_INDEXES view contains information about the indexes on tables that are available to the user. Some of the information listed in this view details the features of the index, such as whether all values in the indexed column are unique. Other information in the view identifies the storage parameters of the index and where the index is stored. Here's an example:

```
SQL> column owner format a10
SQL> column index_name format a15
SQL> column table_name format a12
SQL> column uniqueness format a10
SQL> select owner, index_name, table_name, uniqueness
  2  from all_indexes
  3  where owner = 'SCOTT';
OWNER      INDEX_NAME       TABLE_NAME   UNIQUENESS
---------- ---------------- ------------ ----------
SCOTT      PK_01            EXAMPLE_1    UNIQUE
SCOTT      SYS_C00905       DEPARTMENT   UNIQUE
SCOTT      UK_EMPLOYEE_01   EMPLOYEE     UNIQUE
```

TIP
For those of you following along on your own database, I've shown some useful formatting commands for cleaning up the output from these queries.

The next view is the ALL_USERS view. This view is used to give the current user of the database more information about all users known to the Oracle database:

```
SQL> select * from all_users;
USERNAME                          USER_ID CREATED
----------------------------- --------- ---------
SYS                                 0 23-JUN-99
SYSTEM                              5 23-JUN-99
OUTLN                              11 23-JUN-99
DBSNMP                             18 23-JUN-99
AURORA$ORB$UNAUTHENTICATED         23 23-JUN-99
JASON                              27 18-JUL-00
STUDENT2                           46 30-OCT-00
STUDENT1                           45 30-OCT-00
SPANKY                             43 30-OCT-00
```

```
JASON2                           48 31-OCT-00
SCOTT                            52 19-MAR-01
JASON3                           49 16-NOV-00
JASON10                          50 18-NOV-00
GIANT                            51 08-DEC-00
```

Querying Dictionary Views for Constraints

Here's a trickier example. In keeping with our work on constraints in this chapter, the next few views are related to constraints. Let's look at combining the contents of two views: ALL_CONSTRAINTS and ALL_CONS_COLUMNS. The ALL_CONSTRAINTS view is used to display information about the constraints that have been defined in the database, while ALL_CONS_COLUMNS displays all columns in integrity constraints in Oracle. Consider the following situation. Say we can't remember whether we have followed the book's advice for naming shared columns in multiple tables the same name. Is this a problem? Not with the Oracle data dictionary on hand! We can still determine the referenced column using ALL_CONSTRAINTS and ALL_CONS_COLUMNS, as I've shown in the following block:

```
SQL> column table_name format a12
SQL> column column_name format a12
  SQL> select a.table_name, b.column_name, c.table_name, c.column_name
    2  from all_constraints a, all_cons_columns b, all_cons_columns c
    3  where a.constraint_name = b.constraint_name
    4  and a.r_constraint_name = c.constraint_name;
TABLE_NAME    COLUMN_NAME          TABLE_NAME    COLUMN_NAME
------------  -------------------  ------------  --------------

EMPLOYEE      DEPARTMENT_NUM       DEPARTMENT    DEPARTMENT_NUM
```

Using Other Dictionary Views

Similar information to the contents of ALL_CONS_COLUMNS can be found in ALL_IND_COLUMNS. However, the dictionary view ALL_IND_COLUMNS will contain columns used in constraint-related indexes, as well as columns used in other types of indexes. Check out the following code block:

```
SQL> create index ix_employee_01 on employee (lastname);
Index created.
SQL> select index_name, table_name, column_name, column_position
  2  from all_ind_columns
  3  where table_name = 'EMPLOYEE';
INDEX_NAME      TABLE_NAME    COLUMN_NAME          COLUMN_POSITION
--------------  ------------  -------------------  ---------------
PK_EMPLOYEE_01  EMPLOYEE      EMPID                              1
UK_EMPLOYEE_01  EMPLOYEE      GOVT_ID                            1
IX_EMPLOYEE_01  EMPLOYEE      LASTNAME                           1
```

TIP
You'll learn more about indexes in Chapter 4.

For Review

Be sure you can develop queries against dictionary views. Remember, any query techniques you learned in Chapters 1 and 2 on tables can be applied to dictionary views.

Exercises

1. **Use the following code block to answer this question:**

```
TEXT
---------------------------------------------
declare
  x varchar2(10);
begin
  x := 'hello world';
  dbms_output.put_line(x);
end;
```

A query on which of the following dictionary views could have produced this output?

A. ALL_ERRORS

B. ALL_SOURCE

C. ALL_VIEWS

D. ALL_TRIGGERS

2. **Use the following code block to answer this question:**

```
SQL> select text from all_views where view_name =
  2  'DBA_TABLES';
TEXT
----------------------------------------------------------------

select u.name, o.name,
       decode(bitand(t.property, 4194400), 0, ts.name, null),
```

Which of the following choices identifies a formatting command that can be used for displaying the rest of the output?

A. set long 9999

B. column text format a9999

C. `set long 50`

D. `column text format a50`

3. **To identify some aspects about all users in the database, you would use this view:** _____

Answer Key

1. B. **2.** A. **3.** ALL_USERS.

Manipulating Oracle Data

This section covers the following topics related to manipulating Oracle data:

- Adding new rows to a table

- Making changes to existing row data

- Deleting data from the Oracle database

- The importance of transaction control

I've shown some data-manipulation operations from time to time. Every time I have done so, I've promised to explain what these statements meant later. Well, now is my chance. This section will introduce you to all forms of data-change manipulation. The three types of data-change manipulation in the Oracle database are updating, deleting, and inserting data. These statements are collectively known as the *data-manipulation language* of Oracle, or *DML* for short. We'll also look at *transaction processing*, which is a mechanism that the Oracle database provides in order to facilitate the act of changing data. Without transaction-processing mechanisms, Oracle cannot guarantee that users won't overwrite one another's changes in midprocess or select data that is in the process of being changed by another user.

Adding New Rows to a Table

The first data-change manipulation operation that will be discussed is the act of inserting new rows into a table. Once a table is created, there is no data in the table, unless the table is created and populated by rows selected from another table. Even in this case, the data must come from somewhere. This "somewhere" is from users who enter data into the table via `insert` statements. An `insert` statement has a different syntax from a `select` statement. The general syntax for an `insert` statement is listed in the following code block, which defines several rows to be added to the EMPLOYEE table:

```
SQL> desc employee
 Name                            Null?     Type
 ------------------------------- --------  -------------
 EMPID                           NOT NULL  VARCHAR2(5)
 LASTNAME                        NOT NULL  VARCHAR2(25)
 FIRSTNAME                                 VARCHAR2(25)
 SALARY                                    NUMBER(10,4)
 HIRE_DATE                                 DATE
 DEPT                                      VARCHAR2(10)
SQL>   insert into employee (empid, lastname, firstname,
  2     salary, dept, hire_date)
  3   values ('39334','SMITH','GINA',75000, null, '15-MAR-97');
1 row created.
SQL> insert into employee (empid, lastname, firstname, salary,
  2   dept, hire_date)
  3   values ('49539','LEE','QIAN',90000, '504A', '25-MAY-99');
1 row created.
SQL> insert into employee (empid, lastname, firstname, salary,
  2   dept, hire_date)
  3   values ('60403','HARPER','ROD',45000, '504A', '30-APR-79');
1 row created.
```

TIP

If you want to follow along on your Oracle database, remember that we've created several different versions of EMPLOYEE in the earlier discussion about constraints. Therefore, you need to ensure that your version of the EMPLOYEE table contains all the columns listed in the preceding describe *statement, using the appropriate* alter table *statements, before inserting data into your table.*

The preceding insert statement has two parts. In the first part, the table to receive the inserted row is defined, along with the columns of the table that will have the column values inserted into them. The second portion of the statement defines the actual data values for the row to be added. This latter portion of the statement is denoted by the values keyword.

Oracle is capable of handling several variations on the insert statement. For example, the user generally only needs to define explicit columns of the table when data is not going to be inserted in all columns of the table. Let's look at an example where we don't identify explicit columns because we intend to define values for every column listed in the EMPLOYEE table:

```
SQL> insert into employee values
  2  ('02039','WALLA','RAJENDRA',60000,'01-JAN-96','604B');
1 row created.
SQL> insert into employee values
  2  ('49392','SPANKY','STACY',100000,null,'604B');
1 row created.
```

TIP
Notice how we used the NULL to insert a NULL value for HIRE_DATE in the row entry for user SPANKY.

How does Oracle know which column to populate with what data? The answer is position. Position can matter in tables on the Oracle database; the position of the data in the `insert` statement must correspond to the position of the columns in the table. The user can determine the position of each column in a table by using the `describe` command or the output from the USER_TAB_COLUMNS dictionary view using COLUMN_ID to indicate position as part of the `order by` clause. The order in which the columns are listed in the output from the `describe` command is the same order in which values should be placed to insert data into the table without explicitly naming the columns of the table. Take a look for yourself;

```
SQL> select column_name, column_id
  2  from user_tab_columns
  3  where table_name = 'EMPLOYEE'
  4  order by column_id;
COLUMN_NAME               COLUMN_ID
------------------------  ----------
EMPID                             1
LASTNAME                          2
FIRSTNAME                         3
SALARY                            4
HIRE_DATE                         5
DEPT                              6
SQL> describe employee
 Name                              Null?     Type
 --------------------------------  --------  ------------
 EMPID                             NOT NULL  VARCHAR2(5)
 LASTNAME                          NOT NULL  VARCHAR2(25)
 FIRSTNAME                                   VARCHAR2(25)
 SALARY                                      NUMBER(10,4)
 HIRE_DATE                                   DATE
 DEPT                                        VARCHAR2(10)
```

Another variation on the `insert` theme is the option to populate a table using data obtained from other tables using a `select` statement. This method of populating table data is similar to the method used by the `create table as select` statement. In this case, the `values` clause can be omitted entirely. However, the rules regarding column position of the inserted data still apply in this situation, meaning that if the user can select data for all columns of the table having data inserted into it, the user need not name the columns in the `insert into` clause. Here's an example:

```
SQL> insert into scott.employee (select * from master.employee);
```

TIP
In order to put data into a table, a special privilege must be granted from the table owner to the user who needs to perform the `insert` operation. A more complete discussion of object privileges will appear in Chapter 4.

For Review

Know the statement used to place new data into an Oracle table. Know how to code several derivatives of this statement as well.

Exercises

1. **You are adding data to the PRODUCTS table in an Oracle database. This table contains three columns: PRODUCT_NAME, PRODUCT_TYPE, and PRICE. Which of the following choices does not identify a well-formed `insert` statement on this table?**

   A. `insert into products (product_name, product_type, price) ('BARNEY DOLL','TOYS',49.99);`

   B. `insert into products (product_name, product_type, price) values ('BARNEY DOLL','TOYS',49.99);`

   C. `insert into products values ('BARNEY DOLL','TOYS',49.99);`

   D. `insert into products (select product_name, product_type, price from master_products);`

2. **Examine the following statement:**

```
insert into SALES values ('BARNEY
DOLL','31-MAR-93',29483854.39);
```

Which of the following choices identifies a statement you cannot use to verify whether the correct information is placed into the correct columns?

A. `select * from sales;`

B. `select column_name, column_id from all_tab_columns where table_name = 'SALES';`

C. `describe sales`

D. `select column_name, column_position from all_ind_columns where table_name = 'SALES';`

3. **The absence of a values clause in an insert statement indicates that the insert statement contains a _____.**

Answer Key

1. A. **2.** D. **3.** subquery.

Making Changes to Existing Row Data

Often, the rows in a table will need to be changed. In order to make those changes, the update statement can be used. Updates can be made to any row in a database, except in two cases. One case is where you don't have enough access privileges to update the data. You will learn more about access privileges in Chapter 4. The other case is where some other user on the database is making changes to the row you want to change. You will learn more about transaction control at the end of this section in the discussion titled "The Importance of Transaction Control." Otherwise, you can change data by issuing an update statement, as shown here:

```
SQL> update employee set salary = 99000
  2  where lastname = 'SPANKY';
1 row updated.
```

The typical update statement has three clauses:

- An update clause, where the table that will be updated is named.

- A set clause, where all columns whose values will be changed are named and the new values assigned.

■ The `where` clause (optional), which lists one or more comparison operations to determine which rows Oracle will update. Omitting the `where` clause in an `update` statement has the effect of applying the data change to every row that presently exists in the table.

Advanced Data Changes in Oracle

You can modify the values in more than one column using a single `update` statement, and you can also use subqueries in `update` statements. The following code block illustrates examples of both these statements:

```
SQL> update employee
  2   set firstname = 'ATHENA', lastname = 'BAMBINA'
  3   where empid = '49392';
1 row updated.
SQL> update employee
  2    set lastname = (select ename from emp where empno = 7844)
  3   where empid = '49392';
1 row updated.
```

For Review

Know how to use `update` statements to change data in an Oracle table. Understand the two mandatory clauses, `update` and `set`, and the optional clause, `where`.

Exercises

1. **You are updating data in an Oracle table. Which of the following statements best describes how you may use the `where` clause in an `update` statement?**

   A. You may use whatever expressions are appropriate, except for single-row functions.

   B. You may use whatever expressions are appropriate, except for subqueries.

   C. You may use whatever expressions are appropriate, except for `in` expressions.

   D. You may use whatever expressions are appropriate with no limitations.

2. **You are updating data in an Oracle table. Which of the following choices identifies the keyword that indicates the columns you would like to update the values of?**

A. update

B. set

C. where

D. order by

Answer Key
1. D. 2. D.

Deleting Data from the Oracle Database

The removal of data from a database is as much a fact of life as putting the data
there in the first place. The delete statement in SQL*Plus is used to remove
database rows from tables. The syntax for the delete statement is detailed in the
following code block. Note that in this example, there is no way to delete data from
selected columns in a row in the table; this act is accomplished with the update
statement, with the columns that are to be "deleted" being set to NULL by the
update statement:

```
SQL> delete from employee where lastname = 'TURNER';
1 row deleted.
```

As in the case with database updates, delete statements use the where clause
to help determine which rows are meant to be removed. Like an update or
select statement, the where clause in a delete statement can contain any type
of comparison operation, range operation, subquery, or any other operation
acceptable for a where clause. Like an update statement, if the where clause is
left off the delete statement, the deletion will be applied to all rows in the table.

TIP
*Data deletion should be undertaken with care.
It can be costly to replace data that has been
inappropriately deleted from the database, which is
why the privilege of deleting information should
only be given out to those users who really should
be able to delete records from a table.*

For Review

Be sure you understand how to use `delete` statements to remove data from an Oracle table. Also, understand how to use the mandatory clause, `delete from`, and the optional clause, `where`.

Exercises

1. This is the clause in a `delete` statement that identifies which rows to remove: _____

2. You would like to delete data in the PROFITS column of the SALES table for all rows where PRODUCT_TYPE is set to 'TOYS'. Which of the following choices identifies how to accomplish this task?

   A. `delete from sales where product_type = 'TOYS';`

   B. `delete profits from sales where product_type = 'TOYS';`

   C. `update sales set profits = NULL where product_type = 'TOYS';`

   D. `delete from sales;`

Answer Key

1. `where`. **2.** C.

The Importance of Transaction Control

We've made a great deal of changes to our Oracle database over the last three chapters. Some might say we've even made quite a mess of our data. *However, not a single one of those changes was actually saved to the database, and none are visible to any other user on your database besides you.* How can that be, you ask? It's because of the magic of Oracle transaction control! One of the great benefits Oracle provides is the ability to make changes and then decide later whether we want to save or discard them. Oracle allows you to execute a series of data-change statements together as one logical unit of work, called a *transaction*, that's terminated when you decide to save or discard the work. A transaction begins with your first executable SQL statement.

Underlying Transaction Controls

Transaction processing consists of a set of controls that allow a user issuing an `insert`, `update`, or `delete` statement to declare a beginning to the series of data-change statements he or she will issue. When the user has finished making the changes to the database, the user can save the data to the database by explicitly ending the transaction. Alternatively, if a mistake is made at any point during the transaction, the user can have the database discard the changes made to the database in favor of the way the data existed before the transaction.

Transactions are created with the use of two different elements in the Oracle database. The first element is the set of commands that define the beginning, breakpoint, and end of a transaction. The second element is the special locking mechanisms designed to prevent more than one user at a time from making a change to row information in a database. Locks will be discussed after the transaction control commands are defined. The commands that define transactions are as follows:

- **set transaction**   Initiates the beginning of a transaction and sets key features. This command is optional. A transaction will be started automatically when you start SQL*Plus, commit the previous transaction, or roll back the previous transaction.

- **commit**   Ends the current transaction by saving database changes and starts a new transaction.

- **rollback**   Ends the current transaction by discarding database changes and starts a new transaction.

- **savepoint**   Defines breakpoints for the transaction to allow partial rollbacks.

set transaction

This command can be used to define the beginning of a transaction. If any change is made to the database after the `set transaction` command is issued but before the transaction is ended, all changes made will be considered part of that transaction. The `set transaction` statement is not required, because a transaction begins under the following circumstances:

- As soon as you log into Oracle via SQL*Plus and execute the first command

- Immediately after issuing a `rollback` or `commit` statement to end a transaction

- When the user exits

■ When the system crashes

■ When a data control language command such as `alter database` is issued

By default, a transaction will allow both read and write access unless you override this default by issuing `set transaction read only`. You can set the transaction isolation level with `set transaction` as well. The `set transaction isolation level serializable` command specifies serializable transaction isolation mode as defined in SQL92. If a serializable transaction contains data manipulation language (DML) that attempts to update any resource that may have been updated in a transaction uncommitted at the start of the serializable transaction, the DML statement fails. The `set transaction isolation level read committed` command is the default Oracle transaction behavior. If the transaction contains DML that requires row locks held by another transaction, the DML statement waits until the row locks are released. Here's an example:

```
SQL> SET TRANSACTION READ ONLY;
Transaction set.
SQL> rollback;
Rollback complete.
SQL> SET TRANSACTION READ WRITE;
Transaction set.
SQL> rollback;
Rollback complete.
SQL> SET TRANSACTION ISOLATION LEVEL SERIALIZABLE;
Transaction set.
SQL> rollback;
Rollback complete.
SQL> SET TRANSACTION ISOLATION LEVEL READ COMMITTED;
Transaction set.
SQL> rollback;
Rollback complete.
```

TIP
A `set transaction` command can appear only as the first statement in the beginning of a transaction. Therefore, we must explicitly end each transaction with the `rollback` command before starting another with the `set transaction` command.

commit

The commit statement in transaction processing represents the point in time when the user has made all the changes he or she wants to have logically grouped together, and because no mistakes have been made, the user is ready to save the work. The work keyword is an extraneous word in the commit syntax that is designed for readability. Issuing a commit statement also implicitly begins a new transaction on the database because it closes the current transaction and starts a new one. It is important also to understand that an implicit commit occurs on the database when a user exits SQL*Plus or issues a data-definition language (DDL) command such as a create table statement, used to create a database object, or an alter table statement, used to alter a database object. Here's an example:

```
SQL> COMMIT;
Commit complete.
SQL> COMMIT WORK;
Commit complete.
```

rollback

If you have at any point issued a data-change statement you don't want, you can discard the changes made to the database with the use of the rollback statement. After the rollback command is issued, a new transaction is started implicitly by the database session. In addition to rollbacks executed when the rollback statement is issued, there are implicit rollback statements conducted when a statement fails for any reason or if the user cancels a statement with the CTRL-C cancel command. Here's an example:

```
SQL> ROLLBACK;
Rollback complete.
SQL> ROLLBACK WORK;
Rollback complete.
```

savepoint

In some cases involving long transactions or transactions that involve many data changes, you may not want to scrap all your changes simply because the last statement issued contains unwanted changes. Savepoints are special operations that allow you to divide the work of a transaction into different segments. You can execute rollbacks to the savepoint only, leaving prior changes intact. Savepoints are great when part of the transaction needs to be recovered in an uncommitted transaction.

At the point the `rollback to savepoint so_far_so_good` statement completes in the following code block, only changes made before the savepoint was defined are kept when the `commit` statement is issued:

```
SQL> UPDATE products
  2   SET quantity = 55
  3   WHERE product# = 59495;
1 row updated.
SQL> SAVEPOINT so_far_so_good;
Savepoint created.
SQL> UPDATE spanky.products
  2   SET quantity = 504;
1 row updated.
SQL> ROLLBACK TO SAVEPOINT so_far_so_good;
Rollback complete.
SQL> COMMIT;
Commit complete.
SQL> select quantity from spanky.products
  2   where product# = 59495;
QUANTITY
--------
      55
```

Locks

The final aspect of the Oracle database that allows the user to employ transaction processing is the lock, the mechanism by which Oracle prevents data from being changed by more than one user at a time. There are several different types of locks, each with its own level of scope. Locks available on a database are categorized into table-level locks and row-level locks.

A table-level lock allows only the user holding the lock to change any piece of row data in the table, during which time no other users can make changes anywhere on the table. A table lock can be held in any of several modes: row share (RS), row exclusive (RX), share (S), share row exclusive (SRX), and exclusive (X). The restrictiveness of a table lock's mode determines the modes in which other table locks on the same table can be obtained and held.

A row-level lock is one that allows the user the exclusive ability to change data in one or more rows of the table. However, any row in the table that is not held by the row-level lock can be changed by another user.

TIP
An update *statement acquires a special row-level lock called a "row-exclusive" lock, which means that for the period of time the* update *statement is executing, no other user in the database can view or change the data in the row. The same goes for* delete *or* insert *operations. Another* update *statement—the* select for update *statement—acquires a more lenient lock called the "share row" lock. This lock means that for the period of time the* update *statement is changing the data in the rows of the table, no other user may change that row, but users may look at the data in the row as it changes.*

For Review

1. Be sure you can identify what a transaction is. Know when a transaction begins and when it ends. Be able to use the set transaction, savepoint, commit, and rollback keywords with respect to transaction processing.

2. Know how locks support transactions by preventing other users from seeing the data in your table.

Exercises

1. You have finished your transaction and would like to issue another. Which of the following statements can only appear at the very beginning of the transaction and sets up many characteristics about the transaction?

A. set transaction

B. rollback

C. savepoint

D. commit

2. **You are engaged in transaction processing on your Oracle database. Which command can you use to define logical breakpoints within the transaction?**

   A. `set transaction`

   B. `rollback`

   C. `savepoint`

   D. `commit`

3. **This is the database component that prevents other users from changing data that you are in the process of changing:** _____

Answer Key

1. A. 2. C. 3. Lock.

Chapter Summary

We covered a great deal of ground in this chapter. At the beginning, we discussed how to create tables in the Oracle database. We talked about how to alter our table definitions as well. After covering how to define and change the definition of tables with respect to columns, we spent a great deal of time discussing database constraints. You learned about the five different types of database constraints, as well as how to create them when initially defining the table. You also learned how to create constraints after the fact using the `alter table` command. We then moved on to discuss indexes that can be created with constraints. We covered constraint deferability and how to correct problems when the data in a table column might violate the constraint on that column—two complex topics to know for OCP. After constraints, we discussed how to use the Oracle data dictionary. Finally, we wrapped up the chapter with coverage of how to manipulate data with `insert`, `update`, and `delete` statements, as well as how to engage in Oracle transaction processing.

Two-Minute Drill

- The basic types of data relationships in Oracle include primary keys and functional dependency within a table, as well as foreign-key constraints from one table to another.

- A relational database is composed of objects that store data, objects that manage access to data, and objects that improve performance when accessing data.

- Within database planning, it is necessary to create an entity-relationship diagram that acts as a visual representation of the business process being modeled. The diagram consists of people, places, things, and ideas, all called *entities*, which are related to one another by activities or process flows, called *relationships*.

- Once an entity-relationship diagram has been created for an application, it must be translated into a logical data model. The logical data model is a collection of tables that represent entities and referential-integrity constraints that represent relationships.

- A table can be created with five different types of integrity constraints: PRIMARY KEY, FOREIGN KEY, UNIQUE, NOT NULL, and CHECK.

- Referential integrity often creates a parent/child relationship between two tables—the parent being the referenced table and the child being the referring table. Often, a naming convention that requires child objects to adopt and extend the name of the parent table is useful in identifying these relationships.

- The datatypes available for creating columns in tables are CHAR, VARCHAR2, NUMBER, DATE, RAW, LONG, LONG RAW, ROWID, BLOB, CLOB, NCLOB, and BFILE.

- A table column can be added or modified with the alter table statement.

- Columns can be added with little difficulty if they are nullable, using the alter table add (*column_name datatype*) statement. If a NOT NULL constraint is desired, add the column, populate the column with data, and then add the NOT NULL constraint separately.

- Column datatype size can be increased with no difficulty by using the alter table modify (*column_name datatype*) statement. Column size can be decreased, or the datatype can be changed, only if the column contains NULL for all rows.

■ Constraints can be added to a column only if the column already contains values that will not violate the added constraint.

■ PRIMARY KEY constraints can be added with a table constraint definition by using the `alter table add (constraint constraint_name primary key (column_name))` statement or with a column constraint definition by using the `alter table modify (column_name constraint constraint_name primary key)` statement.

■ UNIQUE constraints can be added with a table constraint definition by using the `alter table add (constraint constraint_name unique (column_name))` statement or with a column constraint definition by using the `alter table modify (column_name constraint constraint_name unique)` statement.

■ FOREIGN KEY constraints can be added with a table constraint definition by using the `alter table add (constraint constraint_name foreign key (column_name) references OWNER.TABLE (column_name) [on delete cascade])` statement or with a column constraint definition by using the `alter table modify (column_name constraint constraint_name references OWNER.TABLE (column_name) [on delete cascade])` statement.

■ CHECK constraints can be added with a table constraint definition by using the `alter table add (constraint constraint_name check (check_condition))` statement or with a column constraint definition by using the `alter table modify (column_name constraint constraint_name check (check_condition))` statement.

■ The `check` condition cannot contain subqueries, references to certain keywords (such as `user`, `sysdate`, and `rowid`), or any pseudocolumns.

■ NOT NULL constraints can be added with a column constraint definition by using the `alter table modify (column_name NOT NULL)` statement.

■ A named PRIMARY KEY, UNIQUE, CHECK, or FOREIGN KEY constraint can be dropped with the `alter table drop constraint constraint_name` statement. A NOT NULL constraint is dropped using the `alter table modify (column_name NULL)` statement.

■ If a constraint that created an index automatically (such as a `primary key` or UNIQUE constraint) is dropped, the corresponding index is also dropped.

■ If the table is dropped, all constraints, triggers, and indexes created for the table are also dropped.

■ Removing all data from a table is best accomplished with the `truncate` command rather than the `delete from table_name` statement, because `truncate` will reset the table's high-water mark and deallocate all the table's storage quickly, thus improving performance on `select count( )` statements issued after the truncation.

■ An object name can be changed with the `rename` statement or with the use of synonyms.

■ Indexes are created automatically in conjunction with `PRIMARY KEY` and `UNIQUE` constraints. These indexes are named after the constraint name given to the constraint in the definition of the table.

■ Tables are created without any data in them, except for tables created with the `create table as select` statement. These tables are created and prepopulated with data from another table.

■ Information is available in the Oracle database to help users, developers, and DBAs know what objects exist in the Oracle database. This information is in the Oracle data dictionary.

■ To find the positional order of columns in a table, or what columns there are in a table at all, the user can issue a `describe` command on that table. The Oracle data dictionary will then list all columns in the table being described.

■ Data dictionary views on database objects are divided into three categories based on the scope of user visibility: USER_, for what is owned by the user; ALL_, for all that can be seen by the user; and DBA_, for all that exists in the database, whether the user can see it or not.

■ New rows are put into a table with the `insert` statement. The user issuing the `insert` statement can insert one row at a time with one statement or can perform a mass `insert` operation with `insert into table_name (select . . .)`.

■ Existing rows in a database table can be modified using the `update` statement. The `update` statement contains a `where` clause similar in function to the `where` clause of `select` statements.

■ Existing rows in a table can be deleted using the `delete` statement. The `delete` statement also contains a `where` clause similar in function to the `where` clause in `update` and `select` statements.

■ Transaction processing controls the change of data in an Oracle database.

■ Transaction controls include commands that identify the beginning, breakpoint, and end of a transaction, as well as the locking mechanisms that prevent more than one user at a time from making changes in the database.

Fill-in-the-Blank Questions

1. This constraint is useful for verifying data entered for a column against a static list of values identified as part of the table definition: _____

2. This transaction-processing command identifies a logical break within the transaction, not an end to the current transaction: _____

3. This datatype is used for identifying each row uniquely in the table: _____

4. All instantiations of this object used for storing data for later query access for the duration of a session or transaction have this scope of availability: _____

5. This five-word command specifies that the transaction should execute every DML statement serially and in isolation, as defined in SQL92: _____

6. This keyword for constraint enablement specifies that Oracle will not check to see whether the data conforms to the constraint until the user commits the transaction: _____

7. This view in Oracle is used for listing every table available to you as the current user: _____

8. This database object in Oracle, created when the primary key is defined, will be dropped when the table is dropped: _____

Chapter Questions

1. **Which of the following integrity constraints automatically create an index when defined? (Choose two.)**

    A. Foreign keys

    B. Unique constraints

    C. not NULL constraints

    D. Primary keys

2. **Which of the following dictionary views gives information about the position of a column in a primary key?**

    A. ALL_PRIMARY_KEYS

    B. USER_CONSTRAINTS

    C. ALL_IND_COLUMNS

    D. ALL_TABLES

3. **Developer ANJU executes the following statement: `create table ANIMALS as select * from MASTER.ANIMALS;`. What is the effect of this statement?**

    A. A table named ANIMALS will be created in the MASTER schema with the same data as the ANIMALS table owned by ANJU.

    B. A table named ANJU will be created in the ANIMALS schema with the same data as the ANIMALS table owned by MASTER.

    C. A table named ANIMALS will be created in the ANJU schema with the same data as the ANIMALS table owned by MASTER.

    D. A table named MASTER will be created in the ANIMALS schema with the same data as the ANJU table owned by ANIMALS.

4. **User JANKO would like to insert a row into the EMPLOYEE table. The table has three columns: EMPID, LASTNAME, and SALARY. This user would like to enter data for EMPID 59694, LASTNAME Harris, but no salary. Which statement would work best?**

    A. `insert into EMPLOYEE values (59694,'HARRIS', NULL);`

    B. `insert into EMPLOYEE values (59694,'HARRIS');`

    C. `insert into EMPLOYEE (EMPID, LASTNAME, SALARY) values (59694,'HARRIS');`

    D. `insert into EMPLOYEE (select 59694 from 'HARRIS');`

5. **No relationship officially exists between two tables. Which of the following choices is the strongest indicator that a parent/child relationship exists between these tables?**

    A. The two tables in the database are named VOUCHER and VOUCHER_ITEM, respectively.

    B. The two tables in the database are named EMPLOYEE and PRODUCTS, respectively.

    C. The two tables in the database were created on the same day.

    D. The two tables in the database contain none of the same columns.

6. **Which of the following are valid database datatypes in Oracle? (Choose three.)**

   A. CHAR

   B. VARCHAR2

   C. BOOLEAN

   D. NUMBER

7. **Omitting the `where` clause from a `delete` statement has which of the following effects?**

   A. The `delete` statement will fail because there are no records to delete.

   B. The `delete` statement will prompt the user to enter criteria for the deletion.

   C. The `delete` statement will fail because of a syntax error.

   D. The `delete` statement will remove all records from the table.

8. **Which line of the following statements will produce an error?**

   A. `create table GOODS`

   B. `(GOODNO number,`

   C. `GOOD_NAME varchar2(20) check(GOOD_NAME in (select NAME from AVAIL_GOODS)),`

   D. `constraint PK_GOODS_01`

   E. `primary key (GOODNO));`

   F. There are no errors in this statement.

9. **The transaction control that prevents more than one user from updating data in a table is which of the following?**

   A. Lock

   B. Commit

   C. Rollback

   D. Savepoint

10. **You are adding columns to a table in Oracle. Which of the following choices indicates what you would do to increase the number of columns accepting NULL values in a table?**

    A. Use the `alter table` statement.

    B. Ensure that all column values are NULL for all rows.

    C. First, increase the size of adjacent column datatypes and then add the column.

    D. Add the column, populate the column, and then add the not NULL constraint.

11. **A user issues the statement `select count(*) from employee`. The query takes an inordinately long time and returns a count of zero. What is the most cost-effective solution to this problem?**

    A. Upgrade the hardware

    B. Truncate the table

    C. Upgrade the version of Oracle

    D. Delete the high-water mark

12. **You are creating some tables in your database as part of the logical data model. Which of the following constraints has an index associated with it that is generated automatically by Oracle?**

    A. Unique

    B. Foreign key

    C. CHECK

    D. not NULL

13. **Each of the following statements is true about referential integrity, except one. Which is it?**

    A. The referencing column in the child table must correspond to a primary key in the parent.

    B. All values in the referenced column in the parent table must be present in the referencing column in the child.

C. The datatype of the referenced column in the parent table must be identical to the referencing column in the child.

D. All values in the referencing column in the child table must be present in the referenced column in the parent.

14. You are managing constraints on a table in Oracle. Which of the following choices correctly identifies the limitations on check constraints?

A. Values must be obtained from a lookup table.

B. Values must be part of a fixed set defined by `create` or `alter table`.

C. Values must include reserved words, such as SYSDATE and USER.

D. The column cannot contain a NULL value.

Fill-in-the-Blank Answers

1. Check

2. `savepoint`

3. ROWID

4. Global temporary table

5. `set transaction isolation level serializable`

6. `novalidate`

7. ALL_TABLES

8. Index

Answers to Chapter Questions

1. B and D. Unique constraints and primary keys

Explanation   Every constraint that enforces uniqueness creates an index to assist in the process. The two integrity constraints that enforce uniqueness are unique constraints and primary keys. Other types of integrity constraints, like check, not NULL, and foreign keys, do not use indexes in any capacity for enforcing data integrity.

2. C. ALL_IND_COLUMNS

Explanation   This view is the only one listed that provides column positions in an index. Because a primary key creates an index, the index created by the primary key will be listed with all the other indexed data. Choice A is incorrect because no view exists in Oracle called PRIMARY_KEYS. Choice B is incorrect because although ALL_CONSTRAINTS lists information about the constraints in a database, it does not contain information about the index created by the primary key. Choice D is incorrect because ALL_TABLES contains no information related to the position of a column in an index.

   3. C. A table named ANIMALS will be created in the ANJU schema with the
      same data as the ANIMALS table owned by MASTER.

Explanation   This question requires you to look carefully at the `create table`
statement in the question and to know some things about table creation. First, a
table is always created in the schema of the user who created it. Second, because
the `create table as select` clause was used, choices B and D are both
incorrect because they identify the table being created as something other than
ANIMALS, among other things. Choice A identifies the schema into which the
ANIMALS table will be created as MASTER, which is incorrect for the reasons just
stated. Refer to the discussion of creating tables for more information.

   4. A. `insert into EMPLOYEE values (59694,'HARRIS', NULL);`

Explanation   This choice is acceptable because the positional criteria for not
specifying column order is met by the data in the `values` clause. When you would
like to specify that no data be inserted into a particular column, one method of
doing so is to insert a NULL. Choice B is incorrect because not all columns in the
table have values identified. When you're using positional references to populate
column data, values must be present for every column in the table. Otherwise, the
columns that will be populated should be named explicitly. Choice C is incorrect
because when a column is named for data insert in the `insert into` clause, a
value must definitely be specified in the `values` clause. Choice D is incorrect
because using the multiple-row `insert` option with a `select` statement is not
appropriate in this situation. Refer to the discussion of `insert` statements for more
information.

   5. A. The two tables in the database are named VOUCHER and
      VOUCHER_ITEM, respectively.

Explanation   This choice implies the use of a naming convention similar to the one
we discussed in this chapter—where tables with foreign key relationships have
similar names. Although there is no guarantee that these two tables are related, the
possibility is strongest in this case. Choice B implies the same naming convention,
but because the two tables' names are dissimilar, there is little likelihood that the
two tables are related in any way. Choice C is incorrect because the date a table is
created has absolutely no bearing on what function the table serves in the database.
Choice D is incorrect because two tables *cannot* be related if there are no common
columns between them. Refer to the discussion of creating tables using integrity
constraints, naming conventions, and data modeling.

6. A, B, and D. CHAR, VARCHAR2, and NUMBER

Explanation   BOOLEAN is the only invalid datatype in this listing. Although BOOLEAN is a valid datatype in PL/SQL, it is not a datatype available on the Oracle database, meaning that you cannot create a column in a table that uses the BOOLEAN datatype. Review the discussion of allowed datatypes in column definitions.

7. D. The `delete` statement will remove all records from the table.

Explanation   There is only one effect produced by leaving off the `where` clause from any statement that allows one—the requested operation is performed on all records in the table.

8. C. `GOOD_NAME varchar2(20) check(GOOD_NAME in (select NAME from AVAIL_GOODS)),`

Explanation   A check constraint cannot contain a reference to another table, nor can it reference a virtual column, such as ROWID or SYSDATE. The other lines of the `create table` statement contain the correct syntax.

9. A. Lock

Explanation   A *lock* is the mechanisms that prevents more than one user at a time from making changes to a database. All other options refer to the commands that are issued to mark the beginning, middle, and end of a transaction. Review the discussion of transaction controls.

10. A. Use the `alter table` statement.

Explanation   The `alter table` statement is the only choice offered that allows you to increase the number of columns per table. Choice B is incorrect because setting a column to all NULL values for all rows does simply that. Choice C is incorrect because increasing the adjacent column sizes simply increases the sizes of the columns, and choice D is incorrect because the listed steps outline how to add a column with a not NULL constraint—something not specified by the question.

11. B. Truncate the table.

Explanation   Choices A and C may work, but an upgrade of hardware and software will cost far more than truncating the table. Choice D is partly correct, because there will be some change required to the high-water mark. However, the change will reset the high-water mark, not eliminate it entirely, and the method used is to issue the `truncate table` command.

12. A. Unique

Explanation Only unique and primary-key constraints require Oracle to generate an index that supports or enforces the uniqueness of the column values. Foreign keys, CHECK constraints, and not NULL constraints do not require indexes. Therefore, choices B, C, and D are incorrect.

13. B. All values in the referenced column in the parent table must be present in the referencing column in the child.

Explanation Referential integrity is from child to parent, not vice versa. The parent table can have many values that are not present in child records, but the child record must correspond to something in the parent. Therefore, the correct answer, in this case, is choice B.

14. B. Values must be part of a fixed set defined by `create table` or `alter table`.

Explanation A check constraint may only use fixed expressions defined when you create or alter the table with the constraint definition. Reserved words such as SYSDATE and USER and values from a lookup table are not permitted, thus making choices A and C incorrect. Finally, NULL values in a column are constrained by not NULL constraints, a relatively unsophisticated form of check constraints. Therefore, choice D is incorrect.

4

Creating Other
Database Objects
in Oracle

n this chapter, you will learn about and demonstrate knowledge in the following areas:

- Creating views
- Other database objects
- Controlling user access

At this point, you should already know how to select data from tables, design database tables, create relationships between those tables, restrict data from entering the tables, and populate tables with data. These functions represent important cornerstones of functionality that Oracle can provide. However, the design of a database does not stop there. There are features in the Oracle architecture that can make certain data available to some users but not to others, speed access to data, and generate sequential numbers for primary keys or other purposes. There is also the issue of creating and managing users and their ability to access data. These are advanced database features of Oracle tested in the OCP Exam 1. The material in this chapter comprises 17 percent of the material covered on the exam.

Creating Views

This section covers the following topics concerning views:

- Creating simple views
- Creating views that enforce constraints
- Creating complex views
- Modifying and removing views

It has been said that the eyes are the windows to the soul. Although this may or may not be true, it is true that your eyes can be used to look at data in a table. In order to make sure the right eyes see the right data, however, some special "windows" on the data in a table can be created. These special windows are called *views*. Recall that we defined views in Chapter 3 as queries stored in Oracle that dynamically assemble data into a virtual table. You can treat this virtual table as though it is a real one, which is exactly what we did on the Oracle data dictionary views of the last chapter. To the person using the view, manipulating the data from the view is just like manipulating the data from a table. In some cases, it is even possible for the user to change data in a view as though the view *were* a table. Let's now explore the topic of creating, using, and managing views in more detail.

TIP

We are deviating somewhat from the Oracle8i DBA OCP Candidate Guide with respect to titles for the topic areas. Although the titles and organization of this content are different from the Candidate Guide, the content covers all the information you need to know for OCP.

Creating Simple Views

Views act like tables by allowing you to query them like tables. However, views are logical representations of data, whereas tables physically store data. Views do not actually store any data. That said, let's start by looking at the simplest example of a `create view` statement—the statement used for creating views in the Oracle database—and perform some simple table-like actions on the view we create. The `create view` statement is shown in bold in the following example:

```
SQL> create view emp_view as
  2  (select * from emp
  3  where job = 'ANALYST');
View created.
SQL> describe emp_view
 Name                           Null?    Type
 ------------------------------ -------- ------------
 EMPNO                          NOT NULL NUMBER(4)
 ENAME                                   VARCHAR2(10)
 JOB                                     VARCHAR2(9)
 MGR                                     NUMBER(4)
 HIREDATE                                DATE
 SAL                                     NUMBER(7,2)
 COMM                                    NUMBER(7,2)
 DEPTNO                                  NUMBER(2)
SQL> select empno, ename from emp_view;
    EMPNO ENAME
--------- ----------
     7788 SCOTT
     7902 FORD
```

Notice the two components of our basic `create view` statement. In the first part, we identify the name of the view we want Oracle to create. In the second part, we define, in parentheses, the query Oracle should use for obtaining data to populate our virtual table. The underlying table whose information is used as the basis for data in the view is sometimes called the *base table*. Views can even act as base tables for other views as well! Once the view is created, we can do anything with it that we might have done with the underlying table. Everything in our view, EMP_VIEW, looks just like the underlying EMP table, except for one small detail: EMP_VIEW only contains employee data for the analysts! Therefore, *a view can add extra security to data by allowing you to restrict data shown to users looking at the view instead of at the real table.*

Appropriately enough, the type of view we just created is known as a *simple view*. Oracle considers this a simple view because it uses data from only one table. Because views contain `select` statements, there are some things you should know about what sorts of `select` statements are allowed in simple views:

- Most any `select` statement on a single table you can issue from SQL*Plus can be used for creating a simple view. Basic queries on single tables in Oracle containing single-row operations such as `decode()`, `nvl()`, and so on, are permitted.

- Query operations containing `order by` clauses are also permitted, so long as the `order by` clause appears outside the parentheses. Here's an example of what I mean: `create view my_view as (select * from emp) order by empno`.

- Oracle also permits view queries to contain `group by` clauses, `connect by` clauses, and group functions such as `count ( )`, so long as each function has an alias.

- Oracle permits views containing the `distinct` keyword, using syntax similar to `create view my_view as (select distinct(job) as my_jobs from emp`.

Although references to more than one table are permitted in the queries used in `create view` commands, the view created is not a simple view. It is a complex view (sometimes called a *join view*). We'll talk more about those views in the next discussion.

TIP
You cannot create a view containing a for update clause.

Hierarchical Queries: A Brief Digression

A word of warning: read this section only if my point about views not allowing queries containing `connect by` clauses has piqued your interest about the type of query known in Oracle as a *hierarchical query*. This topic usually isn't tested on OCP. The hierarchical query can link together the table's rows into a hierarchy. Like most companies, the one whose employees are listed in EMP is a hierarchical one, where every employee reports to another employee all the way up to KING, the president of the company. There is a way to obtain a listing of all employees in that hierarchy using a hierarchical query such as this one:

```
SQL>  select empno, ename, job
  2   from emp
  3   connect by prior empno = mgr;
```

TIP
Like Shakespeare's Polonius, I believe brevity is the soul of wit. Therefore, I won't show the output of this query here because we are digressing from the heart of our topic—views and the OCP exam. However, if you find that you like hierarchical queries and want to play with them on your own time, the Oracle documentation has some interesting things to say about them. Good luck!

And Now, Back to Simple Views

Related to the idea that views can help you secure your data against prying eyes, let's explore the use of certain keywords to ensure data security as well. For example, consider our trusty EMP table. It contains data about employee salaries—something that most organizations typically don't like to publish widely. To batten down the hatches on SAL and COMM data in the EMP table from SCOTT's prying eyes (which are disgruntled by being underpaid), consider the following code block:

```
SQL> create or replace view emp_view as
  2  ( select empno, ename, job, mgr, hiredate,
  3           decode(ename, user, sal, 'KING', sal, 0) as sal,
  4           decode(ename, user, comm, 'KING', comm, 0) as comm,
  5           deptno from emp);
View created.
SQL> select ename, sal from emp_view
  2  where job = 'ANALYST';
ENAME           SAL
----------  ---------
SCOTT           3000
FORD               0
```

Notice a few things about the bold code in the preceding example. We used the decode ( ) function to determine what to return for SAL and COMM information, which we know is allowed. Also notice that we used the keyword user, which is a function that identifies the name of the user logged into the system, in order to figure out whose salary and commission information we'll show and to whom. Next, notice that we also built in some functionality so that KING can see everyone's salary (he is the president of the company, after all). After that, notice that we had to create an alias for that column so Oracle would know what to call the column in our virtual table. Besides being required to create the view, column aliases, as you'll recall, simplify the otherwise confusing column name Oracle would generate based on our use of the single-row function.

Finally, observe our use of the `create or replace view EMP_VIEW` syntax in this example. Before, we simply said `create view EMP_VIEW`; but in this case, our view creation would have failed because EMP_VIEW already exists, if we hadn't included the `or replace` keywords. These keywords are useful when you want to redefine an existing view based on new needs or criteria. Why not simply use the `alter view` command, you ask? Because the only job `alter view` can perform is recompiling an invalid view. We'll discuss `alter view` in more detail later in the section.

Changing Underlying Table Data Through Simple Views

Now, let's try doing something completely different. Say securing the salary data about other employees from the prying eyes of SCOTT wasn't enough to persuade him not to begrudge the company for his lousy pay. Now SCOTT is irritated enough to take matters into his own hands by changing his pay against company rules. Assuming SCOTT doesn't know about the underlying EMP table, let's see if he can change information in that table, anyway, via EMP_VIEW:

```
SQL> update emp_view set sal = 6000
  2  where ename = 'SCOTT';
update emp_view set sal = 6000
                        *
ERROR at line 1:
ORA-01733: virtual column not allowed here
```

Apparently he can't. Remember, we didn't use simple column references for SAL and COMM in our view. Instead, we referred to them by way of the `decode( )` function, which effectively created virtual columns in EMP_VIEW containing salary and commission information that can't be updated. You might think that this "security measure" is more of a technicality than a way to enhance security, and in truth, you're probably right. Nevertheless, we thwarted SCOTT's attempt to defraud the company. However, let's say that now SCOTT is fighting mad and is willing to do anything to get even with the company, even if it means calling the president a fool in front of everyone, as shown in the following code block:

```
SQ> update emp_view set ename = 'FOOL!'
  2  where job = 'PRESIDENT';
1 row updated.
SQL> select ename from emp
  2  where job = 'PRESIDENT';
ENAME
----------
FOOL!
```

Sure enough, SCOTT can call the president of the company a fool by modifying the EMP table via an `update` on EMP_VIEW, although no doubt SCOTT will pay the consequences when KING discovers SCOTT's destructive act.

Changing Data in Underlying Tables Through Simple Views: Restrictions

Now let's extrapolate a general rule: *You can insert, update, or delete information on an underlying table via simple views*, subject to the following restrictions:

- In general, all constraint restrictions defined on the underlying table also apply to modifying data via the view. For example, you can't add data to an underlying table via a view that violates the table's primary key constraint.

- If the underlying table has not NULL constraints on columns not appearing in your view, you will likely have trouble when you try to insert data into a view. This problem can be solved by using default values for the not NULL column(s) in the table definition.

- Generally speaking, you can delete records from underlying tables using the view, even when the view doesn't contain all the columns or all the rows the underlying table contains.

- You cannot update data in a column of an underlying table via a simple view if the column was defined using a single-row function or function-based keywords such as `user` or `sysdate`. You *can* update a column of an underlying table if the simple view did *not* use a single-row function to define the column.

- You may not insert, update, or delete data on the table underlying the simple view if the `select` statement creating the view contains a `group by` clause, group function, or `distinct` clause.

TIP

If you yearn for some adventure as you follow along in your own database, try creating simple views that don't violate these restrictions, but otherwise do odd things. Then see if you can add, change, or remove rows from the underlying table. Here's an example: Try to insert a row into the EMP table via a view created as follows: `create view my_view as (select rowid as row_id, empno from emp)`. *If you find any restrictions in your adventures that I may have missed in the bulleted list, send an e-mail to jcouchman@mindspring.com and I'll acknowledge you by name in my next book.*

For Review

1. Understand what a view is and what it is not. A view is a select statement that generates the contents of a virtual table dynamically. Although views behave like tables, they do not actually contain table data.

2. Know the basic syntax for creating a view in Oracle. Understand the kinds of queries you can use to create a view. Basically, just about anything goes.

3. Be able to identify situations when it is possible to add data to a table via a view, and alternatively, when it is not possible to add data to a table via a view.

Exercises

1. **SCOTT creates a view on the EMP table using the following code block:**

```
SQL> create or replace view emp_view as
  2  ( select empno, ename, job, mgr, hiredate,
  3           decode(ename, user, sal, 'KING', sal, 0) as sal,
  4           decode(ename, user, comm, 'KING', comm, 0) as comm,
  5           deptno from emp);
View created.
```

Which of the following DML statements will successfully make a change to data in the EMP table?

   A. insert into emp_view values (2345,
   'SMITHERS','MANAGER', 7839, 4500, 0, 10);

   B. update emp_view set job = 'CLERK', comm = 0 where
   ename = 'TURNER';

   C. delete from emp_view where ename = 'SMITH';

   D. update emp_view set comm = comm*1.3 where
   ename = 'TURNER';

2. **Use the view shown in the preceding code block to answer this question. User SCOTT logs into Oracle and issues the following query:**

```
SQL> select ename, sal from emp_view
  2  where job = 'ANALYST';
ENAME            SAL
----------  ---------
SCOTT           3000
FORD               0
```

Later, TURNER logs into Oracle and issues the same query. What will be the result listed for SCOTT in TURNER's output?

A. 0

B. 1500

C. 3000

D. 6000

3. **User SCOTT creates a view using the statement in the following code block:**

```
SQL> create or replace view my_view as
  2  (select user as orcl_user, rowid as row_id, empno
  3   from emp
  4   where ename = user)
  5   order by empno;
View created.
```

Then SCOTT issues the following DML statement: `insert into my_view values ('JASON','weraqwetrqwer',3421);`. Which of the following choices correctly identifies how Oracle will respond and why?

A. Oracle will return an error because you cannot perform DML on views created with an `order by` clause.

B. Oracle will return an error because no data can be added on a column defined using `user`.

C. Oracle will return an error because no data can be added on a column defined using the ROWID pseudocolumn.

D. Oracle will insert the new row into the underlying table because the statement contains no errors.

4. **Use the code defined for creating MY_VIEW in the previous question to answer this one. You issue the following statement in Oracle: `delete from my_view where orcl_user = 'SCOTT';`. How many rows are removed from the EMP table?**

A. 0

B. 1

C. 2

D. 14

Creating Views That Enforce Constraints

Tables that underlie views often have constraints that limit the data that can be added to those tables. As I said earlier, views cannot add data to the underlying table that would violate the table's constraints. However, you can also define a view to restrict the user's ability to change underlying table data even further, effectively placing a special constraint for data manipulation through the view. This additional constraint says that insert or update statements issued against the view are not allowed to create rows that the view cannot subsequently select. In other words, if, after the change is made, the view will not be able to select the row you changed, the view will not let you make the change. This viewability constraint is configured when the view is defined by adding the with check option to the create view statement. Let's look at an example to clarify my point:

```
SQL> create or replace view emp_view as
  2  (select empno, ename, job, deptno
  3   from emp
  4   where deptno = 10)
  5  with check option constraint emp_view_constraint;
View created.
SQL> update emp_view set deptno = 20
  2  where ename = 'KING';
update emp_view set deptno = 20
       *
ERROR at line 1:
ORA-01402: view WITH CHECK OPTION where-clause violation
```

TIP
On some systems, you may not get the ORA-01402 error in this context. Instead, Oracle may simply state that zero rows were updated by your change.

Notice, first, the code in bold in the preceding block where the viewability constraint is defined. We've effectively said that no user can make a change to the EMP table via this view that would prevent the view from selecting a row. After that, we test this constraint by attempting to update the DEPTNO column for KING from 10 to 20, thus causing the view not to be able to pick up that row later. Oracle prevents this data change with an ORA-01402 error, as you can see. Finally, take a look again at the `constraint` clause in the line in bold. This optional clause lets us define a name for our view constraint. If we omitted the clause, Oracle would generate its own name for the constraint. By naming it ourselves, we can easily identify the constraint later in dictionary views containing data about constraints, such as USER_CONSTRAINTS. Output for USER_CONSTRAINTS listing our viewability constraint is shown here:

```
SQL> select constraint_name, constraint_type
  2  from user_constraints;
CONSTRAINT_NAME                    C
------------------------------     -
SYS_C00905                         P
SYS_C00903                         C
PK_EMPLOYEE_01                     P
SYS_C00921                         C
CK_EMPLOYEE_01                     C
EMP_VIEW_CONSTRAINT                V
PK_01                              P
PK_PRICES_01                       P
```

TIP
The CONSTRAINT_TYPE column in USER_CONSTRAINTS and ALL_CONSTRAINTS will list the first character of the first word that best describes each type of constraint in Oracle: primary key, foreign key, check, not NULL, unique key, or viewability.

Creating Simple Views That Can't Change Underlying Table Data

In some cases, you may find that you want to create views that don't allow your users to change data in the underlying table. In this case, you can use the `with read only` clause. This clause will prevent any user of the view from making changes to the base table. Let's say that, after reprimanding SCOTT severely for calling him a fool, KING wants to prevent all employees from ever changing data in EMP via the EMP_VIEW again. Here's how he would do it:

```
SQL> create or replace view emp_view
  2  as (select * from emp)
  3  with read only;
```

The next time SCOTT tries to call KING a fool, here's what happens:

```
SQL> update emp_view set ename = 'FOOL!'
  2  where ename = 'KING';
```

```
where ename = 'KING'
      *
ERROR at line 2:
ORA-01733: virtual column not allowed here
```

For Review

1. Be sure you can explain how viewability constraints placed on views work and how to use the `with check option` and `constraint` clause in `create view` statements in order to create this type of constraint.

2. Understand how to use the `with read only` clause in order to prevent users from making changes to underlying base tables via a view on those tables.

Exercises

1. **Use the code in the following block to answer this question:**

```
SQL> create or replace view emp_view as
  2  (select empno, ename, job, deptno
  3   from emp
  4   where job = 'MANAGER')
  5   with check option;
View created.
SQL> select * from emp_view;
    EMPNO ENAME       JOB        DEPTNO
--------- ---------- ---------- ---------
     7566 JONES       MANAGER        20
     7698 BLAKE       MANAGER        30
     7782 CLARK       MANAGER        10
```

Which of the following data changes will *not* be allowed by Oracle on this view?

A. `update emp set job = 'ANALYST' where job = 'MANAGER' and empno = 7566;`

B. `update emp set ename = 'BARNEY' where job = 'MANAGER' and ename = 'JONES';`

C. `update emp set empno = 7999 where job = 'MANAGER' and deptno = 10;`

D. `update emp set deptno = 30 where job = 'MANAGER' and empno = 7782;`

2. Use the contents of the following code block to answer this question:

```
SQL> create or replace view emp_view as
  2  (select empno, ename, job, deptno
  3   from emp
  4   where job = 'MANAGER')
  5   with check option;
View created.
SQL> select constraint_name, constraint_type
  2  from user_constraints;
CONSTRAINT_NAME                      C
------------------------------      -
SYS_C00905                           P
SYS_C00903                           C
SYS_C00921                           C
SYS_C00929                           V
```

Which of the following constraints is the viewability constraint created in support of EMP_VIEW?

A. SYS_C00905

B. SYS_C00903

C. SYS_C00929

D. SYS_C00921

3. Use the following code block to answer this question:

```
SQL> create or replace view emp_view as
  2  (select empno, ename, job, deptno
  3   from emp
  4   where job = 'MANAGER')
  5   with read only;
View created.
```

Which of the following data-change statements will Oracle allow to make changes to the underlying table?

A. `insert into emp_view values (2134, 'SMITHERS','MANAGER',10);`

B. `update emp_view set ename = 'JOHNSON' where empno = 7844;`

C. `delete from emp_view where ename = 'KING';`

D. None of the above

Answer Key

1. A. **2.** C. **3.** D.

Creating Complex Views

I mentioned earlier that you can create views that join data from more than one table. These are called *complex views*. Complex views allow for complicated data models where many base tables are drawn together into one virtual table. Let's take a look at your basic complex view, where we join the contents of the EMP and DEPT tables together to form one virtual table:

```
SQL> create view emp_dept_view as
  2  (select empno, ename, job, dname, loc
  3   from emp e, dept d
  4   where e.deptno = d.deptno
  5   and job in ('ANALYST','CLERK','MANAGER'));
View created.
```

The contents of this view are listed as follows:

```
SQL> select * from emp_dept_view;
   EMPNO ENAME      JOB        DNAME           LOC
--------- ---------- ---------- --------------- -------------
    7782 CLARK      MANAGER    ACCOUNTING      NEW YORK
    7934 MILLER     CLERK      ACCOUNTING      NEW YORK
    7369 SMITH      CLERK      RESEARCH        DALLAS
    7566 JONES      MANAGER    RESEARCH        DALLAS
    7876 ADAMS      CLERK      RESEARCH        DALLAS
    7902 FORD       ANALYST    RESEARCH        DALLAS
    7788 SCOTT      ANALYST    RESEARCH        DALLAS
    7698 BLAKE      MANAGER    SALES           CHICAGO
    7900 JAMES      CLERK      SALES           CHICAGO
```

TIP

The same sorts of `select` *statements permitted for defining simple views are generally allowed on complex views as well. You may want to refer back to the list of* `select` *statements that are allowed in simple views for a refresher on complex views. You can even define complex views using the outer join (+) operator as well!*

Updating Base Tables of a Complex View

Oracle **8i** and higher
For the most part, complex views will not allow you to change data in any of the base tables if you haven't properly defined foreign key and primary key relationships between the joined tables using appropriate Oracle integrity constraints. Let's take a look at what I mean by this statement. The dictionary view USER_UPDATABLE_COLUMNS can tell you whether the columns in a complex view can be modified. Let's take a look:

```
SQL> create or replace view emp_dept_view as
  2  (select empno, ename, job, loc
  3  from emp e, dept d
  4  where e.deptno = d.deptno);
View created.
SQL> select column_name, updatable
  2  from user_updatable_columns
  3  where table_name = 'EMP_DEPT_VIEW';
COLUMN_NAME                      UPD
-------------------------------- ---
EMPNO                            NO
ENAME                            NO
JOB                              NO
LOC                              NO
```

TIP
If you used the `utlsampl.sql` *script to build the SCOTT demonstration tables, you'll have the proper primary and foreign key constraints already created. However, if you used the* `demobld.sql` *script to build the SCOTT demonstration tables, then your primary and foreign key constraints won't exist.*

However, after I properly define my foreign key and primary key relationships between the EMP and DEPT tables, I can create a complex view that will allow partial modification of data in the base tables via the view. Let's look at an example of such a view, which is called an *updatable join view* or *modifiable join view*. A *join view* is simply another name for a complex view, which makes sense, considering that complex views contain join operations. Let's look at the code:

```
SQL> alter table emp add constraint pk_emp_01
  2  primary key (empno);
Table altered.
SQL> alter table dept add constraint pk_dept_01
  2  primary key (deptno);
Table altered.
SQL> alter table emp add constraint fk_emp_01
  2  foreign key (deptno) references dept (deptno);
Table altered.
```

```
SQL> create or replace view emp_dept_view as
  2  (select empno, ename, job, loc
  3  from emp e, dept d
  4  where e.deptno = d.deptno);
View created.
SQL> select column_name, updatable
  2  from user_updatable_columns
  3  where table_name = 'EMP_DEPT_VIEW';
COLUMN_NAME                     UPD
------------------------------- ---
EMPNO                           YES
ENAME                           YES
JOB                             YES
LOC                             NO
```

TIP

Views containing outer joins generally won't contain key-preserved tables unless the outer join generates no NULL values. Even in such a case, the updatability is dependant on your data; so for all intents and purposes, you should just assume that outer join views are not updatable.

That's more like it. Now, when we issue an `update` statement on EMP_DEPT_VIEW that modifies the EMPNO, ENAME, or JOB column, Oracle will let us make the change. Yet, notice that there's still one column that we cannot update. To understand why, we have to talk about the concept of a *key-preserved table*. A key-preserved table is a table in a complex view whose primary key column is present in the view *and whose values are all unique and not NULL in the view*. In a sense, the key-preserved table's primary key can also be thought of as the primary key for the data in the view. In some cases, many tables in the complex view may be key-preserved if the primary key for the view is the primary key in several of the joined tables. Only columns from the key-preserved table can be modified via the complex view. Columns from the non-key-preserved table (the LOC column in DEPT, in this case) cannot be modified via the complex view. In conclusion, you can execute data-change statements on a complex view only when all the following conditions are met:

- The statement must affect only one of the tables in the join.

- For `update` statements, all columns changed must be extracted from a key-preserved table. In addition, if the view is created using the `with check option` clause, join columns and columns taken from tables that are referenced more than once in the view cannot be part of the `update`.

■ For `delete` statements, there may only be one key-preserved table in the join. This table may be present more than once in the join, unless the view has been created using the `with check option` clause.

■ For `insert` statements, all columns in which values are inserted must come from a key-preserved table, and the view must not have been created using the `with check option` clause.

■ The complex view does not contain group functions, `group by` expressions, set operations, the `distinct` keyword, `start with` or `connect by` clauses, or the ROWNUM pseudocolumn. Pseudocolumns are virtual columns in a table that you cannot add data to or change data on.

TIP

Set operations include the UNION, UNION ALL, INTERSECT, and MINUS keywords, used for joining the output of one select statement with the output of another. For example, select empno from emp UNION select sal from emp is a set operation. Set operations are typically not tested on the OCP exam and therefore will not be covered in this book in any great detail.

For Review

1. Be able to define the meaning of a complex or join view. Know how a complex view differs from a simple view. Be sure you can identify the types of `select` statements permitted in defining a complex view.

2. Know the factors that limit your ability to make changes to underlying base tables in a complex view. In particular, understand the importance of constraints in the underlying tables to solidify the relationship between the two tables, and the concept of key-preserved tables.

3. Be sure you can list the items a complex view cannot contain if you want the ability to modify the underlying tables.

Exercises

1. **Your database of sales information consists of four tables: PROFITS lists the profit amount for every product sold by the company, listed by product name, type, sales region, and quarter; PRODUCT_TYPES lists all valid product types that are sold by your company; PRICES lists the name of every product, along with the associated price; and UNIT_SALES lists**

every product sold by the company and units sold of the product by quarter. You create a view on this database using the following block:

```
SQL> create or replace view profits_view as
  2  (select a.product_name, a.product_type, b.product_desc,
  3  c.product_price,
  4  d.unit_sale, a.quarter
  5  from profits a, product_types b, prices c, unit_sales d
  6  where a.product_type = b.product_type
  7  and a.product_name = c.product_name
  8  and a.product_name = d.product_name
  9  and a.quarter = d.quarter);
View created.
```

Assuming all the proper integrity constraints are in place, which of the following tables in this view is not a key-preserved table?

A. PROFITS

B. PRODUCT_TYPES

C. PRICES

D. UNIT_SALES

2. You are developing complex views in Oracle. Which of the following choices identifies an item that may not be included in the query defining the view if you intend to allow users to update key-preserved tables joined in the view?

   A. avg( )

   B. decode( )

   C. nvl( )

   D. to_char( )

3. Key-preserved tables share this in common with the output of complex views they underlie: _____

Answer Key

1. B. 2. A. 3. Primary key.

Modifying and Removing Views

Notice that, on several occasions, we have altered the definition of views that already existed in the database. However, we didn't follow the same precedent with views that we used for other objects, such as tables, when we wanted to modify them. That's because views don't follow the syntax conventions of other database objects. Although there is an `alter view` statement in the Oracle SQL language, it is used for recompiling or revalidating the view *as it exists already*. Here's an example:

```
SQL> alter view emp_dept_view compile;
View altered.
```

When we wanted to alter the underlying data used in the definition of a view, we used the `create or replace view` statement. When a `create or replace view` statement is issued, Oracle will disregard the error that arises when it encounters the view that already exists with that name, and it will overwrite the definition for the old view with the definition for the new one. The following code block illustrates the use of the `create or replace view` statement from the first exercise in the previous discussion:

```
SQL> create or replace view profits_view as
  2  (select a.product_name, a.product_type, b.product_desc,
  3  c.product_price,
  4  d.unit_sale, a.quarter
  5  from profits a, product_types b, prices c, unit_sales d
  6  where a.product_type = b.product_type
  7  and a.product_name = c.product_name
  8  and a.product_name = d.product_name
  9  and a.quarter = d.quarter);
View created.
```

TIP
You'll have to create your own versions of each of these four tables in order to follow along in your Oracle database, using what you know about. When doing so, make sure the datatypes for the shared PRODUCT_NAME, PRODUCT_TYPE, and QUARTER columns match in each of the tables those columns appear in. Also, make sure you define the appropriate primary and foreign key integrity constraints between the tables. There is no script for creating these tables automatically—I believe it's very important that you get hands-on practice developing complex views for OCP!

We see from the last line in the block that Oracle created the view with no errors. If we wanted to verify the status of the view, we could look in the USER_OBJECTS view, as shown here:

```
SQL> column object_name format a20
SQL> select object_name, status
  2  from user_objects
  3  where object_name = 'PROFITS_VIEW';
OBJECT_NAME          STATUS
-------------------- -------
PROFITS_VIEW         VALID
```

TIP

The USER_VIEWS view does not contain the validity status of your view. Be sure you memorize that the status of all your database objects is found in USER_OBJECTS or ALL_OBJECTS for OCP.

Let's now drop the PRICES table, which is a base table for PROFITS_VIEW, as you'll recall from the question. Notice what happens to PROFITS_VIEW:

```
SQL> drop table prices;
Table dropped.
SQL> select object_name, status
  2  from user_objects
  3  where object_name = 'PROFITS_VIEW';
OBJECT_NAME          STATUS
-------------------- -------
PROFITS_VIEW         INVALID
```

So you see, Oracle doesn't remove views from the database if a base table is destroyed. Instead, Oracle simply marks PROFITS_VIEW as invalid to indicate that the object dependency that PROFITS_VIEW had on PRICES is now fractured. Here's what happens when you try to obtain data from PROFITS_VIEW:

```
SQL> select * from profits_view;
select * from profits_view
              *
ERROR at line 1:
ORA-04063: view "SCOTT.PROFITS_VIEW" has errors
```

The way to solve this problem is to re-create the PRICES table and recompile PROFITS_VIEW, as I show in the following block. When the view recompiles successfully, you will be able to select data from the view again:

```
SQL> create table prices
  2  (product_name varchar2(10) primary key,
  3   product_price number(10,4));
Table created.
SQL> alter view profits_view compile;
View altered.
```

TIP
Alternately, to fix a view that has become invalid due to the redefinition or deletion of a table that underlies it, you can modify the view with the `create or replace view` *statement.*

Removing Views

There may come a time when you need to remove a view. The command for executing this function is the `drop view` statement. There are no cascading scenarios that the person dropping a view must be aware of, except in situations in which the view being dropped acts as a base table for another view. In this case, the view that's left will be marked invalid. The following statement illustrates the use of `drop view` for deleting views from the database:

```
SQL> drop view profits_view;
View dropped.
```

For Review

1. Know how to use the `alter view` statement for recompiling views and the `create or replace view` statement for redefining the view query.

2. Know that object dependency is when a database object depends on another database object for information. Views have object dependencies on their base tables. Know what happens to the status of a view when its base table gets dropped, as well as how to repair the problem.

Exercises

1. You have just replaced a base table for a view that was dropped inadvertently. Which of the following statements cannot be used to update the status of the view in one step? (Choose two.)

   A. `create view`

   B. `create or replace view`

C. `alter view`

D. `drop view`

2. **What is the term that describes the relationship between a view and its base table (two words)?** _____

3. **You would like to identify the status of views in your database. Which of the following dictionary views would you use?**

   A. USER_VIEWS

   B. USER_TAB_COLUMNS

   C. USER_OBJECTS

   D. USER_TABLES

Answer Key

1. B and C. **2.** Object dependency. **3.** C.

Other Database Objects

This section covers the following topics related to other database objects in Oracle:

- Overview of other database objects
- Using sequences
- Using indexes
- Using public and private synonyms

So far, you've gotten some exposure to a few of the types of objects available for use in an Oracle database. This section will change that. In this section, you get an overview of many other important objects available in Oracle. You will also get some hands-on exposure to the creation and use of sequences in the Oracle database. After that, you will gain exposure to indexes, Oracle's performance-giving objects in the database. Finally, you will learn about the use of both public and private synonyms on an Oracle database.

Overview of Other Database Objects

Some of the objects that are part of the relational database produced by Oracle and that are used in the functions just mentioned are as follows:

- **Tables, views, and synonyms**   Used to store and access data

- **Indexes and the Oracle RDBMS**   Used to speed access to data

- **Sequences**   Used for generating numbers for various purposes

- **Triggers and integrity constraints**   Used to maintain the validity of data entered

- **Privileges, roles, and profiles**   Used to manage database access and usage

- **Packages, procedures, and functions**   Application PL/SQL code used in the database

TIP
*This is only a partial listing of all the different types of objects available in Oracle. In reality, there are dozens of different types of objects that aren't covered here. But, you do not need to know how to create or use the database object types **not** listed here in order to pass OCP Exam 1. You should know what the objects in the preceding list are, however, because we either have discussed or will discuss these objects at some point during this book.*

For Review

Be sure you can identify the different basic types of objects found in Oracle databases that are listed in this brief discussion. They are discussed in this book. Other database objects exist in Oracle; however, they are not covered on the OCP exam.

Exercises

1. **This is the database object, comprised of PL/SQL code stored in the database, that performs some programmatic task:**

   _____

2. **This is the database object designed to enforce validity rules on data added to the database that does not use PL/SQL code:**

   _____

3. **This is a database object that generates numbers in order:**

   _____

Answer Key

1. Package (*procedure* or *function* is also acceptable). **2.** Constraint. **3.** Sequence.

Using Sequences

A *sequence* is a database object that generates integers according to rules specified at the time the sequence is created. Sequences have many purposes in database systems—the most common of which is to generate primary keys automatically. However, nothing binds a sequence to a table's primary key, so in a sense it's also a sharable object. This task is common in situations in which the primary key is not generally used for accessing data in a table. The common use of sequences to create primary keys has one main drawback: because it is simply a sequential number, the primary key itself and the index it creates are somewhat meaningless. However, if you only need the key to guarantee uniqueness and don't care that you're creating a nonsense key, it is perfectly all right to do so. Sequences are created with the `create sequence` statement. Each clause in the statement is explained here:

- **start with n** Allows the creator of the sequence to specify the first value generated by the sequence. Once created, the sequence will generate the value specified by `start with` the first time the sequence's NEXTVAL virtual column is referenced. If no `start with` value is specified, Oracle defaults to a start value of 1.

- **increment by n** Defines the number by which to increment the sequence every time the NEXTVAL virtual column is referenced. The default for this clause is 1 if it is not explicitly specified. You can set *n* to be positive for incrementing sequences or negative for decrementing or countdown sequences.

- **minvalue n** Defines the minimum value that can be produced by the sequence. If no minimum value is specified, Oracle will assume the default, `nominvalue`.

- **maxvalue n** Defines the maximum value that can be produced by the sequence. If no maximum value is desired or specified, Oracle will assume the default, `nomaxvalue`.

- **cycle** Allows the sequence to recycle values produced when `maxvalue` or `minvalue` is reached. If cycling is not desired or not explicitly specified, Oracle will assume the default, `nocycle`. You cannot specify `cycle` in conjunction with `nomaxvalue` or `nominvalue`. If you want your sequence to cycle, you must specify `maxvalue` for incrementing sequences, or `minvalue` for decrementing or countdown sequences.

- **cache *n*** Allows the sequence to cache a specified number of values to improve performance. If caching is not desired or not explicitly specified, Oracle will assume the default, which is to cache 20 values.

- **order** Allows the sequence to assign values in the order in which requests are received by the sequence. If order is not desired or not explicitly specified, Oracle will assume the default, `noorder`.

Consider now an example for defining sequences. The integers that can be specified for sequences can be negative as well as positive. The following example uses a decrementing sequence. The `start with` integer in this example is positive, but the `increment by` integer is negative, which effectively tells the sequence to decrement instead of increment. When zero is reached, the sequence will start again from the top. This sequence can be useful in programs that require a countdown before an event will occur. Here's the example:

```
SQL> CREATE SEQUENCE countdown_20
  2    START WITH 20
  3    INCREMENT BY -1
  4    MAXVALUE 20
  5    MINVALUE 0
  6    CYCLE
  7    ORDER
  8    CACHE 2;
Sequence created.
```

Once the sequence is created, it is referenced using the CURRVAL and NEXTVAL pseudocolumns. The users of the database can view the current value of the sequence by using a `select` statement. Similarly, the next value in the sequence can be generated with a `select` statement. Because sequences are not tables—they are only objects that generate integers via the use of virtual columns—the DUAL table acts as the "virtual" table from which the virtual column data is pulled. As stated earlier, values cannot be placed into the sequence; instead, they can only be selected from the sequence.

The following example demonstrates how COUNTDOWN_20 cycles when `minvalue` is reached:

```
SQL> select countdown_20.nextval from dual;
   NEXTVAL
---------
        20
SQL> /
   NEXTVAL
---------
        19

   . . .

SQL> /
NEXTVAL
---------
         1
SQL> /
NEXTVAL
---------
         0
SQL> /
NEXTVAL
---------
        20
```

TIP

References to sequences cannot be used in subqueries of `select` statements (including those with `having`), views, `select` statements using set operations (such as `union` and `minus`), or any `select` statement that requires a sort to be performed.

Once the NEXTVAL column is referenced, the value in CURRVAL is updated to match the value in NEXTVAL, and the prior value in CURRVAL is lost. The next code block illustrates this point:

```
SQL> select countdown_20.currval from dual;
   CURRVAL
---------
        20
SQL> select countdown_20.nextval from dual;
```

```
    NEXTVAL
---------
       19
SQL> select countdown_20.currval from dual;
   CURRVAL
---------
       19
```

TIP
CURRVAL is set to the start with *value until NEXTVAL is referenced for the first time after sequence creation. After that, CURRVAL is set to the value for NEXTVAL. Every time NEXTVAL is referenced, CURRVAL changes. Interestingly, the first time you reference NEXTVAL, it gets set to the* start with *value also, so effectively the value for CURRVAL doesn't change!*

Referencing Sequences in Data Changes

Sequence-value generation can be incorporated directly into data changes made by insert and update statements. This direct use of sequences in insert and update statements is the most common use for sequences in a database. When the sequence generates a primary key for all new rows entering the database table, the sequence would likely be referenced directly from the insert statement. Note, however, that this approach sometimes fails when the sequence is referenced by triggers. Therefore, it is best to reference sequences within the user interface or within stored procedures. The following statements illustrate the use of sequences directly in changes made to tables:

```
SQL> INSERT INTO expense(expense_no, empid, amt, submit_date)
  2  VALUES(countdown_20.nextval, 59495, 456.34, '21-NOV-99');
1 row inserted.
SQL> UPDATE product
  2  SET product_num = countdown_20.currval
  3  WHERE serial_num = 34938583945;
1 row updated.
```

TIP
These trivial code block examples are for tables that we may or may not have referred to in earlier discussions. You can formulate your own sequences for similar use on tables we have already worked on or tables of your own design.

Modifying Sequence Definitions

There may come a time when the sequence of a database will need its rules altered in some way. For example, you may want COUNTDOWN_20 to decrement by a different number. Any parameter of a sequence can be modified by issuing the `alter sequence` statement. Here's an example:

```
SQL> select countdown_20.nextval from dual;
NEXTVAL
-------
     16
SQL> alter sequence countdown_20
  2  increment by -4;
Sequence altered.
SQL> select countdown_20.nextval from dual
  2  ;
  NEXTVAL
---------
       12
SQL> /
  NEXTVAL
---------
        8
```

The effect is immediate. In this example, the statement will change COUNTDOWN_20 to decrement each NEXTVAL by 4 instead of 1.

Any parameter of a sequence that is not specified by the `alter sequence` statement will remain unchanged. Therefore, by altering the sequence to use `nocycle` instead of `cycle`, we cause the COUNTDOWN_20 sequence in the following listing to run through one countdown from 20 to 0 only. After the sequence hits 0, no further references to COUNTDOWN_20.NEXTVAL will be allowed:

```
SQL> alter sequence countdown_20
  2  nocycle;
Sequence altered.
SQL> select countdown_20.nextval from dual;
  NEXTVAL
---------
        4
SQL> /
  NEXTVAL
---------
        0
SQL> /
select countdown_20.nextval from dual
*
```

```
ERROR at line 1:
ORA-08004: sequence COUNTDOWN_20.NEXTVAL goes below MINVALUE
and cannot be instantiated
```

Beware of Effects of Modifying Sequences

Modifying sequences is a simple process. However, the impact of the changes can be complex, depending on how an application uses these sequences. The main concern with changing sequences is monitoring the effect on tables or other processes that use the values generated by the sequences.

For example, resetting the value returned by a sequence from 1,150 to 0 is not difficult to execute. However, if the sequence was being used to generate primary keys for a table, for which several values between 0 and 1,150 had already been generated, you will encounter problems when the sequence begins generating values for `insert` statements that depend on the sequence to create primary keys. This problem won't show up when the sequence is altered, but later `insert` operations will have primary-key constraint violations on the table. The only way to solve the problem (other than deleting the records already existing in the table) is to alter the sequence again. Gaps can arise in the values of the primary key from this same premise as well.

Dropping Sequences

When a sequence is no longer needed, it can be removed. To do so, the DBA or owner of the sequence can issue the `drop sequence` statement. Dropping the sequence renders its virtual columns, CURRVAL and NEXTVAL, unusable. However, if the sequence was being used to generate primary-key values, the values generated by the sequence will continue to exist in the database. There is no cascading effect on the values generated by a sequence when the sequence is removed. Here's an example:

```
SQL> DROP SEQUENCE countdown_20;
Sequence dropped.
SQL> select countdown_20.currval from dual;
select countdown_20.currval from dual
       *
ERROR at line 1:
ORA-02289: sequence does not exist
```

TIP
You can find information about your sequences and the sequences available to you in the USER_SEQUENCES and ALL_SEQUENCES dictionary views, respectively.

For Review

1. Be sure you know that a sequence is an object that generates numbers in a sequence you define. Sequences can be used for many purposes, but most commonly they are used for generating unique numbers for primary key columns.

2. Know how to use the `create sequence`, `alter sequence`, and `drop sequence` statements. Also, be sure you can identify the information contained in the CURRVAL and NEXTVAL pseudocolumns of a sequence, as well as what happens to CURRVAL when NEXTVAL is selected.

3. Understand the different ways to refer to a sequence with `select`, `update`, and `insert` statements. Know how to use sequences in conjunction with the DUAL table as well.

Exercises

1. **This sequence pseudocolumn contains the most recently generated value the sequence has derived:** _____

2. **This sequence pseudocolumn contains the last value the sequence has derived:** _____

Answer Key

1. NEXTVAL. 2. CURRVAL.

Using Indexes

Indexes are objects in the database that provide a mapping of all the values in a table column, along with the ROWID(s) for all rows in the table that contain that value for the column. A *ROWID* is a unique identifier for a row in an Oracle database table. Indexes have multiple uses on the Oracle database. Indexes can be used to ensure uniqueness on a database, and they can also boost performance when you're searching for records in a table. The improvement in performance is gained when the search criteria for data in a table includes a reference to the indexed column or columns. In Oracle, indexes can be created on any column in a table except for columns of the LONG datatype. Especially on large tables, indexes make the difference between an application that drags its heels and an application that runs with efficiency. However, many performance considerations must be weighed before you make the decision to create an index. Performance is not improved simply by throwing a few indexes on the table haphazardly.

B-tree Index Structure

The traditional index in the Oracle database is based on a highly advanced algorithm for sorting data, called a *B-tree*. A B-tree contains data placed in layered, branching order, from top to bottom, resembling an upside-down tree. The midpoint of the entire list is placed at the top of the "tree" and is called the *root node*. The midpoints of each half of the remaining two lists are placed at the next level, and so on, as illustrated in Figure 4-1.

By using a "divide and conquer" method for structuring and searching for data, the values of a column are only a few hops away on the tree, rather than several thousand sequential reads through the list away. However, traditional indexes work best when there are many distinct values in the column or when the column is unique.

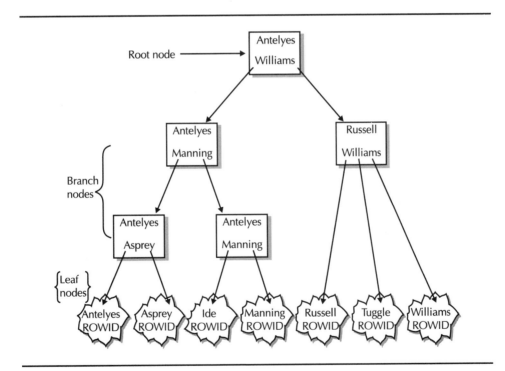

FIGURE 4-1.   *A B-tree index, displayed pictorially*

The algorithm works as follows:

1. Compare the given value to the value in the halfway point of the list. If the value at hand is greater, discard the lower half of the list. If the value at hand is less, discard the upper half of the list.

2. Repeat step 1 for the remaining part of the list until a value is found or the list exhausted.

Along with the data values of a column, each individual node of an index also stores a piece of information about the column value's row location on disk. This crucial piece of lookup data is called a *ROWID*. The ROWID for the column value points Oracle directly to the disk location of the table row corresponding to the column value. A ROWID identifies the location of a row in a data block in the datafile on disk. With this information, Oracle can then find all the data associated with the row in the table.

TIP
The ROWID for a table is an address for the row on disk. With the ROWID, Oracle can find the data on disk rapidly.

Bitmap Index Structure
This topic is pretty advanced, so consider yourself forewarned. The other type of index available in Oracle is the *bitmap index*. Try to conceptualize a bitmap index as being a sophisticated lookup table, having rows that correspond to all unique data values in the column being indexed. Therefore, if the indexed column contains only three distinct values, the bitmap index can be visualized as containing three rows. Each row in a bitmap index contains four columns. The first column contains the unique value for the column being indexed. The next column contains the start ROWID for all rows in the table. The third column in the bitmap index contains the end ROWID for all rows in the table. The last column contains a bitmap pattern, in which there will be one bit for every row in the table. Therefore, if the table being indexed contains 1000 rows, there will be 1000 corresponding bits in this last column of the bitmap index. Each bit in the bitmap index will be set to 0 (off) or 1 (on), depending on whether the corresponding row in the table has that distinct value for the column. In other words, if the value in the indexed column for that row matches this unique value, the bit is set to 1; otherwise, the bit is set to 0. Figure 4-2 displays a pictorial representation of a bitmap index containing three distinct values.

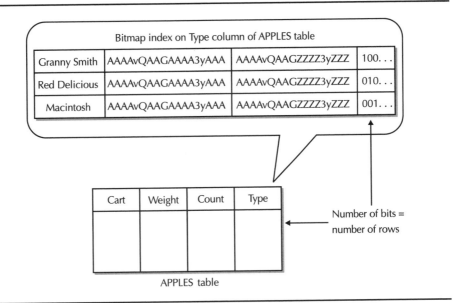

Bitmap index on Type column of APPLES table			
Granny Smith	AAAAvQAAGAAAA3yAAA	AAAAvQAAGZZZZ3yZZZ	100...
Red Delicious	AAAAvQAAGAAAA3yAAA	AAAAvQAAGZZZZ3yZZZ	010...
Macintosh	AAAAvQAAGAAAA3yAAA	AAAAvQAAGZZZZ3yZZZ	001...

Cart	Weight	Count	Type

APPLES table

Number of bits =
number of rows

FIGURE 4-2.   *A bitmap index, displayed pictorially*

Each row in the table being indexed adds only a bit to the size of the bitmap
pattern column for the bitmap index, so growth of the table won't affect the size of
the bitmap index too much. However, each distinct value adds another row to the
bitmap index, which adds another entire bitmap pattern with one bit for each row in
the table. Be careful about adding distinct values to a column with a bitmap index,
because these indexes work better when there are few distinct values allowed for a
column. The classic example of using a bitmap index is where you want to query a
table containing employees based on a GENDER column, indicating whether the
employee is male or female. This information rarely changes about a person, and
there are only two distinct possibilities, so a traditional B-tree index is not useful
here. However, this is exactly the condition where a bitmap index would aid
performance. Therefore, the bitmap index improves performance when traditional
indexes are not useful, and vice versa.

TIP
*Up to 32 columns from one table can be included in
a single B-tree index on that table, whereas a bitmap
index can include a maximum of 30 columns from
the table.*

Creating Indexes

You can create a unique B-tree index on a column manually by using the `create index` statement containing the `unique` keyword. This process is the manual equivalent of creating a unique or primary key constraint on a table. (Remember, unique indexes are created automatically in support of those constraints.)

You can index a column that contains NULL or repeated values, as well, simply by eliminating the `unique` keyword. Creating a composite index with more columns named is possible as well. You can also create a *reverse-key index*, where the contents of the index correspond to a reversed set of data from the indexed column. For example, if you are indexing the LASTNAME column of the EMPLOYEE table, a row containing "COUCHMAN" in that column would have a corresponding value in the reverse-key index of "NAMHCOUC." Reverse-key indexes are often found in Oracle Parallel Server environments to improve parallel query performance. Finally, you can create a bitmap index by substituting the `bitmap` keyword for the `unique` keyword. Here's an example:

```
SQL> -- unique indexes
  2   CREATE UNIQUE INDEX emp_empno_01
  3   ON emp (empno);
Index created.
SQL> -- nonunique indexes
  2   CREATE INDEX emp_sal_01
  3   ON emp (sal);
Index created.
SQL> -- composite indexes
  2   CREATE UNIQUE INDEX employee_empno_ename_indx_01
  3   ON emp (empno, ename);
Index created.
SQL> -- reverse key indexes
  2   CREATE INDEX emp_ename_reverse_indx
  3   ON emp (ename) REVERSE;
Index created.
SQL> -- bitmap indexes
  2   CREATE BITMAP INDEX emp_deptno_indx_01
  3   ON emp (deptno);
Index created.
```

TIP
You can create all these indexes on the EMP table we've been using throughout the book. Alternatively, you can use these code blocks as templates for creating these types of indexes on tables of your own design.

In order to replace the definition of the index, the entire index must be dropped and re-created. However, there are several different ways to find information about the index. The ALL_INDEXES dictionary view displays storage information about the index, along with the name of the table with which the index is associated. The ALL_OBJECTS dictionary view displays object information about the index, including the index status. The ALL_IND_COLUMNS view displays information about the columns that are indexed on the database. This last view is especially useful for determining the order of columns in a composite index.

Creating Function-Based Indexes

The function-based index is a new type of index in Oracle8i that is designed to improve query performance by making it possible to define an index that works when your where clause contains operations on columns. Traditional B-tree indexes won't be used when your where clause contains columns that participate in functions or operations. For example, suppose you have table EMP, with four columns: EMPID, LASTNAME, FIRSTNAME, and SALARY. The SALARY column has a B-tree index on it. However, if you issue the select * from EMP where (SALARY*1.08) > 63000 statement, the RDBMS will ignore the index, performing a full table scan instead. Function-based indexes are designed to be used in situations like this one, where your SQL statements contain such operations in their where clauses. The following code block shows a function-based index defined:

```
SQL> CREATE INDEX ixd_emp_01
  2  ON emp(SAL*1.08);
Index created.
```

By using function-based indexes like this one, you can optimize the performance of queries containing function operations on columns in the where clause, like the query shown previously. As long as the function you specify is repeatable, you can create a function-based index around it. A *repeatable function* is one whose result will never change for the same set of input data. For example, 2 + 2 will always equal 4. In other words, it will never change one day so that it equals 5. Therefore, the addition operation is repeatable. To enable the use of function-based indexes, you must issue two alter session statements, as follows:

```
SQL> alter session set query_rewrite_enabled = true;
Session altered.
SQL> alter session set query_rewrite_integrity=trusted;
Session altered.
```

Oracle **8i** and higher

TIP
Bitmap indexes can also be function-based indexes, and function-based indexes can also be partitioned.

Removing Indexes

When an index is no longer needed in the database, the developer can remove it with the `drop index` command. Once an index is dropped, it will no longer improve performance on searches using the column or columns contained in the index. No mention of that index will appear in the data dictionary anymore, either. You cannot drop the index that is used for a primary key.

The syntax for the `drop index` statement is the same, regardless of the type of index being dropped (unique, bitmap, or B-tree). If you wish to rework the index in any way, you must first drop the old index and then create the new one. Here's an example:

```
SQL> DROP INDEX employee_last_first_indx_01;
Index dropped.
```

Guidelines for Creating Indexes

Although the best performance improvement can be seen when a column containing all unique values has an index created on it, similar performance improvements can be made on columns containing some duplicate values or NULL values. Therefore, data in a column need not be unique in order for you to create an index on the column. There are some guidelines for ensuring that the traditional index produces the performance improvements desired. The guidelines for evaluating performance improvements given by traditional indexes and some consideration of the performance and storage tradeoffs involved in creating these indexes will be presented later in this section of the chapter.

Using indexes for searching tables for information can provide incredible performance gains over searching tables using columns that are not indexed. However, care must be taken to choose the right index. Although a completely unique column is preferable for indexing with a B-tree index, a non-unique column will work almost as well if only about 10 percent of its rows, or even less, have the same values. "Switch" or "flag" columns, such as ones for storing the sex of a person, are not appropriate for B-tree indexes. Neither are columns used to store a few "valid values," or columns that store a token value representing valid or invalid, active or inactive, yes or no, or any such types of values. Bitmap indexes are more appropriate for these types of columns. Finally, you will typically use reverse-key indexes when you have Oracle Parallel Server installed and running and you want to maximize parallelism in the database. Table 4-1 summarizes some handy rules of thumb on the topic of when to create and when not to create indexes.

When to Create an Index	When Not to Create an Index
When you have a large table	When you have a small table
When the table is used mainly for queries	When users make DML changes to the table frequently
When you generally query the table for one or a few distinct values	When your query results contain substantial portions of the data the table actually stores

TABLE 4-1.   *When to Create and When Not to Create an Index*

TIP
The uniqueness of the values in a column is referred to as "cardinality." Unique columns or columns that contain many distinct values have "high cardinality," whereas columns with few distinct values have "low cardinality." Use B-tree indexes for columns with high cardinality and bitmap indexes for columns with low cardinality.

For Review

1. Know what an index is and how to create one. Understand the difference between a unique index and a non-unique index. Also, be sure you can create B-tree, bitmap, function-based, reverse-key, and composite indexes.

2. Be sure you understand that, on unique indexes containing more than one column, uniqueness for the row is determined by unique combinations of all columns in the index.

3. Understand what is meant by cardinality. Know when you might use a B-tree index to improve performance and when you might use a bitmap index to improve performance instead. Know also that you can look in USER_INDEXES and USER_IND_COLUMNS for information about indexes.

Exercises

1. **You want to create an index that will improve performance on salary reviews. The query needs to determine what an employee's salary would**

be if the employee were given a 12% raise. Which of the following `create index` commands would handle this situation?

A. `create index my_idx_1 on employee (salary * 1.12);`

B. `create unique index my_idx_1 on employee (salary);`

C. `create bitmap index my_idx_1 on employee (salary);`

D. `create index my_idx_1 on employee (salary) reverse;`

2. Your table—which contains name and telephone number information for the states of California, New York, and Texas—needs an index on the LASTNAME column. In order to improve performance, which of the following indexes would be most appropriate?

A. `create unique index my_idx_1 on people_phone (lastname);`

B. `create index my_idx_1 on people_phone (lastname);`

C. `create bitmap index my_idx_1 on people_phone (lastname);`

D. `create index my_idx_1 on people_phone (lastname) reverse;`

3. You are creating an index for the US_GOVT_SS table in the U.S. Government Social Security application on the SS_NUM column. Which of the following choices best identifies the statement you will use on this column?

A. `create index my_idx_1 on US_govt_SS (ss_num);`

B. `create bitmap index my_idx_1 on US_govt_SS (ss_num);`

C. `create unique index my_idx_1 on US_govt_SS (ss_num);`

D. `create index my_idx_1 on US_govt_SS (ss_num) reverse;`

4. This word describes the uniqueness of values in an indexed column:

_____

Answer Key

1. A. 2. B. 3. C. 4. Cardinality.

Using Public and Private Synonyms

The objects in Oracle you create are available only in your schema unless you grant access to the objects explicitly to other users. We'll discuss privileges and user access in the next section. However, even when you grant permission to other users for using an object, the boundary created by schema ownership will force other users to prefix the object name with your schema name in order to access your object. For example, SCOTT owns the EMP table. If TURNER wants to access SCOTT's EMP table, he must refer to EMP as SCOTT.EMP. If TURNER doesn't, here's what happens:

```
SQL> connect turner/ike
Connected.
SQL> SELECT * FROM emp
  2  WHERE empno = 7844;
SELECT * FROM emp
              *
ORA-00942: table or view does not exist.
```

TIP

We'll cover the issue of creating TURNER's user ID and the privileges associated with accessing a table in the next section. For now, focus on the issue of schema ownership.

So, TURNER can't even see his own employee data—in fact, Oracle tells him that the EMP table doesn't even exist (pretty sneaky, eh?). Yet, as soon as TURNER prefixes the EMP table with its schema owner, SCOTT, a whole world of data opens up for TURNER, as you can see in the following code block:

```
SQL> connect turner/ike
SQL> SELECT empno, ename, sal FROM SCOTT.emp
  2  WHERE empno = 7844;
    EMPNO ENAME           SAL
--------- ---------- ---------
     7844 TURNER         1500
```

How Synonyms Can Help

If remembering which user owns which table seems unnecessarily complicated, synonyms can be used on the database for schema transparency. *Synonyms* are alternative names that can be created as database objects in Oracle to refer to a table or view. Two types of synonyms exist in Oracle: private synonyms and public synonyms. You can use a private synonym within your own schema to refer to a table or view by an alternative name. Private synonyms are exactly that—they are private to your schema, and therefore usable only by you. Think of private synonyms as giving you the ability to develop "pet names" for database objects in Oracle. You can use public synonyms to allow all users in Oracle to access database objects you own without having to prefix the object names with your schema name. This concept of referencing database objects without worrying about the schema the objects are part of is known as *schema transparency*. Public synonyms are publicly available to all users of Oracle; however, you need special privileges to create public synonyms. We'll talk more about the privilege required for creating public synonyms in the next section. For now, the following code block shows how SCOTT can create private and public synonyms, respectively:

```
SQL> create synonym all_my_emps for emp;
Synonym created.
SQL> create public synonym emp for scott.emp;
Synonym created.
```

TIP
Neither public nor private synonyms alter the details of the table's or view's definition. They just simply act as alternative names for the table or view.

Now that SCOTT has his own private synonym for the EMP table, he can start referring to EMP by his "pet name" right away:

```
SQL> connect scott/tiger
Connected.
SQL> select empno, ename, sal
  2  from all_my_emps
  3  where empno = 7369;
    EMPNO ENAME            SAL
--------- ---------- ---------
     7369 SMITH            800
```

Meanwhile, TURNER no longer needs to refer to EMP using SCOTT's schema prefixed to the table name. He can simply call it EMP, as he does here:

```
SQL> connect turner/ike
Connected.
SQL> select empno, ename, sal
  2  from emp
  3  where empno = 7844;
```

```
    EMPNO ENAME           SAL
--------- ---------- ---------
     7844 TURNER          1500
```

Note another interesting thing about private synonyms: if no public synonym existed for TURNER to use for referencing the EMP table without prefixing SCOTT's schema, TURNER could create his own private synonym for the object, as shown here:

```
SQL> connect turner/ike
Connected.
SQL> create synonym emp for scott.emp;
Synonym created.
SQL> select empno, ename, sal
  2  from emp
  3  where empno = 7844;
    EMPNO ENAME           SAL
--------- ---------- ---------
     7844 TURNER          1500
```

TIP
Synonyms do not give you access to data in a table that you do not already have access to. Only privileges can do that. Synonyms simply allow you to refer to a table without prefixing the schema name to the table reference. When resolving a database table name, Oracle looks first to see whether the table exists in your schema. If Oracle doesn't find the table, Oracle searches for a private synonym. If none is found, Oracle looks for a public synonym.

Dropping Synonyms

Synonyms are dropped using the `drop synonym` command, as shown in the following code block:

```
SQL> connect turner/ike
Connected.
SQL> drop synonym emp;
Synonym dropped.
SQL> connect scott/tiger
Connected.
SQL> drop public synonym emp;
Synonym dropped.
SQL> drop synonym all_my_emps;
Synonym dropped.
```

For Review

1. Understand how synonyms are used to facilitate schema transparency.

2. Know the difference between public synonyms and private synonyms. Know that private synonyms can be referenced only by the user who created them, whereas public synonyms can be referenced by every user in Oracle.

Exercises

1. **User DAVIS would like to access table PROFITS, which is owned by user WATTERSON, without prefixing the schema owner. Assuming the privilege issue is worked out, which of the following choices do *not* resolve the schema transparency issue? (Choose two.)**

    A. `create synonym profits for watterson.profits;` (issued by WATTERSON)

    B. `create public synonym for watterson.profits;` (issued by WATTERSON);

    C. `create synonym profits for watterson.profits;` (issued by DAVIS)

    D. `create synonym profits for profits;` (issued by DAVIS)

2. **This type of synonym is accessible by every user in the Oracle database (two words): _____**

3. **This type of synonym is accessible by the user in the Oracle database who created the synonym (two words): _____**

Answer Key

1. A and D. 2. Public synonym. 3. Private synonym.

User Access Control

In this section, we will cover the following topics related to controlling user access:

■ Creating users

■ Granting and revoking object privileges

■ Using roles to manage database access

The most secure database is one with no users; but take away the users of a database, and the whole point of having a database is lost. In order to address the issues of security within Oracle, a careful balance must be maintained between providing access to necessary data and functions and preventing unnecessary access. Oracle provides a means of doing this with its security model, which consists of several options for limiting connect access to the database and for controlling what a user can and cannot see once a connection is established. This section will focus on security on the Oracle database—from creating users, to administering passwords, to administering security on individual objects in the database.

Creating Users

The basic Oracle database security model consists of two parts. The first part consists of password authentication for all users of the Oracle database. Password authentication is available either directly from the Oracle server or from the operating system supporting the Oracle database. When Oracle's own authentication system is used, password information is stored in Oracle in an encrypted format. For the purposes of OCP Exam 1, we'll focus exclusively on Oracle's own authentication mechanism. The second part of the Oracle security model consists of controlling which database objects a user may access, the level of access a user may have to these objects, and whether a user has the authority to place new objects into the Oracle database. At a high level, these controls are referred to as *privileges*. We'll talk about privileges and database access later in this section.

TIP
In Oracle8i, there are additional components to the Oracle security model, including such features as fine-grained access control, certificate-based authentication, and advanced password-management functions such as password rotation expiry and complexity verification. These features are tested extensively in OCP Exam 2, but not on OCP Exam 1. Oracle9i promises to offer even more security features, such as Oracle Label Security.

How to Create Users

Let's start our discussion of creating users with an example. We referred to user TURNER in an earlier example. He's a divorced salesman working for our company who used to have ties to the music industry. Only privileged users such as the DBA can create other users in Oracle. For now, we'll pretend that user SCOTT is the DBA. SCOTT creates TURNER's userid in Oracle with the `create user` command.

The most basic version of this command defines only the user we want to create, along with a password, as seen here:

```
SQL> connect scott/tiger
Connected.
SQL> create user turner identified by ike;
User created.
```

TIP
Usernames can be up to 30 characters in length and can contain alphanumeric characters, as well as the $, #, and _ characters.

Creating a User Authenticated by the Host

Host authentication isn't used by Oracle databases too often, but it can be. Host authentication means that you create a user in Oracle whose password is validated by the underlying host system. When the user logs into the host with a correct password, Oracle then trusts the host's authentication and allows the user access to Oracle without providing another password. The username identifying the user in Oracle must match that used on the host system, prefixed by OPS$, as shown here:

```
SQL> create user OPS$harvey identified externally;
User created.
```

Later, when HARVEY wants to connect to Oracle from a host system command prompt, he can specify the following to do so and does not need to provide a password:

```
C:\windows> c:\oracle\ora81\bin\sqlplus /
```

TIP
You must first be connected directly to the host system (via Telnet on UNIX or at a DOS prompt) in order for host authentication to work.

Finding Information About Users

Once users are created in Oracle, you can look in the dictionary view ALL_USERS to gain some basic information about them, including username and the day each user was created. Take a look at the following code block:

```
SQL> select * from all_users;
USERNAME                         USER_ID CREATED
------------------------------ --------- ---------
SYS                                    0 23-JUN-99
SYSTEM                                 5 23-JUN-99
OUTLN                                 11 23-JUN-99
DBSNMP                                18 23-JUN-99
PO8                                   26 17-JUL-00
AURORA$ORB$UNAUTHENTICATED            23 23-JUN-99
JASON                                 27 18-JUL-00
STUDENT2                              46 30-OCT-00
STUDENT1                              45 30-OCT-00
SPANKY                                43 30-OCT-00
JASON2                                48 31-OCT-00
SCOTT                                 52 19-MAR-01
JASON3                                49 16-NOV-00
JASON10                               50 18-NOV-00
GIANT                                 51 08-DEC-00
TURNER                                53 21-MAR-01
```

TIP
The USER_USERS dictionary view also gives important information about your own userid, related to the advanced password-management features available in Oracle8i (not tested on OCP Exam 1). Take a look at this view and try to figure out what it contains before moving on to the exercises at the end of this discussion.

Getting Users Started with System Privileges

Now that SCOTT has created user TURNER, let's have SCOTT help TURNER get started by having SCOTT grant TURNER some privileges. Remember, privileges are the second part of the basic Oracle security model. Everything you can possibly do in an Oracle database is regulated by privileges. Two types of privileges exist in Oracle: object privileges and system privileges. *Object privileges* regulate access to database objects in Oracle, such as querying or changing data in tables and views, creating foreign key constraints and indexes on tables, executing PL/SQL programs, and a handful of other activities. Fewer than 10 object privileges can be granted in Oracle, so they are easy to memorize. You'll learn more about object privileges in the next discussion. *System privileges* govern every other type of activity in Oracle, such as connecting to the database, creating tables, creating sequences, creating views, and much, much more.

TIP
All told, more than 80 separate privileges can be granted in Oracle, the vast majority of which are system privileges. We'll focus our discussion only on those system and object privileges tested on OCP Exam 1.

Privileges are given to users with the `grant` command, and they are taken away with the `revoke` command. The ability to grant privileges to other users in the database rests on users who can administer the privileges. The owner of a database object can administer object privileges related to that object, whereas the DBA administers system privileges. We'll keep pretending that SCOTT is the DBA for our system as we take a look at some `grant` commands that give TURNER various system privileges to work on the database:

```
SQL> connect scott/tiger
Connected.
SQL> grant create session to turner;
Grant succeeded.
SQL> grant create table to turner;
Grant succeeded.
SQL> grant create sequence to turner;
Grant succeeded.
SQL> grant create procedure to turner;
Grant succeeded.
```

Now, when TURNER attempts to connect to Oracle and do some work, he'll be able to

```
SQL> connect turner/ike
Connected.
SQL> create table my_table
  2  (my_column number);
Table created.
```

Taking Away System Privileges

Now, let's say that management has decided that TURNER is all washed up with our company. KING hands TURNER a pink slip, and TURNER returns to his cubicle to clean out his desk. SCOTT now has to keep TURNER out of Oracle, but let's say he's too busy to do all the work today. SCOTT can simply revoke TURNER's ability to create sessions by using the following command:

```
SQL> connect scott/tiger
Connected.
SQL> revoke create session from turner;
Revoke succeeded.
```

TURNER is quite steamed about being fired, as you might imagine. He has been with the company for a long time and is going through some serious personal issues. While cleaning out his desk, TURNER decides to get even with his employer by sabotaging the data in Oracle. However, because SCOTT has revoked his ability to create database sessions, here's what happens to TURNER:

```
SQL> connect turner/ike
ERROR:
ORA-01045: user TURNER lacks CREATE SESSION privilege; logon denied
```

TIP
Even though TURNER can no longer log into Oracle, he still has all the other privileges that have been granted to him.

System Privileges to Know for OCP

Several categories of system privileges relate to each object. Those categories determine the scope of ability that the privilege grantee will have. The classes or categories of system privileges are listed here. Note that in the following subtopics, the privilege itself gives the ability to perform the action against your own database objects, and the any keyword refers to the ability to perform the action against any database object of that type in Oracle.

Database Access   These privileges control who accesses the database, when they can access it, and what they can do regarding management of their own session. Privileges include create session, alter session, and restricted session.

Users   These privileges are used to manage users on the Oracle database. Typically, these privileges are reserved for DBAs or security administrators. Privileges include create user, become user, alter user, and drop user.

Tables   You already know that tables store data in the Oracle database. These privileges govern which users can create and maintain tables. The privileges include create table, create any table, alter any table, backup any table, drop any table, lock any table, comment any table, select any table, insert any table, update any table, and delete any table. The create table or create any table privilege also allows you to drop the table. The `create table` privilege also bestows the ability to create indexes on the table and to run the `analyze` command on the table. To be able to truncate a table, you must have the `drop any table` privilege granted to you.

Indexes   You already know that indexes are used to improve SQL statement performance on tables containing lots of row data. The privileges include `create any index`, `alter any index`, and `drop any index`. You should note that there is no `create index` system privilege. The `create table` privilege also allows you to alter and drop indexes that you own and that are associated with the table.

Synonyms   A synonym is a database object that allows you to reference another object by a different name. A public synonym means that the synonym is available to every user in the database for the same purpose. The privileges include `create synonym`, `create any synonym`, `drop any synonym`, `create public synonym`, and `drop public synonym`. The `create synonym` privilege also allows you to alter and drop synonyms that you own.

Views   You already know that a view is an object containing a SQL statement that behaves like a table in Oracle, except that it stores no data. The privileges include `create view`, `create any view`, and `drop any view`. The `create view` privilege also allows you to alter and drop views that you own.

Sequences   You already know that a sequence is an object in Oracle that generates numbers according to rules you can define. Privileges include `create sequence`, `create any sequence`, `alter any sequence`, `drop any sequence`, and `select any sequence`. The `create sequence` privilege also allows you to drop sequences that you own.

Roles   Roles are objects that can be used for simplified privilege management. You create a role, grant privileges to it, and then grant the role to users. Privileges include `create role`, `drop any role`, `grant any role`, and `alter any role`.

Transactions   These privileges are for resolving in-doubt distributed transactions being processed on the Oracle database. Privileges include `force transaction` and `force any transaction`.

PL/SQL   You have already been introduced to the different PL/SQL blocks available in Oracle. These privileges allow you to create, run, and manage those different types of blocks. Privileges include `create procedure`, `create any procedure`, `alter any procedure`, `drop any procedure`, and `execute any procedure`. The `create procedure` privilege also allows you to alter and drop PL/SQL blocks that you own.

Triggers　You know that a trigger is a PL/SQL block in Oracle that executes when a specified DML activity occurs on the table to which the trigger is associated. Privileges include `create trigger`, `create any trigger`, `alter any trigger`, and `drop any trigger`. The `create trigger` privilege also allows you to alter and drop triggers that you own.

Using Dictionary Views to Display Privileges

To display privileges associated with users and roles, you can use the following views:

- **USER_SYS_PRIVS**　Shows all system privileges associated with this user

- **SESSION_PRIVS**　Shows all privileges available in this session

Changing Passwords

Security in the database is a serious matter, so users have to keep their passwords a secret. Most small organizations let the DBA handle database security, but larger ones use a security administrator. However, depending on the environment, developers, DBAs, or even end users may need to understand the options available in the Oracle security model for the version of Oracle the organization uses.

　　Toward that end of tighter security, SCOTT's new responsibilities as DBA require that he change his password to something less obvious. SCOTT must do this because he's worried that TURNER may try to log into Oracle using the SCOTT user ID and password. Like tables, passwords can contain alphanumeric characters (including $, #, and _). Let's look at what SCOTT must do with the `alter user` command in order to change his password:

```
SQL> connect scott/tiger
Connected.
SQL> alter user scott identified by 1#secure_pw;
User altered.
```

TIP
Several other options are available in both the `create user` *and* `alter user` *commands. However, basic user creation and password definition is all that's tested in OCP. If password management piques your interest, you can check out the Oracle documentation to see what other options are available. More advanced user management is tested on OCP Exam 2 in the DBA track.*

For Review

1. Be sure you can identify the two basic components of the Oracle security model: password authentication and privilege administration.

2. Know how to create a user along with her password using the `create user` command. Also, be sure you know how to change a password using the `alter user` command.

3. Understand where to look in the data dictionary for information about users.

4. Be sure you know what system and object privileges are and how to use `grant` and `revoke` to give out and take away privileges.

Exercises

1. User IMADBA wants to give user DAVIS, a brand-new employee who started today, the ability to create tables in the Oracle database. Which of the following choices identifies a step that doesn't need to take place before DAVIS can start creating tables?

   A. `create user davis identified by new_employee;`

   B. `grant create session to davis;`

   C. `grant create table to davis;`

   D. `grant create public synonym to davis;`

2. This is the privilege required for connecting to the Oracle database:

   _____

3. This is the privilege required for creating some public synonyms:

   _____

4. This is the clause used in the `alter user` statement for changing a password: _____

Answer Key

1. D. 2. `create session`. 3. `create public synonym`. 4. `identified by`.

Granting and Revoking Object Privileges

As I mentioned before, every possible activity in Oracle is governed by privileges. We already covered system privileges, so let's talk now about object privileges. All granting of object privileges is managed with the `grant` command. In order to grant an object privilege, the grantor must either have been granted the privilege with the `with grant option` privilege or must own the object. To grant an object privilege, the grantor of the privilege must determine the level of access a user requires on the object. Then, the privilege must be granted.

Available Object Privileges

The object privileges for any database object belong to the user who created that object. Object privileges can be granted to other users for the purpose of allowing them to access and manipulate the object. Object privileges include the following:

- **select**   Permits the grantee of this object privilege to access the data in a table, sequence, view, or snapshot.

- **insert**   Permits the grantee of this object privilege to insert data into a table or, in some cases, a view.

- **update**   Permits the grantee of this object privilege to update data in a table or view.

- **delete**   Permits the grantee of this object privilege to delete data from a table or view.

- **alter**   Permits the grantee of this object privilege to alter the definition of a table or sequence *only*; the `alter` privileges on all other database objects are considered system privileges.

- **index**   Permits the grantee of this object privilege to create an index on a table already defined.

- **references**   Permits the grantee of this object privilege to create or alter a table in order to create a foreign-key constraint against data in the referenced table.

- **execute**   Permits the grantee of this object privilege to run a stored procedure or function.

TIP
*There are less than 10 object privileges in Oracle.
In contrast, there are dozens of system privileges.
If you want an easy way to distinguish the two, try
memorizing the object privileges. Then, you can
simply assume that any privilege you encounter
on the OCP exam that is not an object privilege
is a system privilege.*

Granting Object Privileges in Oracle

The administrative abilities over an object privilege include the ability to grant the
privilege or revoke it from anyone, as well as the ability to grant the object privilege
to another user with administrative ability over the privilege. For these examples,
let's say that KING has reconsidered his haste in firing TURNER and has allowed
TURNER back on a probationary basis. Now, SCOTT has to set up TURNER with
access to the EMP table, as follows:

```
SQL> GRANT select, update, insert ON emp TO turner;
Grant succeeded.
SQL> GRANT references ON emp.empno TO turner;
Grant succeeded.
SQL> GRANT select, update, insert ON emp TO turner;
Grant succeeded.
```

Open to the Public

Another aspect of privileges and access to the database involves a special user on
the database. This user is called PUBLIC. If a system privilege or object privilege is
granted to the PUBLIC user, and then every user in the database has that privilege.
Typically, it is not advised that the DBA should grant many privileges or roles to
PUBLIC, because if a privilege or role ever needs to be revoked, then every stored
package, procedure, or function will need to be recompiled. Let's take a look:

```
SQL> GRANT select, update, insert ON emp TO public;
Grant succeeded.
```

TIP
*Roles can be granted to the PUBLIC user as well.
We'll talk more about roles in the next section.*

Granting Object Privileges All at Once

The keyword all can be use as a consolidated method for granting object privileges related to a table. Note that all in this context is not a privilege; it is merely a specification for all object privileges for a database object. The following code block shows how all is used:

```
SQL> GRANT ALL ON emp TO turner;
Grant succeeded.
```

Giving Administrative Ability Along with Privileges

When another user grants you a privilege, you then have the ability to perform whatever task the privilege allows you to do. However, you usually can't grant the privilege to others, nor can you relinquish the privilege without help of the user who granted the privilege to you. If you want some additional power to administer the privilege granted to you, the user who gave you the privilege must also give you administrative control over that privilege. For example, let's say KING now completely trusts TURNER to manage the creation of tables (a system privilege) and wants to give him access to the EMP table (an object privilege). Therefore, KING tells SCOTT to give TURNER administrative control over both these privileges, as follows:

```
SQL> GRANT CREATE TABLE TO turner WITH ADMIN OPTION;
Grant succeeded.
SQL> GRANT SELECT, UPDATE ON turner TO SPANKY WITH GRANT OPTION;
Grant succeeded.
```

The with admin option clause gives TURNER the ability to give or take away the create table *system* privilege to others. The with grant option clause gives TURNER that same ability for the select and update *object* privileges on table EMP. TURNER can make other users administrators of those privileges as well.

TIP
Finally, if a role is granted using the with admin option *clause, the grantee can alter the role or even remove it. You'll learn more about roles in the next section.*

Revoking Object Privileges in Oracle

Let's say that, once again, KING changed his mind and has fired TURNER. Revoking object privileges is handled with the revoke command. If you want to revoke system or object privileges granted with the with admin option clause or an object privilege granted with the with grant option clause, there is no additional syntax for doing so. Simply revoke the privilege, and the ability to administer that privilege gets revoked, too. You can see some examples of using this command for object privileges in the following code block:

```
SQL> revoke select, update, insert ON emp from turner;
Revoke succeeded.
SQL> revoke references ON emp.empno from turner;
Revoke succeeded.
SQL> revoke select, update, insert on emp from turner;
Revoke succeeded.
```

Cascading Effects of Revoking System Privileges

Consider the following situation related to the cascading effects of system privileges. User SCOTT gives TURNER the ability to create tables with administrative ability, and TURNER turns around and gives the same privilege to FORD, an aging auto factory worker who switched into computer programming:

```
SQL> connect scott/tiger
Connected.
SQL> grant create table to turner with admin option;
Grant succeeded.
SQL> connect turner/ike
Connected.
SQL> create table my_table
  2  (my_column number);
Table created.
SQL> grant create table to ford;
Grant succeeded.
SQL> connect ford/henry
Connected.
SQL> create table my_table
  2  (my_column number);
Table created.
```

SCOTT finds out that TURNER gave the `create table` privilege to FORD, who is only supposed to be able to create PL/SQL programs. SCOTT gets mad at TURNER and revokes the `create table` privilege from TURNER, along with the administrative ability, as follows:

```
SQL> connect scott/tiger
Connected.
SQL> revoke create table from turner;
Revoke succeeded.
```

Will FORD continue to be able to create tables? Let's see:

```
SQL> connect ford/henry
Connected.
SQL> create table my_table_2
  2  (my_column number);
Table created.
```

As you can see, FORD still has the ability to create tables, even though TURNER (the guy who gave FORD the privilege) does not. This means that there are no cascading effects of revoking system privileges from users. FORD keeps his ability to create tables, and TURNER's table, called MY_TABLE, doesn't get dropped. If you want to take away a system privilege from a user, you have to explicitly revoke that privilege directly from the user, as well as drop whatever objects that user has created while having the privilege.

Cascading Effects of Revoking Object Privileges

Now let's consider the same situation, only this time, the privilege in question is an object privilege. SCOTT grants `select` access on EMP to TURNER with administrative ability, who turns around and gives it to FORD. Check it out in the following block:

```
SQL> connect scott/tiger
Connected.
SQL> grant select on emp to turner with grant option;
Grant succeeded.
SQL> connect turner/ike
Connected.
SQL> select ename, job from scott.emp
  2  where empno =7844;
ENAME      JOB
---------- ---------
TURNER     SALESMAN
SQL> grant select on scott.emp to ford;
Grant succeeded.
SQL> connect ford/henry
Connected.
SQL> select ename, job from scott.emp
  2  where empno = 7369;
ENAME      JOB
---------- ---------
SMITH      CLERK
```

SCOTT then finds out what TURNER did and revokes the privilege from TURNER:

```
SQL> connect scott/tiger
Connected.
```

```
SQL> revoke select on emp from turner;
Revoke succeeded.
```

Will FORD still be able to access table EMP? Take a look:

```
SQL> connect ford/henry
Connected.
SQL> select ename, job
  2  from scott.emp
  3  where empno = 7360;
from scott.emp
          *
ERROR at line 2:
ORA-00942: table or view does not exist
```

So, when an object privilege is revoked from a grantor of that privilege, all grantees receiving the privilege from the grantor also lose the privilege. However, in cases in which the object privilege involves update, insert, or delete, if subsequent grantees have made changes to data using the privilege, the rows already changed don't get magically transformed back the way they were before.

Facts to Remember About Granting and Revoking Object Privileges

You should try to remember the following facts about granting and revoking object privileges before taking OCP:

- If a privilege has been granted on two individual columns, the privilege cannot be revoked on only one column—the privilege must be revoked entirely and then regranted on the individual column.

- If the user has been given the references privilege and has used it to create a foreign key constraint to another table, you must use the cascade constraints clause to revoke the references privilege (otherwise, the revoke will fail), as follows: REVOKE REFERENCES ON emp FROM spanky CASCADE CONSTRAINTS.

- The insert, update, and references privileges can be granted on columns within the database object. However, if a user has the insert privilege on several columns in a table but not all columns, the privilege administrator must ensure that no columns in the table that do not have the insert privilege granted are not NULL columns.

- If a user has the ability to execute a stored procedure owned by another user, and the procedure accesses some tables, the object privileges required to access those tables must be granted to the *owner* of the procedure, not the user to whom execute privileges were granted. What's more, the privileges must be granted directly to the user, not through a role.

For Review

1. Be sure you can identify all the object privileges and use the `grant` and `revoke` commands to give the privileges to users and take them away.

2. Know what happens when you grant object privileges to the PUBLIC user. Know when and how to use the `all` keyword when granting object privileges on a table to a user.

3. Understand how to grant administrative abilities over a privilege to other users along with the privilege itself. Memorize the syntax difference between granting system privileges with the `with admin option` clause and granting object privileges with the `with grant option` clause.

4. Be sure you know the differences between system and object privileges with respect to cascading effects of revoking those privileges.

5. Make sure you understand all the points I made about special conditions with respect to granting and revoking object privileges.

Exercises

1. You want to grant user TIMOTHY the ability to update data in the SALES table, as well as the ability to administer that access for others. Which of the following commands would you issue?

   A. `grant update to timothy;`

   B. `grant update on emp to timothy;`

   C. `grant update on emp to timothy with grant option;`

   D. `grant update on emp to timothy with admin option;`

2. User REED can administer the `create session` privilege. User REED grants the same `create session` privilege to MANN using the `with admin option` clause. MANN then grants the privilege to SNOW. REED discovers MANN issued the privilege to SNOW and revokes the privilege from MANN. Who can connect to Oracle?

   A. REED, only

   B. SNOW and MANN, only

   C. REED, MANN, and SNOW

   D. REED and SNOW, only

3. User SNOW owns table SALES, and she grants `delete` privileges to user REED using the `with grant option` clause. REED then grants `delete` privileges on SALES to MANN. SNOW discovers MANN has the privilege and revokes it from REED. Which of the following users can delete data from the SALES table?

   A. MANN, only

   B. SNOW, only

   C. SNOW and MANN, only

   D. REED and MANN, only

4. When this user has the privilege, everyone has the privilege:

   _____

5. When revoking the references privilege after a user has built a foreign key constraint using that privilege, you must include this clause (two words):

   _____

Answer Key

1. C. 2. D. 3. B. 4. public. 5. cascade constraints.

Using Roles to Manage Database Access

When your databases has lots of tables, object privileges can become unwieldy and hard to manage. You can simplify the management of privileges with the use of a database object called a *role*. A role acts in two capacities in the database. First, the role can act as a focal point for grouping the privileges to execute certain tasks. Second, the role can act as a "virtual user" of a database, to which all the object privileges required to execute a certain job function can be granted, such as data entry, manager review, batch processing, and so on. Figure 4-3 illustrates how to manage privileges with roles. In order to use roles, your privilege-management process must consist of four steps:

1. You must logically group certain types of users together according to the privileges they need to do their jobs.

2. You must define a role (or roles) for each user type.

3. You must grant the appropriate privileges to each of the roles.

4. You can then grant the roles to specific users of each type.

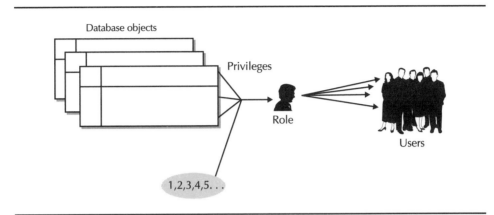

FIGURE 4-3.   *Managing privileges with roles*

Creating Roles to Correspond to User Types

Step 1 is a process that can happen outside the database. You simply sit down and think to yourself, How many different purposes will users be accessing this application for? Once this step is complete, you can create the different roles required to manage the privileges needed for each job function. Let's say there are two different job roles for people using the EMP table: those who can query the table and those who can add records to the table. The next step is to create roles that correspond to each activity. This architecture of using roles as a "middle layer" for granting privileges greatly simplifies administration of user privileges. Let's take a look at how to create the appropriate roles:

```
SQL> connect scott/tiger
Connected.
SQL> create role rpt_writer;
Role created.
SQL> create role data_changer;
Role created.
```

Modifying Roles

Let's say that, after we create our roles, we realize that changing records in the EMP table is serious business. To create an added safeguard against someone making a change to the EMP table in error, the DATA_CHANGER role can be altered to require a password by using the `alter role identified` by statement. Anyone wanting to modify data in EMP with the privileges given via the DATA_CHANGER role must first supply a password. Code for altering the role is shown here:

```
SQL> alter role data_changer
  2  identified by highly#secure;
Role altered.
```

Granting Privileges to Roles

The next step is to grant object privileges to roles. You can accomplish this task using the same command as you would use to grant privileges directly to users—the `grant` command. The following code block demonstrates how to grant privileges to both our roles:

```
SQL> grant select on emp to rpt_writer;
Grant succeeded.
SQL> grant update, delete, insert on emp to data_changer;
Grant succeeded.
```

TIP

Revoking privileges from roles works the same way as it does for users. System privileges are granted and revoked with roles in the exact same way they are with users as well.

Granting Roles to Users

Once a role is created and privileges are granted to it, the role can then be granted to users. This step is accomplished with the `grant` command. Let's see an example of how this is done:

```
SQL> grant rpt_writer to turner;
Grant succeeded.
SQL> grant data_changer to ford;
Grant succeeded.
```

TIP

If a role already granted to a user is later granted another privilege, that additional privilege is available to the user immediately. The same statement can be made for privileges revoked from roles already granted to users, too.

Defining User Default Roles

Now user TURNER can execute all the privileges given to him via the RPT_WRITER role, and user FORD can do the same with the privileges given from DATA_CHANGER. Or can he? Recall that we specified that DATA_CHANGER requires a password in order for the grantee to utilize its privileges. Let's make a little change to FORD's userid so that this status will take affect:

```
SQL> alter user ford default role none;
User altered.
```

TIP
You can use the following keywords in the alter
user default role *command to define default
roles for users:* all, all except rolename, *and*
none. *Note that users usually cannot issue* alter
user default role *themselves to change their
default roles—only a privileged user such as the
DBA can do it for them.*

By default, when a role is granted to a user, that role becomes a default role for
the user. We changed FORD's default role with the preceding code so that FORD
has no role. Let's see how this factor affects things when FORD tries to modify the
contents of the EMP table:

```
SQL> connect ford/henry
Connected.
SQL> insert into scott.emp (empno, ename, job)
  2  values (1234, 'SMITHERS','MANAGER');
insert into scott.emp (empno, ename, job)
                *
ERROR at line 1:
ORA-00942: table or view does not exist
```

TIP
Roles can be granted to other roles!

Enabling the Current Role
FORD knows he is supposed to be able to accomplish this task because he has the
DATA_CHANGER role. Then he remembers that this role has a password on it.
FORD can use the set role command to enable the DATA_CHANGER role in
the following way:

```
SQL> set role data_changer identified by highly#secure;
Role set.
```

Now FORD can make the change he needs to make:

```
SQL> insert into scott.emp (empno, ename, job)
  2  values (1234, 'SMITHERS','MANAGER');
1 row created.
```

Revoking and Dropping Roles

Finally, a role can be revoked by the role's owner or by a privileged administrative user using the revoke statement, much like revoking privileges:

```
SQL> connect scott/tiger
Connected.
SQL> revoke rpt_writer from turner;
Revoke succeeded.
SQL> revoke data_changer from ford;
Revoke succeeded.
```

Roles can be deleted from the database using the drop role statement. When a role is dropped, the associated privileges are revoked from the users granted the role. The following code block shows how to eliminate roles from Oracle:

```
SQL> connect scott/tiger
Connected.
SQL> drop role rpt_writer;
Role dropped.
SQL> drop role data_changer;
Role dropped.
```

Some Predefined Roles Available in Oracle

Some special roles are available to the users of a database. The roles available at database creation from Oracle7 onward include the CONNECT, RESOURCE, DBA, EXP_FULL_DATABASE, and IMP_FULL_DATABASE roles. Additionally, Oracle8i adds the roles DELETE_CATALOG_ROLE, EXECUTE_CATALOG_ROLE, and SELECT_CATALOG_ROLE to the mix, and much more. The predefined roles you might need to know about for OCP Exam 1 include the following:

- **CONNECT** Allows the user extensive development capability within his or her own user schema, including the ability to perform create table, create cluster, create session, create view, create sequence, and more. The privileges associated with this role are platform specific; therefore, the role can contain a different number of privileges, but typically the role never allows the creation of stored procedures.

- **RESOURCE** Allows the user moderate development capability within his or her own user schema, such as the ability to execute create table, create cluster, create trigger, and create procedure. The privileges associated with this role are platform specific; therefore, the role can contain a different number of privileges.

- **DBA** Allows the user to administer and use all system privileges.

Dictionary Views for Roles

The following views are available in the Oracle data dictionary pertaining to role information:

- **USER_ROLE_PRIVS**   Identifies the roles granted to you

- **ROLE_ROLE_PRIVS**   Identifies the roles granted to other roles in the database

- **ROLE_TAB_PRIVS**   Identifies object privileges granted to roles

- **ROLE_SYS_PRIVS**   Identifies system privileges granted to roles

- **SESSION_ROLES**   Identifies roles available to the current session

For Review

1. Know what a role is and how it can assist you in managing privileges in Oracle. Understand the four steps required for managing privileges when you want to do so with roles.

2. Know how to use the `create role`, `alter role identified by`, `alter user default role`, `set role`, and `drop role` commands. Also, understand how to use the `grant` and `revoke` commands with respect to roles.

3. When a role has an associated password, you shouldn't grant it to users as a default role. By granting a role to a user as a non-default role, you force the grantee to enable the role using the `set role identified by` command. This extra step enforces a higher level of security on that user when the user wants to employ the privileges granted by the role.

4. Know the available dictionary views that contain information about roles.

Exercises

1. User THOMAS has been granted the role SALES_ANALYZER, which allows her to access the SALES table for writing reports. However, when she tries to do so, she gets this error: `ORA-00942: table or view does not exist`. Which of the following statements can she issue in order to resolve the problem?

   A. `alter user thomas default role sales_analyzer;`

   B. `set role sales_analyzer;`

C. `grant select on sales to sales_analyzer;`

D. `grant sales_analyzer to thomas;`

2. **User FRANKLIN owns the PROFITS table and the SALES_ANALYZER role, which has already been granted to DAVIS. FRANKLIN grants `select` privileges on PROFITS to the SALES_ANALYZER role. At what point will that privilege be made available to DAVIS?**

   A. The next time DAVIS logs into Oracle

   B. The next time FRANKLIN grants the SALES_ANALYZER role to DAVIS

   C. The next time FRANKLIN grants the privilege to SALES ANALYZER

   D. Immediately after the privilege is granted to SALES_ANALYZER

3. **You are defining default roles for a user. Under which of the following circumstances should a role not be made a default role for a user?**

   A. When the role has object privileges granted to it

   B. When the role has system privileges granted to it

   C. When the role has a password assigned to it

   D. When the role has other roles assigned to it

4. **This dictionary view can identify the roles available to you in your current connection to Oracle:** _____

Answer Key

1. B. 2. D. 3. C. 4. SESSION_ROLES.

Chapter Summary

This chapter has covered a great deal of information you need to know about objects other than tables in the Oracle database. We started the chapter with a lengthy discussion on how to define both simple and complex views. You learned about how to modify data in base tables using a view, as well as when this is not possible in certain circumstances using complex views. We then moved on to cover how to use indexes in the Oracle database. You learned about the different types of indexes available to Oracle, as well as the different uses for those types of indexes. The chapter then covered the use of sequences for generating numbers for various purposes in Oracle. After that, the chapter covered the use of synonyms for creating schema transparency in your database. The chapter then concluded with a discussion of users and access privileges in Oracle. You learned how to create and alter users, as well as how to grant system privileges to those users in order to perform tasks such as connecting to the Oracle database. You learned how to grant, revoke, and administer object privileges in Oracle as well. Finally, we wrapped up the chapter by covering the available roles in the Oracle database.

Two-Minute Drill

- A view is a virtual table defined by a `select` statement.

- Views can distill data from tables that may be inappropriate for some users, and they can hide the complexity of data joined from several tables. You can also mask the complexity that arises when you perform many single-row or group operations on the data returned by the view's query.

- The two types of views are simple and complex.

- Simple views are those that have only one underlying table.

- Complex views are those with two or more underlying tables that have been joined together.

- Data may be inserted into simple views, except in the following cases:

  - If the `with check option` clause is used, the user may not insert, delete, or update data on the table underlying the simple view if the view itself is not able to select that data for the user.

  - The user may not insert, delete, or update data on the table underlying the simple view if the `select` statement creating the view contains `group by`, `order by`, or a single-row operation.

  - No data may be inserted in simple views that contain references to any virtual columns, such as ROWID, CURRVAL, NEXTVAL, and ROWNUM.

  - No data may be inserted into simple views that are created with the `read only` option.

- Data may be inserted into complex views when all the following conditions are true:

  - The statement affects only one of the tables in the join.

- For update statements, all columns changed are extracted from a key-preserved table. In addition, if the view is created with the with check option clause, join columns and columns taken from tables that are referenced more than once in the view are not part of the update.

- For delete statements, there is only one key-preserved table in the join. This table may be present more than once in the join, unless the view has been created with the with check option clause.

- For insert statements, all columns where values are inserted must come from a key-preserved table, and the view must not have been created with the with check option clause.

■ The with check option clause, upon creating a view, allows this simple view to limit the data that can be inserted or otherwise changed on the underlying table by requiring that the data change be selectable by the view.

■ Modifying the data selected by a view requires re-creating the view with the create or replace view statement or dropping the view first and issuing the create view statement.

■ An existing view can be recompiled by executing the alter view statement if for some reason it becomes invalid due to object dependency.

■ A view is dropped with the drop view statement.

■ A sequence generates integers based on rules that are defined by sequence creation.

■ Options that can be defined for sequences include the first number generated, how the sequence increments, the maximum value, the minimum value, whether the sequence can recycle numbers, and whether numbers will be cached for improved performance.

■ Sequences are used by selecting from the CURRVAL and NEXTVAL virtual columns.

■ The CURRVAL column contains the current value of the sequence.

■ Selecting from NEXTVAL increments the sequence and changes the value of CURRVAL to whatever is produced by NEXTVAL.

■ The rules that a sequence uses to generate values can be modified using the alter sequence statement.

■ A sequence can be deleted with the `drop sequence` statement.

   Some indexes in a database are created automatically, such as those supporting the primary key and the unique constraints on a table.

■ Other indexes are created manually to support database performance improvements.

■ Indexes created manually are often on non-unique columns.

■ B-tree indexes work best on columns that have high cardinality—that is, columns that contain a large number of distinct values and few duplicates.

■ B-tree indexes improve performance by storing data in a binary search tree and then searching for values in the tree using a "divide and conquer" methodology, as outlined in this chapter.

■ Bitmap indexes improve performance on columns with low cardinality— that is, columns that contain few distinct values and many duplicates.

■ Columns stored in an index can be changed only by dropping and re-creating the index.

■ Indexes can be deleted by issuing the `drop index` statement.

■ The Oracle database security model consists of two parts: limiting user access with password authentication and controlling object use with privileges.

■ Available privileges in Oracle include system privileges, for maintaining database objects, and object privileges, for accessing and manipulating data in database objects.

■ Changing a password can be performed by a user with the `alter user identified by` statement.

■ Granting system and object privileges is accomplished with the `grant` command.

■ Taking away system and object privileges is accomplished with the `revoke` command.

■ Creating a synonym is accomplished with the `create public synonym` command.

Fill-in-the-Blank Questions

1. Schema transparency can be created in an Oracle database through the use of this type of database object: _____

2. Obtaining a sequence's value without actually changing that value is done by referencing this Oracle pseudocolumn: _____

3. A view containing data from two or more tables, where the user can actually modify values in the underlying tables, is called what?

   _____

4. This type of database index is used for applying a repeatable programmatic operation to all values in a column: _____

5. This type of constraint automatically creates an underlying index in your database: _____

6. This clause allows a view to enforce the rule that if the view, itself, cannot see the data change, the data change is not allowed:

   _____

7. This type of database object can act as an intermediary for consolidating privileges granted to users around job functions:

   _____

8. Obtaining a new value from a sequence is accomplished by querying this Oracle pseudocolumn: _____

Chapter Questions

1. **Dropping a table has which of the following effects on a nonunique index created for the table?**

   A. No effect.

   B. The index will be dropped.

   C. The index will be rendered invalid.

   D. The index will contain NULL values.

2. **Which of the following statements about indexes is true?**

   A. Columns with low cardinality are handled well by B-tree indexes.

B. Columns with low cardinality are handled poorly by bitmap indexes.

C. Columns with high cardinality are handled well by B-tree indexes.

3. **Which of the following choices represents the step you would take to add the number of columns selected by a view?**

   A. Add more columns to the underlying table.

   B. Issue the `alter view` statement.

   C. Use a correlated subquery in conjunction with the view.

   D. Drop and re-create the view with references to select more columns.

4. **Which of the following choices is a valid parameter for sequence creation?**

   A. `identified by`

   B. `using temporary tablespace`

   C. `maxvalue`

   D. `on delete cascade`

5. **The following statement is issued against the Oracle database:**
   ```
   create view EMP_VIEW_01
   as select E.EMPID, E.LASTNAME, E.FIRSTNAME, A.ADDRESS
   from EMPLOYEE E, EMPL_ADDRESS A
   where E.EMPID = A.EMPID
   with check option;
   ```
   Which line will produce an error?

   A. `create view EMP_VIEW_01`

   B. `as select E.EMPID, E.LASTNAME, E.FIRSTNAME, A.ADDRESS`

   C. `from EMPLOYEE E, EMPL_ADDRESS A`

   D. `where E.EMPID = A.EMPID`

   E. `with check option;`

   F. This statement contains no errors.

6. **You are granting privileges on your table to another user. Which object privilege allows the user to create his or her own table with a foreign key on a column in your table?**

   A. `references`

   B. `index`

C. select

D. delete

7. **Which of the following statements are true about roles? (Choose three.)**

   A. Roles can be granted to other roles.

   B. Privileges can be granted to roles.

   C. Roles can be granted to users.

   D. Roles can be granted to synonyms.

8. **You are working with sequences in Oracle. After referencing NEXTVAL, the value in CURRVAL is changed in which of the following ways or to which of the following values?**

   A. Is incremented by one

   B. Is now in PREVVAL

   C. Is equal to NEXTVAL

   D. Is unchanged

9. **The EMP_SALARY table has two columns: EMP_USER and SALARY. EMP_USER is set to be the same as the Oracle username. To support user MARTHA, the salary administrator, you create a view with the following statement:**

   ```
   CREATE VIEW EMP_SAL_VW
   AS SELECT EMP_USER, SALARY
   FROM EMP_SALARY
   WHERE EMP_USER <> 'MARTHA';
   ```

   MARTHA is supposed to be able to view and update anyone's salary in the company, except her own, through this view. Which of the following clauses do you need to add to your view-creation statement in order to implement this functionality?

   A. with admin option

   B. with grant option

   C. with security option

   D. with check option

10. **The INVENTORY table has three columns: UPC_CODE, UNITS, and DELIV_DATE. The primary key is UPC_CODE. New records are added daily through a view. The view was created using the following code:**

```
CREATE VIEW DAY_INVENTORY_VW
AS SELECT UPC_CODE, UNITS, DELIV_DATE
FROM INVENTORY
WHERE DELIV_DATE = SYSDATE
WITH CHECK OPTION;
```

    What happens when you try to insert a record with duplicate UPC_CODE?

    A. The statement fails due to the `with check option` clause.

    B. The statement will succeed.

    C. The statement fails due to the primary key constraint.

    D. The statement will insert everything except the date.

11. **You are cleaning information out of an Oracle database. Which of the following statements will get rid of all views that use a table at the same time you eliminate the table from the database?**

    A. `drop view`

    B. `alter table`

    C. `drop index`

    D. `alter table drop constraint`

12. **You create a view with the following statement:**

```
CREATE VIEW BASEBALL_TEAM_VW
AS SELECT B.JERSEY_NUM, B.POSITION, B.NAME
FROM BASEBALL_TEAM B
WHERE B.NAME = USER;
```

    What will happen when user JONES attempts to select a listing for user SMITH?

    A. The `select` statement will receive an error.

    B. The `select` statement will succeed.

    C. The `select` statement will receive the NO ROWS SELECTED message from Oracle.

    D. The `select` statement will add data only to BASEBALL_TEAM.

Fill-in-the-Blank Answers

1. Synonym

2. CURRVAL

3. Updatable join view

4. Function-based index

5. Primary key (unique constraint also acceptable)

6. with check option

7. Role

8. NEXTVAL

Answers to Chapter Questions

1. B. The index will be dropped.

Explanation   Like automatically generated indexes associated with a table's primary key, the indexes created manually on a table to improve performance will be dropped if the table is dropped. Choices A, C, and D are, therefore, invalid, because the effects listed in those choices do not take place in this context..

2. C. Columns with high cardinality are handled well by B-tree indexes.

Explanation   Columns with low cardinality are the bane of B-tree indexes, thus eliminating choice A. Furthermore, bitmap indexes are primarily used for performance gains on columns with low cardinality, thus eliminating choice B. The correct answer is C. Review the discussion of how B-tree indexes work for more information.

3. D. Drop and re-create the view with references to select more columns.

Explanation   Choice A is incorrect because adding columns to the underlying table will not add columns to the view; instead, it will likely invalidate the view. Choice B is incorrect because the alter view statement simply recompiles an existing view definition, whereas the real solution here is to change the existing view definition by dropping and re-creating the view. Choice C is incorrect because a correlated subquery will likely worsen performance. This underscores the real problem—a column must be added to the view. Review the discussion of altering the definition of a view.

4. C. `maxvalue`

Explanation The `maxvalue` option is a valid option for sequence creation. Choices A and B are both part of the `create user` statement, whereas choice D is a part of a constraint declaration in an `alter table` or `create table` statement. Review the discussion on creating sequences.

5. F. This statement contains no errors.

Explanation Even though the reference to `with check option` is inappropriate, considering that `insert` operations into complex views are not possible, the statement will not actually produce an error when compiled. Therefore, there are no errors in the view. This is not something that can be learned. It requires hands-on experience with Oracle.

6. A. `references`

Explanation The `references` privilege gives the user the ability to refer back to your table in order to link to it via a foreign key from his or her table to yours. Choice B is incorrect because the `index` privilege allows the user to create an index on a table, whereas choice C is incorrect because the `select` privilege allows the user to query data in your table. Finally, choice D is incorrect because the `insert` privilege is only required for allowing the user to insert data into your table.

7. A, B, and C.

Explanation Choice D is the only option not available to managing roles. Roles cannot be granted to synonyms. Refer to the discussion of roles and privileges in this chapter.

8. C. Is equal to NEXTVAL

Explanation Once NEXTVAL is referenced, the sequence increments the integer and changes the value of CURRVAL to be equal to NEXTVAL. Refer to the discussion of sequences for more information.

9. D. `with check option`

Explanation The appropriate clause is `with check option`. You can add this clause to a `create view` statement so that the view will not allow you to add rows to the underlying table that cannot then be selected in the view. The `with {admin|grant} option` clauses are used to assign administrative ability to users, along with granting them privileges. Therefore, choices A and B are incorrect. The `with security option` is fictitious—it does not exist in Oracle. Therefore, choice C is incorrect.

10. C. The statement fails due to the primary-key constraint.

Explanation   It should be obvious that the statement fails—the real question here is why. It is because of the primary-key constraint on UPC_CODE. As soon as you try to add a duplicate record, the table will reject the addition. Although the view has with check option specified, this is not the reason the addition fails. It would be the reason an insert fails if you attempt to add a record for a day other than today, however.

11. A. drop view

Explanation   When a table is dropped, Oracle eliminates all related database objects, such as triggers, constraints, and indexes—except for views. Views are actually considered separate objects, and although the view will not function properly after you drop the underlying table, Oracle will keep the view around after the table is dropped.

12. C. The select will receive the NO ROWS SELECTED message from Oracle

Explanation   Although the query will succeed (translation: you won't receive an error), you must beware of the distracter in choice B. In reality, choice C is the better answer because it more accurately identifies what really will occur when you issue this statement. Oracle will behave as it would for any select statement you issue when you list criteria in the where clause that no data satisfies—by returning the NO ROWS SELECTED message. This is not an error condition, but you wouldn't call it a successful search for data, either, making choices A and B incorrect. Finally, select statements never add data to a table. Therefore, choice D is incorrect.

CHAPTER
5

Introducing PL/SQL

n this chapter, you will learn about and demonstrate knowledge in the following areas:

- Understanding the benefits and basic constructs of PL/SQL
- Writing executable statements
- Writing control structures

PL/SQL is Oracle's own language available for developers to code stored procedures that seamlessly integrate with database object access via the language of database objects, SQL. PL/SQL provides far more execution potential than simple `update`, `select`, `insert`, and `delete` statements. PL/SQL offers a procedural extension that allows for modularity, variable declaration, loops and other logic constructs, and advanced error handling. This chapter will present an overview of PL/SQL syntax, constructs, and usage. This information in this chapter is tested on OCP Exam 1, and it makes up 15 percent of the test material.

Since PL/SQL is used extensively in Oracle development, it is crucial that you understand this language. It is especially recommended that you take some time to work through the material in this chapter before reading Chapter 6, especially if you have no experience with PL/SQL. Don't hesitate to take breaks.

NOTE
The first topic in the Oracle8i DBA OCP Candidate Guide, "Creating Variables," is somewhat misleading. This topic is actually an overview of PL/SQL. Here it is labeled as such.

Overview of PL/SQL

This section presents an overview of PL/SQL, including the following topics:

- Benefits of PL/SQL
- Parts of a PL/SQL block
- Declaring and using variables
- Executing PL/SQL code

PL/SQL offers many advantages over other programming languages for handling the logic and enforcement of business rules in database applications. It is a straightforward language with all the common logic constructs associated with a programming language. It also includes many features that other languages don't have, such as robust error handling and modularization of code blocks. The PL/SQL code used to interface with the database is stored directly in the Oracle database, and it is the only programming language that interfaces with the Oracle database natively and within the database environment.

Benefits of PL/SQL

Chapter 1 already covered several of the benefits of PL/SQL. For review, they are listed again here:

- **PL/SQL is easy to learn and use.**   Professionals with even a modest programming background can usually pick up PL/SQL syntax fairly quickly, and they can develop programs of moderate complexity without much effort. Professionals without a programming background can learn PL/SQL with more effort spent learning basic constructs such as variable declaration, conditional statement processing, and so on.

- **PL/SQL is stored in the Oracle database.**   This means that you only need to compile the code into the Oracle database to make that code available to every user on the system. There is no need for an extended deployment, as there is with traditional client/server applications. The result is code that runs quickly and works natively with your Oracle data.

- **PL/SQL integrates well with the Oracle database.**   No special command syntax is needed to perform SQL operations involving data in the Oracle database. No colons, question marks, or other special characters are required to prefix variables, as are necessary in other languages. One exception to this rule relates to trigger development, which is a hybrid between a database object and PL/SQL.

- **PL/SQL is especially adept at processing large blocks of data.**   Oracle PL/SQL provides a special construct called a `cursor for` loop, which allows you to query several rows of table data, and then process through each row of that data in an iterative fashion. This feature allows you to process large amounts of data in bulk.

■ **PL/SQL comes with a lot of Oracle-supplied code to assist in performing tasks.** Oracle distributes several packages of PL/SQL code with every database shipped. This code enables you to perform highly specialized operations, such as file I/O, Web page retrieval into your database, job scheduling, dynamic SQL operations, interprocess communication, resource management, and much more. You can refer to these Oracle-supplied packages just like any other PL/SQL program.

■ **PL/SQL supports named and anonymous programs.** There are many different types of named programs you can develop in PL/SQL, including stored procedures, functions, and packages. These code blocks are actually compiled and stored in the database and are available for later use. You can also write anonymous programs, which are compiled at the time you submit the code for execution, executed, but not stored in the database.

■ **PL/SQL supports encapsulation and modularization.** *Encapsulation* is using one named PL/SQL program to call another named PL/SQL program. *Modularization* is breaking down a large task into several smaller components and then writing named PL/SQL programs to handle those smaller tasks. The result is code that is easier to read and maintain.

■ **PL/SQL supports overloading.** *Overloading* is when you have several different versions of the same packaged procedure or function, each accepting variables of different datatypes. When you call the overloaded procedure, Oracle dynamically decides which version of the procedure to use based on the datatype of the variable you pass.

■ **PL/SQL allows programmers to package their Oracle code.** Oracle PL/SQL supports a construct called a *package*. This feature allows you to logically group several procedures or functions that work together into a single construct. Procedures grouped together using packages perform better than they would individually, because all procedures in the package will be loaded into memory as soon as one of the procedures is referenced. In contrast, stand-alone procedures are only loaded into memory when called. This reduces the overhead Oracle requires for memory management, thus improving performance.

■ **PL/SQL supports advanced datatypes.** PL/SQL gives users the ability to define abstract datatypes such as records, allowing programmers some object-oriented flexibility in their procedural code. PL/SQL also offers table constructs for variable definition and use, approximating the use of arrays. Finally, PL/SQL allows you to declare REF datatypes, which gives PL/SQL the ability to use datatypes similar to pointers in C.

Centralized Versus Decentralized Business Logic

Many applications that use client/server architecture have one thing in common: difficulty in maintaining the business rules for an application. When business rules are decentralized throughout the application, the developers must make changes throughout the application and implement system testing to determine whether the changes are sufficient. However, in tight scheduling situations, the first deployment item to be omitted is almost invariably testing. One logical design change that should be implemented is to centralize the logic in the application to allow for easier management of changes. In systems that use an Oracle database, a "middle layer" of application logic can be designed with PL/SQL. The benefits are as follows:

- PL/SQL is managed centrally within the Oracle database. You manage source code and execution privileges with the same syntax used to manage other database objects.

- PL/SQL communicates natively with other Oracle database objects.

- PL/SQL is easy to read and has many features permitting code modularity and error handling.

Decentralized computing has increased the capacity of organizations to provide fast, easy-to-use applications to their customers. However, when business logic is stored in the client application, making changes to the business logic involves coding the changes, recompiling the client application (potentially on several different platforms), and installing the new executable versions of the client on every user's desktop. There is also overhead for communication and support to make sure that all users have the correct version of the application.

Some centralization improves the job by allowing the application development shop the ability to eliminate distribution channels for business-logic changes and to focus the client-side developers' efforts on the client application. When developers store application logic centrally, as PL/SQL stored procedures allow, they need to compile a change only once to make it immediately accessible to all users of the application. Figure 5-1 shows an example of the difference between centralized and decentralized business-logic code management.

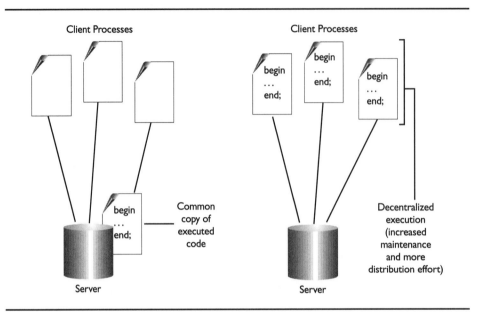

FIGURE 5-1. *Centralized versus decentralized business-logic code management*

For Review

1. Be sure that you can name some benefits of accessing the Oracle database with PL/SQL. If necessary, review the beginning of Chapter 1 for more information.

2. Know the advantages of using PL/SQL to access the database over using other programming languages for database access.

Exercises

1. You develop a PL/SQL named program and compile it. Your PL/SQL program is now stored in which of the following areas?

    A. In an executable program

    B. In a flat file

    C. In the Oracle database

    D. In SQL*Plus

2. **You are using PL/SQL to support code centralization in your organization. Which of the following choices does not identify a feature offered by PL/SQL's centralization?**

   A. More manageable upgrade process

   B. Program that takes advantage of client PC power

   C. Single copy of program available for all users

   D. Native communication with the database

3. **You want to use the feature in PL/SQL that allows different versions of the same procedure to accept information of different datatypes. Which of the following terms best describes this feature?**

   A. Encapsulation

   B. Packages

   C. Modularization

   D. Overloading

Answer Key

1. C. **2.** B. **3.** D.

Parts of a PL/SQL Block

There are three components of named or anonymous PL/SQL blocks:

- **Variable declaration section**   The declaration section, which is optional, identifies all variable constructs that will be used in the code block. A variable can be of any datatype available in the Oracle database, as well as of some other types exclusive to PL/SQL.

- **Executable section**   The executable section of a PL/SQL block is mandatory and starts with the `begin` keyword and ends either with the `end` keyword for the entire code block or with the `exception` keyword.

- **Exception handler**   The final component of a PL/SQL block is the exception handler. This code portion defines all errors that may occur in the block and specifies how they should be handled. The exception handler is optional in PL/SQL.

Here is a basic stored procedure that shows these constructs:

```
SQL> create or replace procedure no_op is
  2  /* declare your variables here*/
  3  begin
  4    null;
  5  exception
  6    when others then
  7      null;
  8  end;
  9  /
Procedure created.
```

NOTE

Comments are indicated in PL/SQL using the / */ syntax, as in C, or using two dashes (--). The null keyword can be used as a statement in PL/SQL. It simply means "do nothing." We'll discuss PL/SQL blocks in detail, such as the contents of the exception clause, in Chapter 6. When we run the preceding statements, Oracle does not actually process the PL/SQL commands we gave it. Instead, Oracle merely parses the commands for syntactic validity and stores the procedure in compiled form inside the Oracle database. Later, we can run the procedure by referencing it either from SQL*Plus or from within another PL/SQL block.*

In a named PL/SQL block such as no_op( ) in the preceding example, the declaration section is found between the is keyword and the begin keyword. PL/SQL blocks can also be nested as sub-blocks inside each other, so that begin, exception, and end keywords could appear inside another PL/SQL block, as we see here in a revised version of no_op( ):

```
SQL> create or replace procedure no_op is
  2    /* declare your variables here */
  3  begin
  4    null;
  5    begin
  6      null;
  7    exception
  8      when others then null;
  9    end;
 10  exception
```

```
11     when others then null;
12   end;
13   /
Procedure created.
```

NOTE
Notice that we used the or replace *keywords to create our revised version of* no_op( )*. Once a procedure is created, you cannot redefine it without either dropping it first or using the* or replace *keywords in the* create procedure *statement.*

Anonymous PL/SQL Blocks

Like a named block, an anonymous block contains a declaration section, an executable section, and an exception handler. It is easy to identify the declaration section of an anonymous PL/SQL block because the declaration section is preceded by the declare keyword.

Note that when we say anonymous block, we really mean a PL/SQL block that has no name. When a PL/SQL block is named, as in the preceding examples, Oracle can store the block in the database in compiled form for later execution. Anonymous blocks, on the other hand, must be compiled every time they are issued against the database, because they are not stored in Oracle.

Take a look at the following anonymous block, which shows the declaration, execution, and exception handler sections in bold:

```
SQL> declare
  2    -- nothing;
  3  begin
  4    null;
  5  exception
  6    when others then null;
  7  end;
  8  /
PL/SQL procedure successfully completed.
```

NOTE
PL/SQL blocks can be nested inside each other in anonymous blocks, too.

When we use the create procedure command, we merely tell Oracle to parse and compile some PL/SQL commands of our own design. When we issue anonymous blocks, Oracle must both parse and execute the commands we gave it.

Thus, when we used `create procedure` in the named block examples shown earlier, Oracle returned a message saying it had successfully created the procedure we defined. When we issue an anonymous block like in the preceding code, Oracle tells us it successfully ran the PL/SQL we issued. This is an important difference you need to understand for the OCP exam.

Named PL/SQL: Procedures, Functions, Packages, and Triggers

Named PL/SQL blocks like `no_op( )` can be stored and referenced by name by other PL/SQL blocks or directly by you from the SQL*Plus command line. When you submit a named block of code to Oracle, the database will parse and compile the block, and store it associated with the name you gave the block. Named blocks of PL/SQL code are divided into four categories: stored procedures, functions, packages, and triggers. The four types of named PL/SQL code blocks are described and demonstrated in the following sections.

Procedure   A *procedure* is a named block of PL/SQL code that consists of a series of statements accepting and/or returning zero or more variables. Let's look at a rewrite of the `no_op( )` procedure as it would look if it accepted a NUMBER value called MYVAR that must be passed in by anyone calling `no_op( )`:

```
SQL> create or replace procedure no_op (myvar in number) is
  2  /* declare your variables here*/
  3  begin
  4    null;
  5  exception
  6    when others then
  7      null;
  8  end;
  9  /
Procedure created.
```

Function   A *function* is a named block of PL/SQL code that consists of a series of statements accepting zero or more variables and returning one value. Because functions always return a value, they are often used for numeric calculations. Let's look at a rewrite of `no_op( )`, called `f_no_op( )`, to see what it would look like as a function:

```
SQL> create or replace function f_no_op
  2  ( myvar in number )
  3  return number is
  4  /*declare variables here */
  5  begin
  6    null;
  7    return myvar;
```

```
 8   exception
 9     when others then null;
10   end;
11   /
Function created.
```

Two important differences should immediately stand out between procedures and functions. First, we needed to define the datatype of the function's return value. Every function must return a value, so this syntax is required. Second, we explicitly defined a return value. Since every function must return a value, Oracle needs to know what to return when this function completes, so we told Oracle to simply give us back the value in MYVAR.

Package   A *package* is a named block of PL/SQL code that consists of a collection of named procedures and functions. A package has two parts. The first part is a *specification*, which lists available procedures and functions and their parameters, constants, and user-defined type declarations. Let's take a look at a package specification:

```
SQL> create or replace package my_pkg is
  2   /*********/
  3      function f_no_op
  4      ( myvar in number)
  5      return number;
  6   /********/
  7      procedure no_op
  8      ( myvar in number);
  9   end;
 10   /
Package created.
```

The second part of a package is a *body*, which contains the actual code for the procedures and functions.

```
SQL> create or replace package body my_pkg is
  2   /*********/
  3      function f_no_op (myvar in number)
  4      return number is
  5       /* declare variables here */
  6      begin
  7         null;
  8         return myvar;
  9      exception
 10         when others then null;
 11      end;
 12   /*********/
 13      procedure no_op (myvar in number) is
```

```
14      /* declare variables here */
15      begin
16        null;
17      exception
18        when others then null;
19      end;
20   end;
21   /
Package body created.
```

Trigger   A *trigger* is a named block of PL/SQL code that consists of a series of PL/SQL statements attached to a database table. Whenever a triggering event (such as update, insert, or delete) occurs, the event's corresponding trigger will fire. For example, an update trigger will fire whenever an update statement occurs, but not when an insert statement occurs.

Triggers can be defined to fire once for an entire table when the triggering event occurs, or they can fire for each row modified by the triggering event. Triggers can also be set to fire only when one column in a row changes.

```
SQL> create or replace trigger emp_trig_01
  2   before delete on emp
  3   begin
  4       null;
  5   exception
  6       when others then null;
  7   end;
  8   /
Trigger created.
```

Modularity in PL/SQL Programs

PL/SQL also permits you to subdivide your program into modules to improve software reusability and to hide the complexity of execution of specific operations. For example, there may be a complex process involved in adding an employee record to a corporate database, which requires records to be added to several different tables for several different applications. Stored procedures may handle the addition of records to each of the systems, making it appear to the user as if the only step required were entering data on one screen. In reality, that screen's worth of data entry may call dozens of separate procedures, each designed to handle one small component of the overall process of adding the employee. These components may even be reused data-entry code blocks from the various pension, health-care, day-care, payroll, and other human resources applications, which have simply been repackaged around this new data-entry screen. Figure 5-2 shows how modularity can be implemented in PL/SQL blocks.

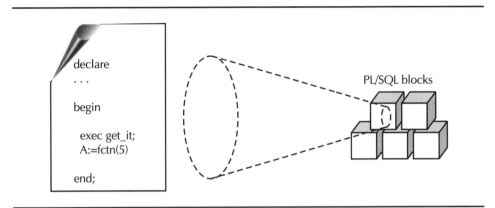

FIGURE 5-2.   *Modularity and PS/SQL blocks*

Process Flow and Logic Constructs

PL/SQL offers logic constructs such as loops, conditional statements, variable assignments, and other expressions. Other logic constructs include PL/SQL tables and records. These "procedural" constructs are the items in PL/SQL that allow it to be both a programming language for supporting business rules and a functional language for providing data.

Cursors

One of the real strengths of PL/SQL is its ability to handle cursors. A *cursor* is a handle to an address in memory that stores the results of an executed SQL statement. Oracle runs most SQL statements in a cursor, and we'll talk more about implicit and explicit cursors in Chapter 6. Cursors are extremely useful for performing operations on each row returned from a `select` statement. Therefore, PL/SQL programmers often use the looping procedural constructs of PL/SQL in conjunction with cursor-manipulation operations.

Error Handling

Errors are called *exceptions* in PL/SQL, and they are checked implicitly anywhere in the code block. We have already seen a few basic exception handlers. If, at any time, an error occurs in the code block, the exception corresponding to that error can be raised. At that point, execution in the executable code block stops and control is transferred to the exception handler. There are many different types of exceptions in Oracle, some defined by the user and others defined by Oracle.

NOTE
Although all the code blocks we've seen so far contained exception handlers, the exception section is not required in PL/SQL blocks.

For Review

1. Be sure that you can identify the three parts of a PL/SQL block: declaration, execution, and exception handler.

2. Know the syntactic and semantic differences between named and anonymous blocks. The most important difference to remember is that named blocks are stored in Oracle as compiled code and can be referenced with a procedure or function call either from other PL/SQL blocks or from the SQL*Plus command line. Anonymous blocks must be parsed and executed every time they are run, and they are usually stored in flat files called from SQL*Plus.

3. Understand that stored PL/SQL, such as procedures, functions, and packages, are stored in the Oracle database, while anonymous block are not.

Exercises

1. **Use the following code block to answer this question:**

```
SQL> create or replace package my_pkg is
  2  /*********/
  3    function f_no_op
  4    ( myvar in number)
  5    return number;
  6  /********/
  7    procedure no_op
  8    ( myvar in number);
  9  end;
 10  /
Package created.
```

Which of the following choices identifies the type of code block shown here?

A. Package specification

B. Package body

    C. Procedure specification

    D. Procedure body

2. **You are creating a function in PL/SQL. Which two of the following components must appear in every function in PL/SQL (without them, Oracle returns an error)?**

    A. Declared variables

    B. A `return` statement

    C. A `begin-end` section

    D. An `exception` section

3. **You are developing PL/SQL programs in Oracle8i. Which of the following choices best describes a possible definition for a trigger?**

    A. A code block containing procedure and function specifications that has an associated body containing the actual code

    B. A code block containing procedure and function bodies that has an associated specification containing the procedure and function definitions

    C. A code block associated with a table that Oracle executes whenever a specified event occurs

    D. An unnamed code block parsed and executed at the same time

---

Answer Key

1. A. **2.** B and C. **3.** C.

Declaring and Using Variables

A variable is a name for an address in memory, which can be used to store a value. You can declare a variable inside your variable declaration section of the PL/SQL block. PL/SQL offers a great deal of flexibility in variable declaration. The string used to identify a variable can contain alphanumeric characters A–Z, a–z, and 0–9. The string can also contain the special characters $, #, and _. It cannot contain any ampersands (&), hyphens (-), or spaces. Be careful not to use a PL/SQL reserved word as the name of a variable; otherwise, Oracle will give you an error when you compile your block.

Database Datatypes Used to Declare Variables

Variables must be declared to have a certain datatype. There are several datatypes that can be used in PL/SQL that correspond to the datatypes used in the database. For a refresher, these types are listed here:

- **NUMBER(*size*[,*precision*])**   Used to store any number.

- **CHAR(*size*), VARCHAR2(*size*)**   Used to store alphanumeric text strings. The CHAR datatype pads the value stored to the full length of the variable with blanks.

- **DATE**   Used to store dates.

- **LONG**   Used to store large blocks of text, up to 2 gigabytes in length.

- **LONG RAW**   Used to store large blocks of data in binary format.

- **RAW**   Used to store smaller blocks of data in binary format.

- **ROWID**   Used to store the special format of ROWIDs in the database.

- **BLOB, CLOB, NCLOB, and BFILE**   Large object datatypes from Oracle8.

Nondatabase Datatypes

There are also several other PL/SQL datatypes you can use for declaring your variables that are not designed for use in storing data to a table. The following are the nondatabase datatypes PL/SQL offers:

- **DEC, DECIMAL, REAL, and DOUBLE_PRECISION**   Numeric datatypes that are a subset of the NUMBER datatype used for variable declaration in PL/SQL.

- **INTEGER, INT, SMALLINT, NATURAL, POSITIVE, and NUMERIC**   Numeric datatypes that are a subset of the NUMBER datatype used for variable declaration in PL/SQL.

- **BINARY_INTEGER, and PLS_INTEGER**   Used to store integers. A variable in either format cannot be stored in the database without conversion first.

- **CHARACTER**   Another name for the CHAR datatype.

- **VARCHAR**   Another name for the VARCHAR2 datatype.

- **BOOLEAN**   Used to store a TRUE/FALSE value.

- **TABLE**   Used to store the equivalent of an array.

- **RECORD**   Used to store variables with composite datatypes.

CAUTION
Be careful when declaring variables using these PL/SQL datatypes. You may experience problems later when you try to add the values to your database.

Variable Declaration and Assignment

Let's take a look at a variation of our anonymous code block example from earlier in the chapter. This version contains a declared variable called MYVAR:

```
SQL> declare
  2    myvar number;
  3  begin
  4     null;
  5  exception
  6     when others then null;
  7  end;
  8  /
PL/SQL procedure successfully completed.
```

It is possible to assign an initial value to a variable in the declaration section of the code block, as shown here:

```
SQL> declare
  2    myvar number default 0;
  3  begin
  4     null;
  5  exception
  6     when others then null;
  7  end;
  8  /
PL/SQL procedure successfully completed.
```

Later, when we want to manipulate some numbers inside the execution portion of the block, we can assign a value to the variable using the assignment character, which is the colon followed by an equal sign (:=):

```
SQL> declare
  2    myvar number default 0;
  3  begin
  4     myvar := 50;
  5  exception
  6     when others then null;
  7  end;
  8  /
PL/SQL procedure successfully completed.
```

TIP
You can also use the assignment operator in place of the default *keyword to assign an initial value to a variable in the declaration section. However, the equality (=) operator is for comparison only in PL/SQL.*

Variable Declaration and Scope

The concept of variable scope is important with respect to variable declaration and nested PL/SQL blocks. Variable scope in PL/SQL refers to Oracle's ability to see variables in parent blocks when executing statements in sub-blocks. Since you can create sub-blocks anywhere you want in your execution section, you can declare variables for that sub-block to use as well. In addition, the variables in the parent block can be referenced, as in the following example:

```
SQL> declare
  2    myvar number;
  3  begin
  4    myvar := 3;
  5      declare
  6        myvar2 number;
  7      begin
  8        myvar2 := myvar;
  9      end;
 10  end;
 11  /
PL/SQL procedure successfully completed.
```

Constant Declaration

It may be useful for you to declare constants in the declaration section of the PL/SQL blocks. Constants make a good substitute for the use of hard-coded values, or *magic numbers*. A magic number in programming is a value that is required to perform an operation or calculation but does not have any sort of meaning in the code block to help others identify why the value is there. For example, let's say we define a function that calculates the area of a circle, which is the number pi times radius squared. The number pi is well known to most people; but if it were not, imagine how difficult it would be to understand the reason for having the number 3.14159265358 in the middle of the function. Declaring pi as a constant makes the purpose of the value clearer in the code block:

```
SQL> create or replace function area_of_a_circle
  2  (p_radius in number) return number is
  3    my_area number default 0;
```

```
   4     pi constant number := 3.14159265358;
   5  begin
   6    my_area := p_radius * p_radius * pi;
   7    return my_area;
   8  end;
   9  /
Function created.
```

CAUTION

Once you've assigned a value to a variable you defined as a constant, you cannot redefine the constant's value later in the executable section of your PL/SQL block. Its value is precisely that—constant! The value passed into the P_RADIUS variable in the function may not be changed, either.

Functions and Variable Assignment

Variable assignment can be accomplished in a variety of ways in the executable section, particularly where functions are concerned. Since functions always return a value, you can reference a function as part of variable assignment to place that return value in the variable, as shown here:

```
SQL> declare
  2    my_area number default 0;
  3  begin
  4    my_area := area_of_a_circle(5);
  5  exception
  6    when others then null;
  7  end;
  8  /
PL/SQL procedure successfully completed.
```

Subtype Declaration

In addition to using standard PL/SQL datatypes, you can also declare a user-defined type as a subtype of a standard datatype. This is accomplished using the `subtype` *mydatatype* is *oracledatatype* command, where *mydatatype* is the name of your subtype, and *oracledatatype* is the name of a standard datatype in Oracle. You then declare your variable as that subtype, as shown in the following block:

```
SQL> declare
  2    subtype birthdates is date;
```

```
3     stacy_birthday birthdates;
4   begin
5     stacy_birthday := '26-JUN-75';
6   end;
7   /
PL/SQL procedure successfully completed.
```

TIP
Subtypes are compatible with each other as long as the base type is the same. Thus, if you had two different subtypes declared as base type DATE, and two variables declared as each subtype, you could assign the value in one variable of one subtype to a variable of a different subtype.

For Review

1. Know that variables declared in your PL/SQL block can be assigned values anywhere in your PL/SQL block, including the declaration section. Also know how to define constants.

2. Be able to distinguish the equality comparison operator from the assignment operator. Know that you can substitute the `default` keyword for the assignment operator when assigning a value to a variable in the declaration section of your PL/SQL block.

3. Understand the database and nondatabase datatypes that can be used in PL/SQL. Know what a subtype is and how to define and declare variables as subtypes. Be sure that you can describe subtype compatibility.

Exercises

1. **Use the following code block to answer this question:**

```
SQL> declare
2    myvar number;
3  begin
4    null;
5     declare
6       myvar2 number;
7     begin
8        myvar2 := 3;
9     end;
```

```
10   myvar := myvar2;
11   end;
12   /
```

Which of the following choices identifies how Oracle will respond when you try to execute this block?

A. Oracle will process the PL/SQL statements successfully.

B. Oracle will return an error stating that the `declare` keyword in line 5 is incorrect.

C. Oracle will return an error stating that the assignment in line 8 is incorrect.

D. Oracle will return an error stating that the assignment in line 10 is incorrect.

2. **Use the following code block to answer this question:**

```
SQL> create or replace function area_of_a_circle
  2   (p_radius in number) return number is
  3     my_area number default 0;
  4     pi constant number := 3.14159265358;
  5   begin
  6     pi := pi + 1;
  7     my_area := p_radius * p_radius * pi;
  8     return my_area;
  9   end;
 10   /
```

Which of the following choices identifies how Oracle will respond to this PL/SQL code?

A. Oracle will create the function successfully.

B. Oracle will return an error stating that the declaration in line 4 is invalid.

C. Oracle will return an error stating that the assignment in line 6 is incorrect.

D. Oracle will return an error stating that the assignment in line 7 is incorrect.

3. **Two variables are declared as different subtypes. The base type for both is VARCHAR2. What happens when you attempt to compare the variables?**

A. Oracle returns an error because subtype comparison is not allowed.

B. Oracle permits the comparison because the base types are identical.

C. Oracle disregards the statement.

D. Oracle converts the subtype of one variable to the subtype of the other for the comparison.

Answer Key

1. D. **2.** C. **3.** A.

Executing PL/SQL Code

After you've developed a code block, there are a number of methods you can use to execute the block. You've seen the easiest method for executing named functions, which is to simply call the function as part of variable assignment in another PL/SQL block. Executing named procedures is even easier. You simply include the name of the block, include values for the parameters passed (if any), and handle any return values the procedure may have. No special syntax is necessary.

The following code block illustrates an example of our procedure no_op ( ), where the procedure both accepts and returns a value, assigning the value in P_VAR to variable P_VAR2:

```
SQL> create or replace procedure no_op
  2  (p_var in number, p_var2 out number) is
  3  begin
  4     p_var2 := p_var;
  5  exception
  6     when others then null;
  7  end;
  8  /
Procedure created.
```

TIP
You can also define variables that both accept values at the beginning of the procedure and return a value at the end using the in out *syntax. Here's an example:* p_var2 in out number.

Now, we can execute no_op ( ) from inside an anonymous PL/SQL block, using the following procedure:

1. We must declare a variable in our anonymous block to store the return value from procedure no_op( ).

2. We call no_op( ) from within the executable section of our anonymous block. The value 5 is passed into no_op( ) and stored in the P_VAR variable.

3. The no_op( ) procedure assigns the value in P_VAR to P_VAR2.

4. When no_op( ) ends, the value in P_VAR2 is passed back to the MYVAR2 variable in our anonymous block for us to use.

Here is the code:

```
SQL> declare
  2  myvar2 number;
  3  begin
  4  no_op(5, myvar2);
  5  end;
  6  /
PL/SQL procedure successfully completed.
```

Executing Anonymous PL/SQL Blocks from Flat Files

If you intend to reuse the code in an anonymous block, you should store the anonymous block in a flat file so you can execute the block as a script. If the anonymous block in the previous example were stored in a script called myblock.sql, we could call it later from SQL*Plus using the get and run commands, as shown here:

```
SQL> get myblock.sql
  1  declare
  2   myvar2 number;
  3  begin
  4   no_op(5, myvar2);
  5  end;
SQL> run
PL/SQL procedure successfully completed.
```

Alternatively, you could use the @ command, as shown here:

```
SQL> @c:\windows\myblock.sql
PL/SQL procedure successfully completed.
```

TIP

If the filename you are getting or running has a .sql *extension, you can type in the filename without the extension for both the* run *and the* @ *commands, and those commands should operate fine. You should specify the path where the file can be found if that file is not located in the directory from which you started SQL*Plus.*

Executing PL/SQL Procedures

If you've loaded a PL/SQL block into the Oracle database as a stored procedure, you can reference it for execution in SQL*Plus by using the execute command, sometimes abbreviated exec. Assuming we still have the version of no_op( ) that accepts no parameters, which we created at the beginning of the chapter, the following code block illustrates how we might execute it:

```
SQL> execute no_op;
PL/SQL procedure successfully completed.
```

Executing procedures that accept parameters is only slightly more complex. You can either pass the parameters positionally or with direct references. Let's take a look at a procedure called divisor( ), which accepts a dividend and a quotient, in that order, and identifies the divisor. Here is one way to pass the parameters into this procedure:

```
SQL> execute divisor(12,60);
PL/SQL procedure successfully completed.
```

Alternatively, you could pass the parameters as follows:

```
SQL> execute divisor(quotient=>60, dividend=>12);
PL/SQL procedure successfully completed.
```

NOTE

This trivial example refers to a code block we haven't created. The => pointer can be used for passing values into parameters that aren't assigned positionally. For now, we are focusing on how to execute the procedure, rather than on the parameters.

Executing Stored Functions and Procedures with Return Values

As a general rule, you must call functions and procedures with return values only from within other PL/SQL code. This is because you need to also declare variables that will store the values returned. Let's revisit an earlier example of an anonymous block that illustrates how to call a function:

```
SQL> declare
  2   my_area number default 0;
  3  begin
  4    my_area := area_of_a_circle(5);
  5  exception
  6    when others then null;
  7  end;
  8  /
PL/SQL procedure successfully completed.
```

Now, let's look at another anonymous block we've already seen, to understand how to call procedures that return values:

```
SQL> declare
  2   myvar2 number;
  3  begin
  4    no_op(5, myvar2);
  5  end;
  6  /
PL/SQL procedure successfully completed.
```

Executing Packaged Procedures and Functions

When you are executing procedures and functions stored in a package, you must prefix the name of the package to the name of the procedure or function. Let's take a look:

```
SQL> declare
  2    myvar number;
  3  begin
  4    myvar := my_pkg.f_no_op(5);
  5    my_pkg.no_op(5);
  6  end;
  7  /
PL/SQL procedure successfully completed.
```

For Review

1. Be able to identify and describe the ways that you can execute anonymous code blocks in SQL*Plus, either by simply typing in the block or by using a script.

2. Know how to execute stored procedures from the SQL*Plus command line.

3. Know how to call stored functions and procedures that return a value from within an anonymous block.

4. Understand how to call a packaged function by prefixing the function with the package it belongs to.

Exercises

1. You have a procedure called `calc_my_assets( )` that accepts two variables and returns one variable. This procedure is stored in a package called FIN_PKG. Which of the following choices identifies how you might call this procedure?

   A. As `fin_pkg.calc_my_assets( )` from the SQL*Plus command line

   B. As `fin_pkg.calc_my_assets( )` from an anonymous block

   C. As `calc_my_assets( )` from the SQL*Plus command line

   D. As `calc_my_assets( )` from an anonymous block

2. You have an anonymous block stored in a flat file for repeated execution. Which of the following choices identifies the commands you would use in SQL*Plus to execute this file in one operation?

   A. Use the `get` command followed by the `run` command.

   B. Use the `get` command followed by the `@` command.

   C. Use the `@` command by itself.

   D. Use the `run` command by itself.

3. You wish to define a procedure that accepts a value into a variable called P_VAR1 and returns the square of that value in a variable called P_VAR2. Which of the following choices identifies how you would define the parameter passing for this procedure?

   A. `create or replace procedure my_proc (P_VAR1 in number,`
      `P_VAR2 in number)`

B. `create or replace procedure my_proc (P_VAR1 in out number, P_VAR2 in number)`

C. `create or replace procedure my_proc (P_VAR1 out number, P_VAR2 out number)`

D. `create or replace procedure my_proc (P_VAR1 in number, P_VAR2 out number)`

Answer Key

1. B. 2. C. 3. D.

Writing Executable Statements

This section covers the following topics related to developing executable PL/SQL code:

- Writing executable PL/SQL statements
- Nesting PL/SQL blocks
- Executing and testing PL/SQL
- Using code conventions

Now that you understand the overall benefits of PL/SQL programming, along with how to code a basic declaration section in your PL/SQL block, let's focus on how to develop the rest of your code. But wait a minute! We've already looked at some developed code blocks, albeit very simple ones. This section backs up to cover the theory that underlies the sample development we've done so far. The first area covered is the significance of the executable section. Then you will learn how to write basic executable statements in PL/SQL, nest PL/SQL blocks inside other blocks, and execute and test PL/SQL code. Finally, you will learn about some basic code conventions used in PL/SQL applications.

Writing Executable PL/SQL Statements

As you have learned, PL/SQL programs consist of lines of text using a specific set of characters. The PL/SQL character set includes the uppercase and lowercase letters A–Z and a–z. The character set also includes the numerals 0 through 9 and the following symbols: ( ) + –* / < > = ! ~ ^ ; : ." @ % , "# $ & _ | { } ? [ ]. You can have tabs, spaces, and carriage returns in a line of PL/SQL code. PL/SQL is not case sensitive, so uppercase letters are equivalent to corresponding lowercase letters, except within string and character literals (such as, `"I am Happy"`), which are usually enclosed in single quotation marks.

A line of PL/SQL text contains groups of characters known as *lexical units*, which can be classified as follows:

- Delimiters (both simple and compound symbols)

- Identifiers, which include reserved words

- Literals, such as text strings or math equations

- Comments

For example, this line of code computes a bonus for an employee:

```
bonus := salary * 0.10; -- compute bonus
```

This line contains several lexical units. The identifiers are `bonus` and `salary`. The delimiters are the compound symbol `:=` and the simple symbols `*` and `;`. It also contains the numeric literal `0.10`. Finally, it has the comment `-- compute bonus`. Single-line comments are preceded by two dashes (--); multiple-line comments are the same as in C (`/* comment */`).

You could type the preceding line of code as follows:

```
bonus:=salary*0.10;--computebonus
```

Oracle would understand what you wanted. I don't recommend you do so, however. To improve your code's readability, you should separate lexical units by spaces. You can also divide lines using carriage returns, and indent lines using spaces or tabs, such as with `if-then` statements, as you will see later. However, you cannot embed spaces in lexical units except for string literals and comments. For example, Oracle returns an error in the following code block because the compound symbol for assignment (:=) is split:

```
SQL> declare
  2    cnt number default 0;
  3  begin
  4    cnt : = cnt + 1;
  5  end;
  6  /
  cnt : = cnt + 1;
          *
ERROR at line 4:
ORA-06550: line 4, column 8:
PLS-00103: Encountered the symbol ":" when expecting one of
  the following: := . ( @ % ;
```

NOTE
Every executable statement in the execution section must be terminated with a semicolon. However, keywords like declare *and* begin *are not immediately followed by semicolons.*

PL/SQL offers the same math operators (like +,–, *, and /), comparison operations, and logic constructs that SQL offers. The same operator precedence that exists in SQL also exists in PL/SQL, and that precedence can also be short-circuited using parentheses; so remember PEMDAS and you should be fine.

TIP
Some people use the following mnemonic to remember PEMDAS: Please Excuse My Dear Aunt Sally. It stands for Parentheses, Exponents, Multiplication, Division, Addition, and Subtraction.

Other than that, there's not a whole lot to say about writing executable statements. The best way to learn how to write PL/SQL statements is to actually develop PL/SQL code. We will explore that topic in detail for the rest of the chapter.

For Review

1. Be sure that you understand the basic syntax and semantics for developing PL/SQL blocks.

2. Know the difference between identifiers, delimiters, literals, and comments in a PL/SQL block.

Exercises

1. **Solve for *x* in the following code block:**

```
declare
   x number default 0;
begin
   x := 24 - 12 + 36 / 6 - 3;
end;
```

A. 3

B. 5

C. 12

D. 15

2. **Use the following code block to answer this question:**

```
declare
    x number default 0;
begin
    x := 24 - 12 + 36 / 6 - 3;
end;
```

Which of the following choices identifies the PL/SQL component highlighted in bold in the code block above?

A. Literal

B. Comment

C. Delimiter

D. Identifier

3. **You are coding PL/SQL blocks. Which of the following compound symbols requires an associated enclosing symbol (or else Oracle returns an error)?**

A. :=

B. /*

C. --

D. @@

Answer Key

1. D. You might think it's silly of me to cover high school mathematics here, in a book about databases, no less! But, believe me, you will see questions about operator precedence on the OCP exam, so sharpen your pencil. 2. A. 3. B.

Nesting PL/SQL Blocks

You have already seen examples of how to nest unnamed PL/SQL blocks inside other blocks. Let's look at another situation, where we nest named PL/SQL sub-blocks inside other blocks. This is done in the declaration section of the PL/SQL block. However, be careful to ensure that all named sub-blocks are declared at the end of the declaration section. The following code block illustrates the development of named sub-blocks inside other blocks:

```
CREATE OR REPLACE PROCEDURE myproc IS      -- declare all other
myproc_x number default 0;                 -- variables and cursors
                                           -- before sub-block

  FUNCTION subfunc RETURN number IS
     subfunc_x number default 50;
   BEGIN                                 -- begin subfunc
     subfunc_x := myproc_x +3;           -- acceptable assignment
     return subfunc_x;                   -- required for function
   END;                                  -- end subfunc

BEGIN                                    -- main procedure
    myproc_x := subfunc;                 -- assignment to call function
END;                                     -- DONE!
```

Variable Scope and Visibility

Just as with nesting unnamed blocks inside other blocks, you must consider variable scope and visibility to use variables in named sub-blocks correctly. In general, variables declared and used by the parent block are local to the parent and global to the sub-block. Thus, we can assign the value in MYPROC_X to SUBFUNC_X in the named sub-block in the preceding code block. Variables declared and used by the sub-block are local to the sub-block only, thus preventing us from assigning the value in SUBFUNC_X to MYPROC_X later in the main block. However, notice that we use the intrinsic nature of functions to our advantage by assigning the value returned from subfunc( ) to MYPROC_X.

Multiple sub-blocks can exist peer-to-peer in the main block. We could have created several other named procedures, functions, or even unnamed blocks as sub-blocks to the procedure myproc( ). However, remember that variables declared and used in sub-blocks are local only to that block. Not only are those variables not visible to the main block, they are not visible in other sub-blocks, either. If you want the sub-blocks to see each other's variables, you must pass them back and forth as parameters (for procedures) or as return values (for functions). Let's take a look:

```
CREATE OR REPLACE PROCEDURE myproc IS      -- declare all other
myproc_x number default 0;                 -- variables and cursors
                                           -- before sub-block

  FUNCTION subfunc1 RETURN number IS
     subfunc_x number default 50;
   BEGIN                                 -- begin subfunc1
     subfunc_x := myproc_x +3;           -- acceptable assignment
     return subfunc_x;                   -- required for function
   END;                                  -- end subfunc

  FUNCTION sub-func2 RETURN number IS
     subfunc_x number default 0;         -- sub-func2 cannot see
```

```
                              -- subfunc_x in subfunc1
  BEGIN                       -- begin sub-func2
    subfunc_x := sub-func1;   -- call sub-func1 to get value
    return subfunc_x;         -- required for function
  END;                        -- end sub-func

BEGIN                         -- main procedure
    myproc_x := sub-func2;    -- Call sub-func2 to get value
END;                          -- DONE!
```

For Review

1. Be sure that you understand the concept of nesting PL/SQL blocks inside other blocks.

2. Be sure that you understand variable visibility and scope when nesting PL/SQL blocks.

Exercises

1. You have a function called **func1 ( )** with three named sub-blocks: func2 ( ), **func3 ( )**, and **func4 ( )**. Each contains a single variable declaration, FX1, FX2, FX3, and FX4, respectively. Which of the following choices correctly identifies the scope of visibility for a variable and code block?

   A. FX1 can be seen from func4 ( ).

   B. FX2 can bee seen from func3 ( ).

   C. FX3 can be seen from func2 ( ).

   D. FX4 can be seen from func1 ( ).

2. Use the following code block to answer this question:

   ```
   Create or replace procedure myproc is
     function myfunc return number is
       var1 number;
     begin
       var1 := 456;
       return var1;
     end;
    var2 number;
    var3 constant varchar2 := 'FLIPPER';
    begin
       var2 := myfunc;
    end;
   ```

Which of the following choices identifies the problem with this code block?

A. The declaration of VAR3 as a constant is inappropriate for this datatype.

B. The assignment of VAR2 is defined incorrectly.

C. The placement of the sub-block is incorrect.

D. The sub-block is not ended properly.

3. **This type of sub-block can appear anywhere in the declaration or executable areas of a PL/SQL block:** _____

Answer Key

1. A. **2.** C. **3.** Unnamed.

Executing and Testing PL/SQL

You have already seen how to execute a block of PL/SQL. The first test of any PL/SQL block in Oracle is whether it will compile. You can debug compilation of your PL/SQL code in SQL*Plus by simply creating your named block with the create [or replace] command. If all goes well, Oracle returns the procedure created, function created, package created, package body created, or trigger created message—whichever is appropriate to your code block. If the compilation didn't go well, then you receive the Warning: procedure created with compilation errors message.

Viewing Compilation Errors

To view compilation errors, use the show errors command in SQL*Plus. The following code block illustrates a ridiculously simple example:

```
SQL> create or replace procedure myproc
  2  is
  3    x, y, z integer;
  4  begin
  5    null;
  6  end;
  7  /
Warning: Procedure created with compilation errors.
SQL> show errors
Errors for PROCEDURE MYPROC:
LINE/COL ERROR
```

```
------------------------------------------------------------------
3/3        PLS-00103: Encountered the symbol "," when expecting one of
           the following:
           constant exception <an identifier>
           <a double-quoted delimited-identifier> table LONG_ double ref
           char time timestamp interval binary national character nchar

3/17       PLS-00103: Encountered the symbol ";" when expecting one of
           the following:
           , from into bulk

7/0        PLS-00103: Encountered the symbol "end-of-file" when expecting
           one of the following:
           function package pragma procedure form
```

Now you know there are three errors in your code, right? Well, not exactly. The bad news is that Oracle is good at telling you that something is wrong, but not always so good at telling you how to fix it. The good news is that you know where to start. The best place to start with your output from the show errors command is with the first error it identified. So, we turn our attention to line 3 in the code block:

```
SQL> 3
  3*  x, y, z integer;
```

In effect, Oracle is telling you that you put a comma where you weren't supposed to. We both know you were trying to declare three variables at once, but Oracle doesn't let you do it that way. Instead, Oracle knows what it expects after you identify a variable name, so it tells you what it expected. It's up to you to realize, based on careful examination of the code (and the examples in this book), that you need to define all your variables separately. The following block shows the fix:

```
SQL> create or replace procedure myproc
  2  is
  3    x integer;
  4    y integer;
  5    z integer;
  6  begin
  7    null;
  8  end;
  9  /
Procedure created.
```

TIP
Of all the errors that may occur in your programming, by far the most common (and thus annoying) is forgetting the semicolon after a line of code. What makes this problem such a drag is that Oracle almost always gives you the wrong line number (usually a line or two below where the error actually exists) when identifying the error. If you encounter a situation where Oracle tells you a line of your code contains an error and you know the line is correct, take a look at the preceding two or three lines to see if there is a missing semicolon.

Debugging Anonymous Blocks

Testing anonymous blocks takes fewer steps than testing named blocks, but it can be a lot more confusing. Since anonymous blocks are compiled and executed at the time the block is submitted to the PL/SQL engine, your debugging effort consists simply of executing the code block until there are no errors in its execution—there is no need for the show errors command. Here is an example:

```
SQL> declare
  2    x, y, z integer;
  3  begin
  4    null;
  5  end;
  6  /
x, y, z integer;
  *
ERROR at line 2:
ORA-06550: line 2, column 3:
PLS-00103: Encountered the symbol "," when expecting one of the
following:
constant exception <an identifier>
<a double-quoted delimited-identifier> table LONG_ double ref
char time timestamp interval binary national character nchar
ORA-06550: line 2, column 17:
PLS-00103: Encountered the symbol ";" when expecting one of the
following:
, from into bulk
ORA-06550: line 6, column 0:
PLS-00103: Encountered the symbol "end-of-file" when expecting
one of the following:
begin function package pragma procedure form
```

We fix this block in the same way as we corrected the code in the previous example:

```
SQL>  declare
    2    x integer;
    3    y integer;
    4    z integer;
    5  begin
    6     null;
    7  end;
SQL> /
PL/SQL procedure successfully completed.
```

For Review

1. Be sure that you understand how to compile named and anonymous blocks of PL/SQL.

2. Know how to identify compilation errors for named blocks using show errors.

Exercises

1. **Use the following code block to answer this question:**

```
SQL> create or replace procedure myproc is
    2    var1 varchar2;
    3    var2 number
    4    function myfunc return number is
    5    begin
    6      return 5;
    7    end;
    8  begin
    9    var1 := myfunc;
   10  end;
   11  /
Warning: Procedure created with compilation errors.
SQL> show errors
Errors for PROCEDURE MYPROC:
LINE/COL ERROR
-------------------------------------------------------------
4/2      PLS-00103: Encountered the symbol "FUNCTION" when
         expecting one of the following:
         := . ( @ % ; not null range default character
```

Which of the following choices identifies the line number containing the error you should correct, based exclusively on this message?

A. 2

B. 3

C. 4

D. 9

2. Use the code block in the preceding question to answer this quesion. Of the errors in other lines not indicated by Oracle in the preceding block, which line will most likely require correction after you correct the error Oracle indicated?

A. 2

B. 3

C. 4

D. 9

3. Again, use the code block in question 1 to answer this question. After you correct the error indicated by Oracle as part of question 2, which of the following lines of code will Oracle next flag as an error?

A. 2

B. 3

C. 9

D. None, Oracle compiles the code successfully.

Answer Key

1. B. Even though Oracle said the error was in line 4, the problem lies in the missing semicolon at the end of line 3. **2.** A. Oracle flags line 2 as erroneous because the VARCHAR2 type is missing a size specification. Other errors Oracle indicates are related to this problem as well. **3.** D. Even though VAR1 in line 9 declared as VARCHAR2 data receives NUMBER data back from the function, Oracle does not consider this an error. Why? Because Oracle can implicitly convert the NUMBER output into VARCHAR2 format on-the-fly.

Using Code Conventions

PL/SQL naming conventions must be followed in order for your code to work as intended. On the other hand, you are free to choose your own programming styles; however, following some basic guidelines will make your code more readable.

Naming Conventions

The same naming conventions apply to all PL/SQL program items and units, including constants, variables, cursors, cursor variables, exceptions, procedures, functions, and packages. Names can be simple, qualified, remote, or both qualified and remote. For example, you might use the procedure name `raise_salary( )` in any of the following ways:

```
raise_salary(...);                          -- simple
emp_actions.raise_salary(...);              -- qualified
raise_salary@newyork(...);                  -- remote
emp_actions.raise_salary@newyork(...);   -- qualified and remote
```

In the first case, you simply use the procedure name. In the second case, you must qualify the name using dot notation because the procedure is stored in a package called `emp_actions`. In the third case, using the remote access indicator (@), you reference the database link `newyork` because the procedure is stored in a remote database. In the fourth case, you qualify the procedure name and reference a database link.

Programming Style

How you program is up to you—the OCP exam doesn't test stylistic guidelines. But whatever way you program, be sure you accomplish two things. First, your code must work. Second, you must understand it so you (or someone else) can rewrite it later. As a matter of stylistic preference, I use the following guidelines.

Use Named Functions Only   I try only to use named functions as sub-blocks to other named code blocks. This is because I find the intrinsic nature of functions returning values to be a more elegant way to program, as opposed to passing values in variables between procedures like hot potatoes.

Indent Code   I indent my sub-blocks, loops, and conditional statements a little bit from the rest of my code so I know where each line fits into the overall puzzle. The examples you see in this book follow that convention.

Forget About It Safely—Add Comments   I like to add a lot of comments so later I can figure out what I wrote. People will ask you to rewrite your programs *endlessly*! I have yet to experience a situation in which a user's request for a 10-minute code change actually takes 10 minutes; it's usually more like 10 hours. The difference between leaving the office at 7 P.M. and 7 A.M. is usually a well-commented program.

KISS Me   I like to follow the KISS method: Keep It Short and Simple! How short? Each individual procedure or function should stay under one printed page if possible. If I need to write a complex program, I try to break it down into smaller procedures that each perform one little part of the job. My main program then looks like a series of calls to other programs.

Put Litter in Its Place   I prefer not to litter my programs with many unnamed sub-blocks. If you are tempted to write something as an unnamed sub-block, think about rewriting it as a named sub-block. Better yet, consider making it a stand-alone procedure or function, so you can use it again later.

Magic Isn't Magical   I try to avoid magic numbers and instead use constants. The beauty of a constant is that you can change the number later in only one place, and your code still works. Leave the smoke and mirrors where they belong—in your boss's office.

TIP
This is by no means a comprehensive list of how to program PL/SQL. Given that OCP doesn't test your elegant style as a programmer, we've probably digressed as far as we ought to on this topic. There are many sources for good PL/SQL programming style guidelines on the Internet, the most important of which is probably www.revealnet.com. Happy coding!

For Review

Be sure to understand the code conventions for calling simple, qualified, and remote objects.

Exercises

1. **You wish to refer to a remote procedure in a distributed database environment. Which of the following displays a possible reference to that procedure?**

    A. `raise_salary( );`

    B. `emp_actions.raise_salary( );`

    C. `raise_salary@newyork( );`

    D. `scott.emp_actions.raise_salary( );`

2. **This coding convention allows you to declare variables inside your executable section of the PL/SQL block (two words):**

_____

Answer Key

1. C. **2.** Unnamed sub-blocks.

Writing Control Structures

This section covers the following topics related to controlling PL/SQL process flow:

■ Constructing an `if-then` statement

■ Using loops

■ Using logic tables

■ Using nested loops and labels

No programming language is complete without the use of semantic devices to control the processing flow of its code. There are a few basic types of control structures for statement processing in PL/SQL:

■ **Conditional control** Sometimes known as an `if-then` statement. A conditional control simply states that if the condition tested is true, then execute the following block of code. Otherwise, don't execute this code.

■ **Iterative control** Also known as a loop. The loop handles repeating the execution of a block of code until some condition changes, indicating that the looping structure should stop.

■ **Sequential control** Sometimes known as a `goto` statement. When a sequential control is encountered, program execution jumps to a different part of the code, whose location is determined by a label.

This section covers the details of using conditional statements and loops to moderate the processing of a PL/SQL block.

Constructing an if-then Statement

The fundamental idea behind conditional processing is that the execution of certain commands in a program depends on the result of comparison operations. All comparison operations can be evaluated for a Boolean (TRUE or FALSE) result.

NOTE
Boolean logic is named for Charles Boole, a mathematician at University College in Cork, Ireland. Boole originally conceived the idea more than 100 years ago.

For example, the statement 3 + 5 = 8 is TRUE because the sum of 3 and 5 equals 8. In another example, 4 = 10, 4 definitely does not equal 10, so the statement is FALSE. Finally, consider the special case of "today = Wednesday." This comparison is interesting in that sometimes today is Wednesday (thus the statement is TRUE), but sometimes today is not Wednesday (thus the statement is FALSE). The validity of the statement depends on when the comparison is made.

The if-then Structure

The general syntax for conditional statements is "if the comparison is TRUE, then do the following," followed by the end if clause to let Oracle know which commands are part of the conditional operation. Let's take a quick look at a program I wrote and ran one Wednesday:

```
SQL> set serveroutput on
SQL> declare
  2     -- nothing to declare
  3  begin
  4    if to_char(sysdate, 'DAY') = 'WEDNESDAY' then
  5       dbms_output.put_line('Today is Wednesday.');
  6    end if;
  7  end;
Today is Wednesday.
PL/SQL procedure successfully completed.
```

Several things are worthy of note in this code block. First, I used the set serveroutput on command in order to let Oracle show the results of my call to the put_line() procedure inside the DBMS_OUTPUT Oracle-supplied package so that

Oracle would actually have some work to do. If I didn't specify `set serveroutput on`, Oracle wouldn't show the printed message. Second, I compare today's date reformatted into DAY format by the `to_char( )` procedure to see if today is Wednesday. Since it is, Oracle wrote the appropriate message, and then ended.

NOTE

You can see that many single-row operations shown in Chapter 1 are allowed in PL/SQL comparison statements, as long as they resolve to a datatype that can be compared properly. If, for example, one side of the comparison operation resolves to a number and the other side is a text string, that will be a problem.

The else Clause

PL/SQL also offers an optional add-on, called `else`, which says, essentially, "otherwise, do whatever the `else` clause says." Consider the previous example. It tells us something when today is Wednesday, but says nothing any other day. Here is a rewrite that has the code always tell us something, whatever day it is:

```
SQL> set serveroutput on
SQL> declare
  2     -- nothing to declare
  3  begin
  4     if to_char(sysdate, 'DAY') = 'WEDNESDAY' then
  5        dbms_output.put_line('Today is Wednesday.');
  6     else
  7        dbms_output.put_line('Today is not Wednesday.');
  8     end if;
  9  end;
Today is not Wednesday.
PL/SQL procedure successfully completed.
```

CAUTION

To end an if statement, the end if keywords must be used. Otherwise, the code after the conditional expression will be treated as part of the else clause when Oracle parses your program and will generate errors from the PL/SQL compiler.

For Review

1. Be sure that you understand the principle of applying Boolean logic to comparison operations.

2. Understand how to use an `if-then` statement, with and without the special `else` clause for multiple conditions.

3. Know how to use the `dbms_output.put_line( )` procedure and the `set serveroutput on` command.

Exercises

1. **You are defining conditional operations in Oracle. Which of the following choices identifies an invalid comparison for use in the database?**

    A. `"turkeys have features"`

    B. `to_char(trunc(hiredate)) = to_char(sysdate)`

    C. `5 + 5 / 7 = 5 / 5 + 7`

    D. `67 * 4520 > 5303935`

2. **This command is used before running PL/SQL code with references to the DBMS_OUTPUT package (three words):** _____

Answer Key

1. A. **2.** `set serveroutput on`.

Using Loops

Another situation that arises in programming is the need to execute a set of statements repeatedly. The repetitions can be controlled in two ways: repeat the code for a specified number of times or repeat the code until some condition is met, thus rendering a comparison operation TRUE. Three types of loops are available in PL/SQL: `loop-exit` statements (also called basic loops), `while-loop` statements, and `for-loop` statements.

loop-exit Statements

The `loop-exit` statement is the simplest type of loop that can be written in PL/SQL. The `loop` keyword denotes the beginning of the code block that will be repeated, and the `end loop` keywords denote the end of the code block that will be repeated. The `exit` keyword specified by itself denotes that the process should break out of the loop, and it can be used inside an `if-then` statement to give the loop some conditional control. Let's take a look at an example:

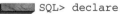

```
SQL> declare
  2    x number default 0;
  3  begin
  4    loop
  5      dbms_output.put_line('Did this ' || to_char(x) || ' times.');
  6      x := x + 1;
  7      if x = 5 then exit;
  8      end if;
  9    end loop;
 10  end;
Did this 0 times.
Did this 1 times.
Did this 2 times.
Did this 3 times.
Did this 4 times.
PL/SQL procedure successfully completed.
```

CAUTION

If you're following along on your own database, make sure that you include the line where we increment the counter x and the `exit` command. If you forget either element, an endless loop will result.

The exit when Clause

The preceding example does its job. The `if-then` statement is designed to determine whether the conditions within the loop are such that the loop should terminate. The `exit` statement instructs the PL/SQL execution mechanism to leave the loop. However, if you don't want to set up an `if-then` statement to determine whether the loop should end, you can use a when condition in the `exit` statement to handle this for you. The when condition contains the comparison operation that the `if-then` statement would have handled. Here is an example:

```
SQL> declare
  2    x number default 0;
```

```
3  begin
4    loop
5      dbms_output.put_line('Did this ' || to_char(x) || ' times.');
6      x := x + 1;
7      exit when x = 5;
8    end loop;
9  end;
Did this 0 times.
Did this 1 times.
Did this 2 times.
Did this 3 times.
Did this 4 times.
PL/SQL procedure successfully completed.
```

while-loop Statements

The previous example did the same job as the loop example shown earlier, but required fewer lines of code and no if-then statement. The exit when clause is useful because it offers an elegant solution to defining when the loop will end. The code in the previous block can be rewritten to include the while-loop statement.

The only difference between the while-loop statement and the loop-exit when statement is where PL/SQL evaluates the exit condition. In a while-loop statement, the exiting condition always must be evaluated at the beginning of the statement; in the loop-exit when statement, the exit condition is evaluated wherever the exit when statement is placed. In one sense, the loop-exit when statement offers more flexibility than the while-loop statement does, because loop-exit when allows the developer to specify the exit condition at any place in the statement. However, the flexibility that the while-loop statement may lack is made up for by its comparative elegance, in that there is no need for an exit statement, as shown here:

```
SQL> declare
2    x number default 0;
3  begin
4    while x < 5 loop
5      dbms_output.put_line('Did this ' || to_char(x) || ' times.');
6      x := x + 1;
7    end loop;
8  end;
Did this 0 times.
Did this 1 times.
Did this 2 times.
Did this 3 times.
Did this 4 times.
PL/SQL procedure successfully completed.
```

for-loop Statements

The `while` loop is great because it can use any type of comparison to determine when to stop looping. However, our examples thus far have employed a special type of loop structure that determines when to stop based on how many times the program has looped already. This type of loop is often called a *counting loop*. As a loop type, counting loops are so frequently used that they have their own special loop construct, called `for loop`, which can simplify development even further. This type of loop allows you to specify exactly the number of times the code will execute before ending. To accomplish this process, the `for-loop` statement specifies a loop counter and a range through which the counter will circulate. The loop counter is then available for use by the statements in the `for-loop` statement, as you see here:

```
SQL> declare
  2    -- nothing to declare
  3  begin
  4    for x in 0..4 loop
  5      dbms_output.put_line('Did this ' || to_char(x) || ' times.');
  6    end loop;
  7  end;
Did this 0 times.
Did this 1 times.
Did this 2 times.
Did this 3 times.
Did this 4 times.
PL/SQL procedure successfully completed.
```

NOTE
There is another type of `for-loop` *statement related to cursor handling that offers the same elegance and utility as the* `for-loop` *statement detailed in the previous code block. Its use, as well as the more general use of cursors, will be covered in Chapter 6.*

Notice that the use of a `for-loop` statement made this code block even more elegant and compact. No longer do we need to increment *x* manually, or even declare it as a variable for that matter, because the `for-loop` statement's built-in counter automatically declares its increment variable and increments itself by 1. You can even circulate through the loop counter in numeric descending order, as shown here:

```
SQL> declare
  2    -- nothing to declare
  3    begin
  4      for x in reverse 0..4 loop
  5        dbms_output.put_line('Did this ' || to_char(x) || ' times.');
  6      end loop;
  7    end;
Did this 4 times.
Did this 3 times.
Did this 2 times.
Did this 1 times.
Did this 0 times.
PL/SQL procedure successfully completed.
```

NOTE
Even when you use the reverse *keyword to decrement the counter, you must still specify the range as* lower_bound .. upper_bound.

PL/SQL does not natively allow you to increment or decrement your counter in the for-loop statement by anything other than 1. However, you can build this functionality by tricking PL/SQL with the use of a mod( ) function in your for-loop statement, as shown in this code block:

```
SQL> declare
  2    -- nothing to declare
  3    begin
  4      for x in reverse 0..4 loop
  5        if mod(x,2) = 0 then
  6          dbms_output.put_line('Did this ' || to_char(x) || ' times.');
  7        end if;
  8      end loop;
  9    end;
Did this 4 times.
Did this 2 times.
Did this 0 times.
PL/SQL procedure successfully completed.
```

For Review

I. Be sure that you can describe how to use a loop-exit statement, and know what happens when you forget the exit command in such a statement. Also, know how to use the exit when clause.

2. Understand how to modify simple loops into `while` loops, and know what the advantages and drawbacks for doing so are.

3. Know how to write a `for` loop. Understand the components of execution that `for` loops handle for you, namely, declaration and incrementation of a counter variable. Be sure that you understand the rules of variable scope for nested `for` loops.

Exercises

1. Use the following code block to answer this question:

```
SQL> declare
  2    x number default 0;
  3  begin
  4    loop
  5      dbms_output.put_line('Did this ' || to_char(x) || ' times.');
  6      x := x + 1;
  7      if x = 5 then exit;
  8      end if;
  9    end loop;
 10  end;
```

Which of the following keywords identifies a type of loop that can be used to reduce the overall number of lines in the PL/SQL block?

A. `loop exit`

B. `loop exit when`

C. `while loop`

D. `for`

2. You are using a `while` loop to perform a certain task in your PL/SQL program. Which of the following choices best identifies how many iterations the `while` loop will execute with respect to your comparison criteria?

A. The `while` loop will execute as long as your comparison is true.

B. The `while` loop will execute as long as your `exit when` comparison is true.

C. The `while` loop will execute until your comparison is true.

D. The `while` loop will execute until your `exit when` comparison is true.

Answer Key

1. D. **2.** C.

Using Logic Tables

In the discussion of if-then statements earlier in this chapter, you saw an example of a program that tests whether it is Wednesday and displays a generic message about whether or not today is Wednesday. Now, suppose that we want a program that will display a special message for both Wednesday and Thursday of the week. Assuming it is Thursday, the following code block shows how we might do this using the if-then-else syntax:

```
SQL> declare
  2    -- nothing to declare
  3    begin
  4      if to_char(sysdate, 'DAY') = 'WEDNESDAY' then
  5        dbms_output.put_line('Today is Wednesday.');
  6      else
  7        if to_char(sysdate, 'DAY') = 'THURSDAY' then
  8          dbms_output.put_line('Today is Thursday.');
  9        end if;
 10      end if;
 11    end;
Today is Thursday.
PL/SQL procedure successfully completed.
```

As shown, this code block will handle the complex conditional operation required. However, it is also hard to read and loaded with potential for problems. For example, if we later want to handle other days of the week, we would need to add each day as a separate if-then-else statement nested inside the else clause of the previous if-then-else statement. We can make it work, but the code looks very messy:

```
Declare
-- nothing to declare
begin
  if to_char(sysdate, 'DAY') = 'WEDNESDAY' then
    dbms_output.put_line('Today is Wednesday.');
  else
    if to_char(sysdate, 'DAY') = 'THURSDAY' then
      dbms_output.put_line('Today is Thursday.');
    else
      if to_char(sysdate, 'DAY') = 'FRIDAY' then
```

```
      dbms_output.put_line('Today is Friday.');
    else
      if to_char(sysdate, 'DAY') = 'SATURDAY' then
        dbms_output.put_line('Today is Saturday.');
      else
        if to_char(sysdate, 'DAY') = 'SUNDAY' then
          dbms_output.put_line('Today is Sunday.');
        else
          if to_char(sysdate, 'DAY') = 'MONDAY' then
            dbms_output.put_line('Today is Monday.');
          else
            if to_char(sysdate, 'DAY') = 'TUESDAY' then
              dbms_output.put_line('Today is Tuesday.');
          end if;
        end if;
      end if;
    end if;
  end if;
end;
```

There is a better way. Instead of adding another `if` statement to our `else` clause, we can use a special keyword called `elsif`, which allows us to use nested `if` statements inside our main `if-then` statement. These nested `if` statements can create a very powerful series of exclusive logical comparisons. These types of comparisons are sometimes referred to as *logic tables*. The following is an example of such a logic table:

```
SQL> declare
  2  -- nothing to declare
  3  begin
  4    if to_char(sysdate, 'DAY') = 'WEDNESDAY' then
  5      dbms_output.put_line('Today is Wednesday.');
  6    elsif to_char(sysdate, 'DAY') = 'THURSDAY' then
  7      dbms_output.put_line('Today is Thursday.');
  8    elsif to_char(sysdate, 'DAY') = 'FRIDAY' then
  9      dbms_output.put_line('Today is Friday.');
 10    elsif to_char(sysdate, 'DAY') = 'SATURDAY' then
 11      dbms_output.put_line('Today is Saturday.');
 12    elsif to_char(sysdate, 'DAY') = 'SUNDAY' then
 13      dbms_output.put_line('Today is Sunday.');
 14    elsif to_char(sysdate, 'DAY') = 'MONDAY' then
 15      dbms_output.put_line('Today is Monday.');
 16    elsif to_char(sysdate, 'DAY') = 'TUESDAY' then
 17      dbms_output.put_line('Today is Tuesday.')
 18    end if;
 19  end;
```

```
Today is Thursday.
PL/SQL procedure successfully completed.
```

NOTE
Take special note of the fact that elsif *has no second* e *in it.*

As you can see, by constructing the if-then operations using the elsif keyword, in effect, we create a logic table of mutually exclusive conditional operations without needing to nest numerous if-then statements inside each other. Although both code blocks are technically acceptable, the latter code block better reflects the exclusivity of the operation being performed; is more elegant; and is easier to read, enhance, and maintain.

For Review

1. Be sure to understand the logical equivalence between logic tables and nested if-then statements.

2. Know how to use the elsif keyword to construct a logic table in your conditional operations.

Exercises

1. **You want to develop a program that will print a special message alerting you to the time of day. Between 12:01 A.M. and 7:59 A.M., you want Oracle to say "Welcome Early Bird!" Between 8:00 A.M. and 11:59 A.M., you want Oracle to say "Good Morning!" From noon to 5:00 P.M., you want Oracle to say "Good Afternoon!" From 5:01 P.M. to midnight, you want Oracle to say "Go Home Nightowl!" Which of the following choices best indicates the general conditional syntax you will use?**

   A. if then else

   B. if then elsif else

   C. if then elsif elsif else

   D. if then elsif elsif elsif else

2. **You are developing a multiconditional if-then statement in Oracle. If you decide not to use logic tables, which of the following choices**

identifies the clause where you must add additional `if-then` statements in order to duplicate this logic?

A. `if`

B. `then`

C. `else`

D. `elsif`

Answer Key

1. C. 2. C.

Using Nested Loops and Labels

Looping constructs can also be nested. This construction method works well for processing multidimensional arrays of information. You can nest a loop inside a loop to create complex stepwise execution of your code across a two-dimensional (or more) set of data to create valid combinational pairings. This example effectively iterates the inner loop once for every element in the outer loop:

```
SQL> declare
  2   -- nothing to declare
  3   begin
  4     for x in 1..3 loop
  5       for y in 1..2 loop
  6         dbms_output.put_line(to_char(x) || ',' || to_char(y));
  7       end loop;
  8     end loop;
  9   end;
1,1
1,2
2,1
2,2
3,1
3,2
PL/SQL procedure successfully completed.
```

The same rules for variable scope that apply to sub-blocks, discussed earlier in this chapter, apply to nested `for` loops. A variable declared in inner `for` loops won't be available to the outer `for` loops, but the variables declared in outer `for` loops will be available in inner `for` loops.

Sequential Processing with Labels

There may be situations in which you need to bail out of a loop. Consider the following example, which harkens back to grammar school. Before the students show up for the first day of class, Mr. Garrison places a pencil on every desk in the classroom. He also writes a PL/SQL program using nested `for` loops to assist him in this task. However, he made one blunder: he didn't buy enough pencils. PL/SQL offers a construct called a *label*, which allows Mr. Garrison to bail out of a loop when he runs out of pencils.

A label is simply a short character string that labels a particular block of *executable* code. The emphasis on *executable* is deliberate, because you cannot place a label in front of nonexecutable statements like end `if`, end `loop`, or the end keyword terminating the code block.

The `goto` statement in PL/SQL allows you to jump directly to the label from the place in the code where the `goto` appears. The syntax for Mr. Garrison's labels and `goto` statements are shown in the following code block:

```
DECLARE
    rownum number;    -- we declare counter variables so we
    desknum number;   -- can refer to them outside the loop
    pencilnum number default 26;
BEGIN
    -- Loop through all rows at the top level
    for rownum in 1..6 loop
        -- Loop through all desks in the current row
        for desknum in 1..10 loop
            -- Mr. Garrison places a pencil on the desk
            pencilnum := pencilnum - 1;
            if pencilnum < 1 then
                goto no_more_pencils;
            end if;
        end loop;
    end loop;
<<no_more_pencils>>
dbms_output.put_line('left off on row: ' || to_char(rownum) ||
'left off on desk: ' || to_char(desknum));
END;
```

Note the peculiarities of constructing code in this way. Although the label is enclosed in << and >>, you do not include those special characters in the `goto` statement referring to the label. Also, the label must precede an executable statement. If you must put a label where no executable statement can be written, use the `null` keyword followed by a semicolon. Remember, this is an executable statement that does no work, and therefore satisfies the semantic needs of labels and the programmatic needs of your application.

Bailout Restrictions

Generally speaking, you can use a `goto` statement to bail out of a conditional structure, code block, or exception handler, but not to "bail into" a conditional structure, code block, or exception handler. Thus, the following example shows illegal use of labeling and `goto` commands:

```
DECLARE
   rownum number;
   desknum number;
   pencilnum number default 0;
BEGIN
goto lose_a_pencil;
-- Loop through all rows at the top level
  for rownum in 1..6 loop
    -- Loop through all desks in the current row
    for desknum in 1..10 loop
      -- process adding a pencil to each desk
      <<lose_a_pencil>>
      pencilnum := pencilnum - 1;
      if pencilnum < 1 then
       goto no_more_pencils;
      end if;
    end loop;
  end loop;
  -- executable statement that does no work follows label
  <<no_more_pencils>>
  null;
END;
```

For Review

1. Know the rules for nesting loops in your PL/SQL code with respect to variable scope.

2. Know how to construct labels and use `goto` statements.

3. Know the restrictions for placing labels in your code, and how to get around this restriction with the `null` keyword.

Exercises

1. **You develop a series of three nested `for` loops. The outermost loop (call it loop 1) uses a counter variable called A, while the inner two loops (one**

inside the other, call them loop 3 inside loop 2) use counter variables called B and C, respectively. Which of the following choices does not identify the proper scope for variables in this loop context?

A. C can be seen inside loop 2.

B. A can be seen inside loop 2.

C. B can be seen inside loop 3.

D. A can be seen inside loop 3.

2. **Use the following code block to answer this question:**

```
DECLARE
   rownum number;
   desknum number;
   pencilnum number default 26;
BEGIN
   -- Loop through all rows at the top level
   for rownum in 1..6 loop
     -- Loop through all desks in the current row
     for desknum in 1..10 loop
       -- process adding a pencil to each desk
       pencilnum := pencilnum - 1;
       if pencilnum < 1 then
        goto no_more_pencils;
       end if;
     end loop;
   end loop;
   <<no_more_pencils>>
END;
```

Which of the following choices identifies the problem with this code block?

A. <<no_more_pencils>> is not defined properly.

B. No executable statement follows <<no_more_pencils>>.

C. The goto keyword cannot jump into the executing loop.

D. The ROWNUM variable is outside the inner loop's scope.

Answer Key

1. A. 2. B.

Chapter Summary

In this chapter, you were introduced to the fundamentals of PL/SQL programming tested on the OCP exam. You learned about the uses and benefits of PL/SQL, along with the basic construction of a PL/SQL program.

We covered the three parts of a PL/SQL program. We also covered how to declare variables and assign values to them. You learned how to write executable statements in PL/SQL and how to handle nesting of PL/SQL blocks inside other blocks. We then focused our attention on more complex syntactic structures for controlling execution of certain statements in our PL/SQL programs. We covered conditional statement processing and iterative statement control using loops. After that, we discussed nesting loops inside other loops. We wrapped up the discussion with coverage of how to handle unconditional statement processing using labels and the goto command.

Two-Minute Drill

- PL/SQL is a programming environment that is native to the Oracle database. It features seamless integration with other database objects in Oracle and with SQL.

- There are three parts to a PL/SQL program: the declaration area, the execution area, and the exception handler.

- There are two categories of PL/SQL blocks: named and anonymous blocks. Named blocks include procedures, functions, packages, and triggers.

- Variables are defined in the declaration section.

- Constants are declared the same way as variables, except that the constant keyword is used to denote a constant and the constant must have a value assigned in the declaration section.

- Variables can have values assigned anywhere in the PL/SQL block using the assignment operator, which is a colon followed by an equal sign (:=). In the declaration section only, a default value for the variable can be assigned using the default keyword.

- PL/SQL is executed using the execute command in SQL*Plus, or simply by referencing the named block in another block.

- Conditional processing is handled in PL/SQL with if-then-else statements.

- `if-then-else` statements rely on Boolean logic to determine which set of statements will execute. If the condition is TRUE, the statements in the `then` clause will execute. If the condition is FALSE, the statements in the `else` clause will execute.

- The `if` statements can be nested into `else` clauses. However, it is better practice to use the `elsif` clause to create logic tables when you need mutually exclusive conditional processing in your application, because the code is easier to read and manage.

- Several loops control the repetition of blocks of PL/SQL statements: `loop-exit`, `while-loop`, and `for-loop` statements

- The `loop-exit` statement is a simple definition for a loop that marks the beginning and end of the loop code. An `if-then` statement tests to see whether conditions are such that the loop should exit. An `exit` statement must be specified explicitly.

- The `if-then` statement can be replaced with an `exit when` statement, which defines the `exit` condition for the loop.

- The `while` statement eliminates the need for an `exit` statement by defining the `exit` condition in the `while-loop` statement.

- If the programmer wants the code to execute a specified number of times, the `for-loop` statement can be used.

- Be sure you understand that labels and `goto` statements can be used for unconditional program redirection.

Fill-in-the-Blanks

1. The keyword used in `if-then` statements to create logic tables:
   _____

2. The keyword used for unconditional control of execution in a PL/SQL block: _____

3. The keyword that can replace the assignment operator for assigning values to variables in the declaration section: _____

4. The clause used in simple loop statements to avoid the need for conditional statement processing to determine the end of the loop (two words): _____

Chapter Questions

1. Developer JANET receives an error due to the following statement in the declaration section: PI CONSTANT NUMBER;
   The problem is because of which of the following causes?

   A. There is not enough memory in the program for the constant.

   B. There is no value associated with the constant.

   C. There is no datatype associated with the constant.

   D. PI is a reserved word.

2. You are constructing PL/SQL process flow into your program. If left out, which of the following would cause an infinite loop to occur in a simple loop?

   A. `loop`

   B. `end loop`

   C. `if-then`

   D. `exit`

3. You are determining the appropriate program flow for your PL/SQL application. Which of the following statements are true about `while` loops?

   A. Explicit `exit` statements are required in `while` loops.

B. Counter variables are required in `while` loops.

C. An `if-then` statement is needed to signal when a `while` loop should end.

D. All `exit` conditions for `while` loops are handled in the `while` clause.

4. **You are preparing to compile a block of PL/SQL code. The lines in the block are shown in the choices here:**

```
CREATE FUNCTION FOO (VAR1 IN VARCHAR2) IS
  VAR2 VARCHAR2(1) default 6;
BEGIN
  IF VAR1 = 6 THEN RETURN (6) ELSE RETURN (8);
  END IF;
END;
```

Which of the lines of PL/SQL code contain an error?

A. CREATE FUNCTION FOO (VAR1 IN VARCHAR2) IS

B. IF VAR1 = 6 THEN RETURN (6) ELSE RETURN (8);

C. END IF;

D. There are no errors in this PL/SQL block

Fill-in-the-Blank Answers

1. `elsif`

2. `goto`

3. `default`

4. `exit when`

Answers to Chapter Questions

1. B. There is no value associated with the constant.

Explanation   A value must be associated with a constant in the declaration section. If no value is given for the constant, an error will result.

2. D. `exit`

Explanation Without an `exit` statement, a simple loop will not stop. Though the `loop` and `end loop` keywords are needed to define the loop, you should assume these are in place and you are only trying to figure out how to end the loop. The `if-then` syntax might be used to determine a test condition for when the loop execution should terminate, but using this syntax is not a requirement for ending the loop process execution.

3. D. All `exit` conditions for `while` loops are handled in the `while` clause.

Explanation There is no need for an `exit` statement in a `while` loop, since the exiting condition is defined in the `while` statement, eliminating choice A. Choice B is also wrong because you don't specifically need to use a counter in a `while` loop the way you do in a `for` loop. Finally, choice C is incorrect because even though the `exit` condition for a `while` loop evaluates to a Boolean value (for example, `exit when (this_condition_is_true)`, the mechanism to handle the exit does not require an explicit `if-then` statement.

4. A. `CREATE FUNCTION FOO (VAR1 IN VARCHAR2) IS`

Explanation There is no definition of a return value datatype in this code block, making the function declaration line the correct answer. Although it may seem that the `if-then` statement in the third line of the code block is incorrect because you are comparing a VARCHAR2 variable to the number 6, Oracle handles this situation just fine because there is an implicit type conversion occurring in the background. Finally, the `select`, `into`, `from`, and `where` clauses of the `fetch` statement are constructed correctly.

CHAPTER

6

Database Programming with PL/SQL

n this chapter, you will learn about and demonstrate knowledge in the following areas:

- Interacting with the Oracle database
- Working with composite datatypes
- Explicit cursor handling
- Understanding advanced explicit cursor topics
- Error handling

In the previous chapter, you learned the basic constructs involved in PL/SQL programming. This chapter takes the discussion further, by showing you how PL/SQL can seamlessly integrate with database object access via SQL.

This chapter will present an overview of how to use PL/SQL in database applications. The information in this chapter is tested on OCP Exam 1, and it makes up about 15 percent of the exam questions. It is highly recommended that you take some time to understand the principles presented in Chapter 5 before starting on this chapter. Again, be sure to take a break occasionally.

Interacting with the Oracle Database

This section covers the following topics related to interacting with Oracle:

- Using select in PL/SQL code
- Declaring PL/SQL variable types dynamically
- Writing DML statements in PL/SQL
- Transaction processing in PL/SQL
- Determining SQL statement outcome

PL/SQL makes it easy to interact with an Oracle database. Any data-manipulation or change operation can be accomplished within PL/SQL, without the additional overhead typically required in other programming environments. There is no ODBC interface, and no embedding is required for database manipulation with PL/SQL. In this section, you will learn how to use regular SQL commands inside PL/SQL code for robust database application development.

NOTE
In contrast to PL/SQL, other programming languages, including those Oracle offers for database development (such as Pro*C), often require special character sequences or even full-blown command syntax to permit database processing inside the native language.

Using select in PL/SQL Code

The integration of PL/SQL and the Oracle database is seamless. There are no special characters or command sequences that must precede the PL/SQL variables in SQL statements. Let's throw a basic query into PL/SQL and see what happens:

```
SQL> connect scott/tiger
SQL> declare
  2    -- nothing to declare
  3  begin
  4    select empno, ename, job, sal
  5    from emp;
  7  end;
declare
*
ERROR at line 1:
ORA-06550: line 4, column 2:
PLS-00428: an INTO clause is expected in this SELECT statement
ORA-06550: line 4, column 2:
PL/SQL: SQL Statement ignored
```

NOTE
We deliberately eliminated the slash (/) required at the end of your SQL*Plus buffer to force Oracle to execute the anonymous block to save space on the page. However, don't forget to use this character in your own development of PL/SQL.

Okay, I may have exaggerated the PL/SQL–database integration just a tiny bit. One very minor concession PL/SQL makes is the into clause, which places the return values from the select statement positionally into variables you declare. If you don't declare some variables to store the values SQL queries return in PL/SQL, then Oracle won't know how to handle the input.

A query containing the `into` clause is sometimes referred to as a *fetch* in PL/SQL. Variables declared to accommodate data fetched from a table must be the same datatype as the associated table column. Let's take a look at a modified PL/SQL code block demonstrating this concept. This time, we'll use the `into` clause, as well as the `dmbs_output.put_line( )` procedure, so we can see the data Oracle obtained for us:

```
SQL> set serveroutput on
SQL> declare
  2    my_empno number(4);
  3    my_ename varchar2(10);
  4    my_job varchar2(9);
  5    my_sal number(7,2);
  6  begin
  7    select empno, ename, job, sal
  8    into my_empno, my_ename, my_job, my_sal
  9    from emp;
 10    dbms_output.put_line(to_char(my_empno) || ' ' || my_ename);
 11    dbms_output.put_line(my_job || ' ' || to_char(my_sal));
 12 end;
declare
*
ERROR at line 1:
ORA-01422: exact fetch returns more than requested number of rows
ORA-06512: at line 7
```

Oh no, not again! It looks like, this time, Oracle didn't like the fact that we were trying to fetch the entire table into just one set of variables, each of which holds only one column value for a row at a time. This is suspiciously similar to how Oracle behaved when our single-row subqueries back in Chapter 2 retrieved more than one row. Let's now restrict our query to the EMP table for employee TURNER:

```
SQL> declare
  2    my_empno number(4);
  3    my_ename varchar2(10);
  4    my_job varchar2(9);
  5    my_sal number(7,2);
  6  begin
  7    select empno, ename, job, sal
  8    into my_empno, my_ename, my_job, my_sal
  9    from emp where empno = 7844;
 10    dbms_output.put_line(to_char(my_empno) || ' ' || my_ename);
 11    dbms_output.put_line(my_job || ' ' || to_char(my_sal));
 12    end;
7844 TURNER
SALESMAN 1500
PL/SQL procedure successfully completed.
```

Finally, we have a PL/SQL block that works! And, in hindsight, once we worked out the kinks, the SQL code embedded into our PL/SQL block does appear quite seamless. We just had to watch out for some hidden booby traps.

NOTE
When using select *statements to fetch values into variables in PL/SQL, use explicit references to the columns you want to fetch in the column clause of your query, as opposed to the more generic* select ** syntax. Oracle must know the explicit columns it needs to obtain in order to match them up positionally with the variables in your* into *clause.*

For Review

I. Always have a purpose in employing select statements in your PL/SQL code. That purpose is to fetch data for later use. Thus, you must declare variables to store the data and use the into clause to fetch that data into appropriate variables.

2. Remember that the variables used for storing table data must be the same datatype as the associated table's column.

3. Your query should only fetch as much data as PL/SQL expects to receive. So far, we've seen an example of single-row fetches. Later in the chapter, we'll work with multiple-row fetches.

Exercises

I. **You are developing PL/SQL to manipulate data in Oracle. Which of the following queries are valid for use in a PL/SQL block that obtains data from the SALES table for the row containing profit information corresponding to PRODUCT_TYPE = 'TOYS'?**

A. select * into my_product_type, my_product_name, my_profit from sales where product_type = 'TOYS';

B. select product_type, product_name, profit from sales where product_type = 'TOYS';

C. select product_type, product_name, profit into my_product_type, my_product_name, my_profit from sales;

    D. select product_type, product_name, profit into
        my_product_type, my_product_name, my_profit
        from sales where product_type = 'TOYS';

2. **This keyword identifies the clause used for storing variable values from table data:** _____

3. **This aspect of the variable used to house a table column's data in the PL/SQL block must be the same as the associated column:**

_____

Answer Key

1. D. 2. into. 3. Datatype.

Declaring PL/SQL Variable Types Dynamically

Suppose that we want to modify the previous PL/SQL block example to obtain MGR column information for TURNER as well. Let's look at a revision of our code to do so:

```
SQL> declare
  2    my_empno number(4);
  3    my_ename varchar2(10);
  4    my_job varchar2(9);
  5    my_sal number(7,2);
  6    my_mgr number(2);
  7  begin
  8    select empno, ename, job, sal, mgr
  9    into my_empno, my_ename, my_job, my_sal, my_mgr
 10    from emp where empno = 7844;
 11    dbms_output.put_line(to_char(my_empno) || ' ' || my_ename);
 12    dbms_output.put_line(my_job || ' ' || to_char(my_sal));
 13    dbms_output.put_line(to_char(my_mgr));
 14  end;
declare
*
ERROR at line 1:
ORA-06502: PL/SQL: numeric or value error:
            number precision too large
ORA-06512: at line 8
```

    What happened, and what does that ORA-06502 error message mean? The error message says that the number precision on a value returned from the EMP table was too large for the variable trying to accommodate it. Apparently, when we added the MY_MGR variable, we didn't make it large enough to accommodate data from the MGR column.

NOTE
*When you make the same mistake on VARCHAR2
or CHAR strings by declaring the variable too small,
the Oracle numeric or value error changes to read*
`character string buffer too small.`

Without further examination of the code and the datatypes of the selected EMP
columns, we won't be able to resolve the problem. Let's take a look at a description
of the EMP table:

```
SQL> desc emp;
 Name                           Null?    Type
 ------------------------------ -------- --------------
 EMPNO                          NOT NULL NUMBER(4)
 ENAME                                   VARCHAR2(10)
 JOB                                     VARCHAR2(9)
 MGR                                     NUMBER(4)
 HIREDATE                                DATE
 SAL                                     NUMBER(7,2)
 COMM                                    NUMBER(7,2)
 DEPTNO                                  NUMBER(2)
```

Aha! In comparing the declaration of the MY_MGR variable in the code block to
the output from the `describe` command, we can see that the code didn't declare the
variable to be large enough to handle data from the column. The code block has
NUMBER(2), but the EMP table has NUMBER(4). Thus, Oracle won't let us put the
MGR value for employee TURNER into variable MY_MGR. Let's make a small
revision to our code block to make the program work:

```
SQL> declare
  2    my_empno number(4);
  3    my_ename varchar2(10);
  4    my_job varchar2(9);
  5    my_sal number(7,2);
  6    my_mgr number(4);
  7  begin
  8    select empno, ename, job, sal, mgr
  9    into my_empno, my_ename, my_job, my_sal, my_mgr
 10    from emp where empno = 7844;
 11    dbms_output.put_line(to_char(my_empno) || ' ' || my_ename);
 12    dbms_output.put_line(my_job || ' ' || to_char(my_sal));
 13    dbms_output.put_line(to_char(my_mgr));
 14  end;
7844 TURNER
```

```
SALESMAN 1500
7698
PL/SQL procedure successfully completed.
```

Using %type as a Shortcut

So, now we know that variables storing data from table columns must be the same size as or larger than the column itself, not to mention the same datatype. However, it's a pain to describe the tables every time you want to develop code against them to obtain the datatype. Fortunately, there's a shortcut. Rather than needing to look up the datatype, you can simply identify the table and column to which this variable's datatype should correspond. This shortcut uses a special keyword known as %type.

When using the %type keyword, all you need to know is the name of the column and the table to which the variable will correspond. Let's take a look at a revision of our code from the previous section:

```
SQL> declare
  2    my_empno emp.empno%type;
  3    my_ename emp.ename%type;
  4    my_job emp.job%type;
  5    my_sal emp.sal%type;
  6    my_mgr emp.mgr%type;
  7  begin
  8    select empno, ename, job, sal, mgr
  9    into my_empno, my_ename, my_job, my_sal, my_mgr
 10    from emp where empno = 7844;
 11    dbms_output.put_line(to_char(my_empno) || ' ' || my_ename);
 12    dbms_output.put_line(my_job || ' ' || to_char(my_sal));
 13    dbms_output.put_line(to_char(my_mgr));
 14  end;
7844 TURNER
SALESMAN 1500
7698
PL/SQL procedure successfully completed.
```

When you use the %type keyword, Oracle dynamically looks up the datatype of the column you referenced and declares the variable using that datatype. In anonymous blocks, this extra step can lead to Oracle needing to perform slightly more work behind the scenes, so you might notice your PL/SQL blocks running just a little slower on less powerful machines when you use %type to declare your variables. However, any performance lost in the use of this feature is more than outweighed by its usefulness in coding PL/SQL database applications quickly.

TIP
If you use the `table_name.table%type`
*syntax to declare your variables used for storing
data from tables, you'll never need to worry about
making sure that the datatype and size of your
variables accommodate the data in the table
column. Furthermore, your PL/SQL procedure
will automatically be kept in sync with any
corresponding changes to the underlying
column's datatype.*

For Review

1. The variables you declare must be large enough to accommodate the data from the table column. The variables can be the same size or larger than their corresponding columns.

2. Understand the use of the `%type` attribute for dynamic variable declaration. By using `%type`, you can avoid problems with the declared variable's type and size.

Exercises

1. Use the following code block to answer this question:

```
SQL> desc profits
 Name                         Null?    Type
 ------------------------     -------- -------------
 PRODUCT_NAME                 NOT NULL VARCHAR2(10)
 PRODUCT_TYPE                          VARCHAR2(5)
 QUARTER                               VARCHAR2(8)
 PROFIT                                NUMBER
 SALES_REGION                          VARCHAR2(10)
```

You want to fetch values from this table for Tickle Me Elmo toys sold by the SOUTHEAST region for the first quarter of 2001. Which of the following datatypes should you use when declaring the variable that stores the region selling this product for this quarter?

A. NUMBER

B. VARCHAR2(5)

    C. VARCHAR2(8)

    D. VARCHAR2(10)

2. **Using the code block and description from the previous question, which of the following choices identifies how to declare the variable storing the name of the region for the quarter mentioned?**

    A. `profits.quarter%type`

    B. `profits.sales_region%type`

    C. `profits.product_name%type`

    D. `profits.product_type%type`

Answer Key
1. D. 2. B.

Writing DML Statements in PL/SQL

Once you've fetched the appropriate values from Oracle in your code block, you can perform other data-manipulation activities based on the data stored in the variable. Let's take a look at how we might use PL/SQL to change the record for employee TURNER to indicate that he is now considered a stellar salesperson, worthy of an increase of $1,000 over his current commission:

```
SQL> declare
  2    my_empno emp.empno%type;
  3    my_comm emp.comm%type;
  4  begin
  5    -- first fetch appropriate record
  6    select empno, comm into my_empno, my_comm
  7    from emp where empno = 7844;
  8    dbms_output.put_line('Old commission: ' || to_char(my_comm));
  9    -- now modify the record
 10    my_comm := my_comm + 1000;
 11    -- now modify the database
 12    update emp set comm = my_comm
 13    where empno = my_empno;
 14    -- tell me what I did
 15    dbms_output.put_line('New commission: ' || to_char(my_comm));
 16  end;
Old commission: 0
New commission: 1000
PL/SQL procedure successfully completed.
```

TIP
We didn't need to select data from EMP to make the update *happen. We could have simply used a hard-coded value for COMM and EMPNO instead. However, using variables better illustrates what the code is doing. As noted in the previous chapter, using variables makes the purpose of your code clearer.*

Once you fetch a value into the variable, you can treat the variable however you want inside the block. You can even refer to that variable in further SQL issued against the database. The same ease of use can be seen in coding delete and insert statements inside your PL/SQL code. The following code block shows how to add a new employee record for SMITHERS, a new manager:

```
SQL> declare
  2    my_empno emp.empno%type default 1234;
  3    my_ename emp.ename%type default 'SMITHERS';
  4    my_job emp.job%type default 'MANAGER';
  5  begin
  6    insert into emp (empno, ename, job)
  7    values (my_empno, my_ename, my_job);
  8  end;
PL/SQL procedure successfully completed.
```

Later, when we realize that SMITHERS won't be coming onboard because she failed her mandatory drug test, we can remove this record from the EMP table with the following code block:

```
SQL> declare
  2    my_empno emp.empno%type;
  3  begin
  4    -- first, obtain my record
  5    select empno into my_empno
  6    from emp where ename = 'SMITHERS';
  7    -- now delete the record
  8    delete from emp where empno = my_empno;
  9  end;
PL/SQL procedure successfully completed.
```

TIP
Of course, you don't always need to fetch a value into a variable in order to delete it. You could always hard-code the value in the delete *statement instead. This example is shown for illustrative purposes only.*

For Review

Understand how to use values fetched into variables by `select` statements later in other types of data-manipulation statements like `insert`, `update`, and `delete`.

Exercises

1. Use the following code block to answer this question:

```
SQL> desc profits
 Name                      Null?    Type
 ------------------------- -------- -------------
 PRODUCT_NAME              NOT NULL VARCHAR2(10)
 PRODUCT_TYPE                       VARCHAR2(5)
 QUARTER                            VARCHAR2(8)
 PROFIT                             NUMBER
 SALES_REGION                       VARCHAR2(10)
SQL> declare
  2  my_profit varchar2(10);
  3  begin
  4   my_profit := '$1,000,000.00';
  5   update profits
  6   set profit = my_profit
  7   where product_type = 'TOYS'
  8   and sales_region = 'SOUTHEAST'
  9   and quarter = '3Q99';
 10  end;
```

Which of the following choices best paraphrases the response Oracle gives when you attempt to execute the code appearing in this block code?

A. Primary key not referenced in the `update` command

B. Datatype mismatch between column EMP.PROFIT and variable MY_PROFIT

C. Value assigned to variable MY_PROFIT too large

D. There is nothing wrong with the PL/SQL code block.

2. Use the following code block and the description of PROFITS from the previous question to answer this question:

```
SQL> declare
  2  my_profit profits.profit%type;
  3  begin
```

```
  4    my_profit := '$1,000,000.00';
  5    update profits
  6    set profit = my_profit
  7    where product_type = 'TOYS'
  8    and sales_region = 'SOUTHEAST'
  9    and quarter = '3Q99';
 10    end;
```

Which of the following choices best paraphrases the response Oracle gives when you attempt to execute the code appearing in this block?

A. Primary key not referenced in the `update` command

B. Datatype mismatch between column EMP.PROFIT and variable MY_PROFIT

C. Value assigned to variable MY_PROFIT too large

D. There is nothing wrong with the PL/SQL code block.

Answer Key

1. C. When a scalar datatype is used for declaring variables into which table values are fetched, Oracle will first resolve every aspect in the code relating to that variable before performing any work against the table. **2.** B. When dynamic datatype references are used, Oracle resolves any datatype mismatching present in the code block first.

Transaction Processing in PL/SQL

The examples of using `insert`, `update`, and `delete` statements in the previous section lacked one critical element that can wreak major havoc on your database systems. Can you guess what that element might be? If you said transaction processing, you're right!

The same options for transaction processing available in SQL statement processing are available in PL/SQL. When you make data changes to your database inside PL/SQL and do not include the appropriate transaction-processing commands to end the transaction initiated by the program, Oracle will not magically end that transaction for you. In other words, all of the previous examples, where we were executing data changes via PL/SQL while connected to Oracle as user SCOTT, will not be available to other users until SCOTT completes his transaction. Thus, if we log into Oracle as user TURNER, we cannot see the change to TURNER's own commission:

```
SQL> connect turner/ike
Connected.
SQL> select comm from scott.emp where ename = 'TURNER';
     COMM
---------
```

Recall that the three transaction specifications available in SQL are `commit`, `rollback`, and `savepoint`. These same commands can be used in PL/SQL to guarantee that changes in the database will be saved or discarded, or to define a logical subunit of work inside your transaction, respectively. Take a look at the following modification of an earlier block, made in SCOTT's existing session, which will change TURNER's commission to 1000 and save the change once and for all:

```
SQL> declare
  2    my_empno emp.empno%type;
  3    my_comm emp.comm%type;
  4  begin
  5    -- first fetch appropriate record
  6    select empno, comm into my_empno, my_comm
  7    from emp where empno = 7844;
  8    dbms_output.put_line('Old commission: ' || to_char(my_comm));
  9    -- now modify the record
 10    my_comm := 1000;
 11    -- now modify the database
 12    update emp set comm = my_comm
 13    where empno = my_empno;
 14    -- save it
 15    commit;
 16    -- tell me what I did
 17    dbms_output.put_line('New commission: ' || to_char(my_comm));
 18  end;
Old commission: 1000
New commission: 1000
PL/SQL procedure successfully completed.
```

Now, let's return to TURNER's existing session and see the change.

```
SQL> connect turner/ike
Connected.
SQL> select comm from scott.emp where ename = 'TURNER';
     COMM
---------
     1000
```

Using DBMS_TRANSACTION

There are some caveats to the transaction-processing strategy used in the previous example. The `set transaction` statement is not available in PL/SQL to denote the beginning of the transaction or to set the transaction's database access to read-only or read-write. To remedy this conundrum, we can use the Oracle-supplied DBMS_TRANSACTION package.

Within the DBMS_TRANSACTION package, there are several functions that allow the user to start, end, and moderate the transaction processing within PL/SQL blocks. The relevant functions are read_only( ), which is equivalent to the set transaction read only command, and read_write( ), which is equivalent to the set transaction read write command. Here is an example of using the read_write( ) function:

```
SQL> declare
   2    my_empno emp.empno%type default 1234;
   3    my_ename emp.ename%type default 'SMITHERS';
   4    my_job emp.job%type default 'MANAGER';
   5  begin
   6    dbms_transaction.read_write;
   7    insert into emp (empno, ename, job)
   8    values (my_empno, my_ename, my_job);
   9    commit;
  10  end;
PL/SQL procedure successfully completed.
```

NOTE
DBMS_TRANSACTION also contains procedures for committing or rolling back your transactions, as well as for declaring savepoints. Because these commands are also implemented directly in PL/SQL, we don't cover the procedures here. Also, remember to prefix the name of the package when referring to procedures in DBMS_TRANSACTION.

For Review

1. Know how to use available transaction-processing features in PL/SQL to avoid problems related to the fact that Oracle does not end your transaction automatically when the PL/SQL block completes.

2. Know that set transaction commands are not available natively in PL/SQL. Instead, you must use relevant procedures from the DBMS_TRANSACTION package.

Exercises

1. **Use the following code block to answer this question:**

```
SQL> declare
   2    my_empno emp.empno%type default 1234;
```

```
 3   my_ename emp.ename%type default 'SMITHERS';
 4   my_job emp.job%type default 'MANAGER';
 5  begin
 6    set transaction read write;
 7    insert into emp (empno, ename, job)
 8    values (my_empno, my_ename, my_job);
 9    commit;
10  end;
```

Which of the following choices identifies the problem with the code block:

A. The `commit` needs to be defined using DBMS_TRANSACTION procedures.

B. The `set transaction` needs to be defined using DBMS_TRANSACTION procedures.

C. The `insert` statement contains inappropriate transaction processing.

D. The datatype for MY_EMPNO is defined inappropriately.

2. This is the DBMS_TRANSACTION procedure for initiating read-only transactions: _____

3. This is the name of the DBMS_TRANSACTION procedure for initiating read-write transactions: _____

Answer Key

1. B. 2. read_only( ). 3. read_write( ).

Determining SQL Statement Outcome

So far, our use of SQL statements in PL/SQL has illustrated a common underlying assumption: we assumed that there is data in the table relevant to the operations we've attempted. This is a bad idea! Recall that in an earlier example, we deleted records from EMP associated with our new manager, SMITHERS. Let's pretend for a moment that we forgot we deleted SMITHERS before and tried to delete her again:

```
SQL> declare
  2    -- nothing to declare;
  3  begin
  4    delete from emp
  5    where ename = 'SMITHERS';
```

```
7    commit;
8    end;
PL/SQL procedure successfully completed.
```

It looks like Oracle did some work in this block. But how do we know for sure? Let's start with a definition in order to answer this question.

SQL statements like `select`, `insert`, `update`, and `delete` in Oracle execute in something Oracle calls an *implicit cursor*. A *cursor* is simply a name for the address in Oracle's memory where Oracle stores the result of the executed SQL statement. After SQL statements execute in their implicit cursor, you can use a feature of that cursor called a *cursor attribute* to determine one of several things that you may care to know about the statement's execution. In the preceding example, we would like to know whether Oracle deleted any data, so let's use a cursor attribute called `%notfound` to find out:

```
SQL> set serveroutput on
SQL>  declare
 2    -- nothing to declare;
 3   begin
 4    delete from emp
 5    where ename = 'SMITHERS';
 6    if sql%notfound then
 7      dbms_output.put_line('We did no work');
 8    end if;
 9    commit;
10   end;
We did no work
PL/SQL procedure successfully completed.
```

Three things are worthy of note about this example:

■ Every time you use a cursor attribute, you must prefix the attribute with the name of the cursor it references. In this case, we are using the cursor attribute on an implicit cursor. Whenever we use cursor attributes on implicit cursors, the name of the cursor referenced is always SQL.

■ Our reference to the `%notfound` cursor attribute is found directly after the SQL statement whose attribute we wanted to detect. This placement is deliberate. If another SQL statement appeared after the `delete` but before our attribute reference, the cursor attribute would have tested the attributes of that implicit cursor instead.

■ Notice our use of the cursor attribute in an `if-then` statement. This should tell you that this cursor attribute resolves to TRUE or FALSE values, depending on the attribute being tested and the conditions present in the cursor. Other attributes resolve to other information, as you will soon see.

NOTE
If the implicit cursor attribute appeared after a `commit, rollback,` *or* `savepoint` *command, the value for the attribute would be whatever value was generated by the implicit cursor executed prior to the* `commit, rollback,` *or* `savepoint`*. These operations don't operate inside implicit cursors.*

Valid Cursor Attributes

The cursor attributes you can use in PL/SQL are as follows:

■ **%notfound**   Identifies whether the executed SQL statement obtained, changed, or removed any row data. If not, this attribute evaluates to TRUE; otherwise, it evaluates to FALSE.

■ **%rowcount**   Identifies the number of rows that were processed by the statement. It returns a numeric value.

■ **%found**   Identifies whether the SQL statement processed any row data. If data was processed, this attribute evaluates to TRUE; otherwise, it evaluates to FALSE.

■ **%isopen**   Identifies whether the cursor referred to is opened and ready for use. It returns TRUE if the cursor is open, and FALSE if the cursor is not. This cursor attribute is most useful for explicit cursors, which are discussed later in this chapter.

For Review

1. Know that SQL statements always run inside an implicit cursor in Oracle.

2. Be able to identify all cursor attributes in PL/SQL, and know how to reference implicit cursor attributes using these special keywords.

3. Understand that the name of all implicit cursors for attribute reference purposes is always SQL.

4. Know where references to cursor attributes should be placed in your PL/SQL programs.

Exercises

1. **Your database has four tables in it. EMP has 14 rows, DEPT has 4 rows, and BONUS has 2 rows. You issue the following block against this database:**

```
DECLARE
-- nothing to declare
BEGIN
    delete from emp;
    delete from dept;
    delete from bonus;
    commit;
    dbms_output.put_line('rows processed by delete:');
    dbms_output.put_line(to_char(sql%rowcount));
END;
```

What result will Oracle display when this code block is run?

A. 2

B. 4

C. 14

D. 20

2. **You have an implicit cursor that you would like to test the results of. Which of the following attributes will return TRUE if a `delete` operation is able to delete data from a table?**

   A. `%notfound`

   B. `%isopen`

   C. `%rowcount`

   D. `%found`

3. **This is the name of every implicit cursor:** _____

Answer Key

1. A. **2.** D. **3.** SQL.

Working with Composite Datatypes

This section covers the following topics related to working with composite datatypes:

- Creating PL/SQL records
- Using `%rowtype` to create records
- Creating PL/SQL tables

■ Creating PL/SQL tables of records

■ Reviewing PL/SQL records, tables, and tables of records

In the previous chapter, we explored how to declare variables using scalar datatypes in Oracle. You will now delve into a more advanced area of variable declaration and use in PL/SQL. This section covers user-defined types in Oracle. The first discussion will explain how to define a PL/SQL record. Next, you will learn how to use a shortcut for defining records associated with tables in your database. You will learn how to declare and use PL/SQL table variables, as well as tables of records.

Creating PL/SQL Records

Think about all the variables we've declared so far in this chapter. Every one of them was an individual variable, and it was up to you, the developer, to understand how they related to row information. While sufficient to store data, these variables weren't very effective for relating entire rows of column data together in a way that mirrors the fact that every unit of information was part of a row. As an alternative, PL/SQL permits you to create your own user-defined datatypes in the form of records.

A *record* is a variable comprised of one or more elements. Each element in the record can be declared as a scalar PL/SQL datatype (VARCHAR2, DATE, INTEGER, and so on), as a dynamically referenced type (using `table.column%type`), or as a user-defined datatype (for example, another record). There are two steps for defining PL/SQL records:

1. Create a special datatype Oracle will use for defining the record variable.

2. Create the variable using its special datatype.

Defining Record Datatypes

To define a PL/SQL record, first you must define the datatype of that record. For this reason, record datatypes are also referred to as *user-defined types.* You define the datatype using the `type is record` statement in the variable declaration section of your PL/SQL code, as shown in the following code block:

```
SQL> declare
  2    -- a new datatype is born!
  3    type t_emp is record (
  4    my_empno emp.empno%type,
  5    my_ename emp.ename%type,
  6    my_job emp.job%type,
  7    my_sal emp.sal%type );
```

```
 8  begin
 9   null;
10  end;
PL/SQL procedure successfully completed.
```

Defining Record Variables

Once you define your record datatype, you need to declare a variable of that datatype in that same PL/SQL block. The record variable is declared just as any other variable would be declared, as follows:

```
SQL> declare
  2    -- a new datatype is born!
  3    type t_emp is record (
  4     my_empno emp.empno%type,
  5     my_ename emp.ename%type,
  6     my_job emp.job%type,
  7     my_sal emp.sal%type );
  8    -- a variable of that type
  9    employee t_emp;
 10  begin
 11   null;
 12  end;
PL/SQL procedure successfully completed.
```

Now you have a variable called EMPLOYEE, consisting of four elements. Each element of the EMPLOYEE variable corresponds to the definition you made inside the type. Thus, your EMPLOYEE record can have four pieces of information stored in it for your use:

- The EMPNO for this employee record

- The ENAME for this employee record

- The JOB for this employee record

- The SALary of this employee record

CAUTION
If you attempt to declare a variable using a user-defined type that is not defined in your PL/SQL code, Oracle returns an error. Oracle also returns an error if you declare your variable using a user-defined type in a line before the line where your user-defined type is declared.

Assigning Values to Record Variable Elements

After you create your record variables, you reference individual elements inside them using dot notation. If you want to assign a value to an element in the record, you first name the record, and then identify the element. The two must be separated by a dot. Let's look at the simplest of examples:

```
SQL> declare
  2    -- a new datatype is born!
  3    type t_emp is record (
  4     my_empno emp.empno%type,
  5     my_ename emp.ename%type,
  6     my_job emp.job%type,
  7     my_sal emp.sal%type);
  8    -- a variable of that type
  9    employee t_emp;
 10  begin
 11    employee.my_empno := 7844;
 12    employee.my_ename := 'TURNER';
 13    employee.my_job   := 'SALESMAN';
 14    employee.my_sal   := 1500;
 15  end;
PL/SQL procedure successfully completed.
```

Assigning Values to Records Wholesale

As long as two record variables are declared using the same record datatype, you can also perform wholesale assignment of values in one record to another. Assignment of one record variable to another is shown in the following code block:

```
SQL> declare
  2    -- a new datatype is born!
  3    type t_emp is record (
  4     my_empno emp.empno%type,
  5     my_ename emp.ename%type,
  6     my_job emp.job%type,
  7     my_sal emp.sal%type);
  8    -- a variable of that type
  9    employee t_emp;
 10    employee_2 t_emp;
 11  begin
 12    employee.my_empno := 7844;
 13    employee.my_ename := 'TURNER';
 14    employee.my_job   := 'SALESMAN';
 15    employee.my_sal   := 1500;
 16    employee_2 := employee;
 17  end;
PL/SQL procedure successfully completed.
```

NOTE
*If two records are declared as two different
user-defined types, you cannot assign one record
variable to another wholesale, even if all elements
in both record types match. Instead, you must go
through all the individual elements one by one,
assigning one element to the other using dot notation.*

Using Dot Notation in SQL Statements

Dot notation is acceptable inside SQL statements in PL/SQL, too. Let's look at
something a little more complex, where we assign values to elements in a record
using a fetch operation:

```
SQL> declare
  2    -- a new datatype is born!
  3    type t_emp is record (
  4      my_empno emp.empno%type,
  5      my_ename emp.ename%type,
  6      my_job emp.job%type,
  7      my_sal emp.sal%type);
  8    -- a variable of that type
  9    employee t_emp;
 10  begin
 11    select empno, ename, job, sal
 12    into employee.my_empno, employee.my_ename,
 13          employee.my_job, employee.my_sal
 14    from emp
 15    where empno = 7844;
 16    dbms_output.put_line(to_char(employee.my_empno) || ' ' ||
 17                         employee.my_ename  || ' ' ||
 18                         employee.my_job || ' ' ||
 19                         to_char(employee.my_sal));
 20  end;
7844 TURNER SALESMAN 1500
PL/SQL procedure successfully completed.
```

Records inside Records

The elements of your record can also be records. To have records inside records,
you must define the datatype for the element inside your record, and then define the
datatype for the record. Later, when you want to assign values to the nested record,
you must do so using dot notation. This is shown in the following code block:

```
SQL> declare
  2    -- two new datatypes are born!
```

```
 3    type t_addr is record (
 4      street varchar2(50),
 5      city varchar2(50),
 6      state varchar2(50),
 7      post  number);
 8    type t_emp is record (
 9      my_empno emp.empno%type,
10      my_ename emp.ename%type,
11      my_job emp.job%type,
12      my_sal emp.sal%type,
13      my_address t_addr );
14    -- a variable of that type
15    employee t_emp;
16  begin
17    employee.my_empno := 7844;
18    employee.my_ename := 'TURNER';
19    employee.my_job   := 'SALESMAN';
20    employee.my_sal   := 1500;
21    employee.my_address.street := '25 PEACH STREET';
22    employee.my_address.city := 'ST. LOIUS';
23    employee.my_address.state := 'MISSOURI';
24    employee.my_address.post := 55555;
25  end;
PL/SQL procedure successfully completed.
```

For Review

1. Be sure that you can identify the two-step process for defining record variables in PL/SQL.

2. Understand the use of dot notation for assigning values to elements inside a PL/SQL record.

Exercises

1. **You are defining and using record datatypes in Oracle. Which of the following choices does not describe an assignment scenario that is possible between records in Oracle?**

   A. Assigning data between records of different datatypes using dot notation

   B. Assigning data between records of different datatypes not using dot notation

   C. Assigning data between records of the same datatype using dot notation

   D. Assigning data between records of the same datatype not using dot notation

  2. Your SALES_FORCE record consists of three elements. Two of the elements (NAME and PRODUCT_LINE) are VARCHAR2 datatypes. The third, PHONE, is of T_PHONE type, which, in turn, consists of three elements: CELL, PAGER, and WORK. Which of the following assigments would not be valid in this PL/SQL block?

    A. `sales_force.name := 'SMITHERS';`

    B. `sales_force.product_line := 'TOYS';`

    C. `sales_force.phone := 4155551212;`

    D. `sales_force.phone.cell := 4155551212`

  3. You are developing a database application in PL/SQL that uses records. Which of the following choices identifies the step that can take place after a value is assigned to the element in a PL/SQL record?

    A. The type must be defined before the variable declared.

    B. The record must be declared before the type is defined.

    C. A record of that same type can be assigned the values in the original record.

    D. The type for that element is then defined.

Answer Key

1. B. **2.** C. **3.** C.

Using %rowtype to Create Records

Type declarations give you a lot of precision over how you define your variables. However, as you can see in the previous examples, the declarations themselves are lengthy, especially considering that we already defined a lot of this datatype information in the table whose record we're storing for processing purposes. You need a lot of dot notation when assigning values to these record variables, too, and that can really bulk up your PL/SQL programs.

    You can avoid a lot of the overhead associated with defining PL/SQL records when all you really want is a variable that will hold the data in a row of your table. The PL/SQL `%rowtype` attribute permits you to create a composite datatype in which all the columns in a table are lumped together into a single record. For example, if we wanted to declare a record variable whose elements could be

used to store every column value in the EMP table for a single row, we could use
`%rowtype`, as shown here:

```
SQL> declare
  2    -- a new datatype is born!
  3    employee emp%rowtype;
  4  begin
  5    select * into employee
  6    from emp where empno = 7844;
  7    dbms_output.put_line(to_char(employee.empno) || ' ' ||
  8                         employee.ename  || ' ' ||
  9                         employee.job || ' ' ||
 10                         to_char(employee.sal));
 11  end;
7844 TURNER SALESMAN 1500
PL/SQL procedure successfully completed.
```

Look at how many lines of code we chopped off this program! Before, it had 20
lines, now it has only 11, and the code that remains is a lot more elegant. Although
we still need to use dot notation when referencing the elements of the EMPLOYEE
record, we no longer need to use dot notation to populate that record with data. We
can also use wildcards to indicate to Oracle that we want values from every column;
and because we used `%rowtype` to define the record, Oracle knows implicitly
where to put all our data.

TIP
*Unlike when you are assigning values in a record of
one user-defined datatype to a record of a different
user-defined type, you can assign records defined
with the `%rowtype` attribute to user-defined
records wholesale, as long as the elements in the
user-defined record match the elements in the
record defined using `%rowtype`.*

For Review

Be sure that you understand how to use the `%rowtype` attribute.

Exercises

1. You wish to declare a PL/SQL record containing elements corresponding
   to rows in the SALES table. Which of the following choices identifies a line
   of PL/SQL code that can be used for doing so?

A. `sales%type`

B. `sales%rowtype`

C. `sales%rowcount`

D. `sales%found`

2. **Use the following code block to answer this question:**

```
SQL> desc profits
 Name                          Null?    Type
 ----------------------------- -------- -------------
 PRODUCT_NAME                  NOT NULL VARCHAR2(10)
 PRODUCT_TYPE                           VARCHAR2(5)
 QUARTER                                VARCHAR2(8)
 PROFIT                                 NUMBER
 SALES_REGION                           VARCHAR2(10)
```

Which of the following elements will not appear in record PROFITS_REC, defined as `PROFITS%rowtype`?

A. PRODUCT_NAME

B. PROFIT

C. QUARTER

D. GROSS_MARGIN

3. **When used, `%rowtype` eliminates this component of defining records in PL/SQL (two words):** _____

Answer Key

1. B. **2.** D. **3.** Type declaration.

Creating PL/SQL Tables

Not content to work only with tables in the database? PL/SQL provides its own table variable construct, allowing you to define variables similar to arrays in other programming languages like C or Pascal. PL/SQL table variables are not to be confused with tables in the Oracle database, although in some cases you can use PL/SQL tables to manipulate Oracle database table data. PL/SQL tables, sometimes called *collections*, are ordered sets of elements of the same type, indexed by an integer. Figure 6-1 shows a diagram of a PL/SQL table used for storing the names of members of a team.

Two types of PL/SQL tables exist in Oracle: index-by tables and nested tables. They are similar, with two main differences. The first difference is that nested tables can be stored in the Oracle database while index-by tables cannot. The second difference is related to the first. Since nested tables can be stored in the Oracle database as columns of a table, the elements in the nested table can use only datatypes allowed in Oracle. Index-by tables, on the other hand, can use all those datatypes identified in Chapter 5 as PL/SQL-only datatypes (INTEGER, BOOLEAN, SMALLINT, and so on).

You declare a PL/SQL table in a manner similar to declaring a record. First, you define the PL/SQL table type using the `type name is table of datatype [index by binary_integer]` command, where *name* is the name of your PL/SQL table type, and *datatype* is the datatype for each element in the table. Including the optional `index by binary_integer` syntax defines the PL/SQL table as an index-by table. The following code block shows the declaration for the PL/SQL index-by table containing the names of members of a team (see Figure 6-1):

```
SQL> declare
  2    type team_type is table of varchar2(10)
  3      index by binary_integer;
  4    my_team team_type;
  5  begin
  6    null;
  7  end;
PL/SQL procedure successfully completed.
```

Here is the declaration for a nested table to contain the team information:

```
SQL> declare
  2    type team_type is table of varchar2(10);
  3    my_team team_type;
  4  begin
  5    null;
  6  end;
PL/SQL procedure successfully completed.
```

TEAM_ARRAY

Smith	Soto	James	Wilson	Hewlett	Sano
(1)	(2)	(3)	(4)	(5)	(6)

FIGURE 6-1. *PL/SQL table for storing the names of members of a team*

NOTE
*We'll work with both nested tables and index-by
tables in this chapter. Index-by tables are the older,
less robust version of PL/SQL tables in Oracle. Using
nested tables affords you the latest and greatest
features in Oracle8i. Index-by tables are provided
mainly for backward compatibility.*

Assigning Values to Index-by Tables

You can assign values to elements in the PL/SQL index-by table by referencing the
subscript that identifies the element in the array. The base element subscript for a
PL/SQL table will always be 1. You can use a loop construct to pass through each
element in the array, assigning a value to that element, as shown in the following
code block:

```
SQL> DECLARE
  2  TYPE team_type IS TABLE OF VARCHAR2(10)
  3     index by binary_integer;
  4   my_team team_type;
  5  BEGIN
  6   for mynum in 1..6 loop
  7    -- assign value to element
  8    if mynum = 1 then
  9     my_team(mynum) := 'SMITH';
 10     elsif mynum = 2 then
 11      my_team(mynum) := 'SOTO';
 12     elsif mynum = 3 then
 13      my_team(mynum) := 'JAMES';
 14     elsif mynum = 4 then
 15      my_team(mynum) := 'WILSON';
 16     elsif mynum = 5 then
 17      my_team(mynum) := 'HOWLETT';
 18     elsif mynum = 6 then
 19      my_team(mynum) := 'SANO';
 20     end if;
 21   end loop;
 22 END;
PL/SQL procedure successfully completed.
```

Assigning Values to Nested Tables

For nested tables, you can assign values to the PL/SQL table variable by means of a *constructor*. A constructor is a special function generated automatically by Oracle whenever you create a nested table, based on the user-defined type you used for creating your nested table. The name of the constructor is the same as the name you gave your user-defined type. The constructor allows you to construct the table based on elements passed to the function. The following code block illustrates how a constructor is used:

```
SQL> DECLARE
  2    TYPE team_type IS TABLE OF VARCHAR2(10);
  3      my_team team_type;
  4    BEGIN
  5      my_team :=    team_type('SMITH','SOTO','JAMES','WILSON','HOWLETT','SANO');
  6    END;
PL/SQL procedure successfully completed.
```

As you can see, using the nested table constructor reduces the amount of coding you need to do to assign that initial set of values to the nested table. Once the values are initialized, you can reference the individual elements in the PL/SQL table using a loop and the subscript notation shown in the preceding section.

Special Attributes and Operations for Nested Tables

You can use some special attributes and operations of PL/SQL tables to achieve certain tasks. For example, consider the problem of figuring out how many elements there are in a PL/SQL table. One solution is to construct a loop that moves through each element, incrementing a counter as you go, and then returning the value in the counter when the end of the table is reached. An easier way is to use the `tablename.count` attribute, which contains the number of elements in the table. The following code block shows how:

```
SQL> DECLARE
  2    TYPE team_type IS TABLE OF VARCHAR2(10);
  3      my_team team_type;
  4      my_cnt number;
  5    BEGIN
  6      my_team := team_type('SMITH','SOTO','JAMES','WILSON','HOWLETT','SANO');
  7      my_cnt := my_team.count;
  8    END;
PL/SQL procedure successfully completed.
```

The other attributes and operations available for PL/SQL tables are as follows (attributes with (*n*) accept one integer parameter):

- **count**   Contains the number of elements found in the PL/SQL table.

- **exists(n)**   Determines if element *n* of the nested table is null. This attribute has no meaning for index-by tables, because those tables contain empty elements as soon as the table is declared.

- **first**   References the first element in the PL/SQL table directly.

- **last**   References the last element in the PL/SQL table directly.

- **prior**   References the element in the PL/SQL table just prior to this one.

- **next**   References the element in the PL/SQL table just after this one.

- **extend(n)**   Adds *n* more elements to the end of the PL/SQL table.

- **trim(n)**   Removes *n* elements from the end of a PL/SQL table. Specifying an integer when referencing this attribute is optional. Without the parameter, this attribute removes one element from the end of the table.

- **delete(n)**   Removes the *n*th element from the PL/SQL table. Thus, `employees.delete(3)` removes the third element from the EMPLOYEES PL/SQL table. Specifying an integer when referencing this attribute is optional. Without the parameter, this attribute removes all elements from the table.

- **delete(m,n)**   Removes a range of elements in the PL/SQL table, starting with element *m* and ending with element *n*.

NOTE

Understanding how PL/SQL tables work may be difficult for the nonprogrammer. Try to work through the examples on a real Oracle database so you understand this important topic.

For Review

1. Know the two types of PL/SQL tables available in the Oracle database. Be able to describe the differences between the two regarding declaration and use.

2. Be sure that you understand the use of the constructor function with respect to nested tables. Also, know that nested tables can be stored in Oracle, as well as the use of nested table attributes in PL/SQL.

Exercises

1. Use the following code block to answer this question:

```
declare
    type tab_type is table of number(5);
    my_table tab_type;
begin
    null;
end;
```

If you want to populate MY_TABLE initially with two numbers, which of the following methods works best?

A. `for n in 1..2 loop. . . end loop;`

B. `while n < 2 loop. . . end loop;`

C. `my_table(1,2)`

D. `my_table.extend(2)`

2. You wish to remove the two elements from MY_TABLE that you began populating in question 1. Which of the following methods will not allow you to do so?

A. `my_table.delete;`

B. `my_table.delete(2);`

C. `my_table.delete(1,2);`

D. `my_table.trim(2);`

3. Use the following code block to answer this question:

```
declare
    type t_table is table of number(5)
      index by binary_integer;
    my_table tab_type;
begin
    null;
end;
```

Which of the following choices does not describe a feature or aspect of the table created in the preceding code block?

A. MY_TABLE contains five NULL elements on code block execution.

B. References to element *x* in MY_TABLE are made as `my_table(x)`.

C. MY_TABLE is known as a collection in Oracle.

D. MY_TABLE can be stored as a table in the database.

Answer Key

1. C. **2.** B. **3.** D.

Creating PL/SQL Tables of Records

You can create PL/SQL tables made up of records as well. Defining PL/SQL tables of records can be quite handy for creating two-dimensional arrays that deal with tables that require many columns of data. After you define your record datatype, you define your PL/SQL table datatype to be the record datatype you just declared. Here is an example:

```
SQL> declare
  2    type t_emp is record (
  3      empno emp.empno%type,
  4      ename emp.ename%type,
  5      job emp.job%type,
  6      sal emp.sal%type);
  7    type t_emp_table is table of t_emp;
  8    my_emp t_emp_table;
  9  begin
 10    null;
 11  end;
PL/SQL procedure successfully completed.
```

CAUTION

You cannot define a PL/SQL table of records when the record contains elements that are also records. If you try to do this, Oracle will return an error.

Populating Elements of Tables of Records

To populate a table of records with a single record element when the table is a nested table, you must complete two steps. First, you assign values to the subelements in the record. Then you assign that record's values to an element in the table of records using the table of record's constructor function. This two-step process satisfies the requirements of the constructor function that must be used to initialize the elements of the nested table. Let's look at an example:

```
SQL> declare
  2    type t_emp is record (
  3      empno emp.empno%type,
  4      ename emp.ename%type,
  5      job emp.job%type,
  6      sal emp.sal%type);
  7    my_rec t_emp;
  8    type t_emp_table is table of t_emp;
  9    my_emp t_emp_table;
 10  begin
 11    my_rec.empno := 7844;
 12    my_rec.ename := 'TURNER';
 13    my_rec.job := 'SALESMAN';
 14    my_rec.sal := 1500;
 15    my_emp := t_emp_table(my_rec);
 16  end;
PL/SQL procedure successfully completed.
```

NOTE
To extend this concept for populating multiple record elements in the table, you may wish to use a loop. In some cases, however, it might be too complicated, as it is in this example, because there is no easy way to loop through the contents of the EMP table following the logic presented here. There are a couple of easier ways, however, which we'll look at shortly.

Using %rowtype in Tables of Records

Unfortunately, the requirements of the constructor complicate things in the previous example. However, you can simplify the process quite a bit by using the `%rowtype` shortcut to define your PL/SQL table elements as the same record datatype as the columns in an Oracle table. The following code block demonstrates how this is accomplished:

```
SQL> declare
  2    type t_emp_table is table of emp%rowtype
  3      index by binary_integer;
```

```
4   my_emp t_emp_table;
5   begin
6     select * into my_emp(1) from emp where empno = 7844;
7   end;
PL/SQL procedure successfully completed.
```

Notice how we eliminate the separate declaration of an explicit record using the `%rowtype` keyword. We already know that this keyword reduces the code size considerably. Also notice how much more straightforward it was for us to assign a value to the elements and subelements of the index-by table. We used the wildcard (*) character, which allowed Oracle to know exactly where to put column values in the subelements. We also used a subscript reference to the individual element in our index-by table when fetching values from the EMP table into our PL/SQL table. This subscript is important, because it allows us to refer to the element and subelements later, as in this code block:

```
SQL> set serveroutput on;
SQL> declare
  2     type t_emp_table is table of emp%rowtype
  3       index by binary_integer;
  4     my_emp t_emp_table;
  5   begin
  6     select * into my_emp(1) from emp where empno = 7844;
  7     if my_emp(1).empno = 7844 then
  8       dbms_output.put_line('My ENAME is: ' || my_emp(1).ename);
  9     end if;
 10   end;
My ENAME is: TURNER
PL/SQL procedure successfully completed.
```

NOTE
Elements of the table of records are referenced using a subscript indicating the element number in the table, followed by the subelement name using dot notation.

For Review

1. Be sure that you understand how to define PL/SQL tables using record datatypes.

2. Know the restriction against elements of the record also being records in PL/SQL tables of records.

Exercises

1. You have created a table of records called MY_SALES in Oracle. MY_SALES's records consist of three elements: PRODUCT_NAME, REGION, and PROFIT. Which of the following choices identifies the proper way to reference elements in this table?

    A. `my_sales(1.profit)`

    B. `my_sales.profit(1)`

    C. `my_sales.(1).profit`

    D. `my_sales(1).profit`

2. You have created a table of records using a nested table. Which of the following methods can be used to assign values to the subelements of this table of records?

    A. Subelement assignment followed by constructor reference

    B. Fetch directly into subelements using subscript notation

    C. Constructor reference for table of records with constructor references for individual records

    D. Subscript notation followed by constructor reference

3. This is the keyword that eliminates the need for the separate declaration of a record for table of records: _____

Answer Key

1. D. 2. A. 3. %rowtype.

Reviewing PL/SQL Records, Tables, and Tables of Records

By this point, you should be familiar with defining records, tables, and tables of records. Here is a review of what each of these items is:

■ A *record* is a composite user-defined datatype, comprised of multiple elements. Each of the elements is either a variable defined using Oracle scalar datatypes or a record.

- A *table* is a one-dimensional array consisting of elements defined using an Oracle scalar datatype. The array is indexed by an integer, which can then be used for subscript referencing of values in the array.

- A *table of records* is a two-dimensional array consisting of elements defined as records. These records must in turn be defined to contain subelements, all of which must be defined using Oracle scalar datatypes (not as records themselves).

You have seen how to define records using scalar datatypes available in PL/SQL, along with how to define records where elements in the record are themselves records. The section on defining PL/SQL tables showed you how to define a one-dimensional array of values using a scalar datatype (remember how we used VARCHAR2 to define the array of members of a team?). Finally, you saw how to define a table of records and the limitations on doing so.

Explicit Cursor Handling

This section covers the following topics related to using cursors in PL/SQL:

- Using explicit cursors

- Using a PL/SQL record variable to fetch data from cursors

- Writing `cursor for` loops

You already know that a cursor is an address in memory where the results of a SQL statement are processed. Implicit cursors are used every time you issue a stand-alone SQL statement in a PL/SQL block. However, Oracle also gives you the ability to create your own cursor variables to control and manipulate the contents of a cursor. Explicit (named) cursors are frequently used in PL/SQL to handle loop processing for a set of values returned by a `select` statement, and they have other uses as well. This discussion will present the uses for cursors, the different types of cursors available in Oracle, guidelines for creating all types of cursors, and the use of the `cursor for` loop for cursor data handling.

Using Explicit Cursors

Every time a user executes SQL statements like `update`, `insert`, `delete`, and `select`, the result is stored in an address in Oracle's memory. This address in memory is called a cursor, as you already know. There are two types of cursors in PL/SQL: implicit and explicit cursors.

The *implicit cursor* is an unnamed address used for storing the result of the SQL statements. When you log into SQL*Plus and issue `select * from EMP` on the command line, the results are stored in an implicit cursor. You have seen how SQL statements issued in PL/SQL are also stored in implicit cursors, and how attributes for that cursor can give you information about the SQL statement results.

NOTE
Every SQL statement executed on the Oracle database is an implicit cursor, and any implicit cursor attribute can be used in conjunction with them.

An *explicit cursor* is a SQL statement that has a name. The name refers to the address in memory where Oracle stores the result of the query. Although cursors can contain `select`, `update`, `insert`, or `delete` commands, we will focus on using queries in our cursors. Any sort of `select` statement can be used in an explicit cursor. The cursor itself is created in the variable declaration section of the PL/SQL block using the `cursor cursor_name is` syntax, as shown here:

```
SQL> declare
  2    cursor my_emps is
  3      select * from emp;
  4  begin
  5    null;
  6  end;
PL/SQL procedure successfully completed.
```

When to Use Explicit Cursors

Explicit cursors are powerful constructs that allow you to exert a great deal of control over the results of your SQL operations. Most serious processing of data records is done with explicit cursors. You should use an explicit cursor when you want to perform some manipulation on each record returned by a `select` operation.

For example, suppose that there is a salary review coming up in our organization. We want to review every employee and grant each a raise according to the employee's job function. This operation might be difficult to code if we were only allowed to use implicit cursors, involving many `select` statements issued against the database and possibly a lot of manual labor. With explicit cursors, the job is a snap. We simply define a cursor containing all of the records from our EMP table. With the contents of table EMP in hand, we can step through each record one by one and apply programming logic to the data in the record to determine how the person's salary should be handled.

Using Explicit Cursors to Control Program Flow
Continuing with the salary review example, a PL/SQL program that addresses this business problem would consist of several steps, as outlined here.

Step 1: Declare the Cursor   You start your cursor usage in PL/SQL by declaring variables for use in the program. The variable declaration section includes a definition of a cursor containing data from the EMP table relevant for the review.

Step 2: Open the Cursor   The next step of the process is to open the cursor in the executable section of our block. Opening a cursor with the open command allows you to use the cursor's contents. This step tells Oracle to accomplish many tasks. First, Oracle finds an address in memory to store the values of the cursor. Then Oracle binds the name of your cursor to that address in memory and identifies the active set of data you wish to work with. Opening a cursor also tells Oracle to execute the query in that cursor and associate the results with your named address in memory.

Step 3: Fetch Values from the Cursor   Unfortunately, you cannot manipulate the contents of a cursor directly. Instead, once the cursor is opened, you can fetch values from it into variables that you can manipulate using PL/SQL code. The fetch operation loads current cursor values into your variable. Every time you issue the fetch command in PL/SQL on an open cursor, Oracle steps through another row of data in the cursor and passes the values in that row to your variables. You can keep fetching data from the cursor until you reach the end of the dataset in that cursor.

Step 4: Close the Cursor   Once you've done everything you need to do with the data in the cursor, you should close it using the close command. Each explicit cursor requires resources from the machine hosting the Oracle database. Even after your PL/SQL block's execution completes, Oracle cannot relinquish those resources back to the host machine until you close your cursor. Thus, you must remember to *always close your cursors* when you have finished working with their contents. If you don't, you could wind up with serious performance problems on your Oracle database.

Cursor Processing: The Salary Review Example
Let's now take a look at how these steps are accomplished in a real PL/SQL program that uses cursors. For the example, let's assume that we're giving out raises in the following way. Analysts at the company are getting a 3% raise. Clerks are getting a 5% raise. Salesmen, as a reward for keeping the company profitable, are getting a

12% raise this year. The president, greedy owner that he is, is getting a 20% raise. Let's see how the program might look before we start feeling too indignant:

```
SQL> declare
  2    cursor csr_emps is
  3      select empno, job, sal from emp; -- step 1
  4    my_empno emp.empno%type;
  5    my_job emp.ename%type;
  6    my_sal emp.sal%type;
  7  begin
  8    open csr_emps;   -- step 2
  9    loop
 10      fetch csr_emps into my_empno, my_job, my_sal; -- step 3
 11      exit when csr_emps%notfound;
 12      if my_job = 'CLERK' then my_sal := my_sal * 1.05;
 13      elsif my_job = 'ANALYST' then my_sal := my_sal * 1.03;
 14      elsif my_job = 'SALESMAN' then my_sal := my_sal * 1.12;
 15      elsif my_job = 'PRESIDENT' then my_sal := my_sal * 1.2;
 16      end if;
 17      update emp set sal = my_sal
 18      where empno = my_empno;
 19    end loop;
 20    close csr_emps; -- step 4
 21    commit;
 22  end;
PL/SQL procedure successfully completed.
```

This is probably the most complex PL/SQL block we've looked at in the book thus far, so let's examine what it does:

- First, our declaration section contains definitions for both the cursor and for enough variables to store each column element from rows later fetched from the cursor.

- Next, the executable section opens the cursor to get the data and immediately enters into a simple loop.

- For each loop iteration, we fetch the current row's worth of data from the cursor into our variables. Oracle accomplishes this step by positionally assigning cursor values to variables.

- Next, exit when csr_emps%notfound tests the value fetched so that we can exit the loop if there is no more data in the cursor.

- After obtaining data from the cursor, we enter a logic table that allows us to give the appropriate raise amount for each employee, depending on the employee's job.

- Finally, we exit the loop, close the cursor, save our work, and end the program.

For Review

1. Know what a cursor is and be able to describe the differences between implicit and explicit cursors.

2. Understand the four steps required for managing cursor processing in a PL/SQL block. Be sure that you know the syntax for defining an explicit cursor, opening the cursor, fetching values from the cursor, and closing the cursor.

3. Know how to construct a basic loop around fetching values from a cursor, as well as how to test the cursor's attributes to determine when the loop should end.

Exercises

1. **You wish to use a simple loop to fetch values from a cursor called MY_CURSOR. Which of the following choices identifies how you might construct the exiting condition test?**

   A. `exit when sql%notfound;`

   B. `exit when sql%found;`

   C. `exit when my_cursor%notfound;`

   D. `exit when my_cursor%found;`

2. **You are handling some cursor processing in Oracle. Which of the following steps is handled after you fetch cursor data into variables?**

   A. The cursor is opened.

   B. A loop construct is defined.

   C. The cursor is closed.

   D. Variables for cursor data are defined.

3. **Review the contents of the following code block:**

   ```
   declare
      cursor my_csr is select * from sales;
   begin
      loop
         fetch my_csr;
         exit when my_csr%notfound;
         if my_csr.profits < 600000 then
   ```

```
                dbms_output.put_line('Region: ' ||
                                my_csr.region || ' is great!');
        end if;
      end loop;
      close my_csr;
    end;
```

Assuming that the SALES table contains the three columns PRODUCT_NAME, REGION, and PROFIT, which of the following choices identifies the response Oracle will give when this code block executes as is?

A. Oracle will respond that the `fetch` statement is incorrect.

B. Oracle will respond that the cursor is not opened.

C. Oracle will respond that direct references to cursor values are not allowed.

D. Oracle will respond by executing this PL/SQL block successfully.

Answer Key

1. C. 2. C. 3. A.

Using PL/SQL Records to Fetch Data from Cursors

The code block in the previous example used independent variables to store the column values from each row in the cursor. Although this program is technically correct, it lacks a certain degree of elegance. After all, the variables each correspond to one particular row, so why not use the record construct to associate the variables together in a meaningful way. This process allows us to assign the values fetched from the cursor directly to the record variable, as opposed to individual variables or even to elements in the record. The following code block shows how to use records to fetch data from cursors:

```
SQL> declare
  2    cursor csr_emps is -- step 1
  3      select empno, job, sal from emp;
  4    type t_emp is record (
  5      empno emp.empno%type,
  6      job emp.ename%type,
  7      sal emp.sal%type );
```

```
 8   my_emp t_emp;
 9  begin
10   open csr_emps; -- step 2
11   loop
12     fetch csr_emps into my_emp;
13     exit when csr_emps%notfound;
14     if my_emp.job = 'CLERK' then my_emp.sal := my_emp.sal*1.05;
15       elsif my_emp.job = 'ANALYST' then my_emp.sal :=my_emp.sal*1.03;
16       elsif my_emp.job = 'SALESMAN' then my_emp.sal := my_emp.sal*1.12;
17       elsif my_emp.job = 'PRESIDENT' then my_emp.sal := my_emp.sal *1.2;
18     end if;
19     update emp set sal = my_emp.sal
20     where empno = my_emp.empno;
21   end loop;
22   close csr_emps; -- step 4
23   commit;
24  end;
PL/SQL procedure successfully completed.
```

CAUTION
The column position of data selected in the cursor must match the element position in the record declaration. If it doesn't, Oracle may inadvertently place your column data in the wrong element, causing errors if the datatypes don't match and confusion if they do.

Using %rowtype Records and Cursors

Okay, maybe I overstated my case on the elegance of using records. Whatever elegance we gained by associating the independent variables together to simplify the `fetch` command, we more than lost with the addition of several lines to the code block, the additional need for dot notation, and the dependence on position for the cursor columns and record elements. Let's take a look at a rewrite of that block using %rowtype to cut down on code size a bit:

```
SQL> declare
  2    cursor csr_emps is -- step 1
  3      select * from emp;
  4    my_emp emp%rowtype;
  5  begin
  6    open csr_emps; -- step 2
  7    loop
  8      fetch csr_emps into my_emp;
```

```
 9      exit when csr_emps%notfound;
10      if my_emp.job = 'CLERK' then my_emp.sal := my_emp.sal*1.05;
11       elsif my_emp.job = 'ANALYST' then my_emp.sal :=my_emp.sal*1.03;
12       elsif my_emp.job = 'SALESMAN' then my_emp.sal := my_emp.sal*1.12;
13       elsif my_emp.job = 'PRESIDENT' then my_emp.sal := my_emp.sal *1.2;
14      end if;
15      update emp set sal = my_emp.sal
16      where empno = my_emp.empno;
17    end loop;
18    close csr_emps; -- step 4
19    commit;
20  end;
PL/SQL procedure successfully completed.
```

This rewrite didn't give us a big improvement, but we were able to shave off about four lines of code. Additionally, we were able to simplify both the cursor definition and the `fetch` command by eliminating references to specific columns. Because we used `%rowtype` in our variable definition, Oracle knows what elements belong in the record and which elements to assign what cursor values. Thus, we avoided the need for explicitly matching the order of columns selected in our cursor definition to the order of elements defined in the record.

For Review

1. Know how to associate the variables needed for cursor-value storage together using records. Understand the benefits and drawbacks for doing so.

2. Understand how you can simplify your use of records for storing cursor data using the `%rowtype` attribute, and know the advantages this process offers over standard records.

Exercises

1. **Use the following code block to answer this question. Assume that the SALES table has only the three columns referenced in the cursor.**

```
declare
  cursor my_csr is select product_name, region, profit
    from sales;
  type t_sales is record (
   product_name sales.product_name%type,
```

```
      profit sales.profit%type,
      region sales.region%type );
    sales_rec t_sales;
  begin
    open my_csr;
    fetch my_csr into sales_rec;
    close my_csr;
  end;
```

Which of the following choices best identifies how Oracle will respond when you attempt to execute this PL/SQL block?

A. Oracle responds with an error because column data is assigned to the wrong record elements.

B. Oracle responds that a loop is necessary to obtain all row data.

C. Oracle responds that you need to reference specific elements in the fetch.

D. Oracle responds that the PL/SQL block is executed successfully.

2. **Use the code block in the preceding question to answer this question. Which of the following choices identifies an aspect of PL/SQL development that will assist you in resolving the problem identified by the correct answer to question 1?**

A. `cursor my_csr is select * from sales; my_sales sales%rowtype;`

B. `loop. . .exit when my_csr%notfound; . . . end loop;`

C. `fetch my_csr into t_sales.product_name, t_sales.profit, t_sales.region;`

D. Nothing, the code block executes successfully.

Answer Key

1. A. 2. A.

Writing cursor for Loops

Each of the examples thus far has contained some overhead for handling the loop process through each record in the cursor. The variables for storing cursor row values must be explicitly declared, the fetch must be enclosed in a loop construct, and the test for the exit condition must be defined explicitly. A special type of PL/SQL loop called the `cursor for` loop is ideal for cursor processing. The `cursor for` loop can handle several loop-creation activities implicitly, including the following:

- Declaring the variable to store values from the cursor

- Opening, parsing, executing, and fetching row data from the cursor

- Determining when the cursor is empty, and thus whether the loop should exit

Defining cursor for Loops in PL/SQL

The features of a `cursor for` loop make it ideal for loop processing in our salary review example. Let's take a look at our PL/SQL block again, this time using a `cursor for` loop statement to handle all cursor processing:

```
SQL> declare
  2    cursor csr_emps is
  3      select * from emp;
  4  begin
  5    for my_emp in csr_emps loop
  6      if my_emp.job = 'CLERK' then my_emp.sal := my_emp.sal*1.05;
  7      elsif my_emp.job = 'ANALYST' then my_emp.sal :=my_emp.sal*1.03;
  8      elsif my_emp.job = 'SALESMAN' then my_emp.sal := my_emp.sal*1.12;
  9      elsif my_emp.job = 'PRESIDENT' then my_emp.sal := my_emp.sal *1.2;
 10      end if;
 11      update emp set sal = my_emp.sal
 12        where empno = my_emp.empno;
 13    end loop;
 14    commit;
 15  end;
PL/SQL procedure successfully completed.
```

Look at how many lines of code we chopped off! Our declaration of MY_EMP is gone, as well as our `exit when` clause. Also, we no longer need to open, fetch, or close our cursor explicitly. The result is a highly elegant and compact reorganization of our employee salary review. You can even reference the SQL statement you want to process directly in the `cursor for` loop, eliminating the need to declare the cursor at all, as shown here:

```
SQL> declare
  2  -- nothing to declare
  3  begin
```

```
4   for my_emp in (select * from emp) loop
5     if my_emp.job = 'CLERK' then my_emp.sal := my_emp.sal*1.05;
6       elsif my_emp.job = 'ANALYST' then my_emp.sal :=my_emp.sal*1.03;
7       elsif my_emp.job = 'SALESMAN' then my_emp.sal := my_emp.sal*1.12;
8       elsif my_emp.job = 'PRESIDENT' then my_emp.sal := my_emp.sal *1.2;
9     end if;
10    update emp set sal = my_emp.sal
11      where empno = my_emp.empno;
12   end loop;
13   commit;
14  end;
PL/SQL procedure successfully completed.
```

CAUTION
One small caveat exists in cursor for *loops.*
When you rely on the loop to declare your variable
used for storing values from the cursor, you cannot
refer to that variable outside the scope of the
cursor for *loop. In other examples in which we*
declared the variable ourselves, we could still
have referenced the variable outside the loop if
we wanted to.

For Review

Know the steps of cursor-statement processing that are handled implicitly by the
cursor for loop: declaring the variable, opening the cursor, fetching cursor
values, and closing the cursor. Remember that even the cursor definition itself
can be eliminated.

Exercises

1. **You are rewriting a PL/SQL cursor application to use cursor for loops.
Which of the following choices indicates an area of overhead processing
required for other types of loops on cursors that is not required for cursor
for loops? (Choose all that apply.)**

   A. Cursor declaration

   B. Variable declaration

   C. Closing the cursor

   D. Fetching values from the cursor

2. **Use the following code block to answer this question:**

```
declare
-- nothing to declare
begin
 for my_emp in (select * from emp) loop
  if my_emp.job = 'CLERK' then my_emp.sal := my_emp.sal*1.05;
   elsif my_emp.job = 'ANALYST' then my_emp.sal :=my_emp.sal*1.03;
   elsif my_emp.job = 'SALESMAN' then my_emp.sal := my_emp.sal*1.12;
   elsif my_emp.job = 'PRESIDENT' then my_emp.sal := my_emp.sal *1.2;
  end if;
  update emp set sal = my_emp.sal
   where empno = my_emp.empno;
 end loop;
  if my_emp.empno = '7844' then
   dbms_output.put_line('Turner is a fool!');
  end if;
end;
```

If this code block is run as is, which of the following choices will best characterize how Oracle responds?

A. Oracle responds that the cursor must be declared.

B. Oracle responds that the changes in the procedure must be committed.

C. Oracle responds that the reference to my_emp.empno in the last if-then statement is out of scope.

D. Oracle responds that the PL/SQL block is executed successfully.

Answer Key

1. A, B, C, and D. **2.** C. **3.**

Understanding Advanced Explicit Cursor Concepts

This section covers the following topics related to advanced explicit cursor concepts:

■ Passing parameters to explicit cursors

■ Using the for update and where current of clauses

■ Using subqueries in cursors

Explicit cursors are extremely flexible in Oracle8i. This section will introduce you to some of the advanced features of explicit cursor development to help you exploit their functionality. You will learn how to extend the use of an explicit cursor using parameters. You will also learn how to reference values in a cursor directly, a feature not available in Oracle prior to Oracle8i. This functionality is supported with the for update and where current of clauses. Finally, you will explore cursors that use subqueries.

Passing Parameters to Explicit Cursors

Let's modify the scope of our previous example and say that instead of giving every employee a raise, we want to process only those employees whose EMPNO falls in a specific range. Furthermore, we may want to rerun the block with different ranges.

The cursors demonstrated thus far select every record in the database or, alternatively, may be designed to select from a table according to hard-coded magic values. To make this change easy, we can extend our existing cursor definition by passing parameters into the cursor. Parameters allow for reuse of cursors by passing in the magic value. Let's look at how we might rewrite our example that used a simple loop to take advantage of parameter passing to the cursor:

```
SQL> declare
  2   cursor my_csr (lowend in number, highend in number) is
  3     select * from emp where empno > lowend and empno < highend;
  4   my_emp emp%rowtype;
  5   begin
  6   open my_csr(7600,7700);
  7   loop
  8     fetch my_csr into my_emp;
  9     exit when my_csr%notfound;
 10     if my_emp.job = 'CLERK' then my_emp.sal := my_emp.sal*1.05;
 11      elsif my_emp.job = 'ANALYST' then my_emp.sal :=my_emp.sal*1.03;
 12      elsif my_emp.job = 'SALESMAN' then my_emp.sal := my_emp.sal*1.12;
 13      elsif my_emp.job = 'PRESIDENT' then my_emp.sal := my_emp.sal *1.2;
 14     end if;
 15     update emp set sal = my_emp.sal
 16     where empno = my_emp.empno;
 17   end loop;
 18   close my_csr;
 19   commit;
 20   end;
PL/SQL procedure successfully completed.
```

Notice that the cursor declaration accommodates two values of the NUMBER datatype and uses those values when evaluating the `select` statement to obtain information. The `open` statement that opens, parses, and executes the cursor now contains two values passed into the cursor creation as parameters. This parameter passing is required for the cursor to resolve into a set of data rows. Let's now take a look at the rewrite of our `cursor for` loop using passed parameters, as well as passing parameters in the next range:

```
SQL> declare
  2    cursor my_csr (lowend in number, highend in number) is
  3      select * from emp where empno > lowend and empno < highend;
  4  begin
  5    for my_emp in my_csr(7700,7800) loop
  6     if my_emp.job = 'CLERK' then my_emp.sal := my_emp.sal*1.05;
  7      elsif my_emp.job = 'ANALYST' then my_emp.sal :=my_emp.sal*1.03;
  8      elsif my_emp.job = 'SALESMAN' then my_emp.sal := my_emp.sal*1.12;
  9      elsif my_emp.job = 'PRESIDENT' then my_emp.sal := my_emp.sal *1.2;
 10     end if;
 11     update emp set sal = my_emp.sal
 12     where empno = my_emp.empno;
 13    end loop;
 14    commit;
 15  end;
PL/SQL procedure successfully completed.
```

NOTE
You cannot use parameter passing in `cursor for` loops when the statement is embedded directly into the `cursor for` loop statement. There is no point in doing so, anyway, since you can simply modify the `where` clause in the query passed!

For Review

1. Know the value that passing parameters into Oracle cursors provides and how to construct the passing of parameters into those cursors.

2. Understand that when a cursor has parameters, you must pass values for those parameters in the `open` command or in the `cursor for` loop.

Exercises

1. **You are using parameters in your cursor manipulations. Which of the following statements are used for passing parameters into the cursor? (Choose two.)**

      A. `cursor for`

      B. `open`

      C. `fetch`

      D. `cursor is`

2. **You are defining parameters for your cursor. Which of the following statements can be used for defining the datatype of the parameters passed?**

      A. `for` *var* `in` *csr* `loop`

      B. `open`

      C. `fetch`

      D. `cursor` *csr* `is`

Answer Key

1. A and B. 2. D.

Using the for update and where current of Clauses

Earlier in the chapter, I told you that you couldn't reference values in the cursor directly. Instead, you need to fetch the values from the cursor into variables, and then manipulate the variables in PL/SQL. Well, there is a small exception to this rule in Oracle8i related to the use of the `cursor for` loop, using the `for update` and `where current of` clauses. Let's start with the `for update` clause.

Using the for update Clause

The `for update` clause in a `select` statement allows you to select data from a table in such a way that Oracle places a share row exclusive lock on each of the rows returned by the query. You are then able to modify data without Oracle needing to do any extra work to acquire a lock on the data you want to change. Here is an example:

```
SQL> select * from emp for update;
```

    The `for update` clause is also valid for use in cursors. Recall in our employee salary review code, we obtained the records in the EMP table, and then updated those records one by one. Oracle's locking mechanisms that exist to support statement-level read consistency work behind the scenes in the `update` statement in the loop, so that Oracle locks the row being changed only when the `update` statement is issued.

In other words, if the EMP table were really large, it is theoretically possible that someone could come along and change the data in an EMP table row while our salary review code was executing, causing a delay to our PL/SQL. The `for update` clause helps us avoid this problem by allowing our code block to lock every record in the EMP table at the time the cursor is opened. Let's look at the use of the `for update` clause in this context:

```
SQL> declare
  2   cursor my_csr is
  3     select * from emp for update;
  4  begin
  5   for my_emp in my_csr loop
  6    if my_emp.job = 'CLERK' then my_emp.sal := my_emp.sal*1.05;
  7     elsif my_emp.job = 'ANALYST' then my_emp.sal :=my_emp.sal*1.03;
  8     elsif my_emp.job = 'SALESMAN' then my_emp.sal := my_emp.sal*1.12;
  9     elsif my_emp.job = 'PRESIDENT' then my_emp.sal := my_emp.sal *1.2;
 10    end if;
 11    update emp set sal = my_emp.sal
 12    where empno = my_emp.empno;
 13   end loop;
 14   commit;
 15  end;
PL/SQL procedure successfully completed.
```

You won't see Oracle return anything special with respect to the rows Oracle locked behind the scenes, but rest assured—the rows *are* locked for you. Of course, the downside is that you need to remember that those rows are locked and handle your transaction processing in the PL/SQL block accordingly, because other users trying to make changes to those rows will need to wait until your transaction ends.

The use of the `for update` clause is exactly the same for queries defined as explicit cursors as it is for queries run as implicit cursors. Again, the rows are locked when they are fetched as part of the query. These two steps happen together when the cursor is opened in your PL/SQL block.

NOTE
The `for update` *clause is not permitted in queries that fetch data from views defined with* `distinct` *or* `group by` *expressions.*

Adding the where current of Clause
When you open your cursor containing a `for update` clause, a magical thing happens—you gain the ability to directly reference elements in a cursor, as opposed to referencing elements in a cursor as values fetched into a variable. Referencing

values directly in the cursor is done using the where current of clause. Here is an example of how to use this technique in our employee salary review code:

```
SQL> declare
  2    cursor my_csr is
  3      select * from emp for update;
  4  begin
  5    for my_emp in my_csr loop
  6      if my_emp.job = 'CLERK' then my_emp.sal := my_emp.sal*1.05;
  7        elsif my_emp.job = 'ANALYST' then my_emp.sal :=my_emp.sal*1.03;
  8        elsif my_emp.job = 'SALESMAN' then my_emp.sal := my_emp.sal*1.12;
  9        elsif my_emp.job = 'PRESIDENT' then my_emp.sal := my_emp.sal *1.2;
 10      end if;
 11    update emp set sal = my_emp.sal
 12    where current of my_csr;
 13    end loop;
 14    commit;
 15  end;
PL/SQL procedure successfully completed.
```

NOTE
The where current of clause should be used only in DML statements appearing inside a loop operating on top of an explicit cursor. Otherwise, the where current of clause will lack any meaningful context. Also, remember that the where current of clause is used only in conjunction with the for update clause.

For Review

1. Be sure that you understand the use of the for update clause in cursors, and the effect it has on data in the table.

2. Be sure that you understand the use of the where current of clause in cursors.

Exercises

1. **Use the following code block to answer this question. Assume that the SALES table has only the columns mentioned in the block.**

```
declare
  cursor my_csr is select product_name, region, profit
    from sales;
begin
  for my_rec in my_csr loop
```

```
      update sales set profit = 0
      where current of my_csr;
   end loop;
end;
```

When this code block is executed in Oracle, which of the following choices indicates how Oracle will respond?

A. Oracle will return an error stating that the `for update` clause must be present.

B. Oracle will return an error stating that direct reference to values in a cursor is illegal.

C. Oracle will return an error stating that the `update` statement must reference MY_REC.

D. Oracle will return a message stating that the PL/SQL block executed successfully.

2. **These are the types of statements in which the `where current of` clause may appear (three words): _____**

Answer Key

1. A. **2.** update, insert, delete.

Using Subqueries in Cursors

Almost any SQL `select` statement that is valid for use against Oracle is valid for use in a cursor. This includes SQL queries that contain subqueries. Recall that a subquery is a query (usually enclosed by parentheses) that appears within another SQL statement. When evaluated, the subquery provides a value or set of values to the statement. Often, subqueries are used in the `where` clause. For example, the following cursor declaration returns employees not located in Chicago:

```
CURSOR c1 IS
  SELECT empno, ename FROM emp
  WHERE deptno IN (SELECT deptno FROM dept
                   WHERE loc <> 'CHICAGO');
```

Using a subquery in the `from` clause, the following cursor returns the number and name of each department with five or more employees:

```
CURSOR c1 IS
   SELECT t1.deptno, dname, "STAFF"
   FROM dept t1, (SELECT deptno, COUNT(*) "STAFF"
                     FROM emp GROUP BY deptno) t2
   WHERE t1.deptno = t2.deptno AND "STAFF" >= 5;
```

Whereas a subquery is evaluated only once per table, a correlated subquery is evaluated once per row. Consider the query in the following example, which returns the name and salary of each employee whose salary exceeds the departmental average. For each row in the EMP table, the correlated subquery computes the average salary for that row's department. The row is returned if that row's salary exceeds the average.

```
CURSOR c1 IS SELECT deptno, ename, sal FROM emp t
   WHERE sal > (SELECT AVG(sal) FROM emp WHERE t.deptno = deptno)
   ORDER BY deptno;
```

For Review

Understand how to use subqueries in your cursors.

Error Handling

This section covers the following areas related to error handling:

- Defining and using different types of PL/SQL exceptions

- Trapping unhandled and unanticipated errors

- Customizing PL/SQL error messages

- Understanding exception propagation in nested blocks

Error handling in PL/SQL is arguably the best contribution PL/SQL makes to commercial programming. In PL/SQL, errors aren't handled with if statements directly within the program. Instead, PL/SQL allows you to *raise exceptions* when an error condition is identified and switch control to a special program area in the PL/SQL block, called the *exception handler*. The code for handling an error does not clutter the executable program logic in PL/SQL, nor is the programmer required to terminate programs with return or exit statements. The exception handler is a cleaner way to handle errors.

Defining a PL/SQL Exception

The three types of exceptions in Oracle PL/SQL are *predefined* exceptions, *internal* exceptions, and *user-defined* exceptions. Exception handling in PL/SQL is simple and flexible. Predefined exceptions offer the developer several built-in problems that can be checked. User-defined and internal exceptions allow for additional flexibility in supporting errors defined by you, the developer of the code.

Predefined Exceptions

In order to facilitate error handling in PL/SQL, Oracle has designed several built-in, or predefined, exceptions. How does a predefined exception work? Let's take a look at an example and find out:

```
SQL> set serveroutput on
SQL> declare
  2    my_var number;
  3  begin
  4    select empno into my_var
  5    from emp where ename = 'SMITHERS';
  6    dbms_output.put_line('We got SMITHERS');
  7  end;
declare
*
ERROR at line 1:
ORA-01403: no data found
ORA-06512: at line 4
```

Remember how we deleted SMITHERS from the EMP table, back in the "Writing DML Statements in PL/SQL" section of this chapter? Well, when we tried to query EMP for that record, Oracle couldn't find one. Rather than just silently playing along with our PL/SQL program and telling us that we obtained SMITHERS, Oracle raises an error telling us that no record for SMITHERS existed in the table. Oracle did so by raising a predefined exception called `no_data_found`, which we need to handle in order for our code block to work right. Let's look at how we would handle this exception in our code:

```
SQL> declare
  2    my_var number;
  3  begin
  4    select empno into my_var
  5    from emp where ename = 'SMITHERS';
  6    dbms_output.put_line('We got SMITHERS');
  7    exception
  8    when no_data_found then
```

```
 9    dbms_output.put_line('SMITHERS does not live here anymore');
10    end;
SMITHERS does not live here anymore
PL/SQL procedure successfully completed.
```

Notice two new things about the code. First, we added an `exception` clause that delineates how Oracle should behave if the exception named in the clause is raised. The other important thing to notice is in the output from the program.

When we execute this code, Oracle raises the `no_data_found` exception and transfers control to the exception handler for that exception. This handler, in turn, writes out a message telling us that SMITHERS isn't in the table. However, notice the other call to `dbms_output.put_line()` in the executable section of the block, the one that tells us we got SMITHERS's record. By every appearance, it should have printed its message, right? After all, it exists in the executable section, and PL/SQL is supposed to execute every statement, right? Well, not exactly.

When an exception is raised in the executable section, Oracle transfers control to the exception handler to process the error condition. When the handler has finished, Oracle transfers control back to the PL/SQL block's caller. Thus, our message about obtaining SMITHERS's record is never printed.

NOTE

In order to trap a predefined exception, there must be an exception handler coded for it in the exception section of the PL/SQL block.

There are many common predefined exceptions that you can handle in your programs. The predefined exceptions are listed here:

- **`invalid_cursor`** An attempt was made to close a cursor that is not open.

- **`cursor_already_open`** An attempt was made to open a cursor that is not closed.

- **`dup_val_on_index`** Unique or primary key constraint violation.

- **`no_data_found`** No rows were selected or changed by the SQL operation.

- **`too_many_rows`** More than one row was obtained by a single-row subquery or in another SQL statement operation where Oracle was expecting one row.

- **`zero_divide`** An attempt was made to divide by zero.

- **rowtype_mismatch** The datatypes of the record to which data from the cursor was assigned are incompatible.

- **invalid_number** An alphanumeric string was referenced as a number.

Internal Exceptions

The list of predefined exceptions is limited, and, overall, they really do nothing other than associate a named exception with an Oracle error. You can extend the list of exceptions associated with Oracle errors within your PL/SQL code by first declaring your new exception and then using the `pragma exception_init` keywords.

The `pragma exception_init` statement is a compiler directive that allows you to declare the Oracle-numbered error to be associated with a named exception in the block. Oracle then raises the exception without requiring you to program an explicit `raise` statement for the exception. For example, assume that we insert a new row into the EMP table, which has a primary key constraint on EMPNO. Instead of allowing the PL/SQL block to terminate with unique constraint violation error `ORA-00001`, we can handle the problem within our program:

```
SQL> declare
  2    cons_violate exception;
  3    pragma exception_init(cons_violate,-0001);
  4  begin
  5    insert into emp (empno, ename, job)
  6      values (7844,'TURNER','SALESMAN');
  7  exception
  8    when cons_violate then
  9      dbms_output.put_line('EMPNO must be unique for each employee');
 10  end;
EMPNO must be unique for each employee
PL/SQL procedure successfully completed.
```

TIP
Defining internal exceptions is useful because Oracle raises the exception for you implicitly. You still need to declare the exception and handle it, but you don't need to raise it.

User-Defined Exceptions

You can create your own exceptions to handle situations that may arise in the code, too. A user-defined exception does not correlate with an Oracle error; instead, user-defined exceptions usually enforce business rules in situations in which an Oracle error would not necessarily occur. Unlike predefined exceptions, which are implicitly raised by

Oracle when the associated error condition arises, a user-defined exception must have explicit code in the PL/SQL block designed to raise it. When writing PL/SQL with user-defined exceptions, you must remember to include code in three areas of the program:

- **Exception declaration**   In the declaration section of the PL/SQL block, the exception name must be declared. This name will be used to invoke, or raise, the exception in the execution section if the conditions of the exception occur.

- **Exception testing**   In the execution section of the PL/SQL block, there must be code that explicitly tests for the user-defined error condition, which raises the exception if the conditions are met.

- **Exception handling**   In the exception handler section of the PL/SQL block, there must be a specified when clause that names the exception and the code that should be executed if that exception is raised. Alternatively, there should be a when others exception handler that acts as a catchall.

The following code block provides an example for coding a user-defined exception. Let's say that we care about situations in which salesmen in the EMP table have a NULL value defined for their commission. The following code obtains salesmen's records from the database; and if the record selected has no commission defined, it raises a user-defined exception to identify the problem with an output message. The code required in all three areas of the block is highlighted in bold:

```
SQL> declare
  2    cursor my_emps is select * from emp
  3      where job = 'SALESMAN';
  4    bad_empno emp.empno%type;
  5    comm_is_null exception;
  6  begin
  7    for my_emp in my_emps loop
  8     if my_emp.comm is null then
  9       bad_empno := my_emp.empno;
 10       raise comm_is_null;
 11     end if;
 12    end loop;
 13   exception
 14    when comm_is_null then
 15     dbms_output.put_line('COMM is NULL for salesman: '
 16                            || to_char(bad_empno));
 17   end;
COMM is NULL for salesman: 7844
PL/SQL procedure successfully completed.
```

NOTE
Remember that the variable used in a `cursor for` *loop is not available outside the scope of that loop. Hence, we needed to declare a variable BAD_EMPNO to pass the EMPNO to the exception handler.*

For Review

1. Know what an exception is and how it simplifies the management of errors in an Oracle PL/SQL application.

2. Understand the three types of exceptions and when and how they are defined, raised, and handled.

3. Be able to identify all of the predefined exceptions in Oracle. Know that Oracle raises these exceptions implicitly during code execution.

4. Know that the keywords used for defining internal exceptions are `pragma exception_init`.

Exercises

1. You wish to define an exception in your PL/SQL block that can be raised by Oracle whenever someone gets an undefined value by dividing SAL by zero. In which of the following areas would you need to define code related to this exception?

A. declare only

B. exception only

C. declare, begin, and exception only

D. declare and exception only

2. You have an exception called `not_enough_pay`, which gets raised whenever someone updates the SAL column on table EMP and does not raise the salary by a basic minimum COLA (cost-of-living allowance). Which of the following areas of your Oracle code indicate where code supporting this exception must be placed?

A. declare only

B. exception only

C. declare, begin, and exception only

D. declare and exception only

Answer Key

1. B. 2. C.

Trapping Unhandled and Unanticipated Errors

Unhandled Oracle-defined exceptions are easy to recognize. Since Oracle always raises its own predefined exceptions in your code, you will be able to spot the Oracle-defined exceptions you didn't code handlers for as soon as you run the code. This is because as soon as your code hits an error, Oracle raises its own exceptions and your program will crash. The code block at the beginning of this section illustrated this principle by demonstrating how Oracle raises the `no_data_found` exception automatically when you attempt to fetch data into a variable and no data is retrieved. The same can be said for internal exceptions where you associated a name you chose with an Oracle error. Since Oracle always catches its own errors, you can be sure that if you don't handle internal exceptions within your program, Oracle will make you aware of your mistake by crashing your program.

Unfortunately, it is a little harder to recognize unhandled user-defined exceptions. You must explicitly raise any exception you define in the PL/SQL programming environment. You might define your own exceptions to handle a situation that crashes the program in a major way or involves data corruption. Unfortunately, if you forget to raise the exception anywhere in your code, the signs of the unhandled exception will be major program failures or data-corruption problems. Careful testing is required for situations to ensure that no unhandled exceptions are propagated to the user level. However, if you define your own exceptions and raise them in your code, and the problem is merely that you forgot to handle your own exception, then the problem is much easier to identify. When you forget to handle your own user-defined exceptions, Oracle tells you with an error, as in this example:

```
SQL> declare
  2    baderror exception;
  3  begin
  4    raise baderror;
  5  end;
  6  /
declare
*
ERROR at line 1:
ORA-06510: PL/SQL: unhandled user-defined exception
ORA-06512: at line 4
```

Writing Exception Handlers

To solve the problem shown in the preceding code block, we could write an exception handler specifically for the exception being raised, such as the exception shown in the following block:

```
exception
  when baderror then
    dbms_output.put_line('You generated a bad error!');
end;
```

This exception has a simple routine that displays an error message designed specifically for the exception we knew would be raised. However, there is another option for us if we suspect that many errors could occur in our program, and we don't want to code explicit exception handlers for every single one of them.

If there is no code explicitly defined for the exception raised, PL/SQL will execute whatever code is defined for a special catchall exception called others. The others exception handler is perhaps the greatest achievement gained by using PL/SQL to write stored procedures in Oracle. Its flexibility and ease of use make it simple to code robust programs with very few lines of code. Because it is designed to handle all exceptions that have not been handled specifically, the others exception handler should appear at the end of the exception section. Let's take a look at a program that handles all possible errors that could arise in the code using the others exception:

```
declare
  my_var number;
  cursor my_emps is select * from emp
   where job = 'SALESMAN';
  bad_empno emp.empno%type;
  comm_is_null exception;
begin
  select empno into my_var
   from emp where ename = 'SMITHERS';
  for my_emp in my_emps loop
   if my_emp.comm is null then
    bad_empno := my_emp.empno;
    raise comm_is_null;
   end if;
  end loop;
exception
  when others then
    dbms_output.put_line('some kind of error occurred');
end;
```

NOTE
*Once an exception is raised, PL/SQL flow control
passes to the exception handler in the current code
block. Once the exception is handled, the PL/SQL
block will be exited. In other words, once the
exception is raised, the execution portion of the
PL/SQL block is over.*

For Review

Be sure that you understand what happens when Oracle raises an exception you
didn't code an exception handler for, and know how to use the `others` exception
to remedy the situation.

Exercises

1. **You are attempting to handle unanticipated errors in your PL/SQL code.
   Which of the following choices does not identify an appropriate use of the
   `others` exception for this purpose?**

   A. The `others` exception can replace all other exceptions in the
   exception handler.

   B. The `others` exception can appear after all other exceptions in the
   exception handler.

   C. The `others` exception can appear between other exceptions in the
   exception handler.

   D. The `others` exception will handle exception scenarios not already
   explicitly handled.

2. **You declare your own exception in a PL/SQL block but do not raise that
   exception in the block. Which of the following choices identifies how
   Oracle alerts you to the possibility that there is an unhandled exception in
   your code block?**

   A. Oracle raises the exception implicitly when the code block is executed.

   B. Oracle will flag the exception during compilation as unhandled.

   C. Oracle raises an error saying you have an unhandled exception in
   your code block.

   D. Oracle does nothing; you need to raise the exception yourself.

Answer Key

1. C. **2.** D.

Customizing PL/SQL Error Messages

In the previous section, you saw how powerful the `others` exception can be for catching any problems that may arise. What you didn't see was `others` communicating the actual error that occurred. No matter what error occurred, you simply end up with a generic-looking message telling you that something bad happened, with no indication of what actually happened or how to fix it. Thus, you need a better way to find out what went wrong in your program.

Using the sqlcode( ) and sqlerrm( ) Functions

To obtain actual error messages from Oracle in your `others` exception (or indeed, any exception or anywhere else in the code for that matter), you can use the Oracle functions `sqlcode( )` and `sqlerrm( )`. These functions work as follows:

- **sqlcode( )**   Accepts no input and returns the error number for any error message raised by Oracle in the course of executing the PL/SQL program. The number returned by `sqlcode( )` is always negative, except when no data is found and when a user-defined exception is raised. In those cases, `sqlcode( )` returns +100 and +1, respectively.

- **sqlerrm( )**   Accepts an error number as input and returns the first 512 characters of the error message corresponding to the number presented by `sqlcode( )`, raised by Oracle in the course of executing the PL/SQL program.

TIP
Although sqlcode( ) and sqlerrm( ) are extremely handy to us in `others` exception handlers to determine exactly what happened to cause your program to crash, these keywords can be used in many other contexts as well. For example, if you made a call to these functions when no error has occurred, then Oracle would return 00000 for sqlcode( ) and Normal, successful execution for sqlerrm( ).

Let's take another look at the code block presented in the previous discussion. This time, we modify the code to take advantage of `sqlcode( )` and `sqlerrm( )` in the `others` exception to tell us exactly what went wrong in our code block:

```
declare
 my_var number;
 my_errmsg varchar2(50);
 cursor my_emps is select * from emp
  where job = 'SALESMAN';
 bad_empno emp.empno%type;
 comm_is_null exception;
begin
 select empno into my_var
  from emp where ename = 'SMITHERS';
 for my_emp in my_emps loop
  if my_emp.comm is null then
   bad_empno := my_emp.empno;
   raise comm_is_null;
  end if;
 end loop;
exception
 when others then
  my_errnum:= sqlcode;
  my_errmsg := substr(sqlerrm(my_errnum),1,50);
  dbms_output.put_line(to_char(my_errnum) || ' ' || my_errmsg);
end;
```

NOTE
You cannot reference sqlcode( ) *and*
sqlerrm( ) *directly in SQL statements. Instead,*
you must assign the values they return to variables
and then reference the variables.

Using the raise_application_error ( ) Procedure

Often, when you develop a large amount of PL/SQL code, with several procedures calling other procedures, it becomes easy to get lost in the shuffle of exception handlers when something goes wrong. To help you keep your sanity when debugging and maintaining code, Oracle allows you to customize the PL/SQL error message propagated to the user level.

Oracle provides a procedure called raise_application_error( ), which lets you issue user-defined error messages from stored programs. That way, you can report errors to your application, avoid returning unhandled exceptions, and spend less time guessing where the error actually came from within your application.

To call raise_application_error( ), use this syntax:

```
raise_application_error(error_number, message[, {TRUE | FALSE}]);
```

The value for *error_number* should be a negative integer between –20000 and –20999. These are the allowed message code numbers allotted to PL/SQL programmers in Oracle. The value for *message* should be a character string up to 2,048 bytes long. If the optional third parameter is TRUE, the error is placed on the stack of previous errors. If the parameter is FALSE (the default), the error replaces all previous errors.

TIP

It is highly advisable that you devise some mechanism that helps you map the integer returned by raise_application_error( ) to the PL/SQL program unit where the error was encountered. This method can greatly reduce the amount of digging you need to do through your code.

An application can call `raise_application_error( )` only from an executing stored subprogram, not from SQL*Plus. Once called, `raise_application_error( )` ends execution of the program that called it and returns the user-defined error number and message to your application.

In the following example, we call `raise_application_ error( )` if an employee's salary is missing:

```
CREATE PROCEDURE raise_salary (emp_id in NUMBER, amount in NUMBER) is
    curr_sal NUMBER;
BEGIN
    SELECT sal INTO curr_sal FROM emp WHERE empno = emp_id;
    IF curr_sal IS NULL THEN
        raise_application_error(-20101, 'Salary is missing');
    ELSE
        UPDATE emp SET sal = curr_sal + amount WHERE empno = emp_id;
    END IF;
END raise_salary;
```

NOTE

The raise_application_error( ) procedure can also be called from within an exception handler. Usually, this is the way that PL/SQL programmers use it.

For Review

Be sure that you understand how to use `sqlcode( )`, `sqlerrm( )`, and `raise_application_error( )`.

Exercises

I. Use the following code block to answer this question. Assume that
ERROR_TABLE contains two columns: ERRNUM and ERRMSG.

```
declare
  my_empno number;
begin
  select empno into my_empno
  from emp where ename = 'SMITH';
exception
  when others then
    insert into error_table (errnum, errmsg)
    values (sqlcode, sqlerrm(sqlcode));
end;
```

Which of the following choices identifies the problem with this
PL/SQL block?

A. Values from `sqlcode( )` and `sqlerrm( )` must be assigned
to a variable.

B. The `others` exception must appear at the end of the exception handler.

C. The `no_data_found` exception is missing from the exception handler.

D. `sqlerrm(-sqlcode)` is needed, because `sqlcode( )` returns
negative numbers.

2. You are using `raise_application_error( )` for your error handling.
Which of the following numbers is appropriate as the error number?

A. –4567

B. –10549

C. –20998

D. –29088

Answer Key

1. A. 2. C.

Understanding Exception Propagation in Nested Blocks.

Once an exception is raised, control is passed to the exception handler of the PL/SQL program unit that was executing when the exception was raised. There is no going back to the execution section, either. Instead, the exception is handled by the corresponding exception handler in that local block's exception section. Alternatively, the others exception handler will catch all exceptions that don't have their own handler. However, in situations where there is no exception handler within the local PL/SQL block equipped to handle this exception, control passes to the exception handler in the PL/SQL block that called this one.

Figure 6-2 shows the control flow in situations where exception handlers don't exist locally for the exception Oracle raises. In Figure 6-2, procedure proc_a( ) is called by the user running SQL*Plus, which in turn calls proc_b( ), which in turn calls proc_c( ). Inside proc_c( ), a query found no data where data was expected, and Oracle raises the no_data_found exception automatically. Control transfers from the execution block in proc_c( ) to the exception handler in that same procedure. If no handler exists for the no_data_found exception or the others exception, this exception is sent to the exception handler of proc_c( )'s caller, proc_b( ). If no handler exists for no_data_found or others in proc_b( ), the exception is raised to proc_b( )'s caller, proc_a( ). As before, if no handler exists for no_data_found or others, the exception is sent to the exception handler of proc_a( )'s caller. Unfortunately, proc_a( )'s caller is not another procedure—it is the user. So, the error gets sent to the user level, and it appears in SQL*Plus as an ORA-1403: no data found error.

This method of propagation is also the case when sub-blocks inside a PL/SQL block cause an exception to be raised. Unhandled exceptions can also affect subprograms. If you exit a subprogram successfully, PL/SQL assigns values to OUT parameters. However, if you exit with an unhandled exception, PL/SQL does not assign values to OUT parameters. Also, if a stored subprogram fails with an unhandled exception, PL/SQL does not roll back database work done by the subprogram.

CAUTION
Exceptions cannot propagate back to their caller when remote procedure calls are made in distributed database environments. If you develop an application that calls PL/SQL procedures in remote databases, take special care to ensure you aren't missing error messages when you test the application.

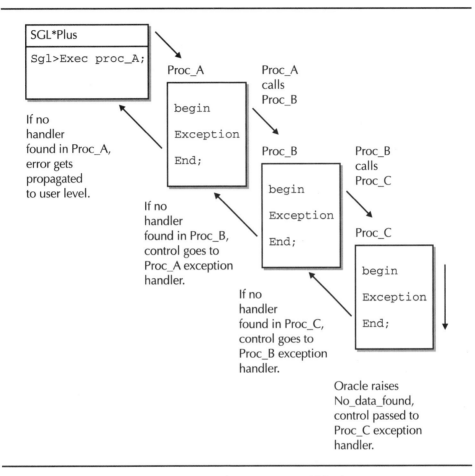

FIGURE 6-2. *Exception propagation between nested blocks*

Continuing Execution Past an Exception

Oracle passes execution control to the exception handler once an exception is raised. Once Oracle completes execution of the exception handler, the rest of the code in the execution section of the current block is ignored, because Oracle then transfers execution control back to the caller of the block. You can use this fact to your advantage by coding portions of your PL/SQL in unnamed sub-blocks and giving those sub-blocks exception handlers of their own.

For example, if we were afraid that our query on the EMP table might turn up NULL results, but knew that a NULL wouldn't adversely affect the rest of the code's execution, we could put just that query and an associated exception handler inside a sub-block. That way, when the sub-block's execution handler completed, Oracle would simply return control to our main block, right where we left off. Observe how to do so in the following code block:

```
declare
  my_var number;
  my_errmsg varchar2(50);
  cursor my_emps is select * from emp
   where job = 'SALESMAN';
  bad_empno emp.empno%type;
  comm_is_null exception;
begin
  -- welcome to the main block
   begin -- now we are in the sub-block
      select empno into my_var
      from emp where ename = 'SMITHERS';
    exception
     when no_data_found then null;
    end; -- sub-block is over
  -- control passes back to the main block
  for my_emp in my_emps loop
   if my_emp.comm is null then
    bad_empno := my_emp.empno;
    raise comm_is_null;
   end if;
  end loop;
exception
 when others then
   my_errnum:= sqlcode;
   my_errmsg := substr(sqlerrm(my_errnum),1,50);
   dbms_output.put_line(to_char(my_errnum) || ' ' || my_errmsg);
end;
```

NOTE
The goto *command (discussed in Chapter 5) cannot be used to branch into or out of an exception handler. However,* goto *can be used to branch from the exception handler into an enclosing block. Be sure that you understand this important fact for the OCP exam.*

Exceptions Raised in the Declaration or Exception Section

If any exceptions are raised in the declaration or exception section, then control passes immediately to the caller of the block where the exception was raised. When might an exception be raised in the declaration or exception section? In the declaration section, an exception could be raised if you tried to assign a default value that was too large for the variable defined, such as `my_var number(3) default 13706`. In this case, control passes immediately to the caller of the block. Exceptions can be raised in the exception section if you attempt to perform an operation such as a SQL `select` that causes a predefined exception to be raised.

For Review

1. Be sure that you understand the propagation of exceptions between nested PL/SQL blocks and to the user level.

2. Be sure that you understand the special cases of exception propagation when exceptions are raised in the declaration and exception sections of a code block.

Exercises

1. Your **insert** statement inside the exception section of a nested sub-block violates an integrity constraint on the table involved. Which of the following choices identifies how PL/SQL handles exception propagation?

   A. Control is transferred to the exception section of the nested block.

   B. Control is transferred to the execution section of the parent block.

   C. Control is transferred to the exception section of the parent block.

   D. Control is transferred to the execution section of the sub-block.

2. Your exception section in a nested sub-block contains reference to a label via **goto**. Which of the following choices identifies a place where the label *may* appear?

   A. In the execution section of the nested sub-block

   B. In the exception section of a sub-block to the current block

   C. In the execution section of the parent block

   D. In the exception section of another sub-block in the parent block

Answer Key
1. C. 2. C.

Chapter Summary

Well, that's it! You've now learned the technical aspects of what you need to know for OCP Exam 1. In this chapter, you learned about database programming in PL/SQL

First, you learned how to embed SQL statements into your PL/SQL code and how to avoid the potential pitfalls in doing so. Next, you learned how to handle composite datatypes in the Oracle database, records, tables, and tables of records. These new variable types can be useful for manipulating data from the Oracle database.

After that, you explored the use of cursors in Oracle. You learned that every SQL statement executes in an implicit cursor, and you also learned how to create your own explicit cursors for powerful manipulation of Oracle data. We discussed the four operations required for cursor processing, as well as the `cursor for` loop, which handles the bulk of cursor statement processing automatically. We then moved onto advanced explicit cursor concepts, including how to manipulate data directly in cursors instead of assigning the values to variables first.

Finally, we wrapped up the chapter with coverage of error handling in PL/SQL. Now you're ready to take the practice exams. After that, you'll be ready to succeed on the OCP exam. Good luck!

Two-Minute Drill

- Variables can have a scalar datatype, such as NUMBER or VARCHAR2, or a referential datatype defined by a table and/or column reference followed by `%type` or `%rowtype`.

- Any SQL statement is valid for use in PL/SQL. This includes all SQL statements, such as `select` and `delete`, and transaction-control statements, such as `commit` and `rollback`.

- Every SQL statement executes in an implicit cursor. An explicit cursor is a named cursor corresponding to a defined SQL statement.

- An explicit cursor can be defined with the `cursor cursor_name is` statement. Cursors can be defined to accept input parameters that will be used in the `where` clause to limit the data manipulated by the cursor.

■ Once declared, a cursor must be opened, parsed, and executed in order to have its data used. This task is accomplished with the `open` statement.

■ In order to obtain data from a cursor, the programmer must fetch the data into a variable. This task is accomplished with the `fetch` statement.

■ The variable used in the fetch can either consist of several loose variables for storing single-column values or a record datatype that stores all column values in a record.

■ A special loop exists to simplify use of cursors: the `cursor for` loop. The `cursor for` loop handles the steps normally done in the `open` statement, and implicitly fetches data from the cursor until the `%notfound` condition occurs. This statement also handles the declaration of the variable and associated record type, if any is required.

■ The `for update` and `where current of` clauses are used within explicit cursors to allow you to reference values directly in a cursor.

■ When the `for update` clause appears alone in a query or in a cursor, Oracle locks rows for data changes when the query fetches the rows.

■ When the `for update` clause is used, you can also use the `where current of` clause to make changes in the row based on the reference in the cursor.

■ You can create arrays in PL/SQL using the `type` *name* `is table of` *datatype* `[index by binary_integer]` command. The optional clause at the end creates an index-by table; omitting that clause creates a nested table. Nested tables can be stored in the Oracle database, while index-by tables cannot.

■ The datatype used to create your PL/SQL table can be a user-defined record type; however, no element in that record can be a composite user-defined datatype. The result is a PL/SQL table of records.

■ The exception handler in PL/SQL handles all error handling. There are user-defined exceptions, predefined exceptions, and pragma exceptions in PL/SQL.

■ Only user-defined exceptions require explicit checks in the execution portion of PL/SQL code to test to see if the error condition has occurred.

■ A named exception can have a `when` clause defined in the exception handler that executes whenever that exception occurs.

■ The others exception is a catchall exception designed to operate if an exception occurs that is not associated with any other defined exception handler.

Fill-in-the-Blanks

1. This keyword allows you to define record variables based on the columns in a table: _____

2. This clause allows you to reference values in a cursor directly from PL/SQL: _____

3. This exception can be used as a blanket catchall for unhandled exceptions in sub-blocks: _____

4. This type of loop construct in PL/SQL can open your cursor, define a variable, and fetch a cursor value into that variable implicitly: _____

5. You can jump to a portion of PL/SQL code identified by a label using this keyword: _____

6. This clause differentiates an index-by table available in older versions of PL/SQL from PL/SQL tables in newer versions of PL/SQL: _____

7. Unless otherwise defined, every SQL statement executes in this type of cursor: _____

8. This feature can extend the use of explicit cursors by allowing you to dynamically assign a value to a variable inside the explicit cursor: _____

Chapter Questions

1. **You are designing your PL/SQL exception handler inside a nested block. Which statement most accurately describes the result of not creating an exception handler for a raised exception?**

   A. The program will continue without raising the exception.

   B. There will be a memory leak.

   C. Control will pass to the PL/SQL block caller's exception handler.

   D. The program will return a `%notfound` error.

2. **You are determining what types of cursors to use in your PL/SQL code. Which of the following statements is true about implicit cursors?**

   A. Implicit cursors are used for SQL statements that are not named.

   B. Developers should use implicit cursors with great care.

   C. Implicit cursors are used in `cursor for` loops to handle data processing.

   D. Implicit cursors are no longer a feature in Oracle.

3. **You are constructing PL/SQL process flow for your program. Which of the following is not a feature of a `cursor for` loop?**

   A. Declares record type declaration

   B. Opens and parses SQL statement

   C. Fetches records from cursor

   D. Requires `exit` condition to be defined

4. **A developer would like to use a referential datatype declaration on a variable. The variable name is EMPLOYEE_LASTNAME, and the corresponding table and column are EMPLOYEE and LASTNAME, respectively. How would the developer define this variable using referential datatypes?**

   A. Use `employee.lastname%type`.

   B. Use `employee.lastname%rowtype`.

C. Look up the datatype for EMPLOYEE column on LASTNAME table and use that.

D. Declare it to be type LONG.

5. **After executing an `update` statement, the developer codes a PL/SQL block to perform an operation based on `sql%rowcount`. What data is returned by the `sql%rowcount` operation?**

A. A Boolean value representing the success or failure of the `update`

B. A numeric value representing the number of rows updated

C. A VARCHAR2 value identifying the name of the table updated

D. A LONG value containing all data from the table

6. **You are defining a check following a SQL statement to verify that the statement returned appropriate data. Which three of the following are implicit cursor attributes?**

A. `%found`

B. `%too_many_rows`

C. `%notfound`

D. `%rowcount`

E. `%rowtype`

7. **You are coding your exception handler. The `others` exception handler is used to handle all of the following exceptions, except one. Which exception does the `others` exception handler *not* cover?**

A. `no_data_found`

B. `others`

C. `rowtype_mismatch`

D. `too_many_rows`

8. **You are defining a cursor in your PL/SQL block. Which line in the following statement will produce an error?**

A. `cursor action_cursor is`

B. `select name, rate, action`

C. `into action_record`

D. from *action_table*;

E. There are no errors in this statement.

9. **You are developing PL/SQL process flow into your program. Which of the following keywords is used to open a `cursor for` loop?**

   A. open

   B. fetch

   C. parse

   D. None, `cursor for` loops handle cursor opening implicitly.

10. **For the following question, assume that before the following PL/SQL block is executed, table MY_TAB contains one column called COLUMN1, and one row with the value FLIBBERJIBBER.**

```
DECLARE
 VAR1 VARCHAR2(1);
 VAR2 VARCHAR2(1);
IS
BEGIN
  SELECT TO_CHAR(CEIL(SQRT(40)))
  INTO VAR2
  FROM DUAL;
  SELECT SUBSTR(COLUMN1,4,1)
  INTO VAR1
  FROM MY_TAB;
  IF VAR1 = 'J' THEN
     VAR2 := '5';
 ELSIF VAR2 = '7' THEN
     VAR2 := 'L';
 ELSE
    VAR2 = '9';
 END IF;
 INSERT INTO MY_TAB VALUES (VAR2);
 COMMIT;
END;
```

   What is the value of COLUMN1 after executing this code block?

   A. 5

   B. 7

   C. L

D. 9

E. J

11. **You create the following PL/SQL block:**

```
DECLARE
  VAR1 CONSTANT NUMBER := 90;
  VAR2 NUMBER := 0;
 BEGIN
  SELECT ACCTNO
  INTO VAR2
  FROM BANK_ACCT
  WHERE NAME = 'LEWIS';
   VAR1 := VAR2 + 3049;
END;
```

Which of the following lines in this block of PL/SQL code will produce an error?

A. VAR2 NUMBER := 0;

B. INTO VAR2

C. WHERE NAME = 'LEWIS';

D. VAR1 := VAR2 + 3049;

E. There are no errors in this PL/SQL block.

12. **You are preparing to compile a block of PL/SQL code. The lines in the block are shown in the choices that follow:**

```
CREATE FUNCTION FOO (VAR1 IN VARCHAR2) IS
  VAR2 VARCHAR2(1);
BEGIN
  SELECT GENDER INTO VAR2 FROM EMP
    WHERE LASTNAME = 'SMITHERS';
  IF VAR1 = 6 THEN RETURN (6) ELSE RETURN (8);
  END IF;
END;
```

Which of the lines of PL/SQL code contains an error?

A. CREATE FUNCTION FOO (VAR1 IN VARCHAR2) IS

B. SELECT GENDER INTO VAR2 FROM EMP

    C. `WHERE LASTNAME = 'SMITHERS';`

    D. `IF VAR1 = 6 THEN RETURN (6) ELSE RETURN (8);`

    E. There are no errors in this PL/SQL block.

Fill-in-the-Blank Answers

    1. `%rowtype`

    2. `where current of`

    3. `others`

    4. `cursor for` loop

    5. `goto`

    6. `index by binary_integer`

    7. `Explicit`

    8. Parameter passing

Answers to Chapter Questions

    1. C. Control will pass to the PL/SQL block caller's exception handler.

Explanation   If the exception raised is not handled locally, PL/SQL will attempt to handle it at the level of the process that called the PL/SQL block. If the exception is not handled there, PL/SQL will attempt to keep finding an exception handler that will resolve the exception. If none is found, the error will be returned to the user.

    2. A. Implicit cursors are used for SQL statements that are not named.

Explanation   Implicit cursors are used for all SQL statements except for those statements that are named. They are never incorporated into `cursor for` loops, nor is much care given to using them more or less, which eliminates choices B and C. They are definitely a feature of Oracle, eliminating choice D.

    3. D. Requires `exit` condition to be defined

Explanation   A `cursor for` loop handles just about every feature of cursor processing automatically, including `exit` conditions.

4. A. Use `employee.lname%type`.

Explanation   The only option in this question that allows the developer to use referential type declarations for columns is choice A. Choice B uses the `%rowtype` referential datatype, which defines a record variable and is not what the developer is after.

5. B. A numeric value representing the number of rows updated

Explanation   `%rowtype` returns the numeric value representing the number of rows that were manipulated by the SQL statement.

6. A, C, and D. `%found`, `%notfound`, and `%rowcount`

Explanation   These three are the only choices that are valid cursor attributes. The `%too_many_rows` attribute does not exist in PL/SQL. `%rowtype` is a keyword that can be used to declare a record variable that can hold all column values from a particular table.

7. B. `others`

Explanation   There is no `others` exception. The `others` exception handler handles all exceptions that may be raised in a PL/SQL block that do not have exception handlers explicitly defined for them. All other choices identify Oracle predefined exceptions that are all caught by the `others` keyword when used in an exception handler. If there is no specific handler for another named exception, the `others` exception handler will handle that exception.

8. C. `into action_record`

Explanation   The `into` clause is not permitted in cursors, nor is it required. Your `fetch` operation will obtain the value in the current cursor record from the cursor.

9. D. None, `cursor for` loops handle cursor opening implicitly.

Explanation   The `cursor for` loops handle, among other things, opening, parsing, and executing named cursors.

10. C. L

Explanation   The square root of 40 is a fraction between 6 and 7, which rounds up to 7 according to the algorithm behind the `ceil( )` function. This means that the VAR2 = '7' flag in the `elsif` will resolve to true. Thus, VAR2 is set to 'L', and then written to the database with the `insert` statement at the end. Be careful not to waste time on reviewing all the intricacies of the PL/SQL block provided.

11. D. `VAR1 := VAR2 + 3049;`

Explanation The main problem with this block of PL/SQL code has to do with the `VAR1 := VAR2 + 3049` statement. VAR1 cannot be assigned a value in this code block because the variable is defined as a constant. `VAR2 NUMBER := 0;` is a proper variable declaration. The `INTO VAR2` clause is appropriate in a PL/SQL `fetch` statement. Finally, the `WHERE NAME = 'LEWIS';` clause is well constructed. All other lines of code in the block not identified as choices are syntactically and semantically correct.

12. A. `CREATE FUNCTION FOO (VAR1 IN VARCHAR2) IS`

Explanation There is no definition of return value datatype in this code block, making the function declaration line the correct answer. Although it may seem that the `if-then` statement in the third line of the code block is incorrect because you are comparing a VARCHAR2 variable to the number "6," in reality, Oracle handles this situation just fine because there is an implicit type conversion occurring in the background. Finally, the `select`, `into`, `from`, and `where` clauses of the `fetch` statement are all constructed correctly.

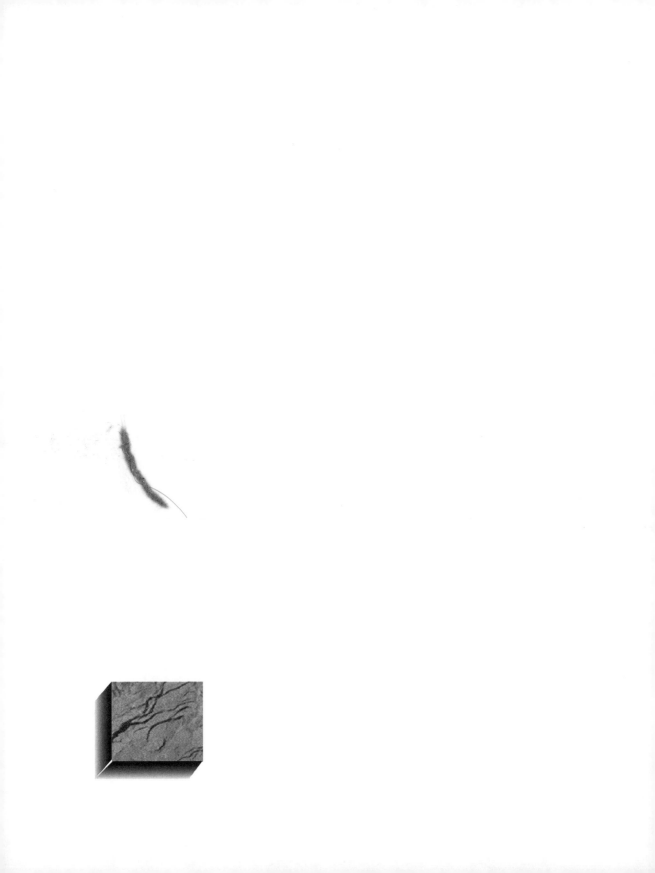

PART

II

OCP Oracle8i DBA
Practice Exams

CHAPTER
7

OCP Exam 1:
Introduction to
SQL and PL/SQL

CP Exam 1 in the Oracle DBA track covers concepts and practices involving the use of SQL and PL/SQL commands. To pass this exam, you need to demonstrate an understanding of the basic SQL constructs available in Oracle, including built-in functions. You should also understand the basic concepts of an Oracle relational database management system (RDBMS). In more recent editions of OCP Exam 1, the focus has included understanding the use of the PL/SQL programming language. In addition, new features in PL/SQL introduced in Oracle8i are tested, so you should also be sure you understand these new features.

Practice Exam 1

1. You are formulating a SQL statement to retrieve data from Oracle. Which of the following SQL statements is invalid?

    A. `select NAME, JERSEY_NO where Jersey_No = 6;`

    B. `select NAME, JERSEY_NO from PLAYERS;`

    C. `select * from PLAYERS where JERSEY_NO = 6;`

    D. `select JERSEY_NO from PLAYERS;`

2. **Use the following PL/SQL code block to answer this question:**

    ```
    DECLARE
    CURSOR My_Employees IS
    SELECT name, title FROM employee;
    My_Name VARCHAR2(30);
    My_Title VARCHAR2(30);
    BEGIN
    OPEN My_Employees;
    LOOP
    FETCH My_Employees INTO My_Name, My_Title;
    EXIT WHEN My_Employees%NOTFOUND;
    INSERT INTO MY_EMPS (MY_EMPNAME, MY_EMPTITLE)
    VALUES (My_Name, My_Title);
    END LOOP;
    CLOSE My_Employees;
    END;
    ```

    If you were rewriting this block of PL/SQL, which of the following types of loops would you use if you wanted to reduce the amount of code by using loop features that handle mundane aspects of processing automatically?

    A. `loop . . . exit when`

    B. `while . . . loop`

    C. `loop . . . loop . . . end`

    D. `cursor for loop`

3. **You are coding a complex PL/SQL block where several procedures call other procedures. You have one outermost procedure that calls all other procedures. If you want to prevent the user of the outermost procedure from having the procedure fail due to an unanticipated problem, which of the following exceptions should you include?**

    A. `no_data_found`

    B. `others`

    C. `zero_divide`

    D. `too_many_rows`

4. **You are attempting to develop a more robust PL/SQL application. Which of the following keywords allows you to associate a user-defined error message with an exception condition?**

    A. `pragma`

    B. `others`

    C. `raise_application_error`

    D. `exception`

5. **You are processing some data changes in your SQL*Plus session as part of one transaction. Which of the following choices does not typically indicate the end of a transaction?**

    A. Issuing an `update` statement

    B. Issuing a `commit` statement

    C. Issuing a `rollback` statement

    D. Ending your session

6. You have just removed 1,700 rows from a table. In order to save the changes you've made to the database, which of the following statements is used?

   A. savepoint

   B. commit

   C. rollback

   D. set transaction

7. To identify the columns that are indexed exclusively as the result of their inclusion in a constraint, which of the following dictionary views is appropriate?

   A. USER_INDEXES

   B. USER_TAB_COLUMNS

   C. USER_COLUMNS

   D. USER_CONS_COLUMNS

8. You are creating some tables in your database as part of the logical data model. Which of the following constraints can only be created as a column constraint (i.e., not as a table constraint) when you either create or alter the table?

   A. UNIQUE

   B. FOREIGN KEY

   C. CHECK

   D. not NULL

9. You have a table with three associated indexes, two triggers, two references to that table from other tables, and a view. You issue the **drop table cascade constraints** statement. Which of the following objects will still remain after the statement is issued?

   A. The triggers

   B. The indexes

   C. The foreign keys in the other tables

   D. The view

10. **You are using SQL operations in Oracle. All of the following DATE functions return a DATE datatype, except one. Which one is it?**

    A. NEW_TIME

    B. LAST_DAY

    C. ADD_MONTHS

    D. MONTHS_BETWEEN

11. **You issue a `select` statement on the BANK_ACCT table containing the `order by` clause. Which of the following uses of the `order by` clause would produce an error?**

    A. `order by acctno DESC;`

    B. `order by 1;`

    C. `order by sqrt(1);`

    D. `order by acctno ASC;`

12. **You execute the query `select 5 + 4 from DUAL`. You have never inserted data into the DUAL table before. Which of the following statements best describes the DUAL table?**

    A. Dictionary view containing two schema names

    B. Table with one column and one row used in various operations

    C. Dictionary view containing two index names

    D. Table with two columns and no rows used in various operations

13. **You issue the following statement:**

    ```
    SELECT DECODE(ACCTNO, 123456, 'CLOSED', 654321, 'SEIZED',
    590395, 'TRANSFER','ACTIVE') FROM BANK_ACCT;
    ```

    If the value for ACCTNO is 503952, what information will this statement display?

    A. ACTIVE

    B. TRANSFER

    C. SEIZED

    D. CLOSED

14. You are entering several dozen rows of data into the BANK_ACCT table from SQL* Plus. Which of the following statements will enable you to execute the same statement again and again, entering different values for variables at statement runtime?

    A. `insert into BANK_ACCT (ACCTNO, NAME) VALUES (123456,'SMITH');`

    B. `insert into BANK_ACCT (ACCTNO, NAME) VALUES (VAR1, VAR2);`

    C. `insert into BANK_ACCT (ACCTNO, NAME) VALUES (&VAR1, '&VAR2');`

    D. `insert into BANK_ACCT (select ACCTNO, NAME from EMP_BANK_ACCTS);`

15. You execute the following SQL statement: `select ADD_MONTHS ('28-APR-97',120) from DUAL`. What will Oracle return?

    A. 28-APR-03

    B. 28-APR-07

    C. 28-APR-13

    D. 28-APR-17

16. On Monday, June 26, 2037, at 10:30 at night, you issue the following statement against an Oracle database:

    ```
    ALTER SESSION SET NLS_DATE_FORMAT =
    'DAY MONTH DD, YYYY: HH:MIAM';
    ```

    Then you issue the following statement:

    ```
    SELECT SYSDATE FROM DUAL;
    ```

    What will Oracle return?

    A. 26-JUN-37

    B. June 26, 2037, 22:30

    C. 26-JUN-2037

    D. MONDAY JUNE 26, 2037: 10:30PM

17. **You wish to join the data from two tables, A and B, into one result set and display that set in your session. Tables A and B have a common column, called C in both tables. Which of the following choices correctly displays the `where` clause you should use if you want to see the data in table A where the value in column C equals 5, even when there is no corresponding value in table B?**

    A. where A.C = 5 AND A.C = B.C;

    B. where A.C = 5 AND A.C = B.C (+);

    C. where A.C = 5 AND A.C (+) = B.C(+);

    D. where A.C = 5;

18. **Each of the following statements is true about associated columns and datatypes, except one. Which of the following statements is not true?**

    A. When declaring a variable designed to hold data from a column in PL/SQL, it must be declared with a datatype large enough to accommodate values from that column.

    B. When creating composite primary keys, the datatypes in all columns within the primary key must be the same datatype.

    C. When creating referential integrity constraints between two tables, the datatype of the referenced column in the parent table must be identical to the referencing column in the child.

    D. When creating record variables designed to hold a row's worth of data, each element's datatype in the record must be large enough to hold the associated column from the table.

19. **You have a group of values from a column in a table, and you would like to perform a group operation on them. Each of the following functions operates on data from all rowss as a group, except for which of the following choices?**

    A. avg( )

    B. sqrt( )

    C. count( )

    D. stddev( )

20. You have a situation in which you need to use the `nvl( )` function. All the following statements about the `nvl( )` function are true except one. Which is it?

A. `nvl( )` returns the second value passed if the first value is NULL.

B. `nvl( )` handles values of many different datatypes.

C. `nvl( )` returns NULL if the first value is not equal to the second.

D. Both the values passed for `nvl( )` must be the same datatype.

21. You are developing a stored procedure that handles table data. The `%rowtype` expression in PL/SQL allows you to declare which of the following kinds of variables?

A. Records

B. VARCHAR2s

C. PLS_INTEGERs

D. NUMBERs

22. You create a sequence with the following statement:

```
CREATE SEQUENCE MY_SEQ
START WITH 394
INCREMENT BY 12
NOMINVALUE
NOMAXVALUE
NOCACHE
NOCYCLE;
```

Three users have already issued SQL statements to obtain NEXTVAL, and four more have issued SQL statements to obtain CURRVAL. If you issue a SQL statement to obtain the NEXTVAL, what will Oracle return?

A. 406

B. 418

C. 430

D. 442

23. Table EMP has 17,394,430 rows in it. You issue a `delete from EMP` statement, followed by a `commit`. Then you issue a `select count(*)` to find out how many rows there are in the table. Several minutes later, Oracle returns 0. Why did it take so long for Oracle to obtain this information?

A. The table was not empty.

B. The high-water mark was not reset.

C. Oracle always performs slowly after a `commit` is issued.

D. The table data did not exist to be counted anymore.

24. After creating a view, you realize that several columns were left out. Which of the following statements should you issue in order to add some columns to your view?

A. `alter view`

B. `create or replace view`

C. `insert into view`

D. `create view`

25. You are testing several SQL statements for accuracy and usefulness. A SQL statement will result in a Cartesian product as the result of which of the following items?

A. A `join` statement without a `where` clause

B. The result of the `sum( )` operation

C. `select * from DUAL`

D. The result of the `avg( )` operation

26. In order to set your SQL*Plus session so that your NLS_DATE_FORMAT information is altered in a specific way every time you log into Oracle, what method should you use?

A. Setting preferences in the appropriate menu option

B. Creating an appropriate `login.sql` file

C. Issuing the `alter user` statement

D. Issuing the `alter table` statement

27. The EMP_SALARY table has two columns: EMP_USER and SALARY. EMP_USER is set to be the same as the Oracle username. To allow user MARTHA, the salary administrator, to see her own salary only, you create a view with the following statement:

```
create view emp_sal_vw
as select emp_user, salary
from emp_salary
where emp_user = 'martha';
```

Later, you decide to deploy this view to other users. Which of the following choices identify a revision of this view that would prevent users from seeing any salary information other than their own?

A. `create or replace view emp_sal_vw as select emp_user,_salary from emp_salary where emp_user <> user;`

B. `create or replace view emp_sal_vw as select emp_user,_salary from emp_salary where emp_user = user;`

C. `create or replace view emp_sal_vw as select emp_user,_salary from emp_salary where emp_user <> 'MARTHA';`

D. `create or replace view emp_sal_vw as select emp_user,_salary from emp_salary where emp_user in (select emp_user from emp_salary where emp_user <> 'MARTHA');`

28. You are developing PL/SQL code to manipulate and store data in an Oracle table. All of the following scalar datatypes in PL/SQL can be stored in an Oracle database, except one. Which is it?

A. CHAR

B. RAW

C. DATE

D. INTEGER

29. You are performing some conversion operations in your PL/SQL programs. To convert a date value into a text string, you should use which of the following conversion functions?

A. CONVERT

B. TO_CHAR

C. TO_NUMBER

D. TO_DATE

30. Your attempt to read the trigger code stored in the Oracle data dictionary view DBA_TRIGGERS has encountered a problem. The contents of the TRIGGER_BODY column appear to be getting cut off at the end. In order to resolve this problem, which of the following measures is appropriate?

A. Grant appropriate `select` privileges on DBA_TRIGGERS to yourself.

B. Increase your memory allocation limit with the `alter user` statement.

C. Use the `set` command to allow for larger LONG column values.

D. Drop and re-create the DBA_TRIGGERS view.

31. You issue the following `update` statement against the Oracle database:

```
UPDATE BANK_ACCT SET NAME = 'SHAW';
```

Which records will be updated in that table?

A. The first record only

B. All records

C. The last record only

D. None of the records

32. You are coding a complex PL/SQL block where several procedures call other procedures. You have one outermost procedure that calls all other procedures. If you only want to prevent the procedure from failing due to a situation in which a `select into` statement receives two or more records, you should include which of the following exceptions?

A. `too_many_rows`

B. `others`

C. `zero_divide`

D. `no_data_found`

33. You create a table, but then subsequently realize you need a few new columns. To add those columns later, you should issue which of the following statements?

A. `create or replace table`

B. `alter table`

C. `create table`

D. `truncate table`

34. You are busy creating your tables based on a logical data model. Which of the following constraints require the `references` privilege in order to be created?

A. UNIQUE

B. FOREIGN KEY

C. CHECK

D. not NULL

35. The INVENTORY table has three columns: UPC_CODE, UNITS, and DELIV_DATE. The primary key is UPC_CODE. You want to add new records daily through a view. The view will be created using the following code:

```
CREATE VIEW DAY_INVENTORY_VW
AS SELECT UPC_CODE, UNITS, DELIV_DATE
FROM INVENTORY
WHERE DELIV_DATE = SYSDATE
ORDER BY UPC_CODE;
```

What happens when you try to create this view?

A. Oracle returns an error stating that the `order by` clause is not permitted on views.

B. Oracle returns an error stating that the `with check option` clause is required for creating this view.

C. Oracle returns an error stating that the select statement must be enclosed in parentheses.

D. Oracle creates the view successfully.

36. You need to search for text data in a column, but you only remember part of the string. Which of the following SQL operations allows the use of wildcard comparisons?

A. in

B. exists

C. between

D. like

37. You have a script you plan to run using SQL*Plus that contains one SQL statement that inserts data into one table. Which of the following options is the easiest way for this script to allow you to specify values for variables once in the script, in a way in which there is no user interaction at the SQL*Plus prompt?

   A. Use `define` to capture values.

   B. Use `accept` to capture values for each run.

   C. Use & to specify values at runtime for the statement.

   D. Use hard-coded values in the statement.

38. You join data from two tables, EXPNS and EMP, into one result set and display that set in your session. The tables have a common column called EMPID. Which of the following choices correctly displays the `where` clause you would use if you want to see the data in table EMP where the value in column EMPID equals 39284, but only when there is a corresponding value in table EXPNS?

   A. `where EMP.EMPID = 39284 AND EMP.EMPID = EXPNS.EMPID;`

   B. `where EMP.EMPID = 39284 (+) AND EMP.EMPID = EXPNS.EMPID;`

   C. `where EMP.EMPID = EXPNS.EMPID;`

   D. `where EMP.EMPID = 39284 AND EMP.EMPID = EXPNS.EMPID (+);`

39. The `%type` expression in PL/SQL can be used to declare which of the following kinds of variables?

   A. DATE variables

   B. TEXT variables

   C. PLS_INTEGER variables

   D. REAL variables

40. Review the following transcript of a SQL*Plus session:

```
INSERT INTO INVENTORY (UPC_CODE, PRODUCT )
VALUES (503949353,'HAZELNUT COFFEE');
INSERT INTO INVENTORY (UPC_CODE, PRODUCT)
VALUES (593923506,'SKIM MILK');
INSERT INTO INVENTORY (UPC_CODE, PRODUCT)
VALUES (402392340,'CANDY BAR');
```

```
SAVEPOINT INV1;
UPDATE INVENTORY SET UPC_CODE = 50393950
WHERE UPC_CODE = 402392340;
UPDATE INVENTORY SET UPC_CODE = 4104930504
WHERE UPC_CODE = 402392340;
COMMIT;
UPDATE INVENTORY SET PRODUCT = (
SELECT PRODUCT FROM INVENTORY
WHERE UPC_CODE = 50393950)
WHERE UPC_CODE = 593923506;
ROLLBACK;
```

Which of the following UPC codes will not have records in the INVENTORY table as a result of this series of operations?

A. 593923506

B. 503949353

C. 4104930504

D. 50393950

41. **You are removing a table from the Oracle database. When you issue the `drop table` command to remove the table, what happens to any of the views that may have an object dependency on that table?**

   A. The views get dropped automatically along with the table.

   B. Views in the same schema as the table will be dropped automatically, but views outside that schema will not be dropped.

   C. Views in the same database as the table will be dropped automatically, but views that access the table via a database link will not be dropped.

   D. Views with object dependencies on the table being dropped will be rendered invalid automatically but will not be dropped.

42. **You want to join data from four tables into one result set and display that set in your session. Table A has a column in common with table B, table B with table C, and table C with table D. You want to further restrict data returned from the tables by only returning data where values in the common column shared by A and B equal 5. How many conditions should you have in the `where` clause of your `select` statement?**

A. 2

B. 3

C. 4

D. 5

43. **You are developing some code in PL/SQL. If you want to declare variables that could be used to store table column values, but don't know the actual datatype of that column, PL/SQL allows you to declare which of the following kinds of variables?**

    A. `%rowtype` variables

    B. `%type` variables

    C. FLOAT variables

    D. VARCHAR2 variables

44. **You are attempting to explain the Oracle security model for an Oracle database to the new security administrator. What are two components of the Oracle database security model?**

    A. Password authentication and granting privileges

    B. Password authentication and creating database objects

    C. Creating database objects and creating users

    D. Creating users and password authentication

45. **You have a script you plan to run using SQL*Plus that contains several SQL statements that manage milk inventory in several different tables based on various bits of information. You want the output to go into a file for review later. Which command should you use?**

    A. `prompt`

    B. `echo`

    C. `spool`

    D. `define`

46. **Your application's business logic aligns closely with an Oracle internal error. If you want to associate that internal error with a named exception for handling in your application, in which of the following areas in your procedure code must you include some support of this exception?**

    A. Declaration and exception only

    B. Declaration, execution, and exception

    C. Exception only

    D. No coding, definition, or exception handlers are required to raise this exception.

47. **You have a table called TEST_SCORE that stores test results by student personal ID number, test location, and date the test was taken. Tests given in various locations throughout the country are stored in this table. A student is not allowed to take a test for 30 days after failing it the first time, and there is a check in the application preventing the student from taking a test twice in 30 days at the same location. Recently, it has come to everyone's attention that students are able to circumvent the 30-day rule by taking a test in a different location. Which of the following SQL statements would be useful for identifying the students who have done so?**

    A. `select A.STUDENT_ID, A.LOCATION, B.LOCATION from TEST_SCORE A, TEST_SCORE B where A.STUDENT_ID = B.STUDENT_ID AND A.LOCATION = B.LOCATION AND trunc(A.TEST_DATE)+30 <= trunc(B.TEST_DATE) AND trunc(A.TEST_DATE)-30 >= trunc(B.TEST_DATE);`

    B. `select A.STUDENT_ID, A.LOCATION, B.LOCATION from TEST_SCORE A, TEST_SCORE B where A.STUDENT_ID = B.STUDENT_ID AND A.LOCATION <> B.LOCATION AND trunc(A.TEST_DATE)+30 >= trunc(B.TEST_DATE) AND trunc(A.TEST_DATE)-30 <= trunc(B.TEST_DATE);`

    C. `select A.STUDENT_ID, A.LOCATION, B.LOCATION from TEST_SCORE A, TEST_SCORE B where A.STUDENT_ID = B.STUDENT_ID AND A.LOCATION = B.LOCATION AND trunc(A.TEST_DATE)+30 >= trunc(B.TEST_DATE) AND trunc(A.TEST_DATE)-30 <= trunc(B.TEST_DATE);`

    D. `select A.STUDENT_ID, A.LOCATION, B.LOCATION from TEST_SCORE A, TEST_SCORE B where A.STUDENT_ID = B.STUDENT_ID AND A.LOCATION <> B.LOCATION AND trunc(A.TEST_DATE)+30 <= trunc(B.TEST_DATE) AND trunc(A.TEST_DATE)-30 >= trunc(B.TEST_DATE);`

48. **In an expense application, you are searching for employee information in the EMPLOYEE table corresponding to an invoice number you have. The**

INVOICE table contains EMPID, the primary key for EMPLOYEE. Which of the following options is appropriate for obtaining data from EMPLOYEE using your invoice number?

A. `select * from EMPLOYEE where empid = &empid;`

B. `select * from EMPLOYEE where empid = 69494;`

C. `select * from EMPLOYEE where empid = (select empid from invoice where invoice_no = 4399485);`

D. `select * from EMPLOYEE;`

49. Which of the following uses does not describe an appropriate use of the **having** clause?

    A. To put returned data into sorted order

    B. To exclude certain data groups based on known criteria

    C. To include certain data groups based on unknown criteria

    D. To include certain data groups based on known criteria

50. You are managing data access for an application with 163 tables and 10,000 users. Which of the following objects would assist in managing access in this application by grouping privileges into an object that can be granted to users at once?

    A. Sequences

    B. Tables

    C. Indexes

    D. Roles

51. After logging into Oracle the first time to access table EMP, user SNOW is told to change his password. Which of the following statements allows him to do so?

    A. `alter user`

    B. `alter table`

    C. `alter role`

    D. `alter index`

52. User SNOW executes the following statement: `select * from EMP`. This statement executes successfully, and SNOW can see the output. Table EMP is owned by user REED. What object is required in order for this scenario to happen?

    A. User SNOW needs the role to view table EMP.

    B. User SNOW needs the privileges to view table EMP.

    C. User SNOW needs a synonym for table EMP.

    D. User SNOW needs the password for table EMP.

53. You develop a PL/SQL block containing a complex series of data changes. A user then executes your PL/SQL block. At what point will the data changes made be committed to the database?

    A. When the PL/SQL block finishes

    B. After each individual `update`

    C. Whenever the `commit` command is issued

    D. When you, the creator of the PL/SQL block, disconnect from your session

54. If you would like to code your PL/SQL block to select some data from a table, and then run through each row of output and perform some work, which of the following choices best identifies how you would do so?

    A. Implicit cursors with a `cursor for` loop

    B. Implicit cursors with implicit cursor attributes

    C. Explicit cursors with a `cursor for` loop

    D. Explicit cursors with implicit cursor attributes

55. You have the following code block declaration in PL/SQL:

```
DECLARE
CURSOR EMP_1 IS
SELECT * FROM EMP
WHERE EMPID = '40593';
CURSOR EMP_2 IS
SELECT * FROM EMP
WHERE EMPID = '50694';
BEGIN...
```

How could you rewrite this declaration block to reduce the number of explicit cursors used in your program?

A. Using `cursor for` loops

B. Using `%rowtype`

C. Using `%notfound`

D. Passing EMPID values as parameters to the cursor

56. **You issue the following statement in Oracle:**

```
SELECT * FROM EMP WHERE DEPT IN
(SELECT DEPT FROM VALID_DEPTS
WHERE DEPT_HEAD = 'SALLY'
ORDER BY DEPT);
```

Which of the following choices best indicates how Oracle will respond to this SQL statement?

A. Oracle returns the data selected.

B. Oracle returns data from EMP but not VALID_DEPTS.

C. Oracle returns data from VALID_DEPTS but not EMP.

D. Oracle returns an error.

57. **You would like to query a table in your PL/SQL block. What special syntactic attribute must you precede the SQL statement with in order to make the PL/SQL block compile?**

A. Put a colon in front of all variables.

B. Use /*and*/ to surround the SQL code.

C. Prefix the command exec SQL in front of the statement.

D. No special syntax is required.

58. **You are coding SQL statements in SQL*Plus. Which of the following is a valid SQL statement?**

A. `select nvl(sqrt(59483)) from dual;`

B. `select to_char(nvl(sqrt(59483), 0)) from dual;`

C. `select to_char(nvl(sqrt(59483), 'VALID')) from dual;`

D. `select (to_char(nvl(sqrt(59483), '0')) from dual;`

59. The following output is from a SQL*Plus session:

```
select PLAY_NAME||', ' || AUTHOR play_table from PLAYS;
My Plays and Authors
------------------------------------
Midsummer Night's Dream, SHAKESPEARE
Waiting For Godot, BECKETT
The Glass Menagerie, WILLIAMS
```

Which of the following SQL*Plus commands produced it?

A. column PLAY_TABLE alias 'My Plays and Authors'

B. column PLAY_TABLE format a12

C. column PLAY_TABLE heading 'My Plays and Authors'

D. column PLAY_TABLE as 'My Plays and Authors'

60. You create a view with the following statement:

```
CREATE VIEW BASEBALL_TEAM_VW
AS SELECT B.JERSEY_NUM, B.POSITION, B.NAME
FROM BASEBALL_TEAM B
WHERE B.NAME = (SELECT UNAME FROM MY_USERS);
```

The contents of the MY_USERS table are listed as follows:

```
UNAME
-----
JONES
SMITH
FRANK
JENNY
```

Which of the following players will not be listed when user JONES attempts to query the view?

A. JONES

B. SMITH

C. BABS

D. JENNY

Practice Exam 2

I. **Which of the following choices identifies a PL/SQL block containing the correct syntax for a `cursor for` loop?**

A.
```
DECLARE
   CURSOR My_Employees IS
    SELECT * FROM employee;
   My_NameVARCHAR2(30);
   My_Title VARCHAR2(30);
BEGIN
    OPEN My_Employees;
     FOR csr_rec IN My_Employees LOOP
        INSERT INTO MY_EMPS (MY_EMPNAME,
MY_EMPTITLE)
        VALUES (My_Name, My_Title);
      END LOOP;
   CLOSE My_Employees;
END;
```

B.
```
DECLARE
   CURSOR My_Employees IS
     SELECT * FROM employee;
   csr_rec VARCHAR2(30);
BEGIN
   FOR csr_rec IN My_Employees LOOP
      EXIT WHEN My_Employees%NOTFOUND;
         INSERT INTO MY_EMPS (MY_EMPNAME,
MY_EMPTITLE)
         VALUES (csr_rec.name, csr_rec.title);
       END LOOP;
   END;
```

C.
```
DECLARE
   CURSOR My_Employees IS
     SELECT name, title FROM employee;
BEGIN
   FOR csr_rec IN My_Employees LOOP
        INSERT INTO MY_EMPS (MY_EMPNAME,
MY_EMPTITLE)
        VALUES (csr_rec.name, csr_rec.title);
      END LOOP;
   END;
```

```
D. DECLARE
     CURSOR My_Employees IS
       SELECT name, title FROM employee;
     My_Name VARCHAR2(30);
     My_Title VARCHAR2(30);
   BEGIN
       OPEN My_Employees;
        LOOP
             FETCH My_Employees INTO My_Name, My_Title;
             EXIT WHEN My_Employees%NOTFOUND;
            INSERT INTO MY_EMPS (MY_EMPNAME,
   MY_EMPTITLE)
             VALUES (My_Name, My_Title);
           END LOOP;
       CLOSE My_Employees;
   END;
```

2. **Your attempt to read the view-creation code stored in the Oracle data dictionary has encountered a problem. The view code appears to be getting cut off at the end. In order to resolve this problem, which of the following measures is appropriate?**

   A. Increase the size of the dictionary view.

   B. Increase your user view allotment with the `alter user` statement.

   C. Use the `set long` statement.

   D. Use the `set NLS_DATE_FORMAT` statement.

3. **Inspect the following SQL statement:**

   ```
   SELECT FARM_NAME, COW_NAME,
   COUNT(CARTON) AS NUMBER_OF_CARTONS
   FROM COW_MILK
   GROUP BY COW_NAME;
   ```

   Which of the following choices contains the line with the error?

   A. `select FARM_NAME, COW_NAME,`

   B. `count(CARTON) as NUMBER_OF_CARTONS`

   C. `from COW_MILK`

   D. `group by COW_NAME;`

   E. There are no errors in the statement.

4. **All of the following types of PL/SQL blocks are stored within the Oracle database for reusability, except for one type. Which type is it?**

   A. Functions

   B. Procedures

   C. Package specs

   D. Package bodies

   E. Anonymous blocks

   F. Triggers

5. **Inspect the following SQL statement:**

```
SELECT COW_NAME,
   MOD(CARTON, FILL_STATUS)
FROM COW_MILK
GROUP BY COW_NAME;
```

   Which of the following lines contains an error?

   A. `select COW_NAME,`

   B. `mod(CARTON, FILL_STATUS)`

   C. `from COW_MILK`

   D. `group by COW_NAME;`

   E. There are no errors in this statement.

6. **You are writing queries against an Oracle database. Which of the following queries takes advantage of an inline view?**

   A. `select * from EMP_VW where EMPID = (select EMPID from INVOICE where INV_NUM = 5506934);`

   B. `select A.LASTNAME, B.DEPT_NO from EMP A, (select EMPID, DEPT_NO from DEPT) B where A.EMPID = B.EMPID;`

   C. `select * from EMP where EMPID IN (select EMPID from INVOICE where INV_NUM > 23);`

   D. `select 'select * from EMP_VW where EMPID is NOT NULL;' from USER_TABLES;`

7. For the following question, assume that before the following PL/SQL block is executed, table MY_TAB contains one column called COLUMN1, and one row with the value 'FLIBBERJIBBER'.

```
DECLARE
 VAR1 VARCHAR2(1);
 VAR2 VARCHAR2(1);
IS
BEGIN
  SELECT TO_CHAR(CEIL(SQRT(40)))
  INTO VAR2
  FROM DUAL;
  SELECT SUBSTR(COLUMN1,4,1)
  INTO VAR1
  FROM MY_TAB;
  IF VAR1 = 'J' THEN
     VAR2 := '5';
  ELSIF VAR2 = '7' THEN
     VAR2 := 'L';
  ELSE
     VAR2 = '9';
  END IF;
  INSERT INTO MY_TAB VALUES (VAR2);
  COMMIT;
END;
```

What is the value of COLUMN1 after executing this code block?

A. 5

B. 7

C. L

D. 9

E. J

8. User LEWIS's account balance, stored in the BANK_ACCOUNT table, is 50650. To manipulate his balance, you create the following PL/SQL block:

```
DECLARE
   VAR1 NUMBER := 90;
   VAR2 NUMBER := 0;
 BEGIN
  SELECT BALANCE
  INTO VAR2
```

```
FROM BANK_ACCT
WHERE NAME = 'LEWIS';
  VAR1 := VAR2 + 3049;
END;
```

Which of the following choices identifies the value in VAR1 at the end of this PL/SQL block's execution?

A. 90

B. 3049

C. 50650

D. 53699

9. **You are preparing to compile the following block of PL/SQL code:**

```
CREATE FUNCTION FOO (VAR1 IN VARCHAR2) IS
  VAR2 VARCHAR2(1);
BEGIN
  SELECT GENDER INTO VAR2 FROM EMP
    WHERE LASTNAME = 'SMITHERS';
  IF VAR1 = 6 THEN RETURN (6) ELSE RETURN (8);
END;
```

Which line of PL/SQL code contains an error?

A. create function foo(VAR1 IN VARCHAR2) is

B. select GENDER into VAR2 FROM EMP

C. where LASTNAME = 'SMITHERS';

D. if VAR1 = 6 then return (6) else return (8);

E. There are no errors in this PL/SQL block.

10. **You have several indexes on a table that you want to remove. You want to avoid removing the indexes associated with constraints, however. Each of the following statements will remove the index associated with a constraint, except one. Which choice will not remove the index associated with a constraint?**

A. drop index

B. alter table drop primary key cascade

C. alter table drop constraint

D. drop table

11. **You are managing constraints on a table in Oracle. Which of the following choices correctly identifies the limitations on primary key constraints?**

A. Every primary key column value must be unique.

B. No primary key column value can be NULL.

C. Every primary key column value must be unique and none can be NULL.

D. Every primary key column must be the same datatype as other columns in the table.

12. **Review the following statement:**

```
CREATE TABLE FOOBAR
( MOO VARCHAR2(3),
  BOO NUMBER);
```

This table contains 60,000,000 rows. You issue the following statement:

```
SELECT MOO, BOO FROM FOOBAR WHERE MOO = 'ABC'
```

This value is unique in column MOO, yet the query takes several minutes to resolve. Which of the following explanations is the best reason why?

A. Oracle didn't use the existing primary-key index.

B. select statements that do not use views take longer to resolve.

C. Table FOOBAR has no primary-key and, therefore, no index on MOO.

D. The table had been dropped and re-created.

13. **You have created a table called EMP with a primary key called EMP_PK_01. In order to identify any objects that may be associated with that table and primary key, what dictionary views and characteristics would you look for?**

A. USER_SEQUENCES, sequences created at the same time

B. USER_TABLES, tables with the same number of columns

C. USER_IND_COLUMNS, constraints with the same name as the table

D. USER_INDEXES, indexes with the same name as the constraint

14. **You are designing your database, and you are attempting to determine the best method for indexing your tables. Which of the following is a main advantage of using bitmap indexes on a database?**

A. To improve performance on columns with many unique values

B. To improve performance on columns with few unique values

C. To improve performance on columns with all unique values

D. To improve performance on sequences with all unique values

15. **Use the following PL/SQL code block to answer this question:**

```
DECLARE
  CURSOR CARTON_CRSR IS
  SELECT CARTON FROM MILK;
  MY_CARTON MILK.CARTON%TYPE;
BEGIN
    OPEN CARTON_CRSR;
      LOOP
        FETCH CARTON_CRSR INTO MY_CARTON;
        INSERT INTO MY_MILK_CRATE (CARTON)
        VALUES (MY_CARTON);
      END LOOP;
    CLOSE CARTON_CRSR;
END;
```

What is wrong with this PL/SQL block?

A. It will not work unless the loop is rewritten as a `cursor for` loop.

B. The exception handler must be defined if the cursor is not declared.

C. The user does not have permission to execute the block.

D. A loop exit condition must be defined.

E. There are no errors in this code block.

16. **Your PL/SQL block includes the following statement:**

```
SELECT EMP_ID
INTO MY_EMPID
FROM EMPLOYEE
WHEN LASTNAME = 'FRANKLIN';
```

You want Oracle to process the situation in which no data is retrieved for that LASTNAME value. Which of the following actions should you take?

A. Include the `%found` implicit cursor attribute.

B. Include the `%notfound` implicit cursor attribute.

C. Include the `when rowtype_mismatch` exception.

D. Nothing, Oracle raises this as an exception automatically.

17. User JANKO would like to insert a row into the EMPLOYEE table that has three columns: EMPID, LASTNAME, and SALARY. The user would like to update salary data for employee number 59694. Which statement would work best?

    A. `update employee set salary = 5000 where empid = 59694;`

    B. `update employee set empid = 45939 where empid = 59694;`

    C. `update employee set lastname = 'HARRIS' where empid = 59694;`

    D. `update employee set salary = 5000 where lastname = 'HARRIS';`

18. You join data from two tables, COW_MILK (C) and CARTON_CRATE (C1), into one result set and display that set in your session. The tables have a common column, called CARTON_NUM in both tables. You want to see the data in table COW_MILK for BESS the cow and all corresponding information in CARTON_CRATE; but if there is no data in CARTON_NUM, you don't want to see the data in COW_MILK. Which of the following choices correctly displays the `where` clause you should use?

    A. `where C.COW_NAME <> 'BESS' AND C.CARTON_NUM = C1.CARTON_NUM;`

    B. `where C.CARTON_NUM = C1.CARTON_NUM;`

    C. `where C.COW_NAME = 'BESS';`

    D. `where C.COW_NAME = 'BESS' AND C.CARTON_NUM = C1.CARTON_NUM;`

    E. `where C.COW_NAME = 'BESS' AND C.CARTON_NUM = C1.CARTON_NUM (+);`

19. You create a table with a primary key that is populated on `insert` with a value from a sequence, and then you add several hundred rows to the table. You then drop and re-create the sequence with the original sequence code. Suddenly, your users are getting constraint violations. Which of the following explanations is most likely the cause?

    A. Dropping a sequence also removes any associated primary keys.

    B. Any cached sequence values before the sequence was dropped are unusable.

    C. The table is read-only.

    D. The `insert` statements contain duplicate data due to the reset sequence.

20. You are developing SQL statements for the application. Which of the following SQL operations requires the use of a subquery?

    A. `in`

B. exists

C. between

D. like

21. **Review the following transcript from a SQL*Plus session:**

```
SELECT CEIL(4093.505) FROM DUAL;
CEIL(4093.505)
-------------------
              4094
```

Which single-row function could not be used to produce 4093 from the number passed to the `ceil( )` function?

A. round( )

B. trunc( )

C. floor( )

D. abs( )

22. **You have a script you plan to run using SQL*Plus that contains several SQL statements that update banking information for one person in several different tables based on name. Since the script only changes information for one person, you want the ability to enter the name only once and have that information reused throughout the script. Which of the following options is the best way to accomplish this goal in such a way that you don't need to modify the script each time you want to run it?**

A. Use define to capture the name value for each run.

B. Use accept to capture the name value for each run.

C. Use the & character to specify lexical substitution for names at runtime.

D. Hard-code names in all SQL statements, and change the value for each run.

23. **You need to undo some data changes. Which of the following data changes cannot be undone using the `rollback` command?**

A. update

B. truncate

C. delete

D. insert

24. **You are developing some code to handle transaction processing. Each of the following items signifies the beginning of a new transaction, except one. Which is it?**

    A. savepoint

    B. set transaction

    C. Opening a new session

    D. commit

25. **The following SQL statement is invalid:**

    ```
    SELECT   PRODUCT, BRAND
    WHERE UPC_CODE = '650-35365656-34453453454-45';
    ```

    Which of the following choices indicates an area of change that would make this statement valid?

    A. A select clause

    B. A from clause

    C. A where clause

    D. An order by clause

26. **Use the following PL/SQL code block to answer this question:**

    ```
    DECLARE
      CURSOR UPC_CODE_CRSR IS
        SELECT UPC_CODE FROM INVENTORY;
      MY_UPC_CODE INVENTORY%ROWTYPE;
    BEGIN
        OPEN UPC_CODE_CRSR;
          LOOP
              FETCH UPC_CODE_CRSR INTO MY_UPC_CODE;
              EXIT WHEN UPC_CODE_CRSR%NOTFOUND;
            INSERT INTO MY_SHOPPING_CART (UPC_CODE)
            VALUES (UPC_CODE_CRSR);
          END LOOP;
      CLOSE UPC_CODE_CRSR;
    END;
    ```

    What is wrong with this PL/SQL block?

    A. It will not work unless the loop is rewritten as a cursor for loop.

    B. The exception handler must be defined if a cursor is not declared.

C. The user does not have permission to execute the block.

D. Values from a cursor cannot be referenced directly.

27. **You are coding a PL/SQL block. PROC_A calls PROC_B, which then calls PROC_C, and PROC_B has no exception handler. If you want to prevent the PROC_A procedure from failing due to a situation in PROC_B where the divisor in a division statement is zero, how could you address this in your code?**

   A. Use an `if sql%zero_divide` statement immediately following the math operation.

   B. Code a `when zero_divide` exception handler in PROC_C.

   C. Code a `when others` exception handler in PROC_A.

   D. Code a `when others` exception handler in PROC_C.

28. **If you want to define an exception that causes no Oracle errors but represents a violation of some business rule in your application, in which of the following areas in your procedure code must you include some support for this exception?**

   A. Declaration and exception only

   B. Declaration, execution, and exception

   C. Exception only

   D. No coding or definition is required to raise this exception.

29. **You are at the beginning of your current transaction and want to prevent your transaction from being able to change data in the database. To prevent any statements in the current transaction from altering database tables, which statement is used?**

   A. `set transaction`

   B. `rollback`

   C. `commit`

   D. `savepoint`

30. Your application searches for data in the EMP table on the database on a nullable column indicating whether a person is male or female. To improve performance, you decide to index the table. The table contains more than 2,000,000 rows, and the column contains few NULL values. Which of the following indexes would be most appropriate?

    A. Nonunique B-tree index

    B. Unique B-tree index

    C. Bitmap index

    D. Primary-key index

31. Your employee expense application stores information for invoices in one table. Each invoice can have several items, which are stored in another table. Each invoice may have one or more items, or none at all, but every item must correspond to one invoice. The relationship between the INVOICE table and INVOICE_ITEM table is best described as which of the following?

    A. Parent to child

    B. Detail to master

    C. Primary key to foreign key

    D. Foreign key to primary key

32. You issue the following statement:

    ```
    SELECT DECODE(UPC_CODE, 40390, 'DISCONTINUED', 65421, 'STALE',
    90395, 'BROKEN', 'ACTIVE') FROM INVENTORY;
    ```

    If the value for ACCTNO is 20395, what information will this statement display?

    A. DISCONTINUED

    B. STALE

    C. BROKEN

    D. ACTIVE

33. In considering the correspondence of logical aspects to physical aspects of a database, which of the following choices best represents the mapping of physical datafiles to their logical counterparts?

A. Extents

B. Tablespaces

C. Segments

D. Blocks

34. **You are comparing the storage implementation strategy employed by Oracle to the strategy for storage implementation used in hierarchical database systems like IMS. Which of the following choices represent advantages of the RDBMS implementation that are not present in hierarchical databases? (Choose three.)**

    A. RDBMS requires that you define how to obtain data.

    B. RDBMS defines how to obtain data for you.

    C. RDBMS can model master/detail relationships.

    D. RDBMS allows flexibility in changing data relationships.

    E. RDBMS is able to model relationships other than master/detail.

35. **Which of the following choices is not a benefit of using PL/SQL in developing an Oracle RDBMS application?**

    A. Ease of accessing data stored in Oracle

    B. Ease of integrating programs written in different languages

    C. Ability to manipulate cursor data

    D. Ability to handle errors without explicit conditional operations

36. **You are developing advanced queries for an Oracle database. Which of the following where clauses makes use of Oracle's ability to logically test values against a set of results returned without explicitly knowing what the set is before executing the query?**

    A. `where COL_A = 6`

    B. `where COL_A in (6,7,8,9,10)`

    C. `where COL_A between 6 AND 10`

    D. `where COL_A in (select NUM from TAB_OF_NUMS)`

37. You are developing a multiple-row query to handle a complex and dynamic comparison operation in the Olympics. Two tables are involved. CONTESTANT lists all contestants from every country, and MEDALS lists every country and the number of gold, silver, and bronze medals they have. If a country has not received one of the three types of medals, a zero appears in the column. Thus, a query will always return data, even for countries that haven't won a medal. Which of the following queries shows only the contestants from countries with more than 10 medallists of any type?

A. select NAME from CONTESTANT C, MEDALS M where C.COUNTRY = M.COUNTRY;

B. select NAME from CONTESTANT where COUNTRY C in (select COUNTRY from MEDALS M where C.COUNTRY = M.COUNTY)

C. select NAME from CONTESTANT where COUNTRY C = (select COUNTRY from MEDALS M where C.COUNTRY = M.COUNTY)

D. select NAME from CONTESTANT where COUNTRY in (select COUNTRY from MEDALS where NUM_GOLD + NUM_SILVER + NUM_BRONZE > 10)

38. You issue the following query in a SQL*Plus session:

```
SELECT NAME, AGE, COUNTRY FROM CONTESTANT
WHERE (COUNTRY, AGE) IN ( SELECT COUNTRY, MIN(AGE)
FROM CONTESTANT GROUP BY COUNTRY);
```

Which of the following choices identifies both the type of query and the expected result from the Oracle database?

A. Single-row subquery, the youngest contestant from one country

B. Multiple-row subquery, the youngest contestant from all countries

C. Multiple-column subquery, the youngest contestant from all countries

D. Multiple-column subquery, Oracle will return an error because = should replace in.

39. The contents of the CONTESTANTS table are listed as follows:

```
NAME                      AGE COUNTRY
----------------    --------------- ---------------
BERTRAND                  24 FRANCE
GONZALEZ                  29 SPAIN
HEINRICH                  22 GERMANY
```

```
TAN                      39 CHINA
SVENSKY                  30 RUSSIA
SOO                      21
```

You issue the following query against this table:

```
SELECT NAME FROM CONTESTANT
WHERE (COUNTRY, AGE) IN ( SELECT COUNTRY, MIN(AGE)
FROM CONTESTANT GROUP BY COUNTRY);
```

Which of the following contestants will not be listed among the output?

A. SOO

B. HEINRICH

C. BERTRAND

D. GONZALEZ

40. **An object in Oracle contains many columns that are functionally dependent on the key column for that object. The object requires segments to be stored in areas of the database other than the data dictionary. The object in question is correctly referred to as which of the following objects?**

A. Cursor

B. Table

C. Sequence

D. View

41. **You are defining where to place information in a PL/SQL block. If you want the block to contain a conditional operation that determines whether a portion of code will be executed based on the value returned from a query, which section of the PL/SQL block should you write the code into?**

A. Declaration

B. Executable

C. Exception

D. Package specification

42. Use the following PL/SQL block to answer this question:

```
DECLARE
  CURSOR UPC_CODE_CRSR IS
    SELECT UPC_CODE FROM INVENTORY;
  BEGIN
    MY_UPC_CODE INVENTORY%ROWTYPE;
    OPEN UPC_CODE_CRSR;
      LOOP
        FETCH UPC_CODE_CRSR INTO MY_UPC_CODE;
        EXIT WHEN UPC_CODE_CRSR%NOTFOUND;
        INSERT INTO MY_SHOPPING_CART (UPC_CODE)
        VALUES (UPC_CODE_CRSR);
      END LOOP;
    CLOSE UPC_CODE_CRSR;
END;
```

What is wrong with this code block?

A. The variable is declared incorrectly.

B. Appropriate looping values are not used.

C. The `insert` statement is incorrectly defined.

D. The loop must be closed in the exception handler.

43. You need to execute a PL/SQL procedure. Which of the following choices does *not* represent a way to do so?

A. With the `execute` command from SQL*Plus

B. From within a procedure

C. From within a `select` statement

D. Using the `start` command

44. You are declaring variables in PL/SQL. Which of the following choices are not methods that can be used to define variables with an initial value? (Choose two.)

A. `VAR_1 CONSTANT NUMBER(3) :=96;`

B. `VAR_1 NUMBER(3) :=96;`

C. `VAR_1 NUMBER(3) DEFAULT 96;`

D. `VAR_1 NUMBER(3) INITIAL 96;`

45. You are developing a PL/SQL block in Oracle. Which of the following standard parts of a PL/SQL block is required for proper compilation and use?

A. Declaration section

B. Exception section

C. Execution section

D. Parameter passing

46. Use the following PL/SQL block to answer this question:

```
DECLARE
PROCEDURE UPDATE_EMP_SAL ( P_EMPID IN NUMBER, P_SAL IN NUMBER) IS BEGIN
UPDATE EMP SET SALARY = SAL WHERE EMPID = P_EMPID;
END;
MY_EMPID NUMBER := 12345;
MY_SAL NUMBER DEFAULT 50000;
BEGIN
UPDATE_EMP_SAL (MY_EMPID, MY_SAL);
END;
```

What is wrong with this PL/SQL block?

A. Blocks containing named subprograms must also be named.

B. Variables passed as parameters must have the same name as the parameter.

C. The nested block must be defined after variables used in the main block.

D. The `default` keyword is invalid in PL/SQL.

47. Your application uses database objects in distributed systems owned by many users. In masking complexity added by referencing those various objects, which of the following choices identifies a situation in which use of synonyms is *not* permitted?

A. Package constants in the local procedure

B. Procedures in a remote system

C. Procedures owned by another user

D. Tables owned by another user in a remote system

48. You are developing a complex PL/SQL routine. Which of the following control structures in PL/SQL can be used for unconditional branching to a particular area of the code block?

A. `if true then`

B. `loop`

C. `if-then-else`

D. `goto`

49. The contents of the CONTESTANTS table are listed as follows:

```
NAME                         AGE COUNTRY
----------------    --------------- ---------------
BERTRAND                     24 FRANCE
GONZALEZ                     29 SPAIN
HEINRICH                     22 GERMANY
TAN                          39 CHINA
SVENSKY                      30 RUSSIA
SOO                          21
```

Use the following PL/SQL block to answer this question:

```
DECLARE
 VAR1 VARCHAR2(20);
 VAR2 NUMBER := 0;
BEGIN
 SELECT NAME INTO VAR1 FROM CONTESTANT
 WHERE COUNTRY = 'JAPAN';
 IF VAR1 = 'GERMANY' THEN
   VAR2 := LENGTH(VAR1);
ELSIF VAR1 = 'RUSSIA' THEN
 VAR2 := LENGTH(VAR1) + 15;
ELSIF VAR1 = 'FRANCE' THEN
 VAR2 := LENGTH(VAR1) + 25;
ELSIF VAR1 = 'GERMANY' THEN
 VAR2 := LENGTH(VAR1) + 35;
ELSIF VAR1 = 'CHINA' THEN
 VAR2 := LENGTH(VAR1) + 45;
ELSE
  VAR2 := LENGTH(VAR1) + 55;
END IF;
END;
```

What is the value of VAR2 at the end of this code block?

A. 7

B. 21

C. 55

D. NULL

50. **The contents of the CONTESTANTS table are listed as follows:**

```
NAME                          AGE COUNTRY
----------------    --------------  ---------------
BERTRAND                      24 FRANCE
GONZALEZ                      29 SPAIN
HEINRICH                      22 GERMANY
TAN                           39 CHINA
SVENSKY                       30 RUSSIA
SOO                           21
```

Use the following PL/SQL block to answer this question:

```
DECLARE
    JUNK VARCHAR2(20);
    i PLS_INTEGER := 0;
BEGIN
SELECT NAME INTO JUNK FROM CONTESTANT
WHERE COUNTRY = 'RUSSIA';
  FOR i IN 1..50 LOOP
    IF JUNK = 'SVENSKY' THEN
      GOTO END_LOOP;
    END IF;
    JUNK := 'RIZENFRANZ';
  <<end_loop>>
  END LOOP;
END;
```

What is wrong with this PL/SQL block?

A. The label is not followed by an executable statement.

B. The endless loop must be modified.

C. The looping variable must be assigned a default value.

D. There is nothing wrong with this statement.

51. **You want to create a user-defined record corresponding to the columns in table CONTESTANT. The columns in this table include**

```
NAME - VARCHAR2(20)
AGE - NUMBER(5)
COUNTRY - VARCHAR2(30)
```

Which of the following code fragments handle this declaration properly?

A. CONTESTANT_RECORD_NAME VARCHAR2(20);
CONTESTANT_RECORD_AGE NUMBER(5);
CONTESTANT_RECORD_COUNTRY VARCHAR2(30);

B. TYPE cont_rec IS (
NAME VARCHAR2(20),
AGE NUMBER(5),
COUNTRY VARCHAR2(30));
CONTESTANT_RECORD cont_rec;

C. CONTESTANT_RECORD CONTESTANT%ROWTYPE;

D. CONTESTANT_RECORD RECORD OF TABLE CONTESTANT;

52. You are loading data into the CONTESTANTS table, which contains the following columns:

```
NAME   - VARCHAR2(20)
AGE    - NUMBER(5)
COUNTRY - VARCHAR2(30)
```

To use a PL/SQL table for loading data, which of the following code fragments identifies how you should declare it?

A. CONTESTANT_TABLE is table of VARCHAR2(20), NUMBER(5),
VARCHAR2(30) index by BINARY_INTEGER;

B. type CONT_REC is (
NAME VARCHAR2(20),
AGE NUMBER(5),
COUNTRY VARCHAR2(30));
CONTESTANT_TABLE is table of CONT_REC%TYPE index by
BINARY_INTEGER;

C. CONTESTANT_TABLE is table of CONTESTANT%ROWTYPE;

D. CONTESTANT_TABLE is table of CONTESTANT%ROWTYPE index
by BINARY_INTEGER;

53. Examine the following code block:

```
DECLARE
 CONTESTANT_NAME_TABLE IS TABLE OF
 CONTESTANT.NAME%TYPE INDEX BY BINARY_INTEGER;
 CURSOR CONTESTANT_CSR IS SELECT NAME
   FROM CONTESTANT;
 MYVAL BINARY_INTEGER := 0;
```

```
BEGIN
  FOR MY_CONT_REC IN CONTESTANT_CSR LOOP
    CONTESTANT_NAME_TABLE(MYVAL)  := MY_CONT_REC.NAME;
    MYVAL := MYVAL + 1;
  END LOOP;
- -  HOW MANY ROWS IN TABLE?
END;
```

If you want to find out the number of rows in the table, what methods can you use to do so in the fewest number of program lines possible? (Choose two.)

A. `select count(1) from CONTESTANT_NAME_TABLE;`

B. Value in `MYVAL`

C. `CONTESTANT_NAME_TABLE.COUNT`

D. Use another loop to cycle through the records in `CONTESTANT_TABLE`.

54. **You are developing a PL/SQL block designed for bulk data operations. When attempting to store table data for multiple rows in a PL/SQL variable, which of the following choices identifies the mechanism best suited for the task?**

A. Record

B. Cursor

C. PL/SQL table

D. PL/SQL table of records

55. **You declare a cursor as follows: `cursor c1 is select * from CONTESTANT for update`. Which of the following choices correctly describes what happens when this cursor is opened?**

A. Oracle returns an error because the way that the records should be updated is not defined.

B. Oracle retrieves all records in the CONTESTANT table only.

C. Oracle retrieves all records in the CONTESTANT table into the cursor and locks those rows for `update`.

D. Oracle updates all records in the CONTESTANT table as specified in the open statement.

56. You develop a PL/SQL block that will be used in an overall application that records grants for political asylum for Olympic athletes to the country where the games are held. The cursor definition in this block is `cursors asy_csr is select NAME from CONTESTANT`. As you loop through the cursor, you want the ability to update the record back in the table that corresponds to the record in the cursor. Which of the following choices best identifies the way to do so without explicit comparison between the NAME value in the cursor and the NAME value in the table?

A. `update CONTESTANT set COUNTRY = 'USA' where current of asy_csr;`

B. Redefine the cursor as `cursor cnt_csr is select NAME from CONTESTANT for update;`

C. `update CONTESTANT set COUNTRY = 'USA' where NAME = asy_csr.NAME;`

D. You cannot achieve this functionality with PL/SQL.

57. You want to define a cursor that contains a subquery. Which of the following choices best identifies how PL/SQL allows you to handle this situation?

A. PL/SQL does not allow cursors to contain subqueries.

B. PL/SQL only allows cursors to contain subqueries resolving to inline views.

C. PL/SQL only allows cursors to contain subqueries resolving to a set of comparison values for a where clause.

D. PL/SQL allows cursors to contain the same types of subqueries permitted in any SQL query.

58. You develop a PL/SQL program with several blocks three layers deep. PROC_A calls PROC_B, which in turn calls PROC_C. Which of the following choices correctly identifies how Oracle will propagate the error in order to find an exception handler that will resolve an exception being raised in the innermost block?

A. PROC_B, PROC_A, PROC_C

B. PROC_C, PROC_B, PROC_A

C. PROC_A, PROC_B, PROC_C

D. Exception is propagated directly to the user level.

59. You are developing PL/SQL process flow into your program. Which of the following methods can be used for eliminating the declaration of a cursor when using a cursor for loop?

A. Using the `execute immediate` command

B. Using the DBMS_SQL package

C. Passing a SQL statement directly into the `cursor for` loop

D. You cannot eliminate the declaration of a cursor when using a `cursor for` loop.

60. You are defining records for storing the data in a table in your PL/SQL program. Which of the following choices identifies a record type that simplifies declaration of records for this context?

A. PL/SQL table

B. PL/SQL table of records

C. `%rowtype` record

D. Nested table

Practice Exam 3

1. **You are implementing transaction control in a PL/SQL block. Which of the following choices best describes the use of autonomous transactions in your database?**

   A. A developer wants records to be added to an EXIT_STATUS table, regardless of whether or not the transaction completed successfully.

   B. Two users on the Oracle database are modifying records in different tables at the same time.

   C. Two users on the Oracle database are modifying different records in the same table at the same time.

   D. Two users on the Oracle database are modifying the same records in the same table at the same time.

2. **You need to compute an *N*-dimensional cross-tabulation in your SQL statement output for reporting purposes. Which of the following Oracle8i clauses can be used for this purpose?**

   A. `having`

   B. `cube`

   C. `rollup`

   D. `trim( )`

3. **You are using summaries in the Oracle8i database for data warehousing. Which of the following clauses is implicitly added by Oracle8i to queries in order to take advantage of summary management?**

   A. `order by`

   B. `group by`

   C. `cube`

   D. `rollup`

4. **You are managing a data warehouse using Oracle8i. Which of the following choices identifies a key aspect of dimension creation that must be addressed when the dimension is created?**

    A. cube operation

    B. rollup operation

    C. Summary management

    D. Level hierarchy

5. **You need to define a collection type for student exam records in an Oracle8i database. Each record will consist of student vital information, along with the answers each student gave on every exam the student took in the class. You want the ability to reference specific questions on exams for individual students for comparison purposes. Which of the following choices identifies the best way to do it?**

    A. Scalar datatypes

    B. User-defined type

    C. VARRAY

    D. Nested table

6. **You are indexing Oracle data in an application. The index will be on a column containing sequential numbers with at least seven significant digits. Most, if not all, entries will start with 1. Which of the following indexes is best suited for the task?**

    A. B-tree indexes

    B. Reverse-key indexes

    C. Bitmap indexes

    D. Descending indexes

7. **You need to store a large block of text data in Oracle. These text blocks will be around 3,500 characters in length. Which datatype should you use for storing these large objects?**

    A. VARCHAR2

    B. CLOB

    C. BLOB

    D. BFILE

8. **Two users exist on an Oracle8i system, named FLUFFY and MUFFY. MUFFY owns a PL/SQL procedure called `foobar( )`, defined as follows:**

```
create procedure FOOBAR
authid current_user
is
 var1 number;
begin
 select * into var1 from foo;
end;
```

To use procedure `foobar( )`, what privileges does FLUFFY need granted to her? (Choose as many as appropriate.)

   A. `create procedure` on schema MUFFY

   B. `execute` on procedure `foobar( )`

   C. `update` on table FOO

   D. `select` on table FOO

9. **User MILTON issues the following code block in his SQL*Plus session:**

```
CREATE OR REPLACE PROCEDURE upd_tran
( PVAL1 IN VARCHAR2) IS
    PRAGMA AUTONOMOUS_TRANSACTION;
    MY_VAL2 NUMBER(10);
BEGIN
    SELECT COL_1 INTO MY_VAL2
    FROM TAB_2 WHERE COL_2 = PVAL1;
    UPDATE TAB_1 SET COL_1 = PVAL1
    WHERE COL_2 = PVAL2;
    COMMIT;
END;
```

Later, user GOETHE defines another procedure called `my_tran( )`, which calls `upd_tran( )` as part of an application. Which of the following statements is true about this application?

   A. Any transaction in progress in `my_tran( )` when `upd_tran( )` is called will be committed when `upd_tran( )` completes.

   B. Any uncommitted changes made to table TAB_2 by `my_tran( )` will not be seen by `upd_tran( )`.

   C. Procedure `upd_tran( )` has no problem updating TAB_1 if `my_tran( )` has already done so without issuing a `commit` before the call to `upd_tran( )`.

D. User GOETHE needs to have `update` privileges on TAB_1 to execute
procedure `upd_tran( )`.

10. **Developer JANET receives an error due to the following statement in the
declaration section:**

`PI CONSTANT NUMBER;`

The problem is because of which of the following causes?

A. There is not enough memory in the program for the constant.

B. There is no value associated with the constant.

C. There is no datatype associated with the constant.

D. `pi` is a reserved word.

11. **You are designing your PL/SQL exception handler inside a nested block.
Which statement most accurately describes the result of not creating an
exception handler for a raised exception?**

A. The program will continue without raising the exception.

B. There will be a memory leak.

C. Control will pass to the PL/SQL block caller's exception handler.

D. The program will return a `%notfound` error.

12. **You are determining what types of cursors to use in your PL/SQL code.
Which of the following statements is true about implicit cursors?**

A. Implicit cursors are used for SQL statements that are not named.

B. Developers should use implicit cursors with great care.

C. Implicit cursors are used in `cursor for` loops to handle data processing.

D. Implicit cursors are no longer a feature in Oracle.

13. **You are constructing PL/SQL process flow for your program. Which of the
following is not a feature of a `cursor for` loop?**

A. Declares record type

B. Opens and parses SQL statements

C. Fetches records from cursor

D. Requires `exit` condition to be defined

14. **A developer would like to use a referential datatype declaration on a variable. The variable name is EMPLOYEE_LASTNAME, and the corresponding table and column are EMPLOYEE and LASTNAME, respectively. How would the developer define this variable using referential datatypes?**

    A. Use `EMPLOYEE.LASTNAME%type`.

    B. Use `EMPLOYEE.LASTNAME%rowtype`.

    C. Look up datatype for EMPLOYEE column on LASTNAME table and use that.

    D. Declare it to be type LONG.

15. **After executing an `update` statement, the developer codes a PL/SQL block to perform an operation based on `SQL%rowcount`. What data is returned by the `SQL%rowcount` operation?**

    A. A Boolean value representing the success or failure of the `update`

    B. A numeric value representing the number of rows updated

    C. A VARCHAR2 value identifying the name of the table updated

    D. A LONG value containing all data from the table

16. **You are defining a check following a SQL statement to verify that the statement returned appropriate data. Which of the following are implicit cursor attributes? (Choose three.)**

    A. `%found`

    B. `%too_many_rows`

    C. `%notfound`

    D. `%rowcount`

    E. `%rowtype`

17. **You are constructing PL/SQL process flow into your program. If left out, which of the following would cause an infinite loop to occur in a simple loop?**

    A. `loop`

    B. `end loop`

    C. `if-then`

    D. `exit`

18. You are coding your exception handler. The `others` exception handler is used to handle all of the following exceptions, except one. Which exception does the `others` exception handler not cover?

    A. `no_data_found`

    B. `others`

    C. `rowtype_mismatch`

    D. `too_many_rows`

19. You are defining a cursor in your PL/SQL block. The following options each show a line in the statement. Which line in the statement will produce an error?

    A. `cursor action_cursor is`

    B. `select name, rate, action`

    C. `into action_record`

    D. `from action_table;`

    E. There are no errors in this statement.

20. You are developing PL/SQL process flow into your program. The command used to open a `cursor for` loop is which of the following keywords?

    A. `open`

    B. `fetch`

    C. `parse`

    D. None, `cursor for` loops handle cursor opening implicitly.

21. You are determining the appropriate program flow for your PL/SQL application. Which of the following statements are true about `while` loops?

    A. Explicit `exit` statements are required in `while` loops.

    B. Counter variables are required in `while` loops.

    C. An `if-then` statement is needed to signal when a `while` loop should end.

    D. All `exit` conditions for `while` loops are handled in the `exit when` clause.

22. For the following question, assume that before the following PL/SQL block is executed, table OPERATIONS contains one column called STATUS and one row with the value PROCESSING.

```
DECLARE
 VAR1 VARCHAR2(1);
 VAR2 VARCHAR2(1);
IS
BEGIN
  SELECT TO_CHAR(CEIL(SQRT(40)))
  INTO VAR2
  FROM DUAL;
  SELECT SUBSTR(STATUS,4,1)
  INTO VAR1
  FROM OPERATIONS;
  IF VAR1 = 'H' THEN
     VAR2 := '5';
  ELSIF VAR1 = 'C' THEN
      VAR2 := 'L';
  ELSE
     VAR2 = '9';
  END IF;
  INSERT INTO OPERATIONS VALUES (VAR2);
  COMMIT;
END;
```

What is the value of the STATUS column after executing this code block?

A. 5

B. 7

C. L

D. 9

E. J

23. You create the following PL/SQL block:

```
DECLARE
  MYVAR1 CONSTANT NUMBER := 100;
  MYVAR2 NUMBER := 0;
 BEGIN
  SELECT ITEM
  INTO VAR2
  FROM ITEM_TABLE
```

```
     WHERE NAME = 'SMITH';
       VAR1 := VAR2 + 3079;
   END;
```

Which of the following lines in this block of PL/SQL code will produce an error?

A. MYVAR2 NUMBER := 0;

B. into VAR2

C. where NAME = 'SMITH';

D. VAR1 := VAR2 + 3079;

E. There are no errors in this PL/SQL block.

24. You are preparing to compile the following block of PL/SQL code:

```
CREATE FUNCTION OPERATION_A (VAR1 IN VARCHAR2) RETURN NUMBER IS
   VAR2 VARCHAR2(1);
BEGIN
   SELECT GENDER INTO VAR1 FROM EMP
     WHERE LASTNAME = 'SMITHERS';
   IF VAR1 = 6 THEN RETURN (6) ELSE RETURN (8);
   END IF;
END;
```

Which of the lines of PL/SQL code contains an error?

A. create function operation_a (VAR1 in VARCHAR2) return NUMBER is

B. select GENDER into VAR1 from EMP

C. where LASTNAME = 'SMITHERS';

D. if VAR1 = 6 then return (6) else return (8);

E. There are no errors in this PL/SQL block.

25. Dropping a table has which of the following effects on a nonunique index created for the table?

A. It has no effect.

B. The index will be dropped.

C. The index will be rendered invalid.

D. The index will contain NULL values.

26. **Which of the following statements about indexes is true?**

    A. Columns with low cardinality are handled well by B-tree indexes.

    B. Columns with low cardinality are handled poorly by bitmap indexes.

    C. Columns with high cardinality are handled well by B-tree indexes.

27. **Which of the following methods should you use to add to the number of columns selected by a view?**

    A. Add more columns to the underlying table.

    B. Issue the `alter view` statement.

    C. Use a correlated subquery in conjunction with the view.

    D. Drop and re-create the view with references to select more columns.

28. **Which of the following choices is a valid parameter for sequence creation?**

    A. `identified by`

    B. `using temporary tablespace`

    C. `maxvalue`

    D. `on delete cascade`

29. **The following options each show a line in a statement issued against the Oracle database. Which line will produce an error?**

    A. `create view EMP_VIEW_01`

    B. `as select E.EMPID, E.LASTNAME, E.FIRSTNAME, A.ADDRESS`

    C. `from EMPLOYEE E, EMPL_ADDRESS A`

    D. `where E.EMPID = A.EMPID`

    E. `with check option;`

    F. This statement contains no errors.

30. **You are granting privileges on your table to another user. Which object privilege allows the user to create his or her own table with a foreign key on a column in your table?**

    A. `references`

> **B.** index
>
> **C.** select
>
> **D.** delete

31. **Which of the following statements about roles are true? (Choose three.)**

    A. Roles can be granted to other roles.

    B. Privileges can be granted to roles.

    C. Roles can be granted to users.

    D. Roles can be granted to synonyms.

32. **After referencing NEXTVAL, what happens to the value in CURRVAL?**

    A. It is incremented by one.

    B. It is now in PREVVAL.

    C. It is equal to NEXTVAL.

    D. It is unchanged.

33. **The EMP_SALARY table has two columns: EMP_USER and SALARY. EMP_USER is set to be the same as the Oracle username. To support user MARTHA, the salary administrator, you create a view with the following statement:**

    ```
    CREATE VIEW EMP_SAL_VW
    AS SELECT EMP_USER, SALARY
    FROM EMP_SALARY
    WHERE EMP_USER <> 'MARTHA';
    ```

    MARTHA is supposed to be able to view and update anyone's salary in the company, except her own, through this view. Which of the following clauses do you need to add to your view-creation statement in order to implement this functionality?

    A. with admin option

    B. with grant option

    C. with security option

    D. with check option

34. **The INVENTORY table has three columns: UPC_CODE, UNITS, and DELIV_DATE. The primary key is UPC_CODE. New records are added daily through a view. The view was created using the following code:**

```
CREATE VIEW DAY_INVENTORY_VW
AS SELECT UPC_CODE, UNITS, DELIV_DATE
FROM INVENTORY
WHERE DELIV_DATE = SYSDATE
WITH CHECK OPTION;
```

What happens when a user tries to insert a record with duplicate UPC_CODE?

   A. The statement fails due to `with check option` clause.

   B. The statement will succeed.

   C. The statement fails due to primary key constraint.

   D. The statement will insert everything except the date.

35. **You are cleaning information out of the Oracle database. Which of the following statements will get rid of all views that use a table at the same time you eliminate the table from the database?**

   A. `drop view`

   B. `alter table`

   C. `drop index`

   D. `alter table drop constraint`

36. **You create a view with the following statement:**

```
CREATE VIEW BASEBALL_TEAM_VW
AS SELECT B.JERSEY_NUM, B.POSITION, B.NAME
FROM BASEBALL_TEAM B
WHERE B.NAME = USER;
```

What will happen when user JONES attempts to `select` a listing for user SMITH?

   A. The `select` will receive an error.

   B. The `select` will succeed.

   C. The `select` will receive NO ROWS SELECTED.

   D. The `select` will add data only to BASEBALL_TEAM.

37. Which of the following integrity constraints automatically create an index when defined? (Choose two.)

A. Foreign keys

B. UNIQUE constraints

C. NOT NULL constraints

D. Primary keys

38. Which of the following dictionary views gives information about the position of a column in a primary key?

A. ALL_PRIMARY_KEYS

B. USER_CONSTRAINTS

C. ALL_IND_COLUMNS

D. ALL_TABLES

39. Developer ANJU executes the following statement: `create table ANIMALS as select * from MASTER.ANIMALS;`. What is the effect of this statement?

A. A table named ANIMALS will be created in the MASTER schema with the same data as the ANIMALS table owned by ANJU.

B. A table named ANJU will be created in the ANIMALS schema with the same data as the ANIMALS table owned by MASTER.

C. A table named ANIMALS will be created in the ANJU schema with the same data as the ANIMALS table owned by MASTER.

D. A table named MASTER will be created in the ANIMALS schema with the same data as the ANJU table owned by ANIMALS.

40. User JANKO would like to insert a row into the EMPLOYEE table that has three columns: EMPID, LASTNAME, and SALARY. The user would like to enter data for EMPID 59694 and LASTNAME Harris, but no salary. Which statement would work best?

A. `insert into EMPLOYEE values (59694,'HARRIS', NULL);`

B. `insert into EMPLOYEE values (59694,'HARRIS');`

C. `insert into EMPLOYEE (EMPID, LASTNAME, SALARY) values (59694,'HARRIS');`

D. `insert into EMPLOYEE (select 59694 from 'HARRIS');`

41. No relationship officially exists between two tables. Which of the following choices is the strongest indicator of a parent/child relationship?

A. Two tables in the database are named VOUCHER and VOUCHER_ITEM, respectively.

B. Two tables in the database are named EMPLOYEE and PRODUCTS, respectively.

C. Two tables in the database were created on the same day.

D. Two tables in the database contain none of the same columns.

42. Which of the following are valid database table datatypes in Oracle? (Choose three.)

A. CHAR

B. VARCHAR2

C. BOOLEAN

D. NUMBER

43. Omitting the `where` clause from a `delete` statement has which of the following effects?

A. The `delete` statement will fail because there are no records to delete.

B. The `delete` statement will prompt the user to enter criteria for the deletion.

C. The `delete` statement will fail because of syntax error.

D. The `delete` statement will remove all records from the table.

44. The following options each show a line in a statement. Which line will produce an error?

A. `create table GOODS`

B. `(GOODNO NUMBER,`

C. `GOOD_NAME VARCHAR2(20) check(GOOD_NAME in (select NAME from AVAIL_GOODS)),`

D. `constraint PK_GOODS_01`

E. `primary key (GOODNO));`

F. There are no errors in this statement.

45. **Which of the following is the transaction control that prevents more than one user from updating data in a table?**

    A. Locks

    B. Commits

    C. Rollbacks

    D. Savepoints

46. **Which of the following methods should you use to increase the number of nullable columns for a table?**

    A. Use the `alter table` statement.

    B. Ensure that all column values are NULL for all rows.

    C. First, increase the size of adjacent column datatypes, and then add the column.

    D. Add the column, populate the column, and then add the `NOT NULL` constraint.

47. **A user issues the statement `select count(*) from EMPLOYEE`. The query takes an inordinately long time and returns a count of zero. Which of the following is the most cost-effective solution?**

    A. Upgrade the hardware.

    B. Truncate the table.

    C. Upgrade the version of Oracle.

    D. Delete the high-water mark.

48. **You are creating some tables in your database as part of the logical data model. Which of the following constraints have an index associated with them that is generated automatically by Oracle?**

    A. UNIQUE

    B. FOREIGN KEY

    C. CHECK

    D. not NULL

49. Each of the following statements is true about referential integrity, except one. Which is it?

A. The referencing column in the child table must correspond to a primary key in the parent.

B. All values in the referenced column in the parent table must be present in the referencing column in the child.

C. The datatype of the referenced column in the parent table must be identical to the referencing column in the child.

D. All values in the referencing column in the child table must be present in the referenced column in the parent.

50. You are managing constraints on a table in Oracle. Which of the following choices correctly identifies the limitations on CHECK constraints?

A. Values must be obtained from a lookup table.

B. Values must be part of a fixed set defined by create or alter table.

C. Values must include reserved words like sysdate and user.

D. Column cannot contain a NULL value.

51. Which of the following is not a group function?

A. avg( )

B. sqrt( )

C. sum( )

D. max( )

52. In order to perform an inner join, which criteria must be true?

A. The common columns in the join do not need to have shared values.

B. The tables in the join need to have common columns.

C. The common columns in the join may or may not have shared values.

D. The common columns in the join must have shared values.

53. Once defined, how long will a variable remain defined in SQL*Plus?

   A. Until the database is shut down

   B. Until the instance is shut down

   C. Until the statement completes

   D. Until the session completes

54. You want to change the prompt Oracle uses to obtain input from a user. Which two of the following choices are used for this purpose? (Choose two.)

   A. Change the prompt in the `config.ora` file.

   B. Alter the `prompt` clause of the `accept` command.

   C. Enter a new prompt in the `login.sql` file.

   D. There is no way to change a prompt in Oracle.

55. No search criteria for the EMPLOYEE table are known. Which of the following options is appropriate for use when search criteria are unknown for comparison operations in a `select` statement? (Choose two.)

   A. `select * from EMPLOYEE where EMPID = &empid;`

   B. `select * from EMPLOYEE where EMPID = 69494;`

   C. `select * from EMPLOYEE where EMPID =`
      `(select empid from invoice where INVOICE_NO = 4399485);`

   D. `select * from EMPLOYEE;`

56. Which of the following is the default character for specifying substitution variables in `select` statements?

   A. Ampersand

   B. Ellipses

   C. Quotation marks

   D. Asterisk

57. A user is setting up a join operation between tables EMPLOYEE and DEPT. There are some employees in the EMPLOYEE table that the user wants returned by the query, but the employees are not assigned to department heads yet. Which **select** statement is most appropriate for this user?

A. `select e.empid, d.head from EMPLOYEE e, dept d;`

B. `select e.empid, d.head from EMPLOYEE e, dept d where`
`e.dept# = d.dept#;`

C. `select e.empid, d.head from EMPLOYEE e, dept d where`
`e.dept# = d.dept# (+);`

D. `select e.empid, d.head from EMPLOYEE e, dept d where`
`e.dept# (+) = d.dept#;`

58. Which of the following uses of the **having** clause are appropriate? (Choose three.)

A. To put returned data into sorted order

B. To exclude certain data groups based on known criteria

C. To include certain data groups based on unknown criteria

D. To include certain data groups based on known criteria

59. Which of the following best describes a Cartesian product?

A. A group function

B. Produced as a result of a join `select` statement with no `where` clause

C. The result of fuzzy logic

D. A special feature of Oracle server

60. Which of the following methods is used to change the default character that identifies runtime variables?

A. Modifying the `init.ora` file

B. Modifying the `login.sql` file

C. Issuing the `define variablename` command

D. Issuing the `set define` command

Answers to Practice Exam 1

1. A.   `select NAME, JERSEY_NO where JERSEY_NO = 6;`

Explanation   SQL statements in Oracle must have a `from` clause. A SQL statement can lack a `where` clause, in which case, all of the data in the table will be returned. However, if the statement does not have a `from` clause, Oracle will not know what table to retrieve data from. Recall that a special table called DUAL assists in situations in which you don't want to retrieve data from a table, but instead only want to manipulate expressions. **(Topic 2.2)**

2. D.   `cursor for` loop

Explanation   Any time you see a PL/SQL block where the cursor is opened and manipulated manually, you can revise the code into a `cursor for` loop to take advantage of Oracle automatically managing many aspects of cursor manipulation for you. The other choices simply rewrite the existing structure and may save a line or two of coding, but the `cursor for` loop will tremendously reduce your coding burden in this situation. **(Topic 22.3)**

3. B.   `others`

Explanation   A special exception handler called `others` exists in PL/SQL that will handle all unhandled exceptions captured at that level of processing. Although Oracle will raise the `zero_divide` exception automatically whenever you attempt to divide a number by zero, coding an exception handler for `zero_divide` only defines what happens when `zero_divide` is raised. It does not, for example, handle situations in which another exception is raised, as `others` does. The `no_data_found` and `too_many_rows` exceptions are raised when no data or too much data is returned by an implicit or explicit cursor, respectively. **(Topic 24.4)**

4. C.   `raise_application_error`

Explanation   The `raise_application_error` function allows Oracle to return a user-defined error message when an exception condition is raised. The `pragma exception_init` keywords (of which `pragma` is a subset) indicate a compiler directive where you tell Oracle you want to associate an internal error with an exception name that you choose. The `others` exception is a catchall for processing exceptions that would otherwise escape unhandled. Finally, the `exception` keyword is used to denote the exceptions section of your code block. **(Topic 24.6)**

5. A.   Issuing an `update` statement

Explanation   The only choice that does not end a transaction is the one that continues the transaction, namely, issuing another `update` statement. A `commit` tells Oracle to save your data changes and end the transaction. A `rollback` tells Oracle to discard your data changes and end the transaction. Closing SQL*Plus or otherwise ending the session is usually treated as an implicit `commit` and ends your transaction as well. **(Topic 10.3)**

6. B.   `commit`

Explanation   In order to save any change you make in Oracle, you use the `commit` command. The `savepoint` command merely identifies a logical breakpoint in your transaction that you can use to break up complex units of work. The `rollback` command discards every change you made since the last `commit`. Finally, the `set transaction` command sets up the transaction to be read-only against the Oracle database. **(Topic 10.5)**

7. D.   USER_CONS_COLUMNS

Explanation   The USER_CONS_COLUMNS dictionary view shows you all of the columns in tables belonging to that user that are part of indexes used to enforce constraints. USER_INDEXES is incorrect because that view only displays information about the index itself, not the columns in the index. USER_TAB_COLUMNS displays all the columns in all tables owned by that user. Finally, USER_COLUMNS is not an actual view in the Oracle database. **(Topic 14.2)**

8. D.   not NULL

Explanation   not NULL integrity constraints can only be declared as column constraints, meaning that the actual syntax for defining the constraint will appear next to the constrained column, as opposed to at the end of the column listing. Choices A, B, and C all identify constraints that can be defined as table constraints or as column constraints. **(Topic 12.1)**

9. D.   The view

Explanation   When you drop a table with the `cascade constraints` option, Oracle removes from other tables all associated indexes, triggers, and constraints that reference that table. Oracle does not remove the views that use that table, however. You must remove a view manually with the `drop view` statement. **(Topic 11.5)**

10. D.   MONTHS_BETWEEN

Explanation   Each of the choices accepts as input a DATE datatype and returns a DATE datatype, with one exception. The MONTHS_BETWEEN function returns a number indicating how many months there are between the two dates you give it. This number will be displayed with numbers to the right of the decimal point, which you can round off if you like. **(Topic 4.2)**

11. C.   `order by sqrt(1);`

Explanation   The `order by` clause in the `select` clause of the `select` statement allows you to refer to the column you want the table order determined by, either by the column name or by the number representing the column order. However, you cannot perform any sort of numeric function on that column-order number. Both the `asc` and `desc` keywords are valid for the `order by` clause, indicating ascending order (default) and descending order, respectively. **(Topic 3.2)**

12. B.   Table with one column and one row used in various operations

Explanation   The DUAL table is a special table in Oracle used to satisfy the requirement of a `from` clause in your SQL statements. It contains one column and one row of data. It is not a dictionary view; rather, it is an actual table. You could use the DUAL table in arithmetic expressions and not actually pull real data from the database. You should never insert data into the DUAL table under any circumstances. **(Topic 2.1)**

13. A.   ACTIVE

Explanation   The `decode( )` function is used as a "case" statement, where Oracle will review the value in the column identified in the first parameter (in this case, ACCTNO). If that value equals the second parameter, the third parameter is returned. If that value equals the fourth parameter, the fifth parameter will be returned, and so on. If the value equals no parameter, the default value provided in the last parameter (in this case, ACTIVE) is returned. TRANSFER would be returned if ACCTNO equaled 590395, SEIZED would be returned if ACCTNO equaled 654321, and CLOSED would be returned if ACCTNO equaled 123456. **(Topic 4.1)**

14. C.   `insert into BANK_ACCT (ACCTNO, NAME) VALUES (&VAR1, '&VAR2');`

Explanation   In order to have statement reusability where you can enter a value on-the-fly, you must use lexical references as runtime variables. These references are preceded by an ampersand (`&`) character, as in the correct answer. Although you can use nested subqueries in your `insert` statements, this has the effect of inserting multiple rows at once without requiring input from the user. **(Topic 9.1)**

15. B.   28-APR-07

Explanation   For this question, you really need to put on your thinking cap. ADD_MONTHS adds a specified number of months, indicated by the second parameter to the value in the first parameter. The parameter 120 months is 10 years; so if you add 10 to the year in the date given, you should come up with 28-APR-07, which is the correct answer. When you are taking the exam, beware of having too much of your time sucked up by this sort of "brain-teaser" question. **(Topic 4.2)**

16. D.   MONDAY JUNE 26, 2037: 10:30PM

Explanation   The first statement in this question alters the date format shown in your SQL*Plus session. The second statement returns the current date and time in that specific format. In this case, your format is the day of the week, followed by the month of the year, the date, the year, and the time in AM/PM format. This being the case, the correct answer is MONDAY JUNE 26, 2037: 10:30PM. **(Topic 9.2)**

17. B.   where A.C = 5 AND A.C = B.C (+);

Explanation   The correct choice illustrates the use of Oracle's outer join function. The question indicates that you want to see data in table A, no matter whether there is corresponding data in table B or not. Thus, you place the outer join operation (it looks like a (+)) next to the reference to the C column in table B. If the outer join operation is removed, Oracle will only return data from table A for which there is corresponding data in table B. If the outer join operator is used for both tables, you will get a syntax error. If you omit the join operator comparing values from table A to table B, Oracle will return a Cartesian product of the data you requested from A with all the data from table B. **(Topic 5.2)**

18. B.   When creating composite primary keys, the datatypes in all columns within the primary key must be the same datatype.

Explanation   No restriction exists on column datatypes for composite primary keys requiring that all columns in the primary key have the same datatype. Choice A is incorrect because you must ensure that the variables designed to hold data from table columns are large enough for the values in those columns. Choice D is incorrect for largely the same reason. Finally, choice C is incorrect because Oracle forces you to declare the column in a child table with the exact same datatype as it has in the parent table. **(Topic 12.1)**

19. B.   sqrt()

Explanation All the choices indicate `group by` functions, except for the `sqrt( )` function. `sqrt( )` is a single-row function acting on each value in each column row, one at a time or individually. `avg( )` processes data from multiple rows in a column and produces one result, the average value for all of them. `count( )` processes all values in a column or columns and counts the number of row values in that column or columns. The `stddev( )` function takes all values in a column of rows and determines the standard deviation for that set of values. **(Topic 6.1)**

20. C. `nvl( )` returns NULL if the first value is not equal to the second.

Explanation The only statement that is not true is `nvl( )` returns NULL if the first value is not equal to the second. `nvl( )` is specifically designed to avoid returning NULL for a column, by substituting another value that you pass as the second parameter. `nvl( )` handles many different datatypes, and both values passed must be the same datatype. **(Topic 4.1)**

21. A. Records

Explanation `%rowtype` is a special keyword in PL/SQL that allows you to define a record that conforms to the datatypes for rows in a particular table, as in `EMP%rowtype` for a set of datatypes in a row from the EMP table. Although that row may contain columns of VARCHAR2 or NUMBER datatype, a record datatype is a more accurate way to describe this feature. Because PLS_INTEGER data cannot be stored in Oracle tables, you will never see this datatype in a `%rowtype` record. **(Topic 21.2)**

22. C. 430

Explanation The key here is being able to distinguish between CURRVAL and NEXTVAL. Only NEXTVAL will actually change the sequence value. CURRVAL only selects the current value, so you can factor out the four people who have issued statements requesting CURRVAL and pay attention to those users requesting NEXTVAL. There are three of those, so the sequence, which started at 394, has been incremented twice by 12. 394 + 12 +12 = 430. **(Topic 15.2)**

23. B. The high-water mark was not reset.

Explanation The `select count(*)` statement takes a long time because Oracle needed to inspect the table in its entirety in order to derive the row count, even though the table was empty. To avoid this situation on large tables, use the `truncate` statement rather than `delete`. `truncate` resets the high-water mark on your table, thus reducing the time it takes Oracle to perform `select count(*)` operations. **(Topic 11.5)**

24. B. `create or replace view`

Explanation The column definitions for a view can be changed only by re-creating the view with the `create or replace view` statement. The `alter view` command is used only to recompile a view. `insert into view` is not a valid SQL statement. Although `create view` will technically work, you must first drop the view you want to re-create, which requires two statements, not one. `create or replace view` is the most accurate choice offered. **(Topic 13.2)**

25. A. A `join` statement without a `where` clause

Explanation Cartesian products are the result of `select` statements that contain malformed `where` clauses. `sum( )` and `avg( )` operations are group functions and do not produce Cartesian products. Selecting data from the DUAL table will not produce a Cartesian product because only one table is involved—and a table with only one row at that! **(Topic 5.1)**

26. B. Creating an appropriate `login.sql` file

Explanation SQL*Plus shows its roots in UNIX systems through the `login.sql` file. This file is used to specify settings used in your session. `login.sql` runs automatically after you log into Oracle. SQL*Plus in Windows environments does not have a Preferences menu, eliminating that choice. You shouldn't attempt to use the `alter table` or `alter user` statements for this purpose, either. **(Topic 9.5)**

27. B. `create or replace view emp_sal_vw as select emp_user, salary from emp_salary where emp_user = user;`

Explanation Explanation The command in choice B is correctly defined for creating a view that will only allow users to see their own salary information from the underlying table. Choice A is incorrect because the view defined will show all salary information except for salary data for the user issuing the query. Choices C and D are incorrect because the view will show only salary data for users other than MARTHA. **(Topic 13.3)**

28. D. INTEGER

Explanation Although you can declare variables in PL/SQL blocks using the INTEGER datatype, you cannot store INTEGER datatype data in Oracle tables. All other datatypes shown— CHAR, RAW, and DATE—can be stored in the Oracle database and also be used as datatypes for PL/SQL variables. **(Topic 11.3)**

29. B. TO_CHAR

Explanation   TO_CHAR is used to convert DATE values, numbers, and other things into text strings. The CONVERT operation is used to convert a text string from one character set to another. The TO_NUMBER operation converts numeric text to true numbers. The TO_DATE function is used to convert a properly formatted text string into a DATE value. **(Topic 4.3)**

30. C.   Use the `set` command to allow for larger LONG column values.

Explanation   The TRIGGER_BODY column in the DBA_TRIGGERS view is declared as a LONG datatype column, and SQL*Plus is most likely cutting off data from the output. Choice A is incorrect because the question says you are a ble to see some of the data in the view, just not all the data. Choice B is incorrect because memory allocation has nothing to do with the problem identified in the question. Finally, choice D is incorrect because there is nothing wrong with the DBA_TRIGGERS view. The problem lies instead with how SQL*Plus is currently configured to display LONG column data. **(Topic 9.2)**

31. B.   All records

Explanation   Since the `update` statement does not contain a `where` clause, the change will be made to every record in the table. There is no way to accurately update only the first or last record in the table. None of the records will be updated only if there is something wrong with the `update` statement, such as a column being referenced incorrectly. **(Topic 10.1)**

32. A.   `too_many_rows`

Explanation   The answer to this question is `too_many_rows`, an Oracle predefined exception that is raised automatically in the situation described in the question. The `others` exception handler is a catchall that handles any exception that would otherwise go unhandled at this level of execution. `zero_divide` is raised automatically whenever you attempt to divide by 0. Finally, `no_data_found` is the conceptual opposite of the correct answer. **(Topic 24.3)**

33. B.   `alter table`

Explanation   The `alter table` statement allows you to easily add columns after the table is created, with minimal impact to your system. Unlike when you want to change views, you do not use the `or replace` keyword for this effort, thus creating a powerful distraction for the user who is more familiar with views than with underlying tables. The `create table` statement could be used for the task, but you would first need to issue the `drop table` statement to get rid of the initial table. **(Topic 11.4)**

34. B.   `FOREIGN KEY`

Explanation   Foreign-key relationships require that you grant `references` privileges on a table to the user who is creating the foreign-key relationship from his or her table to yours. There is no particular special privilege that must be granted to create `UNIQUE`, `CHECK`, or `NOT NULL` constraints other than `create table`. **(Topic 16.3)**

35. D.   Oracle creates the view successfully.

Explanation   When you issue the `create view` command shown in the question, Oracle creates the view successfully. A view can be created with the `order by` clause, making choice A incorrect. You do not need to enclose the `select` statement in your `create view` command in parentheses, as choice C suggests. Finally, Choice B is incorrect because you do not need to use the `with check option` clause for creating a view. **(Topic 13.4)**

36. D.   `like`

Explanation   For a situation in which you want to use wildcards, Oracle offers the `like` comparison operator. This operator allows you to search for text strings like the one you're looking for. The `in` operator specifies a set of values to which the comparison value can be equal to one of. `exists` allows you to use a subquery as a lookup validity test for some piece of information. `between` specifies a range comparison, such as `between 1 AND 5`. **(Topic 3.1)**

37. A.   Use `define` to capture values.

Explanation   The `define` command can be used to identify a variable and assign it a value for use throughout a script running in SQL*Plus. This is useful when you are executing a number of SQL statements in batch. Although the `accept` command can perform the same function, the key factor that makes this the wrong answer is the mention of no user interaction in the question. Hard-coded values will work, but they make the script almost completely not reusable. Finally, although lexical references using an ampersand (&) followed by a label will provide statement reusability, your users will need to keep entering values every time a statement containing the lexical reference is processed. **(Topic 9.4)**

38. A.   `where EMP.EMPID = 39284 AND EMP.EMPID = EXPNS.EMPID;`

Explanation   Since you only want data from either table where there is a match in the other, you are performing a regular join or "equijoin" operation. In Oracle, you would not use the outer join (+) operator for this purpose. This eliminates both of the answer choices that contain an outer join operator. **(Topic 5.1)**

39. A.   DATE variables

Explanation   %type can be used to declare a variable as the same datatype as a table column, as in EMPLOYEE.LASTNAME%type for the LASTNAME column of the EMPLOYEE table. All other datatypes offered as choices are valid datatypes in PL/SQL, but not in Oracle tables, so you could not use the %type keyword to reference these datatypes in your code. Of the choices given, only DATE variables can be used as column datatypes in Oracle. **(Topic 19.2)**

40. C.   4104930504

Explanation   The only record that will not be present from the choices given is 4104930504, because UPC code #402392340 does not exist at the time this statement is issued. It was already changed to 50393950, and thus the 4104930504 update statement fails when you issue it. In order to get the answer right, you need to read the question for a long time, and that wastes time when you're taking the OCP exams. Be aware that this question can take up an enormous amount of time if you're not careful. **(Topic 10.5)**

41. D.   Views with object dependencies on the table being dropped will be rendered invalid automatically but will not be dropped.

Explanation   Oracle does not remove views when you drop underlying tables. Instead, Oracle merely marks the view as invalid. Thus, since choices A, B, and C all indicate in various different ways that the view will be dropped, all those choices are incorrect. **(Topic 13.5)**

42. C.   4

Explanation   The general rule of thumb here is that, if you have *n* tables you want to join—four in this case—you will generally need *n* – 1 comparison operations in your where clause joined together by AND—three in this case. In addition, the question states that you want to further restrict return data based on values in the first table. Thus, your where clause would have four conditions, and may look something like the following block:

```
WHERE
A.COLUMN1 = 5           AND
A.COLUMN1 = B.COLUMN1   AND
B.COLUMN2 = C.COLUMN2   AND
C.COLUMN3 = D.COLUMN3
```

(Topic 5.1)

43. B. `%type` variables

Explanation   You would use the `%type` keyword to assign the datatype of a variable dynamically according to the datatype in a column of a table. `%rowtype` is used for declaring variable records according to all columns in a table, so it is almost, but not quite, correct. VARCHAR2 variables might be the result of using `%type`, but remember that you didn't know the datatype of the variable you were declaring—only that it was the same for a particular column of a table. Finally, you will never wind up with a FLOAT variable, because Oracle does not allow FLOAT variables to be used as datatypes in table columns. **(Topic 19.2)**

44. A.   Password authentication and granting privileges

Explanation   Although in order to get database access you need to create user privileges, the two real components of Oracle's security model are password authentication and granting privileges. When users are created, they will still not be able to connect to Oracle unless they are granted a privilege (`create session`), and even when they connect, they still cannot see anything unless someone gives them permission via the `grant` command. **(Topic 16.1)**

45. C. `spool`

Explanation   The `spool` command makes SQL*Plus write an output file containing all information transacted in the session, from the time you turn spooling on and identify the output file to the time you either turn spooling off or end the session. `prompt` causes SQL*Plus to prompt you to enter data using a custom request message. `echo` causes an error because it is not a valid command in SQL*Plus. Finally, the `define` command is used for variable definition and variable assignment in SQL*Plus scripts. **(Topic 2.3)**

46. A.   Declaration and exception only

Explanation   The declaration section of your code block must contain the `pragma` keyword, a compiler directive used to associate named exceptions with internal Oracle errors. The exception handler must contain an exception handler for the named exception. The only area that does not require coding is the execution section of your code block, because Oracle will automatically raise your named exception whenever the internal error occurs in code execution. **(Topic 24.1)**

47. B.   `select A.STUDENT_ID, A.LOCATION, B.LOCATION from TEST_SCORE A, TEST_SCORE B where A.STUDENT_ID = B.STUDENT_ID AND A.LOCATION <> B.LOCATION AND trunc(A.TEST_DATE)+30 >= trunc(B.TEST_DATE) AND trunc(A.TEST_DATE)-30 <= trunc(B.TEST_DATE);`

Explanation Because it ensures that the student is the same and that the date the test was taken violated the 30-day rule, and that the test location is not the same, choice B is the correct answer. This question is probably the hardest on the exam. Even if you have a bit of SQL experience, this question will take you a while. When taking the OCP exam, the last thing you need is time-waster questions to throw you off. A good technique to avoid having questions like this one consume all your time is to skip it if you cannot answer it within 30 seconds. You'll most likely have some time at the end of the exam to review the questions you skipped. **(Topic 5.3)**

48. C. `select * from EMPLOYEE where empid = (select empid from invoice where invoice_no = 4399485);`

Explanation If you can use a subquery, you should do so. There is only one choice that displays a subquery, so that one must be the correct answer. All the other choices depend on the EMPID being provided, not using the invoice number. **(Topic 7.1)**

49. A. To put returned data into sorted order

Explanation The `having` clause is best used to include or exclude certain data groups, not to return data in sort order. The `order by` clause handles that task. **(Topic 6.4)**

50. D. Roles

Explanation Roles allow you to group privileges together into one object and grant the privileges to the user at one time. There are no privileges related to indexes other than the privilege to access the associated table. Tables and sequences both require privileges to be granted to a user or role; they do not simplify the act of privilege management in any way. **(Topic 16.2)**

51. A. `alter user`

Explanation The `alter user` statement with the `identified by` clause is used to change a user's password. `alter role` is used for modifying the actual role object, and affects users insofar as the user has been granted the role. Of the remaining choices, although user SNOW may be able to execute those statements depending on what privileges he is granted, none of these privileges will handle what the question requires. **(Topic 16.1)**

52. C.   User SNOW needs a synonym for table EMP.

Explanation   User SNOW needs a synonym in order to refer to a table he doesn't own without prefixing that reference with a schema owner. Without privileges, SNOW would not see the data, but even with the appropriate privileges granted, SNOW still needs to prefix the table name with the schema information if no synonym exists for the table in that schema. If there is no synonym, SNOW still must prefix references to EMP with REED, as in REED.EMP. Tables don't have passwords, databases do, so that choice is patently incorrect. **(Topic 15.4)**

53. C.   Whenever the `commit` command is issued

Explanation   In PL/SQL, data changes are committed using the `commit` command, and they will take place only when that command is issued. Oracle will not automatically `commit` data changes when the PL/SQL block ends, eliminating that choice. Only if a `commit` command is present after each individual `update` will the change be committed. Finally, if you are the creator of the block, when you disconnect from Oracle has nothing to do with another user making changes to data with your code. **(Topic 19.4)**

54. C.   Explicit cursors with a `cursor for` loop

Explanation   Using explicit cursors with a `cursor for` loop is the way to go for this situation. You would first need to write an explicit cursor so that you could work with each row individually, which eliminates all the implicit cursor choices. There is no way to "write" an implicit cursor, because implicit cursors are handled by the Oracle RDBMS in a way that is transparent to the user. However, the second part of the question is how you will move through each row of output. Here, you need a loop more than you need cursor attributes. **(Topic 22.1)**

55. D.   Passing EMPID values as parameters to the cursor

Explanation   You would reduce the number of cursors declared by having a single cursor that accepted a value for EMPID as a parameter. Although you might use the cursor in a `cursor for` loop, you wouldn't rely on that feature to reduce the overall number of cursors in your database. The variable declaration keyword `%rowtype` helps you reduce the amount of work you need to do to set up a record variable, but does nothing to reduce the number of cursors you declare. Finally, `%notfound` is an implicit cursor attribute that again has nothing to do with how many cursors you need to declare in your code block. **(Topic 23.1)**

56. D.   Oracle returns an error.

Explanation   In this situation, you cannot use the `order by` clause in a subquery. Oracle will return an error. Thus, no data will be returned from any table, so all of the other choices are wrong. **(Topic 7.4)**

57. D.   No special syntax is required.

Explanation   No special syntax is required to place SQL statements into your PL/SQL block. The **/*and*/** markers are used for commenting out portions of your code. `exec SQL` and colons are required only when embedding SQL statements into Pro*C programs, a topic not covered by this exam. **(Topic 19.3)**

58. B.   `select to_char(nvl(sqrt(59483), 0)) from dual;`

Explanation   The `select to_char(nvl(sqrt(59483), 0)) from dual;` statement is a valid statement. The `select nvl(sqrt(59483)) from dual;` statement does not pass enough parameters to the `nvl( )` function. The `select TO_CHAR(nvl(sqrt(59483), 'VALID')) from dual;` statement breaks the rule in `nvl( )` that states that both parameters passed into the function must be the same datatype. The `select (to_char(nvl(sqrt(59483), '0')) from dual;` statement is missing a matching closing parenthesis after `'0'`. **(Topic 4.2)**

59. C.   `column PLAY_TABLE heading 'My Plays and Authors'`

Explanation   The `heading` clause to the `column` command in SQL*Plus acts in the same way as a `column` alias does in SQL—it modifies the output of the query to use a heading of your design. Despite its similarity, however, the `heading` clause is not the same as an alias in SQL. Thus, both the choice identifying the `alias` clause and the choice using the `as` keyword are incorrect. The choice containing the `format` clause should be easy to eliminate. **(Topic 9.2)**

60. C.   BABS

Explanation   Since BABS is not listed in the contents of the MY_USERS table, JONES will not see BABS when he queries the view. Choices A, B, and D all identify users who are listed in the MY_USERS view, and thus will be seen by JONES when he queries BASEBALL_TEAM_VW. **(Topic 13.3)**

Answers to Practice Exam 2

1. C.

```
DECLARE
  CURSOR My_Employees IS
    SELECT name, title FROM employee;
BEGIN
  FOR csr_rec IN My_Employees LOOP
      INSERT INTO MY_EMPS (MY_EMPNAME, MY_EMPTITLE)
      VALUES (csr_rec.name, csr_rec.title);
    END LOOP;
END;
```

Explanation   If you understand the nature of a cursor for loop, you should be able to easily identify the correct answer. Otherwise, you should skip this question and come back to it because you will wind up wasting a lot of time reading the code for each choice—time better spent answering other easier questions. A cursor for loop does three things for you: it declares the fetch variable (csr_rec in the code block) implicitly, handles the exit condition automatically, and takes care of opening and closing the cursor without requiring you to code explicit open and close commands. **(Topic 23.3)**

2. C.   Use the set long statement.

Explanation   The set long command allows you to increase the buffer size SQL*Plus will use to retrieve LONG data values. This statement is used because the view text is stored in a LONG column in the appropriate dictionary view. The dictionary view itself does not need to be increased, nor can you somehow solve this problem with the alter user statement. Finally, the set NLS_DATE_FORMAT statement is used for formatting DATE values, not LONG columns. **(Topic 13.1)**

3. D.   group by COW_NAME;

Explanation   The problem with this statement is that not enough leading columns from the query are referred to in the group by clause. As a result, you will receive the ORA-00979 (not a group by expression) error. The correct group by clause would read group by FARM_NAME, COW_NAME;. All other areas of the statement are syntactically and semantically correct. **(Topic 6.3)**

4. E.   Anonymous blocks

Explanation All PL/SQL blocks are blocks that Oracle can store within the database, except for anonymous blocks. These are compiled and run when you submit them to Oracle, and then eventually discarded. There is little opportunity for you to reuse the code unless you store the code as a text file and rerun it in your session. **(Topic 17.1)**

    5. B. `mod(CARTON, FILL_STATUS)`

Explanation The line containing reference to the `mod( )` operation is the one containing the error. Because this is a single-row function, it cannot be used as the `group by` expression in a SQL statement. The rest of the statement is correct. If you substituted a grouping expression like `sum( )`, `avg( )`, or `count( )`, you would have a correct statement. **(Topic 6.2)**

    6. B. `select A.LASTNAME, B.DEPT_NO from EMP A, (select EMPID,`
        `DEPT_NO from DEPT) B where A.EMPID = B.EMPID;`

Explanation An inline view is an undeclared view consisting only of a parenthetical `select` statement in a `from` clause. This subquery is then treated like a view in other areas of the main query. While choices A and C involve the use of subqueries, only the use of a subquery in the `from` clause of a `select` statement constitutes an inline view. Choice D is not really a subquery at all, but rather a way to get SQL*Plus to write a `select` statement for every line of output from the query. **(Topic 8.3)**

    7. C. L

Explanation The square root of 40 is a fraction between 6 and 7, which rounds up to 7 according to the algorithm behind the `ceil( )` function. This means that the VAR2 = '7' flag in the `elsif` will resolve to true. Thus, VAR2 is set to `'L'`, and then written to the database with the `insert` statement at the end. Be careful not to waste time on reviewing all of the intricacies of the PL/SQL block provided. **(Topic 20.2)**

    8. D. 53699

Explanation Since you've fetched Lewis's balance of 50650 into VAR2 and then added 3,049 to it, you will be left with a value of 53699 in VAR1. Although VAR1 starts with a value of 90, your later manipulations eliminate that original value, making choice A incorrect. Choice B is incorrect because 3,049 isn't placed into VAR1: 50650 + 3049 is. Choice C is incorrect because 3049 is added to 50650 to give you the value of 53699 in VAR1. **(Topic 17.4)**

9. A. ``create function foo(VAR1 IN VARCHAR2) is``

Explanation   There is no definition of return value datatype in this code block, making the function declaration line the correct answer. Although it may seem that the ``if-then`` statement in the third line of the code block is incorrect because you are comparing a VARCHAR2 variable to the number 6, in reality, Oracle handles this situation just fine because there is an implicit type conversion occurring in the background. Finally, the ``select``, ``into``, ``from``, and ``where`` clauses of the fetch statement are all constructed correctly. **(Topic 17.2)**

10. D. ``drop table``

Explanation   This is not an easy question. To rid your table of an index associated with a constraint, you will need to modify the table to remove the constraint. The ``alter table drop constraint`` statement works for removing indexes associated with unique constraints, and the ``alter table drop primary key`` statement works for indexes associated with primary keys. Dropping the table removes all associated database objects, including indexes. However, simply dropping the index with the ``drop index`` statement is not possible. **(Topic 15.3)**

11. C. Every primary-key column value must be unique and none can be NULL.

Explanation   A primary-key column must contain all unique, non-NULL values, or else the primary-key constraint will be violated. Choices A and B are both partly correct, but each choice only tells part of the story. Choice D is patently false, and you should have been able to eliminate it immediately. **(Topic 12.2)**

12. C.   Table FOOBAR has no primary key and, therefore, no index on MOO.

Explanation   Because table FOOBAR has no primary key, you cannot obtain data from it rapidly the way you could if the MOO column were set up as the primary key, and thus indexed. So, although Oracle not using the primary key is technically true, the more accurate answer is that the table had no primary key to use and, therefore, no index on MOO. There are no views involved, and the table has not been dropped. **(Topic 11.2)**

13. D.   USER_INDEXES, indexes with the same name as the constraint

Explanation   Since an associated index is generated automatically by Oracle, you will look in the USER_INDEXES view to find the associated object. And, since Oracle uses the name of the constraint in order to name the index created with that constraint, you will look for indexes that have the name EMP_PK_01. There is little correlation between tables and sequences, other than sequences can be used to populate the columns of a table. The USER_TABLES view will offer little value either, since only the EMP table will appear in it, and you are not looking for another table with the same name. **(Topic 14.1)**

14. B.   To improve performance on columns with few unique values

Explanation   Bitmap indexes are primarily designed to improve performance on searches that involve column data that is static and has few unique values. The ideal example of this is a column that indicates whether a person is male or female—it usually doesn't change, and these are the only two choices. All of the other answer choices referring to table columns in this question identify when it is appropriate to use B-tree indexes, the other main type of index available in Oracle. Also, understand that indexes do not improve performance on sequences. **(Topic 15.1)**

15. D.   A loop exit condition must be defined.

Explanation   No loop exit condition is defined for this code block. You don't need an exception handler in this code block for it to execute properly, and since it is anonymous, you don't need execute permission on it, eliminating those answers. Finally, you don't have enough information to determine if the user cannot insert into the table, because you haven't been able to compile it yet. **(Topic 20.3)**

16. D.   Nothing, Oracle raises this as an exception automatically.

Explanation   Oracle raises an exception automatically when an attempt to `select` data `into` a fetch variable fails. However, to handle that exception, you would use the `no_data_found` exception, not `rowtype_mismatch`, making that choice incorrect. You also do not need to include an implicit cursor variable for Oracle to detect this situation, making the `%found` and `%notfound` choices incorrect as well. **(Topic 19.5)**

17. A.   `update employee set salary = 5000 where empid = 59694;`

Explanation   The statement in choice A correctly changes values in the table according to the criteria set forth in the question. Choices B and C are incorrect because the `set` clause changes the EMPID column and LASTNAME column, respectively, not the SALARY column. Finally, choice D is incorrect because although the SALARY column is changed, the change is made based on values in the LASTNAME column, rather than the EMPID column. **(Topic 10.2)**

18. D.   `where C.COW_NAME = 'BESS' AND C.CARTON_NUM = C1.CARTON_NUM;`

Explanation   Two components are required in your `where` clause—you need a join clause and something that only pulls records from COW_MILK for BESS. The right answer is `where C.COW_NAME = 'BESS' AND C.CARTON_NUM = C1.CARTON_NUM`. Another choice is similar to this one, but since it uses the "not equal" (`<>`) clause for getting information only for BESS, it is not the choice you want. The other two choices are incomplete, and therefore wrong. **(Topic 5.1)**

19. D. The `insert` statements contain duplicate data due to the reset sequence.

Explanation The correct answer is that the `insert` statements contain duplicate data due to the reset sequence. When you drop and re-create the sequence from its original code, you reset the start value for that sequence. Subsequent `insert` statements will then attempt to add rows where the value in the primary key is duplicated information. There is no information about read-only status in the question, so you should assume that the answer concerning the table being read-only is not correct. Dropping a sequence does nothing to a table's primary key—there is no relationship between the two. Finally, although it is true that any cached sequence values that existed when the sequence was dropped are now unusable, this point has little relevance to the question at hand. **(Topic 15.2)**

20. B. `exists`

Explanation Only when using the `exists` statement must you use a correlated subquery. Although you can use a subquery with your use of `in`, you are not required to do so because you can specify a set of values instead. The `between` keyword indicates a range of values and does not allow the use of a subquery. The `like` keyword is used for wildcard comparisons and also does not allow the use of a subquery. **(Topic 7.2)**

21. D. `abs()`

Explanation All of the functions except for `abs()` will give you a result of 4093 when you pass them 4093.505. `abs()` returns the absolute value of the number you pass into the function. `round()` can give you a result of 4093 if you also pass in a second parameter defining the precision to which you want to round the function, while `trunc()` will give you a result of 4093 with only 4093.505 as input. `floor()` gives you a result of 4093, because it is the logical opposite of the `ceil()` function. **(Topic 4.2)**

22. B. Use `accept` to capture the name value for each run.

Explanation The `accept` command is the best way to handle the situation. Although you could use `define` to assign a value to a variable used throughout the script, only `accept` allows you to dynamically enter a value for that variable. Lexical substitutions identified with the `&` character will only work for the current statement, meaning that the same value assigned in one statement will not be used in the next statement unless you reenter it. **(Topic 9.1)**

23. B.   `truncate`

Explanation   Once a `truncate` operation is complete, that's it—the change is made and saved. This is because `truncate` is not a DML operation that can be performed as part of a transaction. The `truncate` command is a DDL operation, and as such, it has an implied `commit` at the end of its execution. If you want to get the data back after truncating, you need to recover it. For the other operations listed as choices in this question—`insert`, `update`, and `delete` statements—Oracle allows you to discard the changes using the `rollback` command. **(Topic 11.5)**

24. A.   `savepoint`

Explanation   `savepoint` operations simply act as logical breakpoints in a transaction. They do not cause Oracle to save or discard data, but merely act as a breakpoint with which you can perform partial transaction rollbacks later. The `set transaction` and `commit` commands indicate the beginning of a new transaction. Creating a new session with Oracle implicitly begins a transaction as well. **(Topic 10.5)**

25. B.   A `from` clause

Explanation   No SQL statement can survive without a `from` clause. For this reason, Oracle provides you with the DUAL table, so that you can perform arithmetic operations on expressions and not on table data while still satisfying this syntactic construct. Since this statement already has a `select` clause, you don't need to add another. The `where` clause is optional; but since the statement already has one, you don't need to add another. Finally, your SQL statement does not require an `order by` clause. **(Topic 2.2)**

26. D.   Values from a cursor cannot be referenced directly.

Explanation   The problem lies in the line reading `...VALUES (UPC_CODE_CRSR);`. You cannot reference the cursor directly in this way because a cursor is merely an address in memory. Instead, you need to reference the values as they are fetched into a variable. The cursor-looping mechanism itself is fine and does not need to be rewritten. The exception handler does not need to be defined for the PL/SQL block, either. Finally, since this is an anonymous block, there is no concept of "having permission" to execute it—if you submit it, you can execute it. **(Topic 22.1)**

27. C.   Code a when others exception handler in PROC_A.

Explanation   The others exception handler in PROC_A will prevent exception propagation to the user level if no exception handler exists in PROC_B. Remember that Oracle always raises its own exceptions. If that exception is not handled locally, it is propagated to the next level up, where there must be either an explicit exception handler or the when others handler. **(Topic 18.3)**

28. B.   Declaration, execution, and exception

Explanation   The exception you define is a user-defined exception. You must include support for this type of exception in the declarative, execution, and exception sections of the PL/SQL block. Support for an Oracle predefined exception needs only to be included in the exception handler. If you wanted to associate an internal error with a named exception, you would code support for it in the declaration and exception section of your code block. **(Topic 24.1)**

29. A.   set transaction

Explanation   The set transaction command is used to define the transaction state to be read-only. rollback and commit statements are used to end the transaction. The savepoint command denotes logical breakpoints for the transaction. **(Topic 10.5)**

30. C.   Bitmap index

Explanation   Bitmap indexes work well in situations in which the data in the column is static. In this case, the column contains gender information, which rarely if ever changes. The number of distinct possible values is limited to only two as well. Thus, this column is a bad candidate for B-tree indexes of any sort, but perfect for bitmap indexes. Remember that B-tree indexes work well for columns with high cardinality or number of distinct values corresponding to the overall number of entries in the column. **(Topic 15.1)**

31. A.   Parent to child

Explanation   This question describes the relationship between the INVOICE and INVOICE_ITEM table, and the appropriate answer is parent to child. This is because the relationship described between invoices and invoice items is optional, given that invoices may have no invoice items, but that all invoice items must have a corresponding invoice. **(Topic 12.1)**

32. D.   ACTIVE

Explanation   The decode ( ) function acts as a case statement. The first parameter indicates the column whose values you want decoded. If the value in the column equals parameter 2, then decode( ) returns parameter 3. If the value in the column equals parameter 4, decode( ) returns parameter 5, and so on. If the value in the column doesn't equal any of the other parameters specified, then decode( ) returns the default value specified as the last parameter. Thus, since the column value is not specified for any of the parameters, the returned value is the default, ACTIVE. **(Topic 4.3)**

33. B.   Tablespaces

Explanation   A tablespace, the logical object used for storing database objects like tables and indexes, maps most directly to a datafile because tablespaces can have one or many datafiles. Although segments and extents are stored in datafiles, the mapping is much closer between tablespace and datafile because both are storage containers. Finally, although both containers are comprised of Oracle blocks, the concept of Oracle blocks has less meaning at the file-system level, where the datafile will look just like any other file in the host system. **(Topic 1.1)**

34. B, D, and E.   RDBMS defines how to obtain data for you, RDBMS allows flexibility in changing data relationships, *and* RDBMS is able to model relationships other than master/detail.

Explanation   A relational database differs from hierarchical databases like IMS in many ways. First, the RDBMS handles data-access methods implicitly within the engine, shielding users from defining how to access data physically on the machine (such as, "open this file," "search for this text string," and soon). Hierarchical systems require that you define methods to traverse the master/detail relationships to obtain information. Both hierarchical databases and RDBMS systems can store data in master/detail fashion, which eliminates one choice. Also, because hierarchical databases require that you store all data in master/detail format and define the methods used to access the data, hierarchical databases are less flexible than RDBMS systems when it comes to changing the way data relates to other data. Finally, RDBMS systems can model data in relationships other than master/detail. **(Topic 1.2)**

35. B.   Ease of integrating programs written in different languages

Explanation   Developers typically don't use PL/SQL if they need to integrate programs written in different languages as part of one application. Although later versions of Oracle allow integration with C using EXTPROC, integrating with other languages like COBOL, ADA, and FORTRAN generally makes better use of the Oracle precompilers. However, a developer might choose to use PL/SQL if it is important to have easy access to SQL, the ability to handle cursors, or the ability to handle error situations without necessarily needing to code an explicit conditional operation for every type of error encountered. **(Topic 1.3)**

36. D.   where COL_A in (select NUM from TAB_OF_NUMS)

Explanation   The where clause in choice D is an excellent example of the definition of a subquery, which is the example being asked for in the question. Choice A is not a comparison operation between a column and a set of values, because there is only one value being compared. Choice B is a comparison of a column to a set of values, but the set is static and defined at the time the query is issued. Choice C is a range-comparison operation, a variant on choice B, and therefore also wrong. Only choice D allows Oracle to dynamically generate the list of values to which COL_A will be compared. **(Topic 7.2)**

37. D.   select NAME from CONTESTANT where COUNTRY in (select COUNTRY from MEDALS where NUM_GOLD + NUM_SILVER + NUM_BRONZE > 10)

Explanation   The query in choice D is correct because it contains the subquery that correctly returns a subset of countries that have contestants who won 10 or more medals of any type. Choice A is incorrect because it contains a join operation, not a subquery. Choice B is simply a rewrite of choice A to use a multiple-row subquery, but does not go far enough to restrict return data. Choice C is a single-row subquery that does essentially the same thing as choice B. **(Topic 7.3)**

38. C.   Multiple-column subquery, the youngest contestant from all countries

Explanation   Since the main query compares against the results of two columns returned in the subquery, this is a multiple-column subquery that will return the youngest contestant from every country in the table. This multiple-column subquery is also a multiple-row subquery; but since the defining factor is the fact that two columns are present, you should focus more on that fact than on the rows being returned. This fact eliminates choices A and B. The subquery does return multiple rows, however. You should also be sensitive to the fact that the main query must use an in clause, not the equal sign (=), making choice D incorrect as well. **(Topic 8.1)**

39. A.   SOO

Explanation   The correct answer is SOO because the subquery operation specified by the in clause ignores NULL values implicitly. Thus, because SOO has no country defined, that row is not selected as part of the subquery. As a result, SOO won't show up as having the youngest age in the results of this query. **(Topic 8.2)**

40. B.   Table

Explanation   The object being referred to is a table. A table has many columns, each of which is functionally dependent on the key column. Choice A is incorrect because a cursor is simply the result of a query, which may or may not have been against a table, and does not require any kind of storage in a segment. A sequence is a number generator in Oracle that, again, does not require storage in a segment other than a dictionary segment, making choice C incorrect. Finally, a view is similar to a table in that it contains many columns, each of which is functionally dependent on the key. However, views contain no data needing to be stored in a segment, so choice D is wrong as well. **(Topic 11.1)**

41. B.   Executable

Explanation   The executable section of a PL/SQL block is where the main operation of the block is written. Thus, any conditional operation such as the one referred to by the question would be written in the executable section of the PL/SQL block. The declaration section is used to declare variables, eliminating choice A. The exception section is where exception handlers are defined for error management, eliminating choice C as well. Finally, no executable code appears in a package specification, eliminating choice D. **(Topic 17.2)**

42. A.   The variable is declared incorrectly.

Explanation   Variables must be declared in the declaration section of a code block, making choice A the correct answer. The looping mechanism is set up correctly, eliminating choice B. The `insert` statement is correct as well, eliminating choice C. Finally, choice D is incorrect because the loop does not need to be closed in an exception handler. It can be closed in the executable section as well. It is simply important that the cursor be closed somewhere. **(Topic 17.3)**

43. D.   Using the `start` command

Explanation   The `start` command in SQL*Plus is designed for executing the contents of a file. This file may or may not contain any of the other methods listed as choices. Thus, choice D is the correct answer. The `execute` command is definitely a way to execute PL/SQL blocks in SQL*Plus, and it is possible to execute PL/SQL blocks from within other PL/SQL blocks. These facts eliminate choices A and B. Finally, you can execute PL/SQL blocks from within `select` statements as long as the PL/SQL block being executed is a function. **(Topic 17.5)**

44. A and D.   `VAR_1 CONSTANT NUMBER(3) :=96;` *and*
        `VAR_1 NUMBER(3) INITIAL 96;`

Explanation   Declaring variables with initial values in Oracle PL/SQL is accomplished either by assigning a value to the variable at the time of declaration with the assignment operator (`:=`) or the `default` keyword. If you do not use either of these methods, your initial value declaration will not be correct. Choice A identifies the correct way to declare a constant; but, unfortunately, once a constant is declared you cannot assign another value to it. The `initial` keyword is used in storage declarations for database objects, not as part of the PL/SQL command syntax. **(Topic 17.4)**

45. C.   Execution section

Explanation   Only the execution section, as denoted by the begin and end keywords, is required in order for the PL/SQL block to compile. The declaration section is not required; but if it does appear, it must appear before the execution section. Thus, choice A is incorrect. The exception section is also not required, and can appear either at the end of the execution section or at any point within the execution section. Thus, choice B is incorrect. Finally, the "parameter passing" section or named PL/SQL block declaration section is not required because anonymous blocks are permitted in Oracle, thus making choice D incorrect as well. **(Topic 18.1)**

46. C.   The nested block must be defined after variables used in the main block.

Explanation   In PL/SQL, the rule about nested blocks is that the sub-block must be defined after the variables, cursors, and constants defined for use in the main block. Thus, choice C is correct. You can have named subprograms in anonymous blocks in PL/SQL, and there is no requirement in PL/SQL that variables passed to other blocks must have the same name as the parameter defined in the sub-block. In fact, there are compelling reasons not to do so. Finally, the default keyword is used as an alternative to the assignment operator in PL/SQL for giving a declared variable an initial value, thus making choice D incorrect as well. **(Topic 18.3)**

47. A.   Package constants in the local procedure

Explanation   You would not use synonyms to identify package constants in the local procedure, nor would you need to, since these constants would be available in the local procedure without any scoping difficulties. Choices B, C, and D all identify the types of situations in which synonyms are useful. These situations include reference to stand-alone procedures and tables in distributed databases, or reference to procedures and tables in the same database that are owned by different users. **(Topic 18.5)**

48. D.   goto

Explanation   Of the control structures given, only the goto command allows you to jump to a different portion of the PL/SQL block unconditionally. Even the if true statement, which always executes the block of code contained in the if-then (and thus, an if-then-else) structure, is not correct because it does not allow you to jump to a completely different section of code without running any kind of test. For this reason, choices A and C are incorrect. Finally, choice B is incorrect because a loop statement simply iterates through a block of code for as many times as specified by the looping construct. **(Topic 20.1)**

49. D.   NULL

Explanation   Because there is no row in the table where the country is Japan, the select statement returned no value. Thus, the length of VAR1 will be NULL. Anything evaluated in conjunction with NULL becomes NULL as well, and thus VAR2 is assigned when the length of VAR1 plus 55 is executed. Thus, choice D is the correct answer. **(Topic 20.4)**

50. A.   The label is not followed by an executable statement.

Explanation   All labels in PL/SQL statements must be unique within their scope and must also precede an executable statement. In this case, the label precedes an end loop clause, which is not an executable statement unto itself. Instead, the end loop clause is part of the overall iteration construct used to define the loop. Thus, you must have an executable statement following the label and before the end loop clause. Note that the NULL keyword can be used in this context following the label, because NULL by itself followed by a semicolon actually constitutes an executable statement. **(Topic 20.5)**

51. B.   TYPE cont_rec IS (
NAME VARCHAR2(20),
AGE NUMBER(5),
COUNTRY VARCHAR2(30));
CONTESTANT_RECORD
cont_rec;

Explanation   Choice B is the correct answer because the question asks you to define a user-defined record. This means that you need to first define the elements of this record using the type declaration command, and then define a variable as that type. Choice A simply has you declaring stand-alone variables for each of the elements in the record, which will work correctly but is not a user-defined record. Choice C is a representation of how to define a record using the %rowtype attribute, which is the most efficient way to define this record but is not a user-defined record unto itself. Finally, choice D identifies an invalid command syntax. **(Topic 21.1)**

52. D. CONTESTANT_TABLE is table of CONTESTANT%rowtype index by BINARY_INTEGER;

Explanation To declare a PL/SQL table of records where each record corresponds to a particular table in the Oracle database, you can use the %rowtype attribute in the table declaration itself, thus making choice D correct. Choice A is incorrect because you cannot define a PL/SQL table of records using native datatypes in the form of a multidimensional array, as the syntax in that choice's command would suggest. Choice B is also incorrect because the use of the %type attribute gives only one column datatype, thus making the PL/SQL table a one-dimensional table. Furthermore, the manner in which the type declaration is constructed is incorrect in that choice as well. Finally, choice C is missing the all-important indexing mechanism required in your PL/SQL table of record, making that choice incorrect as well. **(Topic 21.4)**

53. B and C. Value in MYVAL *and* CONTESTANT_NAME_TABLE.COUNT

Explanation After exiting the cursor for loop, the value in the MYVAL variable will represent the number of records in the PL/SQL table, so referencing that variable is one quick way to get the number of rows in the PL/SQL table. Another is to use the count attribute, available on every PL/SQL table. While you can develop another for loop to count the number of rows in the PL/SQL table, as indicated by choice D, this would require several additional lines of code. This is not as efficient as choices B or C, so choice D is wrong. Finally, you cannot reference a PL/SQL table using group functions in SQL the way you can in an Oracle database table, making choice A incorrect. **(Topic 21.3)**

54. D. PL/SQL table of records

Explanation When dealing with bulk data operations, if you want to use a PL/SQL variable to hold data from multiple table rows, your best bet is a PL/SQL table of records. This is because each record can act as a row of data, while the PL/SQL table indexing mechanism allows you to store each row as an element of an array. In essence, you store and treat the table data as a two-dimensional array. Choice A is incorrect because only a single row of data can be stored in a record. Choice B is incorrect because even though the cursor object can be used to refer to an entire table's worth of information, the cursor itself is merely an address in memory of an executed SQL statement, not an actual variable. Choice C is incorrect because a PL/SQL table is only a one-dimensional array, so only tables with single columns could be stored in it. **(Topic 21.5)**

55. C. Oracle retrieves all records in the CONTESTANT table into the cursor and locks those rows for update.

Explanation The `for update` clause allows you to simultaneously collect one or several rows from a table and place a lock on those rows in the table for change during the code block. The change will not be made until you issue an `update` statement, however, making choice D incorrect. Because Oracle does not try to update the statement, choice A is incorrect, too. It is important to remember that the `for update` clause also locks rows from the original table; otherwise, the cursor would simply select all of the data, and choice B would be correct. **(Topic 24.2)**

    56. A. `update CONTESTANT SET COUNTRY = 'USA' where current of asy_csr;`

Explanation The `where current of` clause allows you to reference back to the original table record corresponding to this cursor record without explicitly defining a `where` clause to do so in the `update` statement. Thus, you achieve the same functionality in choice A as you would get with choice C; but since choice C is attempting to reference the actual cursor value rather than the variable into which that cursor record's values were fetched, choice C is actually invalid. Choice B is also incorrect because the `for update` clause only locks the records for update, it doesn't actually change any records at all. Finally, because choice A is the correct answer, choice D is inherently incorrect. **(Topic 24.3)**.

    57. D. PL/SQL allows cursors to contain the same types of subqueries permitted in any SQL query.

Explanation Any subquery permitted in a SQL `select` statement is also fair game for a cursor. Choices B and C both identify types of subqueries permitted in cursors; but because both statements are correct, neither choice by itself is the complete answer, so both are wrong. Choice A is also wrong inherently. **(Topic 24.4)**

    58. B. PROC_C, PROC_B, PROC_A

Explanation PL/SQL first looks at the exception section in the current code block to find a handler for the exception being raised. If none is found, Oracle goes to the procedure caller's exception section to find a handler. This process continues either until an exception handler is identified or until the error is returned to the user level. However, Oracle will not return an error to the user level automatically in any situation; it will always attempt to identify an exception handler first. **(Topic 24.5)**

    59. C. Passing a SQL statement directly into the cursor `for` loop.

Explanation You can pass a SQL statement directly into a cursor `for` loop by enclosing the SQL statement in parentheses, eliminating the need for an explicitly declared cursor. Choices A and B are incorrect because you don't need to use dynamic SQL to perform this task. Finally, since you can pass SQL statements directly into cursor `for` loops, choice D is incorrect. **(Topic 22.3)**

60. C. %rowtype record

Explanation Since you're obtaining data from a table to place in a record, you should know immediately that this situation is perfect for records declared using the %rowtype keyword. The beauty of this method is that most of the work for creating the record is set up implicitly for you. The other choices identify records that require some explicit setup, and thus are incorrect. **(Topic 20.3)**

Answers to Practice Exam 3

1. A. A developer wants records to be added to an EXIT_STATUS table, regardless of whether or not the transaction completed successfully.

Explanation Autonomous transactions allow for procedures to execute their own transaction within the scope of their procedure, without interfering with the transaction that may have been going on within the calling procedure. This feature would allow the developer to create a procedure to add records to an EXIT_STATUS table and commit those records without disrupting the rollback of the transaction that would need to occur in the calling procedure if that transaction failed. Normal transaction processing in Oracle allows two users to make changes to different rows in different tables or the same table at the same time. Thus, choices B and C are eliminated. No user can make a change to the same row at the same time as another user. Table locks in Oracle prevent it. Thus, choice D is also eliminated. **(Topic 19.4)**

2. B. cube

Explanation The cube keyword included in a group by clause of a SQL statement in Oracle8i allows you to perform *N*-dimensional cross-tabulations within the Oracle database, returning the result set directly to the client. This keyword is useful in queries within data warehouses. Choice C is incorrect because even though the rollup keyword was also added to SQL queries in Oracle8i, this keyword supports subtotal and grand total calculations of grouped data. Although the having expression is also available in group operations, choice A is incorrect because you do not need to define a having clause in order to use either cube or rollup. Finally, choice D is incorrect because the trim( ) function combines the abilities of ltrim( ) and rtrim( ). **(Topic 6.1)**

3. B. group by

Explanation The group by clause is added by Oracle8i within the scope of summary management implicitly. This allows for query rewrite, and thus enhanced performance in the data warehouse. The order by clause is not implicitly added, thus making choice A incorrect. And, though `cube` and `rollup` may be used to add additional information to the output of the grouped query, this information is not added implicitly by summary management. **(Topic 6.1)**

4. D.   Level hierarchy

Explanation   When creating a dimension, two aspects must be defined. First, the various levels must be defined for the dimension. Second, the hierarchy between those levels must be defined. `cube` and `rollup` operations do not need to be defined, so choices A and B are incorrect. Also, summary management is not defined as part of the dimension definition, so choice C is incorrect. **(Topic 15.1)**

5. D.   Nested table

Explanation   Oracle recommends that, if individual items in the collection object must be accessed, you use TABLE; otherwise, use VARRAY. Since you want to access individual items in the collection object, choice D is correct and choice C is wrong. Choice A is wrong because although you'll want to use scalar types in the definition of the nested table type, the overall type will be a nested table, not scalar. Finally, choice B is wrong because even though the table type will be user defined, the specific choice of nested table more accurately reflects the answer. **(Topic 21.5)**

6. B.   Reverse-key indexes

Explanation   A reverse-key index is one in which the contents of the indexed column are reversed. This gives a higher amount of lead-in selectivity than a straight B-tree index would, because the cardinality of the root node in the B-tree would be low. This is based on the fact that most records would begin with 1 (recall the question content if you don't understand why), whereas the reverse of that key would have greater cardinality. Be careful of choice A, because although cardinality is high, choice B gives a better option for performance. Choice C is incorrect because bitmap indexes are designed for low-cardinality records like status or gender. Finally, choice D indicates an index type that wouldn't suit this situation. **(Topic 15.1)**

7. A.   VARCHAR2

Explanation   Since the text blocks are within the size limits imposed in Oracle8i for the VARCHAR2 datatype, it is best to use the scalar type rather than a large object for simplicity sake. If the block was larger than 4,000 bytes, you would most likely use a CLOB; but since the size requirement is less than 4,000 bytes, choice C is incorrect. You would use a BLOB to store binary large objects, making choice B incorrect. Finally, the text block is not stored as an external file (you would not use the BFILE type), making choice D incorrect. **(Topic 11.3)**

8. B and D.   `execute on procedure foobar( )` *and* `select on table FOO`

Explanation   Since the procedure contains the line AUTHID CURRENT_USER, this procedure will use invoker's rights execution. Thus, FLUFFY not only needs permission to run the procedure, but the user needs permission to perform all actions specified within the procedure, as well. Since no procedure is being created, choice A is incorrect. Since no table is being updated, choice C is incorrect. **(Topic 19.4)**

9. B.   Any uncommitted changes made to table TAB_2 by `my_tran( )` will not be seen by `upd_tran( )`.

Explanation   Any uncommitted transaction in a procedure that calls a second procedure defined to use autonomous transactions will not be seen by that second procedure. Since the transaction in `upd_tran( )` is autonomous, however, it will not `commit` changes made in `my_tran( )`, eliminating choice A. The `upd_tran( )` procedure will also encounter a deadlock if `my_tran( )` already has a lock on TAB_1, eliminating choice C. Finally, this procedure does not define invoker's rights execution, eliminating choice D. **(Topic 19.4)**

10. B.   There is no value associated with the constant.

Explanation   A value must be associated with a constant in the declaration section. If no value is given for the constant, an error will result. **(Topic 17.3)**

11. C.   Control will pass to the PL/SQL block caller's exception handler.

Explanation   If the exception raised is not handled locally, PL/SQL will attempt to handle it at the level of the process that called the PL/SQL block. If the exception is not handled there, PL/SQL will keep attempting to find an exception handler that will resolve the exception. If none is found, the error will be returned to the user. **(Topic 24.5)**

12. A.   Implicit cursors are used for SQL statements that are not named.

Explanation   Implicit cursors are used for all SQL statements except for those statements that are named. They are never incorporated into `cursor for` loops, nor is much care given to using them more or less, which eliminates choices B and C. They are definitely a feature of Oracle, eliminating choice D. **(Topic 22.1)**

13. D.   Requires `exit` condition to be defined

Explanation   A `cursor for` loop handles just about every feature of cursor processing automatically, including `exit` conditions. **(Topic 22.3)**

14. A.   Use `EMPLOYEE.LASTNAME%type`.

Explanation   The only option in this question that allows the developer to use referential type declarations for columns is choice A. Choice B uses the `%rowtype` referential datatype, which defines a record variable and is not what the developer is after. **(Topic 19.2)**

15. B.   A numeric value representing the number of rows updated

Explanation   `%rowtype` returns the numeric value representing the number of rows that were manipulated by the SQL statement. **(Topic 21.2)**

16. A, C, and D.   `%found`, `%notfound`, `%rowcount`

Explanation   These three are the only choices that are valid cursor attributes. The `%too_many_rows` attribute does not exist in PL/SQL. The `%rowtype` is a keyword that can be used to declare a record variable that can hold all column values from a particular table. **(Topic 19.5)**

17. D.   `exit`

Explanation   Without an `exit` statement, a simple loop will not stop. Though the `loop` and `end loop` keywords are needed to define the loop, you should assume these are in place and you are only trying to figure out how to end the loop. The `if-then` syntax might be used to determine a test condition for when the loop execution should terminate, but it is not required in and of itself to end the loop process execution. **(Topic 20.3)**

18. B.   `others`

Explanation   There is no `others` exception. The `others` exception handler handles all exceptions that may be raised in a PL/SQL block that do not have exception handlers explicitly defined for them. All other choices identify Oracle predefined exceptions that are all caught by the `others` keyword when used in an exception handler. If there is no specific handler for another named exception, the `others` exception handler will handle that exception. **(Topic 24.4)**

19. C.   `into action_record`

Explanation   The `into` clause is not permitted in cursors, nor is it required. Your fetch operation will obtain the value in the current cursor record from the cursor. **(Topic 22.1)**

20. D.   None, `cursor for` loops handle cursor opening implicitly.

Explanation   The `cursor for` loops handle, among other things, the opening, parsing, and executing of named cursors. **(Topic 22.3)**

21. D.   All `exit` conditions for `while` loops are handled in the `exit when` clause.

Explanation   There is no need for an `exit` statement in a `while` loop, since the exiting condition is defined in the `while` statement, eliminating choice A. Choice B is also wrong because you don't specifically need to use a counter in a `while` loop the way you do in a `for` loop. Finally, choice C is incorrect because even though the `exit` condition for a `while` loop evaluates to a Boolean value (for example, `exit when (this_condition_is_true)`, the mechanism to handle the exit does not require an explicit `if-then` statement. **(Topic 20.3)**

22. C.   L

Explanation   The fourth letter in the word *processing* is C, which means that the portion of the `if-then` statement where VAR1 = C will be used to determine the value for VAR2 (L in this case). Thus, VAR2 is set to `'L'`, and then written to the database with the `insert` statement at the end. During the OCP exam, be careful not to waste time on reviewing all of the intricacies of the PL/SQL block provided. **(Topic 20.2)**

23. D.   VAR1 := VAR2 + 3079;

Explanation   The main problem with this block of PL/SQL code has to do with the VAR1 := VAR2 + 3079 statement. This is because VAR1 cannot be assigned a value in this code block because the variable is defined as a constant. `MYVAR2 NUMBER := 0;` is a proper variable declaration. The `into VAR2` clause is appropriate in a PL/SQL fetch statement. Finally, the `where NAME = 'SMITH';` clause is well constructed. All other lines of code in the block not identified as choices are syntactically and semantically correct. **(Topic 17.2)**

24. B.   select GENDER into VAR1 from EMP

Explanation   The assignment of a value to an "in" variable defined in function creation is not permitted, thus making choice B correct. There is a definition of return value datatype in this code block, making the function declaration line an incorrect answer. Although it may seem that the `if-then` statement in the third line of the code block is incorrect because you are comparing a VARCHAR2 variable to the number 6, Oracle handles this situation just fine because there is an implicit type conversion occurring in the background. Finally, the `where` clauses of the fetch statement are all constructed correctly. **(Topic 20.2)**

25. B.   The index will be dropped.

Explanation   Like automatically generated indexes associated with a table's primary key, the indexes created manually on a table to improve performance will be dropped if the table is dropped. Choices A, C, and D are therefore invalid. **(Topic 15.3)**

26. C.   Columns with high cardinality are handled well by B-tree indexes.

Explanation   Columns with low cardinality are the bane of B-tree indexes, eliminating choice A. Furthermore, bitmap indexes are primarily used for performance gains on columns with low cardinality, eliminating choice B. **(Topic 15.1)**

27. D.   Drop and re-create the view with references to select more columns.

Explanation   Choice A is incorrect because adding columns to the underlying table will not add columns to the view, but will likely invalidate the view. Choice B is incorrect because the `alter view` statement simply recompiles an existing view definition, whereas the real solution here is to change the existing view definition by dropping and re-creating the view. Choice C is incorrect because a correlated subquery will likely worsen performance, and underscores the real problem—a column must be added to the view. **(Topic 13.2)**

28. C.   `maxvalue`

Explanation   The `maxvalue` option is a valid option for sequence creation. Choices A and B are both part of the `create user` statement, while choice D is a part of a constraint declaration in an `alter table` or `create table` statement. **(Topic 15.2)**

29. F.   This statement contains no errors.

Explanation   Even though the reference to `with check option` is inappropriate, considering that inserts into complex views are not possible, the statement will not actually produce an error when compiled. Therefore, there are no errors in the view. This is not something that can be learned. It requires hands-on experience with Oracle. **(Topic 15.3)**

30. A.   `references`

Explanation   The `references` privilege gives the user the ability to refer back to your table in order to link to it via a foreign key from his or her table to yours. Choice B is incorrect because the `index` privilege allows the user to create an index on a table, while choice C is incorrect because the `select` privilege allows users to query data in your table. Finally, choice D is incorrect because the `delete` privilege is only required for allowing the other user to delete data into your table. **(Topic 16.3)**

31. A, B, and C. Roles can be granted to other roles, privileges can be granted to roles, *and* roles can be granted to users.

Explanation   Choice D is the only option not available to managing roles. Roles cannot be granted to synonyms. **(Topic 16.2)**

32. C.   It is equal to NEXTVAL.

Explanation   Once NEXTVAL is referenced, the sequence increments the integer and changes the value of CURRVAL to be equal to NEXTVAL. **(Topic 15.2)**

33. D. `with check option`

Explanation   The appropriate clause is `with check` option. You can add this clause to a `create view` statement so that the view will not allow you to add rows to the underlying table that cannot then be selected in the view. The `with admin option` and `with grant option` clauses are used to assign administrative ability to users along with granting them a privilege. The `with security` option is a work of fiction—it does not exist in Oracle. **(Topic 16.4)**

34. C.   The statement fails due to primary-key constraint.

Explanation   It should be obvious that the statement fails—the real question here is why. The reason is because of the primary-key constraint on UPC_CODE. As soon as you try to add a duplicate record, the table will reject the addition. Although the view has `with check option` specified, this is not the reason the addition fails. It would be the reason an `insert` fails if you attempt to add a record for a day other than today, however. **(Topic 13.4)**

35. A. `drop view`

Explanation   When a table is dropped, Oracle eliminates all related database objects, such as triggers, constraints, and indexes. The exception is views. Views are actually considered separate objects; and although the view will not function properly after you drop the underlying table, Oracle will keep the view around after the table is dropped. **(Topic 13.5)**

36. C.   The `select` will receive NO ROWS SELECTED.

Explanation   Although the query will succeed (translation—you won't receive an error), you must beware of the distracter in choice B. In reality, choice C is the better answer because it more accurately identifies what really will occur when you issue this statement. This view will behave as any `select` statement would when you list criteria in the `where` clause that no data satisfies, by returning NO ROWS SELECTED. This is not an error condition, but you wouldn't call it a successful search for data, either, making both those choices incorrect. Finally, select statements never add data to a table. **(Topic 13.3)**

37. B and D.   UNIQUE constraints *and* primary keys

Explanation   Every constraint that enforces uniqueness creates an index to assist in the process. The two integrity constraints that enforce uniqueness are UNIQUE constraints and primary keys. **(Topic 12.2)**

38. C.   ALL_IND_COLUMNS

Explanation   This view is the only one listed that provides column positions in an index. Since primary keys create an index, the index created by the primary key will be listed with all the other indexed data. Choice A is incorrect because no view exists in Oracle called ALL_PRIMARY_KEYS. Choice B is incorrect because, although USER_CONSTRAINTS lists information about the constraints in a database, it does not contain information about the index created by the primary key. Choice D is incorrect because ALL_TABLES contains no information related to the position of a column in an index. **(Topic 14.2)**

39. C.   A table named ANIMALS will be created in the ANJU schema with the same data as the ANIMALS table owned by MASTER.

Explanation   This question requires you to look carefully at the create table statement in the question and to know some things about table creation. First, a table is always created in the schema of the user who created it. Second, since the create table as select clause was used, choices B and D are both incorrect because they identify the table being created as something other than ANIMALS, among other things. Choice A identifies the schema into which the ANIMALS table will be created as MASTER, which is incorrect for the reasons just stated. **(Topic 11.2)**

40. A.   insert into EMPLOYEE values (59694, 'HARRIS', NULL);

Explanation   This choice is acceptable because the positional criteria for not specifying column order are met by the data in the values clause. When you would like to specify that no data be inserted into a particular column, one method of doing so is to insert a NULL. Choice B is incorrect because not all columns in the table have values identified. When using positional references to populate column data, there must be values present for every column in the table. Otherwise, the columns that will be populated should be named explicitly. Choice C is incorrect because when a column is named for data inserted in the insert into clause, a value must definitely be specified in the values clause. Choice D is incorrect because using the multiple row insert option with a select statement is not appropriate in this situation. **(Topic 10.2)**

41. A.   Two tables in the database are named VOUCHER and VOUCHER_ITEM, respectively.

Explanation   This choice implies the use of a naming convention similar to the one we discussed in the chapter, where the two tables with a foreign-key relationship are given similar names. Although there is no guarantee that these two tables are related, the possibility is strongest in this case. Choice B implies the same naming convention; and since the two tables' names are dissimilar, there is little likelihood that the tables are related in any way. Choice C is incorrect because the date a table is created has absolutely no bearing on what function the table serves in the database. Choice D is incorrect because two tables *cannot* be related if there are no common columns between them. **(Topic 12.1)**

42. A, B, and D.   CHAR, VARCHAR2, *and* NUMBER

Explanation   BOOLEAN is the only invalid datatype in this listing. Although BOOLEAN is a valid datatype in PL/SQL, it is not a datatype available in the Oracle database, meaning that you cannot create a column in a table that uses the BOOLEAN datatype. **(Topic 11.3)**

43. D.   The `delete` statement will remove all records from the table.

Explanation   There is only one effect produced by leaving off the `where` clause from any statement that allows one: the requested operation is performed on all records in the table. **(Topic 10.4)**

44. C.   GOOD_NAME VARCHAR2 (20) check (GOOD_NAME in (select NAME from AVAIL_GOODS)),

Explanation   A CHECK constraint cannot contain a reference to another table, nor can it reference a virtual column, such as ROWID or SYSDATE. The other lines of the `create table` statement contain correct syntax. **(Topic 11.2)**

45. A.   Locks

Explanation   Locks are the mechanisms that prevent more than one user at a time from making changes to the database. All other options refer to the commands that are issued to mark the beginning, middle, and end of a transaction. Remember, the `commit` and `rollback` keywords end the current transaction and begin a new one, while the `savepoint` keyword marks a logical breakpoint within the transaction. **(Topic 10.5)**

46. A.   Use the `alter table` statement.

Explanation   The `alter table` statement is the only choice offered that allows the developer to increase the number of columns per table. Choice B is incorrect because setting a column to all NULL values for all rows does simply that. Choice C is incorrect because increasing the adjacent column sizes simply increases the sizes of the columns. Choice D is incorrect because the listed steps outline how to add a column with a `NOT NULL` constraint, something not specified by the question. **(Topic 11.4)**

47. B.   Truncate the table.

Explanation   Choices A and C may work, but an upgrade of hardware and software will cost far more than truncating the table (choice B). Choice D is partly correct, as there will be some change required to the high-water mark, but the change is to reset, not eliminate entirely. **(Topic 11.5)**

48. A.   `UNIQUE`

Explanation   Only `UNIQUE` and `PRIMARY KEY` constraints require Oracle to generate an index that supports or enforces the uniqueness of the column values. `FOREIGN KEY`, `CHECK`, and `not NULL` constraints do not require an index. **(Topic 12.1)**

49. B.   All values in the referenced column in the parent table must be present in the referencing column in the child.

Explanation   Referential integrity is from child to parent, not vice versa. The parent table can have many values that are not present in child records, but the child record must correspond to something in the parent. Thus, the correct answer is all values in the referenced column in the parent table must be present in the referencing column in the child. **(Topic 12.1)**

50. B.   Values must be part of a fixed set defined by `create` or `alter table`.

Explanation   A `CHECK` constraint may only use fixed expressions defined when you create or alter the table with the constraint definition. The reserved words like `sysdate` and `user`, or values from a lookup table, are not permitted, making those answers incorrect. Finally, NULL values in a column are constrained by `NOT NULL` constraints, a relatively unsophisticated form of check constraints. **(Topic 11.2)**

51. B.   `sqrt( )`

Explanation   Square root operations are performed on one column value. **(Topic 6.3)**

52. B. The tables in the join need to have common columns.

Explanation It is possible that a join operation will produce no return data, just as it is possible for any `select` statement not to return any data. Choices A, C, and D represent the spectrum of possibilities for shared values that may or may not be present in common columns. However, joins themselves are not possible without two tables having common columns. **(Topic 5.1)**

53. D. Until the session completes

Explanation A variable defined by the user during a session with SQL*Plus will remain defined until the session ends or until the user explicitly undefines the variable. **(Topic 9.1)**

54. B and C. Alter the `prompt` clause of the `accept` command *and* enter a new prompt in the `login.sql` file.

Explanation Choice D should be eliminated immediately, leaving the user to select between A, B, and C. Choice A is incorrect because `config.ora` is a feature associated with Oracle's client/server network communications product. Choice C is correct, because you can use the `set sqlprompt` command within your `login.sql` file. This is a special Oracle file that will automatically configure aspects of the SQL*Plus session, such as the default text editor, column and NLS data formats, and other items. **(Topic 9.5)**

55. A and C. `select * from EMPLOYEE where EMPID = &empid;` *and*
`select * from EMPLOYEE where EMPID =`
`(select empid from invoice where INVOICE_NO = 4399485);`

Explanation Choice A details the use of a runtime variable that can be used to have the user input appropriate search criteria after the statement has begun processing. Choice C details the use of a subquery that allows the user to select unknown search criteria from the database using known methods for obtaining the data. Choice B is incorrect because the statement simply provides a known search criterion; choice D is incorrect because it provides no search criteria at all. **(Topic 9.1)**

56. A. Ampersand

Explanation The ampersand (&) character is used by default to define runtime variables in SQL*Plus. **(Topic 9.1)**

57. C.   `select e.empid, d.head from EMPLOYEE e, dept d where`
`e.dept# = d.dept# (+);`

Explanation   Choice C details the outer join operation most appropriate to this user's needs. The outer table in this join is the DEPT table, as identified by the `(+)` marker next to the DEPT# column in the comparison operation that defines the join. **(Topic 5.2)**

58. B, C, and D.   To exclude certain data groups based on known criteria, to include certain data groups based on unknown criteria, *and* to include certain data groups based on known criteria

Explanation   All exclusion or inclusion of grouped rows is handled by the `having` clause of a `select` statement. Choice A is not an appropriate answer because sort order is given in a `select` statement by the `order by` clause. **(Topic 6.4)**

59. B.   Produced as a result of a join `select` statement with no `where` clause

Explanation   A Cartesian product is the result dataset from a `select` statement where all data from both tables is returned. A potential cause of a Cartesian product is not specifying a `where` clause for the join `select` statement. **(Topic 5.1)**

60. D.   Issuing the `set define` command

Explanation   Choice A is incorrect because a change to the `init.ora` file will alter the parameters Oracle uses to start the database instance. Choice B is incorrect because, although the `login.sql` file can define many properties in a SQL*Plus session, the character that denotes runtime variables is not one of them. Choice C is incorrect because the `define` command is used to define variables used in a session, not an individual statement. **(Topic 9.2)**

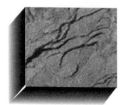

Index

INTERNATIONAL CONTACT INFORMATION

AUSTRALIA
McGraw-Hill Book Company Australia Pty. Ltd.
TEL +61-2-9417-9899
FAX +61-2-9417-5687
http://www.mcgraw-hill.com.au
books-it_sydney@mcgraw-hill.com

CANADA
McGraw-Hill Ryerson Ltd.
TEL +905-430-5000
FAX +905-430-5020
http://www.mcgrawhill.ca

GREECE, MIDDLE EAST,
NORTHERN AFRICA
McGraw-Hill Hellas
TEL +30-1-656-0990-3-4
FAX +30-1-654-5525

MEXICO (Also serving Latin America)
McGraw-Hill Interamericana Editores S.A. de C.V.
TEL +525-117-1583
FAX +525-117-1589
http://www.mcgraw-hill.com.mx
fernando_castellanos@mcgraw-hill.com

SINGAPORE (Serving Asia)
McGraw-Hill Book Company
TEL +65-863-1580
FAX +65-862-3354
http://www.mcgraw-hill.com.sg
mghasia@mcgraw-hill.com

SOUTH AFRICA
McGraw-Hill South Africa
TEL +27-11-622-7512
FAX +27-11-622-9045
robyn_swanepoel@mcgraw-hill.com

UNITED KINGDOM & EUROPE
(Excluding Southern Europe)
McGraw-Hill Education Europe
TEL +44-1-628-502500
FAX +44-1-628-770224
http://www.mcgraw-hill.co.uk
computing_neurope@mcgraw-hill.com

ALL OTHER INQUIRIES Contact:
Osborne/McGraw-Hill
TEL +1-510-549-6600
FAX +1-510-883-7600
http://www.osborne.com
omg_international@mcgraw-hill.com

Knowledge is power. To which we say,

crank up the power.

Are you ready for a power surge?

Accelerate your career—become an **Oracle Certified Professional (OCP)**. With Oracle's cutting-edge *Instructor-Led Training*, *Technology-Based Training*, and this *guide*, you can prepare for certification faster than ever. Set your own trajectory by logging your personal training plan with us. Go to **http://education.oracle.com/tpb**, where we'll help you pick a training path, select your courses, and track your progress. We'll even send you an email when your courses are offered in your area. If you don't have access to the Web, call us at 1-800-441-3541 (Outside the U.S. call +1-310-335-2403).

Power learning has never been easier.

ORACLE
University

Get Your FREE Subscription to *Oracle Magazine*

Oracle Magazine is essential gear for today's information technology professionals. Stay informed and increase your productivity with every issue of *Oracle Magazine*. Inside each **FREE,** bimonthly issue you'll get:

- Up-to-date information on Oracle Database Server, Oracle Applications, Internet Computing, and tools
- Third-party news and announcements
- Technical articles on Oracle products and operating environments
- Development and administration tips
- Real-world customer stories

Three easy ways to subscribe:

1. Web   **Visit our Web site at www.oracle.com/oramag/. You'll find a subscription form there, plus much more!**

2. Fax   Complete the questionnaire on the back of this card and fax the questionnaire side only to **+1.847.647.9735.**

3. Mail   Complete the questionnaire on the back of this card and mail it to P.O. Box 1263, Skokie, IL 60076-8263.

If there are other Oracle users at your location who would like to receive their own subscription to *Oracle Magazine*, please photocopy this form and pass it along.

☐ YES! Please send me a FREE subscription to *Oracle Magazine*.   ☐ NO

To receive a free bimonthly subscription to *Oracle Magazine*, you must fill out the entire card, sign it, and date it (incomplete cards cannot be processed or acknowledged). You can also fax your application to **+1.847.647.9735. Or subscribe at our Web site at www.oracle.com/oramag/**

SIGNATURE (REQUIRED)	X	DATE	

NAME		TITLE	
COMPANY		TELEPHONE	
ADDRESS		FAX NUMBER	
CITY		STATE	POSTAL CODE/ZIP CODE
COUNTRY		E-MAIL ADDRESS	

☐ From time to time, Oracle Publishing allows our partners exclusive access to our e-mail addresses for special promotions and announcements. To be included in this program, please check this box.

You must answer all eight questions below.

1 What is the primary business activity of your firm at this location? *(check only one)*
- ☐ 03 Communications
- ☐ 04 Consulting, Training
- ☐ 06 Data Processing
- ☐ 07 Education
- ☐ 08 Engineering
- ☐ 09 Financial Services
- ☐ 10 Government—Federal, Local, State, Other
- ☐ 11 Government—Military
- ☐ 12 Health Care
- ☐ 13 Manufacturing—Aerospace, Defense
- ☐ 14 Manufacturing—Computer Hardware
- ☐ 15 Manufacturing—Noncomputer Products
- ☐ 17 Research & Development
- ☐ 19 Retailing, Wholesaling, Distribution
- ☐ 20 Software Development
- ☐ 21 Systems Integration, VAR, VAD, OEM
- ☐ 22 Transportation
- ☐ 23 Utilities (Electric, Gas, Sanitation)
- ☐ 98 Other Business and Services

2 Which of the following best describes your job function? *(check only one)*
CORPORATE MANAGEMENT/STAFF
- ☐ 01 Executive Management (President, Chair, CEO, CFO, Owner, Partner, Principal)
- ☐ 02 Finance/Administrative Management (VP/Director/ Manager/Controller, Purchasing, Administration)
- ☐ 03 Sales/Marketing Management (VP/Director/Manager)
- ☐ 04 Computer Systems/Operations Management (CIO/VP/Director/ Manager MIS, Operations)

IS/IT STAFF
- ☐ 07 Systems Development/ Programming Management
- ☐ 08 Systems Development/ Programming Staff
- ☐ 09 Consulting
- ☐ 10 DBA/Systems Administrator
- ☐ 11 Education/Training
- ☐ 14 Technical Support Director/ Manager
- ☐ 16 Other Technical Management/Staff
- ☐ 98 Other

3 What is your current primary operating platform? *(check all that apply)*
- ☐ 01 DEC UNIX
- ☐ 02 DEC VAX VMS
- ☐ 03 Java
- ☐ 04 HP UNIX
- ☐ 05 IBM AIX
- ☐ 06 IBM UNIX
- ☐ 07 Macintosh
- ☐ 09 MS-DOS
- ☐ 10 MVS
- ☐ 11 NetWare
- ☐ 12 Network Computing
- ☐ 13 OpenVMS
- ☐ 14 SCO UNIX
- ☐ 24 Sequent DYNIX/ptx
- ☐ 15 Sun Solaris/SunOS
- ☐ 16 SVR4
- ☐ 18 UnixWare
- ☐ 20 Windows
- ☐ 21 Windows NT
- ☐ 23 Other UNIX _____
- ☐ 98 Other _____
- 99 ☐ **None of the above**

4 Do you evaluate, specify, recommend, or authorize the purchase of any of the following? *(check all that apply)*
- ☐ 01 Hardware
- ☐ 02 Software
- ☐ 03 Application Development Tools
- ☐ 04 Database Products
- ☐ 05 Internet or Intranet Products
- 99 ☐ **None of the above**

5 In your job, do you use or plan to purchase any of the following products or services? *(check all that apply)*
SOFTWARE
- ☐ 01 Business Graphics
- ☐ 02 CAD/CAE/CAM
- ☐ 03 CASE
- ☐ 05 Communications
- ☐ 06 Database Management
- ☐ 07 File Management
- ☐ 08 Finance
- ☐ 09 Java
- ☐ 10 Materials Resource Planning
- ☐ 11 Multimedia Authoring
- ☐ 12 Networking
- ☐ 13 Office Automation
- ☐ 14 Order Entry/Inventory Control
- ☐ 15 Programming
- ☐ 16 Project Management
- ☐ 17 Scientific and Engineering
- ☐ 18 Spreadsheets
- ☐ 19 Systems Management
- ☐ 20 Workflow

HARDWARE
- ☐ 21 Macintosh
- ☐ 22 Mainframe
- ☐ 23 Massively Parallel Processing
- ☐ 24 Minicomputer
- ☐ 25 PC
- ☐ 26 Network Computer
- ☐ 28 Symmetric Multiprocessing
- ☐ 29 Workstation

PERIPHERALS
- ☐ 30 Bridges/Routers/Hubs/Gateways
- ☐ 31 CD-ROM Drives
- ☐ 32 Disk Drives/Subsystems
- ☐ 33 Modems
- ☐ 34 Tape Drives/Subsystems
- ☐ 35 Video Boards/Multimedia

SERVICES
- ☐ 37 Consulting
- ☐ 38 Education/Training
- ☐ 39 Maintenance
- ☐ 40 Online Database Services
- ☐ 41 Support
- ☐ 36 Technology-Based Training
- ☐ 98 Other _____
- 99 ☐ **None of the above**

6 What Oracle products are in use at your site? *(check all that apply)*
SERVER/SOFTWARE
- ☐ 01 Oracle8
- ☐ 30 Oracle8*i*
- ☐ 31 Oracle8*i* Lite
- ☐ 02 Oracle7
- ☐ 03 Oracle Application Server
- ☐ 04 Oracle Data Mart Suites
- ☐ 05 Oracle Internet Commerce Server
- ☐ 32 Oracle *inter*Media
- ☐ 33 Oracle JServer
- ☐ 07 Oracle Lite
- ☐ 08 Oracle Payment Server
- ☐ 11 Oracle Video Server

TOOLS
- ☐ 13 Oracle Designer
- ☐ 14 Oracle Developer
- ☐ 54 Oracle Discoverer
- ☐ 53 Oracle Express
- ☐ 51 Oracle JDeveloper
- ☐ 52 Oracle Reports
- ☐ 50 Oracle WebDB
- ☐ 55 Oracle Workflow

ORACLE APPLICATIONS
- ☐ 17 Oracle Automotive
- ☐ 35 Oracle Business Intelligence System
- ☐ 19 Oracle Consumer Packaged Goods
- ☐ 39 Oracle E-Commerce
- ☐ 18 Oracle Energy
- ☐ 20 Oracle Financials
- ☐ 28 Oracle Front Office
- ☐ 21 Oracle Human Resources
- ☐ 37 Oracle Internet Procurement
- ☐ 22 Oracle Manufacturing
- ☐ 40 Oracle Process Manufacturing
- ☐ 23 Oracle Projects
- ☐ 34 Oracle Retail
- ☐ 29 Oracle Self-Service Web Applications
- ☐ 38 Oracle Strategic Enterprise Management
- ☐ 25 Oracle Supply Chain Management
- ☐ 36 Oracle Tutor
- ☐ 41 Oracle Travel Management

ORACLE SERVICES
- ☐ 61 Oracle Consulting
- ☐ 62 Oracle Education
- ☐ 60 Oracle Support
- ☐ 98 Other _____
- 99 ☐ **None of the above**

7 What other database products are in use at your site? *(check all that apply)*
- ☐ 01 Access
- ☐ 02 Baan
- ☐ 03 dbase
- ☐ 04 Gupta
- ☐ 05 IBM DB2
- ☐ 06 Informix
- ☐ 07 Ingres
- ☐ 08 Microsoft Access
- ☐ 09 Microsoft SQL Server
- ☐ 10 PeopleSoft
- ☐ 11 Progress
- ☐ 12 SAP
- ☐ 13 Sybase
- ☐ 14 VSAM
- ☐ 98 Other _____
- 99 ☐ **None of the above**

8 During the next 12 months, how much do you anticipate your organization will spend on computer hardware, software, peripherals, and services for your location? *(check only one)*
- ☐ 01 Less than $10,000
- ☐ 02 $10,000 to $49,999
- ☐ 03 $50,000 to $99,999
- ☐ 04 $100,000 to $499,999
- ☐ 05 $500,000 to $999,999
- ☐ 06 $1,000,000 and over

If there are other Oracle users at your location who would like to receive a free subscription to *Oracle Magazine*, please photocopy this form and pass it along, or contact Customer Service at **+1.847.647.9630**

Form 5

OPRESS

About the BeachFrontQuizzer™ CD-ROM

BeachFrontQuizzer provides interactive certification exams to help you prepare for certification. With the enclosed CD, you can test your knowledge of the topics covered in this book with more than 500 multiple choice and fill-in-the-blank questions.

Installation

To install BeachFrontQuizzer:

1. Insert the CD-ROM in your CD-ROM drive.

2. Follow the Setup steps in the displayed Installation Wizard. (When the Setup is finished, you may immediately begin using BeachFrontQuizzer.)

3. To begin using BeachFrontQuizzer, enter the 12-digit license key number: **375428343723**

Study Sessions

BeachFrontQuizzer tests your knowledge as you learn about new subjects through interactive quiz sessions. Study Session Questions are selected from a single database for each session, dependent on the subcategory selected and the number of times each question has been previously answered correctly. In this way, questions you have answered correctly are not repeated until you have answered all the new questions. Questions that you have missed previously will reappear in later sessions and keep coming back to haunt you until you get the question correct. In addition, you can track your progress by displaying the number of questions you have answered with the Historical Analysis option. You can reset the progress tracking by clicking on the Clear History button. Each time a question is presented the answers are randomized so you will memorize a pattern or letter that goes with the question. You will start to memorize the correct answer that goes with the question concept.

Practice Exams

For advanced users, BeachFrontQuizzer also provides Simulated and Adaptive certification exams. Questions are chosen at random from the database. The Simulated Exam presents a specific number of questions directly related to the real exam. The Adaptive Exam presents a Minimum of 15 Questions with a maximum number of questions ranging from 25 to 35 questions depending on the exam. After you finish the exam, BeachFrontQuizzer displays your score and the passing score required for the test. You may display the exam results of this specific exam from this menu. You may review each question and display the correct answer.

NOTE
For further details of the feature functionality of this BeachFrontQuizzer software, consult the online instructions by choosing Contents from the BeachFrontQuizzer Help menu.

Technical Support

If you experience technical difficulties please call (888) 992-3131. Outside the U.S. call (281) 992-3131. Or, you may e-mail **bfquiz@swbell.net**.